CW01084101

ON THE LITERATURE AND THOUGHT OF THE GERMAN CLASSICAL ERA

On the Literature and Thought of the German Classical Era

Collected Essays

Hugh Barr Nisbet

OpenBook Publishers

https://www.openbookpublishers.com

© 2021 Hugh Barr Nisbet

ISBN Paperback: 9781783747696
ISBN Hardback: 9781783747702
ISBN Digital (PDF): 9781783747719
ISBN Digital ebook (epub): 9781783747726
ISBN Digital ebook (mobi): 9781783747733
ISBN XML: 9781783747740
DOI: 10.11647/OBP.0180

Cover image: Photo by Nathaniel Shuman on Unsplash at https://unsplash.com/photos/vZvNSeXzmwY

Cover design: Anna Gatti

Contents

Foreword

These are my essays on some of the central products of the German Classical Era. The topics they explore are key to the literature and thought of that period. All the essays have previously been published in journals or collections, dating from 1979 to 2010, and therefore span a considerable portion of my research into the German Enlightenment. I have selected them as the most important items in connection with problems presented by the major thinkers and writers working at that time.

In so doing, I wished to provide as wide a coverage as possible of topics and authors within the German classical period. The essays consequently deal with literature (including lyric poetry, the verse epic, the novel, drama and prose dialogue), philosophy, history, history of science, history of ideas, art history, theology and religion, and with writers and thinkers including Lucretius, Winckelmann, Lessing, Herder, Goethe, Schiller, Kant, Hegel, and many others. I have in addition tried to include only those items the main conclusions of which have not, to the best of my knowledge, been superseded or substantially qualified by later research. In re-editing the work, I have confined myself largely to minor corrections, essential updating, and deletion of some passages which I no longer consider strictly relevant.

I would not have assembled this collection of essays without the encouragement and wisdom of Professor Roger Paulin. Bringing together a selection of my key research in a single volume provides an opportunity to review some of the most important developments in western thought. I hope that this book will help to shed light on the historical and philosophical context in which ideas that are of fundamental significance to the world in which we live were originally developed. I am therefore most grateful to Roger for his foresight in identifying the value of such an initiative. Equally, I wish to thank him for his kindness in supporting the arrangements for preparing and editing the manuscript of these essays.

I would also like to thank Karl Guthke, a colleague of many decades and a great support to me, who has been instrumental in the approval of this collection for publication. My thanks extend to Alessandra Tosi of Open Book Publishers for her professional guidance and forbearance as I have gone through the time-consuming process of revisiting my past research and preparing this volume for publication. I am also greatly indebted to Dr John Williams of the University of St. Andrews. John is an old friend and colleague as well as a leading authority on the German Enlightenment. He has generously spared a considerable amount of his time to assist me in compiling a detailed index to this collection. I wish to thank him for his tireless and meticulous work and for accomplishing the task with impressive resolve. My colleagues at Sidney Sussex College, Cambridge, have provided friendship and kindness to me for many years. I am particularly grateful to the College for organising funding for the work necessary to finalise the manuscript of these essays. I also wish to thank my son, Marcus, who has assisted me in co-ordinating many of the practical steps necessary to bring this project to fruition.

Finally, I would like to pay tribute to my late wife, Angela, who was a dear companion to me for nearly thirty years and a devoted supporter of my endeavours. I duly dedicate this volume to her.

H. B. Nisbet
December 2020

GOETHE,

Nach dem Oelgemälde von Georg Oswald May, 1779.

Johann Wolfgang von Goethe. Etching by W. Unger after G. O. May (1779). Wellcome Library, London. Wellcome Images, CC BY 4.0, https://commons. wikimedia.org/wiki/File:Johann_Wolfgang_von_Goethe._Etching_by_W._ Unger_after_G._O._Wellcome_V0002292.jpg

1. Lucretius in Eighteenth-Century Germany

With a Commentary on Goethe's Poem 'Metamorphosis of Animals'[1]

John Ruskin, who had read Lucretius's *De rerum natura* in his student days as a set book at Oxford, commented in later years: 'I have ever since held it the most hopeless sign of a man's mind being made of flint-shingle if he liked Lucretius'.[2] Such antipathy to the Roman poet was nothing new, of course, particularly towards his philosophy. Though his poetry was admired from when it first appeared around the middle of the first century BC, his Epicureanism was unacceptable to the Stoics who so often dominated Roman philosophy. And his materialism was obnoxious to the Christians—so much so that his work was fortunate to survive the Middle Ages. But it is not just that many people have admired his poetry and rejected his philosophy. His reception is more complex than that—more complex, in fact, than that of any other poet I am familiar with. For *De rerum natura* contains so many and disparate strands that it has of necessity appealed in part to many, but as a whole to few. It incorporates a metaphysics of nature and a system of physical science; a moral philosophy with practical guidance on living; numerous observations on natural history; a conjectural history of human society;

---

1   An earlier version of this chapter was originally published as 'Lucretius in Eighteenth-Century Germany. With a Commentary on Goethe's "Metamorphose der Tiere"', *Modern Language Review*, 81 (1986), 97–115.

2   Ruskin, *Works*, ed. by E. T. Cook and Alexander Wedderburn, 39 vols (London and New York, NY: George Allen and Longmans Green & Co., 1903–12), XXXV, 613.

   https://doi.org/10.11647/OBP.0180.01

and a powerful statement on religion, culminating in a denial of human immortality and, to all intents and purposes, of the gods. As poetry, it is almost as varied: it contains superb lyrical passages in a descriptive, idyllic, or hymnic vein, along with tracts of abstract—and at times arid—philosophical verse, and there are fiercely satirical and polemical passages as well. Consequently, this unique composition has tended to be used over the centuries as a quarry by poets, philosophers, and scientists, rather than endorsed as a whole or imitated directly in the way that more homogeneous forms such as the elegy, epigram, satire, or ode have been.

Nevertheless, Lucretius had a particular appeal to the eighteenth century,[3] and the reasons are not hard to identify. His uncompromising intellectualism, his belief that knowledge alone—especially knowledge obtained through causal, scientific explanation—is the path to human salvation, was congenial to the post-Newtonian age. The Enlightenment's increasing preoccupation with nature to the detriment of theology, and the immense popularity of didactic poetry as a means of disseminating the new knowledge, made his work more accessible than ever before. In Germany, however, which was generally more conservative than France or England in the century of the Enlightenment, there were greater obstacles than elsewhere to his reception—above all in religious quarters. This no doubt explains why the first complete translation of De rerum natura to appear in German was not published until 1784,[4] over a century after that of Thomas Creech had appeared in England[5] and that of Michel de Marolles in France.[6] In fact, interest in the poem in Germany did not reach its height until the last two decades of the century, when the heyday of didactic poetry was already over.

---

3   See, for example, Peter Gay, The Enlightenment: An Interpretation, I, The Rise of Modern Paganism (New York, NY: Knopf Doubleday, 1967), pp. 98–105.

4   Titus Lukretius Carus, Von der Natur der Dinge, translated, with notes, by Franz Xaver Mayr, 2 vols (Leipzig and Vienna: Johann Georg Mössle, 1784); Mayr's translation is in prose. For comprehensive details of German translations of Lucretius, see Cosmo Alexander Gordon, A Bibliography of Lucretius (London: Hart-Davis, 1962), pp. 212–14, 260–69.

5   Titus Lucretius Carus. The Epicurean Philosopher: His Six Books, De Natura Rerum, done into English Verse with Notes by Thomas Creech (Oxford: Anthony Stephens, 1682); see also Gordon, p. 170 (who gives the date as 1683).

6   Michel de Marolles, Le Poète Lucrèce, latin et français (Paris: T. Quinet, 1650); see also Gordon, p. 154. The first Italian translation was published in 1717 (Gordon, p. 147).

The reception of Lucretius in France and England has been fairly fully documented.[7] But there is not, so far as I am aware, a detailed study of his reception in Germany during that (or indeed any other) period.[8] Such a study would have to take account of responses to Lucretius on the part of Brockes, Haller, and many lesser didactic poets such as Kästner, Creuz, and Dusch; of Frederick the Great, Lessing, Nicolai, Lichtenberg, Wieland, Thümmel, Kant, Herder, Goethe, Schiller, Heinse, Schelling, and Steffens; and, if it extended further into the nineteenth century, of Hegel, Schopenhauer, Büchner, Marx, Nietzsche, and many others. The aim of this essay, which is intended as a preliminary survey, is altogether more modest. (It appears to me in any case that a chronological survey of individual responses to Lucretius would be of limited value, precisely because, as I said before, his reception is so piecemeal and diversified.) The first priority, I believe, is to identify the main areas in which his influence made itself felt, and the pattern of individual responses should

---

7   On the reception of Lucretius in France, see C.-A. Fusil, 'Lucrèce et les philosophes du XVIIIe siècle', *Revue d'histoire littéraire de la France*, 35 (1928), 194–210; C.-A. Fusil, 'Lucrèce et les littérateurs, poètes et artistes du XVIIIe siècle', in the same journal, 37 (1930), 161–76; Gustav René Hocke, *Lukrez in Frankreich von der Renaissance bis zur Revolution* (Cologne: Kerschgens, 1935); and the very full account in Johan Werner Schmidt, 'Diderot and Lucretius: The De rerum natura and Lucretius's Legacy in Diderot's Scientific, Aesthetic, and Ethical Thought', *Studies on Voltaire and the Eighteenth Century*, 208 (1982), 183–294. On England, see Wolfgang Bernard Fleischmann, *Lucretius and English Literature 1680–1740* (Paris: Nizet, 1964); T. J. B. Spencer, 'Lucretius and the Scientific Poem in English', in *Lucretius*, ed. by D. R. Dudley (London: Routledge, 1965), pp. 131–64; Bernhard Fabian, 'Lucrez in England im siebzehnten und achtzehnten Jahrhundert', in *Aufklärung und Humanismus*, ed. by Richard Toellner (Heidelberg: Schneider, 1980), pp. 107–29; of Fabian's various studies of Lucretius and individual English poets, I will mention only his 'Pope and Lucretius: Observations on An Essay on Man', *Modern Language Review*, 74 (1979), 524–37. On the influence of Lucretius on the Enlightenment as a whole, see Wolfgang Bernard Fleischmann, 'The Debt of the Enlightenment to Lucretius', *Studies on Voltaire and the Eighteenth Century*, 25 (1963), 631–43, and the discussion by Peter Gay already referred to (see note 3 above). On his influence throughout history, see George Depue Hadzsits, *Lucretius and his Influence* (New York, NY: Cooper Square Publishers, 1963).

8   Even the last three works referred to in the previous note have relatively little to say on Germany. More useful in this connection is Wolfgang Schmidt, 'Lucrez und der Wandel seines Bildes', *Antike und Abendland*, 2 (1946), 193–219, which, despite its general title, has more material on Germany than on other countries. Gerhard Sauder, *Der reisende Epikuräer: Studien zu Moritz August von Thümmels 'Reise in die Mittäglichen Provinzen von Frankreich'* (Heidelberg: C. Winter, 1968) contains an informative account of the revival of Epicurean ethics in eighteenth-century Germany (pp. 181–94).

then become more intelligible. I shall accordingly try to define the main strands of Lucretius's influence in eighteenth-century Germany, and then, with reference to representative individuals, to examine one or two of the more important of them more closely.

There is firstly the scientific legacy—less obvious, perhaps, in the Enlightenment than in the seventeenth century with the revival of atomism by Gassendi, Boyle, and others, but still discernible.[9] Then there is the impact on metaphysics and religion, in which Lucretius is hotly refuted by Christian apologists and at the same time continues to act as a subversive influence and a stimulus to freethinking. In moral philosophy, he plays a part in the revival of Epicurean ethics (for example, in the hedonism of the Rococo) as a reaction to the Stoicism of the Baroque era.[10] In the poetic sphere, there is a wave of Lucretian— or more often, anti-Lucretian—poetry in the early to mid-eighteenth century.[11] Then there is a protracted debate in Germany on the whole status and legitimacy of didactic poetry, a debate which stretches from Gottsched and Lessing to Weimar Classicism and on to the Romantics and Hegel, and in which Lucretius is frequently cited as a cardinal instance.[12] And in the closing decades of the century, the question is finally faced as to whether a new *De rerum natura*, incorporating a unified

---

9   It is clearly visible, for example, in Kant's *Allgemeine Naturgeschichte und Theorie des Himmels* of 1755, and in much of Herder's thinking on scientific matters: see my *Herder and the Philosophy and History of Science* (Cambridge: MHRA, 1970) (hereafter 'Nisbet'), pp. 98–100, 107, and further references under 'Lucretius' in the index to that work.

10 For further comments on this reaction, see Gerhard Sauder, *Empfindsamkeit*, Vol. I, *Voraussetzungen und Elemente* (Stuttgart: Metzler, 1974), pp. 98–99 and 104–05, and Thomas P. Saine, 'Was ist Aufklärung?', in *Aufklärung, Absolutismus und Bürgertum in Deutschland*, ed. by Franklin Kopitzsch (Munich: Nymphenburger Verlagshandlung, 1976), p. 331. See also Sauder (1968), pp. 181–94.

11 A good deal of groundwork on this area has been done by Walter Schatzberg, *Scientific Themes in the Popular Literature of the German Enlightenment, 1720–1760* (Berne: Herbert Lang, 1973). Schatzberg comments on many Lucretian and anti-Lucretian poems in the period (see references under 'Lucretius' in his index), and he remarks on the need for a study of Lucretius in eighteenth-century Germany. See also Leif Ludwig Albertsen, *Das Lehrgedicht. Eine Geschichte der antikisierenden Sachepik in der neueren deutschen Literatur* (Aarhus: Akademisk Boghandel, 1967), especially pp. 316–28 ('Das große antimaterialistische Lehrgedicht'). Christoph Siegrist, *Das Lehrgedicht der Aufklärung* (Stuttgart: Metzler, 1974) contains little, however, on Lucretius and his influence.

12 See, in particular, Bernhard Fabian, 'Das Lehrgedicht als Problem der Poetik', in *Die nicht mehr schönen Künste*, ed. by H. R. Jauss (Munich: Fink, 1968), pp. 67–89; also Albertsen, pp. 339–48.

view of the cosmos and the findings of post-Newtonian science, can be written, and if so, by whom.[13] It would further be instructive to consider which passages from Lucretius are most frequently quoted by German writers of the period (for example, the opening lines of Books I and II), and to examine the function of such quotations. Lastly, there is the history of the first German translation of Lucretius's poem,[14] particularly the hexameter version by Karl Ludwig von Knebel, in the preparation of which Goethe and Herder were intensively involved; this translation, although it was begun in the 1790s, was not published in its completed form until 1821.[15] (There are also, of course, various Latin editions of *De rerum natura* and philological commentaries on it during the period in question; but these belong to the history of classical scholarship rather than to that of the poem's reception.)

Work has been done in several of the above areas (as I have indicated in the footnotes), but rarely from the perspective of the reception of Lucretius, which is usually treated only incidentally. It is from this perspective that I propose now to look at two major areas, one philosophical, the other poetic: briefly and selectively, at the effects of Lucretius's materialism as a threat to traditional religious values in Germany; and in more detail, at the ambitious plan, in which Goethe played a leading part, to write a neo-Lucretian epic of nature for the modern age.

Along with Spinoza, Lucretius provided the eighteenth century with one of its main models for a rigorously naturalistic explanation of all reality, and the radical Enlightenment with one of its weapons against teleological and providential views of nature and human history.[16]

---

13 This episode is discussed, in relation to the development of science, by Alexander Gode-von Aesch, *Natural Science in German Romanticism* (New York, NY: Columbia University Press, 1941), pp. 240–66. See also Albertsen, *Das Lehrgedicht*, pp. 349–69, and Margarete Plath, 'Der Goethe-Schellingsche Plan eines philosophischen Naturgedichts: Eine Studie zu Goethes "Gott und Welt"', *Preußische Jahrbücher*, 106 (1901), 44–74.

14 For bibliographical details of these, see the reference to Gordon in note 4 above.

15 See H. B. Nisbet, 'Karl Ludwig von Knebel's Hexameter Translation of Lucretius', *German Life and Letters*, 41 (1988), 413–25; also ibid., 'Herder und Lukrez', in *Johann Gottfried Herder 1744–1803*, ed. by Gerhard Sauder (Hamburg: Meiner, 1987), 77–87.

16 The ideas of Spinoza are explicitly coupled with the materialism of Lucretius and Epicurus in one of the most notorious anti-religious tracts of the early Enlightenment, the anonymous *Traité des trois imposteurs*, first published in 1719 and later reissued by the Baron d'Holbach (see Pierre Retat's edition of the *Traité* (Lyons: Universités de la Région Rhone-Alpes, 1973), pp. 12 and 81). La Mettrie also couples the two,

Lucretius's arguments against religion, immortality, and the fear of death are continually cited by the *philosophes*: the line *tantum religio potuit suadere malorum* ('so powerful was religion in persuading [people to perform] evil deeds'),[17] with which Lucretius deplores the superstitions that led to the sacrifice of Iphigenia, is perhaps the most frequently cited. Such radicalism is, of course, extremely rare in Germany, at least in the first half of the century. But in 1729. in his poem 'Thoughts on Reason, Superstition, and Unbelief ', Albrecht von Haller does echo Lucretius's anti-clerical sentiments and his theory that religion is a product of fear, and quotes the famous *tantum religio...* as a footnote to his own line 'What evil has occurred that was not the work of a priest?'[18] He directs these sentiments not, however, at the Protestant faith he grew up in but at false religion (by which he means Roman Catholicism). Frederick the Great, on the other hand, had no such reservations. He described *De rerum natura* as his breviary, to which he resorted in moments of despondency and which he carried with him on the battlefield; his own 'Épître au Maréchal Keith' ('Epistle to Marshal Keith') is closely modelled on Book III of Lucretius's poem, and consists of a polemic against the fear of death and the belief in immortality.[19] Those didactic poets of the time who wrote poems on the natural universe in imitation of Lucretius usually took care to distance themselves from his views on providence and religion.[20] Nevertheless, some of these compositions, such as the young Wieland's long didactic poem (his first major work) *Die Natur der Dinge* (*The Nature of Things*) of 1751 and Friedrich Carl Casimir von Creuz's *Lucrezische Gedanken* (*Lucretian Thoughts*) of 1763–

---

and is fond of citing Lucretius in support of his own materialism: see Julien Offray de la Mettrie, *Œuvres philosophiques*, 2 vols (Hildesheim: Georg Olms Verlag, 1970), I, 214, 219, 224 and II, 203. On Lucretius and Hume, see Gay, I, 356–57.

17   *De rerum natura*, I, 101; subsequent otherwise unidentified references in the text by Roman and Arabic numbers are to book and line of Lucretius's poem.

18   Haller, *Gedichte*, ed. by Ludwig Hirzel, 2 vols (Frauenfeld and Leipzig: Huber, 1917), II, 53; this poem is full of Lucretian sentiments, which are countered towards the end by an appeal to Christian faith.

19   See Henri de Catt, *Frederick the Great. The Memoirs of his Reader*, translated by F. S. Flint, 2 vols (London: Constable & Co., 1916), I, pp. xv, 198, and 390; also *Die Werke Friedrichs des Großen in deutscher Übersetzung*, 10 vols (Berlin: R. Hobbing, 1913–14), IX, 124–32 (the epistle to Keith) and VII, 264 (endorsement of Lucretius's denial of immortality). See also Gay, I, 102 and Fleischmann (1963), pp. 631–32.

20   See, for example, Albertsen, pp. 152, 242–43 and Schatzberg, pp. 206, 244, and 266–67.

64, make substantial concessions to the independent creative power of nature.[21] The young philosopher Kant, in his epoch-making work on cosmogony, the *Universal Natural History and Theory of the Heavens* of 1755 (the earliest statement of what later became known as the Kant-Laplace theory of stellar evolution), attempts in his preface to dissociate himself from Lucretian materialism and to uphold the doctrine of divine providence.[22] Nevertheless, he proceeds to explain the evolution of the solar system by combining Newtonian mechanics with the Epicurean theory of a random concourse of atoms (Kant, II, 266). His pupil Herder made copious notes from *De rerum natura* in 1766, and his posthumous papers suggest that he was seriously preoccupied with philosophical materialism around this time.[23] In Wieland's novel *The History of Agathon* of 1766–67, Epicureanism has become a central theme: the hero Agathon is plagued by doubts concerning providence, doubts which are reinforced by the arguments of the Sophist Hippias, who adopts a Mephistophelean role in undermining the young hero's Platonic idealism. Hippias is an Epicurean; his doctrines of the soul's mortality, of random creation by the movement of atoms in space, his contention that religion is based solely on fear and that the gods, if they exist at all, are indifferent to human affairs—all this is Epicurean philosophy, taken for the most part from Lucretius (who is mentioned or alluded to on several occasions).[24]

---

21 As Gode-von Aesch (pp. 39–40) observes, Wieland's poem incorporates two distinct conceptions of God, one transcendent, the other immanent; see also Wieland's preface to the poem, where he speaks of God as the 'Seele der Welt' ('soul of the world'), in Wieland, *Gesammelte Schriften*, ed. by the Königlich-Preußische Akademie der Wissenschaften (Berlin: Weidmann, 1909–), Erste Abteilung, I, 7. Creuz's poem envisages the creation of living creatures other than man by purely natural processes, and parts company with Lucretius only when it comes to the human soul: see C. C. von Creuz, *Oden und andere Gedichte*, 2 vols (Frankfurt a. M.: Varrentrapp, 1769), II, 199–226 (p. 217): 'Lucretius, I can no longer be your pupil!'

22 Kant, *Gesammelte Schriften*, ed. by the Königlich-Preußische Akademie der Wissenschaften (Berlin: Reimer, 1902–), I, 221–28; but even in the preface, Kant admits: 'I shall not deny that the theory of Lucretius or his forerunners Epicurus, Leucippus and Democritus has much similarity with mine.' Compare Hermann Hettner, *Geschichte der deutschen Literatur im achtzehnten Jahrhundert*, ed. by Georg Witkowski, 4 vols (Leipzig: Paul List Verlag, 1928), II, 160: 'At school, Lucretius was his [Kant's] favourite object of study, and at university, Newton.'

23 See Nisbet, *Herder and the Philosophy and History of Science*, pp. 48, 100, and 126–27.

24 Wieland, *Geschichte des Agathon* (first version), ed. by Fritz Martini (Stuttgart: Reclam, 1979), p. 36 (doubts on providence), pp. 58–60 and 89 (Hippias's Epicureanism), and pp. 183 and 405 (references to Lucretius and to *De rerum natura*, II, 14). The narrator's description of Hippias's calm on seeing Agathon's passions boil over

Hippias's philosophical position is never properly refuted either by Agathon or by the narrator; it is only his thorough-going hedonism, that dedication to sensual pleasure which has been popularly known for centuries as 'Epicureanism' (and which goes far beyond anything to be found in Lucretius), that is decisively rejected. In an age in which Christian doctrine was being steadily eroded, it is the moral rather than the theological position which, as in so many other writers of the time, remains firm. Agathon's philosophical and religious uncertainty, however, suggests that Wieland's earlier efforts to refute Lucretius in his poem *The Nature of Things* had by no means silenced his own doubts on such matters. It is also worthy of note that, in Wieland's later novel *The Abderites* of the 1770s, the only positive character described at length in a society of fools is the atomistic philosopher Democritus, the direct intellectual ancestor of both Epicurus and Lucretius.

It seems that nearly all the major writers in Germany around this time had their crises of faith and doubts concerning providence. When such crises occur, it is often either Lucretius or Spinoza who provides the unsettling influence. Schiller is no exception. His early poem 'The Plague', published in 1782, describes the horrors of the plague in a way which recalls the vivid account of the plague in Athens with which Lucretius (VI, 1138–1286) concludes his work.[25] Schiller's poem ends with the bitterly ironic comment on providence: 'In terrible fashion the plague gives praise to God'. The young Goethe's most famous outburst against the gods, his poem 'Prometheus', is full of the Lucretian spirit of religious defiance; its opening challenge to Zeus to practise his thunderbolts on oaks and mountain-tops like a boy beheading thistles is, plainly an allusion to those lines in Book VI of *De rerum natura* in which the gods are ridiculed, and thereby denied, for wasting their projectiles on obviously random targets: 'Why [...] do they [the gods] aim at deserts and waste their labour? Or are they then practising their arms and strengthening their muscles? [...] And why does he [Jupiter]

('The Sophist observed this storm as calmly as someone who, from the safety of the shore, observes the wild turmoil of the waves from which he has fortunately escaped' (p. 339)) is a paraphrase of the celebrated passage in *De rerum natura*, II, 1–4.

25   Friedrich Schiller, *Anthologie auf das Jahr 1782*, ed. by Katharina Mommsen (Stuttgart: J. B. Metzler, 1973). As the editor, who also notices the influence of Spinoza on the early poems, remarks, 'his model was Lucretius' (pp. 18–19).

generally attack high places, why do we see most traces of his fire on the mountain tops?'[26] And in 1789, Goethe declares in a letter to Stolberg, 'that I personally adhere more or less to the doctrine of Lucretius and confine all my pretensions to the sphere of life'.[27]

Lucretius, along with Spinoza, is one of the chief inspirations of that consistent naturalism which Goethe professes in his classical period at the time when his scientific studies were at their height. He constantly discussed Lucretius with his friend Knebel, who was translating the poem, and himself planned to write a long essay on the subject (Grumach, I, 348–49), but, since he became increasingly attached in his later years to a belief in some kind of personal immortality, he now felt obliged to distance himself from Lucretius's polemics against the fear of death. He did so in a humorous manner, likening them to Frederick the Great's outburst at the Battle of Kolin to a group of his grenadiers who hesitated to mount a frontal assault on an enemy battery: 'You dogs, do you then want to live for ever!' (p. 348).

Even from these few scattered examples, it is apparent that Lucretius provided a constant encouragement to secular ways of thinking in the second half of the eighteenth century in Germany. None of the major thinkers of the time adopted his philosophy as a whole, of course; it simply helped to undermine the Christian beliefs they had inherited. There are, however, at least two lesser-known figures who became thorough-going philosophical materialists, and both were members of the Weimar circle. One is Knebel, the translator of Lucretius, whose posthumous essays 'On Immortality', 'Reflections on Lucretius', and 'Atheism' fully endorse the Epicurean philosophy.[28] The other is August

---

26 *De rerum natura*, VI, 396–97 and 421–22. The translation is from the bilingual edition of Lucretius, *De rerum natura*, with an English translation by W. H. D. Rouse, ed. by Martin Ferguson Smith, Loeb Classical Library (Cambridge, Massachusetts and London: Harvard University Press and William Heinemann, 1975), pp. 523–25.

27 Goethe to F. L. von Stolberg, 2 February 1789, in Ernst Grumach, *Goethe und die Antike. Eine Sammlung*, 2 vols (Berlin: De Gruyter, 1949), I, 348–49. All of Goethe's explicit comments on Lucretius are assembled in Grumach, I, 335–52. Karl Bapp, 'Goethe und Lucrez', *Jahrbuch der Goethe-Gesellschaft*, 12 (1926), 47–67 is largely a list of Goethe's references to Lucretius, but some of the Lucretian allusions in Goethe's writings are also noted.

28 See *Knebels Litterarischer Nachlaß und Briefwechsel*, ed. by K. A. Varnhagen von Ense and Theodor Mundt, 3 vols, 2nd edn (Leipzig: Gebrüder Reichenbach, 1840), III, 352–56, 455–56, and 489–90; compare Knebel to Herder, July 1793, in *Von und an Herder*, ed. by Heinrich Düntzer and F. G. von Herder, 3 vols (Leipzig: Dyk'sche

von Einsiedel, an eccentric figure whose unpublished reflections on atoms and the struggle for existence Herder copied out for his private use.[29] And when, in the nineteenth century, materialism finally came out into the open in Germany, its classical origins were still evident. The young Karl Marx wrote his doctoral dissertation on Democritus and Epicurus and their philosophies of nature. His strong sympathy with Epicurus, and with his most eloquent disciple, Lucretius, is evident throughout.[30]

So much for Lucretius as a subversive philosophical influence. I want to consider now the poetic issue of neo-Lucretian experiments and the plan for a new 'De rerum natura' for the modern age.

The philosophico-scientific poem is one of the most characteristic poetic genres of the eighteenth century.[31] The aim of such poetry, especially in the first half of the century, is to reconcile the findings of modern science and natural philosophy with Christian theology, usually by means of the argument from design. All such poems, from Richard Blackmore's 'Creation' of 1712 to Charles Claude Genest's 'Principes de Philosophie' of 1716 and Barthold Hinrich Brockes's nine-volume collection *Irdisches Vergnügen in Gott* (*Earthly Delight in God*) of 1721–48, are anti-Lucretian works, whether or not Lucretius is explicitly mentioned in them (as he frequently is). Of those which are specifically directed against Lucretius's poem, and consciously modelled on it as their formal archetype, the most celebrated at the time was Cardinal de Polignac's Latin *Anti-Lucretius* published posthumously in 1747.

Buchhandlung, 1862), III, 91–92: 'For it nevertheless remains true *for me* at least that the Lucretian principles are based on nature, that is, on truth.' For further information on Knebel's Lucretian studies, including fifteen previously unpublished letters of Knebel to Goethe, see Regine Otto, '"Lukrez bleibt immer in seiner Art der Einzige": Karl Ludwig von Knebel an Goethe. Ungedruckte Briefe aus den Jahren 1821 und 1822', in *Impulse. Aufsätze, Quellen, Berichte zur deutschen Klassik und Romantik*, Folge 5, ed. by Walter Dietze and Peter Goldammer (Berlin and Weimar: Aufbau-Verlag, 1982), pp. 229–63.

29   See August von Einsiedel, *Ideen*, ed. by Wilhelm Dobbek (Berlin: Akademie-Verlag, 1957); as Dobbek observes, 'Fundamental for August von Einsiedel is his allegiance to Democritus, the most significant representative of materialistic philosophy in ancient Greece' (p. 11).

30   See 'Über die Differenz der Demokritischen und Epikureischen Naturphilosophie', in Karl Marx, *Frühe Schriften*, ed. by Hans-Joachim Lieber and Peter Fürth (Stuttgart: Cotta, 1962), I, 18–106; also S. S. Prawer, *Karl Marx and World Literature* (Oxford: Oxford University Press, 1976), who observes that Epicurus and Lucretius were for Marx a lever that might help to dislodge simplistic religious beliefs (p. 27).

31   See Spencer, 'Lucretius and the Scientific Poem in English' p. 137.

Polignac conceived the idea of his poem around the beginning of the century, possibly after an argument about providence with the French sceptic Pierre Bayle.[32] Despite its title, it is directed mainly against modern thinkers such as Hobbes, Spinoza, Locke, Gassendi, and (unfortunately for the later reputation of Polignac who was a Cartesian in scientific matters) Isaac Newton. It is probable that Polignac's poem gave Wieland the idea of writing his own *The Nature of Things* of 1751, for Polignac is extravagantly praised in that work.[33] These poems, despite their Lucretian trappings (Wieland, for example, invokes Minerva and Clio, in parallel to Lucretius's invocations of Venus and Calliope), are little more than versified philosophy. Mercifully, Wieland's poem (of which he was later ashamed) contains a mere 4,177 lines, as against the 7,415 lines of Lucretius himself and the 11,931 lines of Polignac's (albeit unfinished) poem.

Such versified treatises and rhyming encyclopaedias of natural history helped to bring the long didactic poem into disrepute. It was condemned by Lessing,[34] and by others down to the time of Hegel,[35] as unpoetic. Even Goethe and Schiller, although they wrote didactic poems themselves, joined in the criticism;[36] they did, however, leave the way open for a didactic poetry which might overcome the defects of past attempts.[37] The ultimate authority behind all such condemnations

---

32   This anecdote is reported in, for example, Johann Jakob Dusch, *Briefe zur Bildung des Geschmacks*, 6 vols, rev. edn (Leipzig: Meyer, 1773), II, 118. The first two volumes of this work deal solely with didactic poetry, and the long section on Lucretius (Vol. II, Letters 1–5) translates substantial parts of *De rerum natura* into German prose. For further details on Polignac, see Wolfgang Bernard Fleischmann, 'Zum *Anti-Lucretius* des Kardinals de Polignac', in *Romanische Forschungen*, 77 (1965), 42–63.

33   Wieland, *Gesammelte Schriften*, I, 21: 'You, great Polignac, you crown of our age,/ Have long since consigned his [Epicurus's] host of atoms to the void.'

34   Lessing, *Sämtliche Schriften*, ed. by Karl Lachmann and Franz Muncker, 23 vols (Stuttgart, Leipzig and Berlin: Göschen, 1886–1924), VI, 409–45 (*Pope a Metaphysiker!*): 'Lucretius and his like are versifiers, but not poets' (p. 415).

35   Hegel, *Theorie-Werkausgabe*, ed. by Eva Moldenhauer and Karl Markus Michel, 20 vols (Frankfurt a. M.: Suhrkamp, 1970), XIII, 541 (*Lectures on Aesthetics*): 'Didactic poetry cannot be included among the true forms of art.' Hegel includes Lucretius in his condemnation.

36   See Goethe, Weimar edition (henceforth WA), 133 vols (Weimar: Böhlau, 1887–1919), I. Abteilung, XLI/2, 225–27 (*On Didactic Poetry*) and Schiller, *Werke*, Nationalausgabe (Weimar: Böhlau, 1943–), XX, 453 (*On Naïve and Sentimental Poetry*).

37   Goethe's criticisms of the genre in *On Didactic Poetry* (1825) are by no means unqualified, and his own plan of 1799 to write a great epic of nature shows considerable faith in its possibilities (*Briefwechsel zwischen Goethe und Knebel*

was, of course, Aristotle, who had denied that the philosophical verse of Empedocles was poetry (*Poetics*, Chapter I). Herder, however, had a more favourable opinion of the genre, and he took issue directly with Aristotle in its defence: characteristically, he employed the historical argument that poetry has evolved further since Aristotle's time, so that Aristotle's strictures are not applicable to more recent forms. The latter include the work of Lucretius himself, who is always for Herder the supreme example of the didactic poet.[38] In his early years, he even planned himself to write what he called 'a philosophical epic on the human soul' (that is, on psychology).[39] But he soon abandoned this scheme—Herder's poetic talents were modest—and began to call on others to make the discoveries of modern science the subject of a new Lucretian poem (SW I, 470; V, 295, 320; XXIII, 247; etc.). In 1801, he put forward the suggestion, which Schelling soon afterwards developed at length, that scientific systems have an inherently poetic quality which makes them especially suitable for poetic treatment: 'every system is itself a poem in so far as it is independent, whole and pure' (SW XXIII, 243; see also XI, 293 and XXIV, 299).

It is indeed remarkable how often terms such as 'Dichtung', 'Poesie', and even 'Roman' are applied to scientific theories in eighteenth-century Germany—often, but by no means always, pejoratively. But the idea that scientific systems may have an inherently poetic quality is perhaps more comprehensible in relation to the sciences of those days than to the exact sciences of today. Those which attempted to explain the history of the earth or the universe, for example, are often vivid, imaginative reconstructions of cosmic events and processes, comparable in some respects to the science fiction of today. This is

---

(*1774–1832*), ed. by G. E. Guhrauer, 2 vols (Leipzig: Brockhaus, 1851), I, 210, Goethe to Knebel, 22 January 1799). Similarly, Schiller, in condemning Erasmus Darwin's *Botanic Garden* (Schiller to Goethe, 30 January 1798), adds 'I don't believe that the material is impermissible and completely unsuited to poetry', and goes on to suggest how such a poem might be successfully accomplished: *Briefwechsel zwischen Schiller und Goethe*, ed. by Franz Muncker, 4 vols (Stuttgart: Cotta, 1892), III, 29.

38 Herder, *Sämtliche Werke* (SW) ed. by Bernhard Suphan, 33 vols (Berlin: Weidmann, 1877–1913), IV, 282 and 290. For further details, see Nisbet, 'Herder und Lukrez' (note 15 above).

39 See Herder to Merck, March 1771, in Herder, *Briefe. Gesamtausgabe 1763–1803*, ed. by Karl-Heinz Hahn and others (Weimar: Böhlau, 1977–), I, 319. For Bernard Suphan's comments on this project see SW I, 547–48.

true of such works as William Whiston's *New Theory of the Earth*, in which the earth's origin and Noah's Flood are explained as the effects of a comet passing close to the sun, and of later versions such as the cosmogony of Buffon, whose *Époques de la nature* (1778) contains equally bold speculations on earth history which seemed fantastic to many of his contemporaries. It was perhaps in France that the word 'roman' ('novel') was first applied to imaginative theories of the universe. Meusnier de Querlon, in 1777, applied it to 'De rerum natura' itself, which he described as 'le roman physique de Lucrèce (Fusil (1930), p. 163). In 1780, Goethe finds the word entirely appropriate to Buffon's *Époques*, which he praises for its comprehensiveness: 'for which reason also Frenchmen, and Franco-Germans and Germans say that he wrote a novel, which is very well put, because the honourable public knows everything extraordinary only through the novel'.[40] This use of the word *Roman* to denote an imaginative, systematic account of the world's origins explains what Goethe must have had in mind when he planned, in the early 1780s, to write a 'novel on the universe'; it seems to have been conceived as an imaginative account of earth history, possibly in letter form,[41] and the highly poetic essay *On Granite* of 1784 may have been connected with it. It was never written, of course. But it is possible that the novel *The Elective Affinities* of 1808, in which fundamental human relationships are likened to basic chemical reactions so as to suggest that all of nature is a single, unitary whole, is, in its conception, a late echo of the earlier project.

By the 1790s, after repeated promptings by Herder, Knebel had begun to translate Lucretius. Goethe in turn began, with Knebel's encouragement, to consider ways of expressing his own scientific ideas in poetry. One of his earlier attempts is probably the curious poetic

---

40   Goethe to Merck, 11 October 1780, in WA, IV. Abteilung, IV, 311; but see also his letter to Merck of 7 April 1780 (IV, 202), in which he objects to others dismissing Buffon's work as 'a hypothesis or a novel'. Compare Herder's pejorative use of the term a few years earlier (SW, VII, 17), when he speaks of 'Buffon's novels of the origin of animals' (see also Nisbet, *Herder and the Philosophy and History of Science*, p. 306).

41   The surviving evidence on Goethe's plan is assembled in H. G. Gräf, *Goethe über seine Dichtungen*, 9 vols (Frankfurt a. M.: Rütten & Loening, 1901–14:), I/1, pp. 285–95. For a useful discussion of this and Goethe's subsequent plan for a neo-Lucretian poem, see Erich Trunz's remarks in *Goethes Werke*, Hamburg edition (HA), 14 vols (Hamburg: Wegner, 1948–64), I, 569–73.

fragment entitled 'Jussieu's Classes of Plants', a kind of mnemonic which, before breaking off in the middle of the fourteenth line, classifies the main families of plants as defined in Antoine Laurent de Jussieu's botanical system of 1789. The first seven lines set the pattern for the rest:

> For a handy reminder of the 15 natural classes
> As given to us by Jussieu, I attempted the following verses.
> Without bearing seeds, the sponges, the algae and liverwort
> Grow with the rest of the mosses, the ferns and naiadaceae.
> The core of the seed is simple, and all the stamina
> Are placed on top of the fruit in simple blossoming flowers,
> As in araceae and typha, the cyperaceae and grasses.

(WA, I. Abteilung, V (2), 405)

No date is given for this fragment in the Weimar edition, but it may well have been written in 1793, when Goethe acquired a copy of Jussieu's work,[42] or in 1794, when he laid out his garden in flowerbeds corresponding to Jussieu's classification.[43] The metre is that of Lucretius, the hexameter, and the subject is natural history. But the enumerative presentation recalls the encyclopaedic verse of the first half of the century rather than the 'De rerum natura'. The next step comes with the elegy 'The Metamorphosis of Plants', written in June 1798, which expresses Goethe's botanical theories in poetic form. But although it has some Lucretian touches, it is for several reasons (apart from its brevity) not a Lucretian poem. The ideas in it, especially the central idea of plant growth as the successive transformation of an archetypal, leaf-like organ, are very much Goethe's own;[44] its metre is the elegiac couplet, not the Lucretian hexameter; and it has the quality of a personal love lyric. It is addressed to the poet's beloved, and the climactic moment of plant growth, the moment of reproduction (lines 55–58), becomes a symbol and reaffirmation of their love (lines 71–80). Besides, its poetic

---

42 See *Goethes Bibliothek. Katalog*, ed. by Hans Ruppert (Weimar: Arion Verlag, 1958), p. 679, no. 4734; edition of Jussieu's *Genera plantarum* (Zurich: Ziegler, 1791; first published Paris, 1789), acquired September 1793.

43 See Goethe, *Begegnungen und Gespräche*, ed. by Ernst and Renate Grumach (Berlin: De Gruyter, 1965–), IV, 107: the botanist F. G. Dietrich reports on the work done in 1794.

44 See Gertrud Overbeck, 'Goethes Lehre von der Metamorphose der Pflanzen und ihre Widerspiegelung in seiner Dichtung', *Publications of the English Goethe Society*, 31 (1961), 38–59, for a detailed correlation (pp. 41–46) of the poem with Goethe's botanical theories.

affinities are modern rather than classical. A few months before he wrote it, Goethe, in a letter to Schiller, had strongly criticised another botanical poem, Erasmus Darwin's 'The Botanic Garden', whose second section, 'The Loves of the Plants', was published in 1789. He found it poetically inadequate and overloaded with prosaic factual detail. Schiller agreed, calling it 'versified erudition', but added that he considered the material capable of genuinely poetic treatment.[45] The elegy 'The Metamorphosis of Plants', with its erotic associations and nuptial imagery, looks much more like a poetic response by Goethe to Darwin's 'The Loves of the Plants' than an attempt to write Lucretian poetry. To cite only one example, the climax of Darwin's poem, as of Goethe's, is a multiple wedding, in which the stamens and pistils within the flower unite to produce the seed. But whereas Goethe's version, though poetically heightened, bears a clear relation to the botanical process it describes, Darwin's (characteristically lubricious) lines require a learned footnote to remind the reader that it is floral reproduction rather than human promiscuity that is referred to. The German text reads like a corrective to the English:

> And it quickly furls, contracts; the most delicate structures
> Twofold venture forth, destined to meet and unite.
> Wedded now they stand, those delighted couples, together.
> Round the high altar they form multiple, ordered arrays.
> Hymen, hovering, nears, and pungent perfumes, exquisite,
> Fill with fragrance and life all the environing air.
>
> (lines 51–56, transl. Christopher Middleton)

> Pair after pair, along his sacred groves
> To Hymen's fane the bright procession moves;
> [...] On wings of gossamer soft Whispers fly,
> And the sly Glance steals side-long from the eye.
> —As round his shrine the gaudy circles bow,
> And seal with muttering lips the faithless vow,
> Licentious Hymen joins their mingled hands,
> And loosely twines the meretricious bands.—[46]

---

45 See Goethe to Schiller, 26 January 1798, and Schiller to Goethe, 30 January 1798, in *Briefwechsel zwischen Schiller und Goethe*, III, 26–30; see also the quotation from Schiller's letter in note 37 above.

46 Erasmus Darwin, *The Botanic Garden*, 2 vols (London: Jones & Co., 1789–91), II, 164–65 ('The Loves of the Plants', Canto IV, lines 389–90 and 397–402).

Encouraged by the warm reception which 'The Metamorphosis of Plants' received among his friends, Goethe began to consider the much vaster project of a Lucretian poem for the modern age. Knebel urged him to use the hexameter, and Goethe declared that he hoped to use Knebel's translation of Lucretius, which was now well advanced, as the basis of his own poem.[47] He did not write it, of course. Nor did he write the poem on magnetism he planned in the same context.[48] But he did write the poem 'Metamorphosis of Animals', traditionally dated 1806, but probably written by 1800 at the latest. As Erich Trunz points out, Goethe abandoned his plan for a Lucretian poem in 1800, and he was also turned against using the hexameter around this time by the carpings of metrical purists such as Johann Heinrich Voss and August Wilhelm Schlegel; hence it is improbable that he would have written the poem after that date (HA, I, 546–47, 573, and 585–86). (Besides, the editors of the Weimar edition comment that a surviving draft of the poem 'perhaps belongs, to judge by the handwriting and character of the paper, to the 1790s' (WA, I. Abteilung, LIII, 549–50)).

Metamorphosis of Animals

1   Now if your mind is prepared to venture upon the final
Step to this summit, give me your hand and view with an
    open
Gaze the abundance of Nature before you. Everywhere richly
Gifts she has lavished around, the Goddess, but never she
    worries
5   After the manner or mortal women, regarding the nurture
Offspring need in a steady supply, that isn't her wont, for
Doubly she has determined the ultimate law: with a limit,
Set to each life and need in its measure, and then without
    measure
Gifts she has scattered, easy to find, and she quietly favours
10   Motley toils for her children, seeing their needs are so many;
So they will flock and yearn, untrained, for the ends that are
    set them.

---

47   See Knebel to Goethe, 18 July 1798 and Goethe to Knebel, 22 January 1799, in *Briefwechsel zwischen Goethe und Knebel (1774–1832)*, I, 182 and 201.

48   See Goethe to Knebel, 16 July 1798, in *Briefwechsel zwischen Goethe und Knebel*, I, 181.

Every animal *is* an end in itself, it issues
Perfect from Nature's womb and its offspring are equally
    perfect.
All its organs are formed according to laws that are timeless,
15   Even a form very rare will hold to its type, though in secret.
Every mouth is designed to admit particular foodstuffs,
Such as befit the body; an animal feeble and toothless,
One with jaws that are toothed and massive—a suitable organ
Each will possess for channelling food to the rest of its body.
20   Also the feet, whether long or short, will always be moving
Tuned to the animal's every need and every intention.

Thus has the Mother ordained the health complete and
    unbroken
Each of her children enjoys, and the limbs of each, being vital,
Never conflicting the one with the other, have life as their
    function.
25   So the shape of an animal patterns the manner of living,
Likewise their manner of living, again, exerts on the animals'
Shapes a massive effect: all organised structures are solid,
Thus, which are prone to change under pressure from
    outward conditions.
Deep within the more noble creatures, indeed, a power
30   Dwells enclosed in the holy ring of vital formation.
Here are the limits no god can alter, honoured by Nature:
Only a limit enables a form to rise to perfection.

Deep within, however, a spirit may seem to be wrestling:
How shall he rupture the ring and cause the forms to be
    random,
35   Random the will? Yet all his efforts they come to nothing;
For, if he burrows his way right through to this organ or that
    one,
Making it grander by far, then other organs will dwindle,
Disproportionate weight and excess of it quickly destroying
All the beauty of form and all pure litheness of movement.
40   So if you see that a creature possesses a certain advantage,
Put the question at once: What is the fault that afflicts it
Elsewhere?—and seek to discover the defect, always
    inquiring;
Then at once you will find the key to the world of formation.
For there has never existed an animal into whose jawbone

45   Teeth are pegged that had a horn sprout out of its forehead;
      Therefore a lion with a horn the Eternal Mother could never

      Possibly make, though she drew on all her potent resources;
      For she has not measures sufficient to plant in a being
      Rows of teeth, complete, together with horns or with antlers.

50   May this beautiful concept of power and limit, of random
      Venture and law, freedom and measure, of order in motion,
      Defect and benefit, bring you high pleasure; gently
            instructive,
      Thus, the sacred Muse in her teaching tells you of harmonies.
      Moral philosophers never attained to a concept sublimer,
55   Nor did men of affairs, nor artists imagining; rulers,
      Worthy of power, enjoy their crowns on this account only.
      So be glad of it, Nature's loftiest creature, now feeling
      Able to follow her loftiest thought on her wings of Creation.
      Stand where you are, be still, and looking behind you,
            backward,
60   All things consider, compare, and take from the lips of the
            Muse then,
      So that you'll see, not dream it, a truth that is sweet and is
            certain.

                    (HA, I, 201–03; transl. Christopher Middleton)

The 'Metamorphosis of Animals' is Goethe's closest approximation to Lucretian poetry—a good deal closer, I believe, than has hitherto been realised. It is complete in itself, but its opening lines suggest that it was intended to form part of a longer poem, for they seem to presuppose an earlier consideration of lower forms of nature before the animal kingdom is dealt with:

> Now if your mind is prepared to venture upon the final
> Step to this summit, give me your hand and view with an open
> Gaze the abundance of nature before you.

                                        (lines 1–3)

The following lines personify nature as a mother goddess, herself immortal, who has lavished her gifts of life in profusion (lines 3–4). This brief evocation of nature is, in fact, a shorter equivalent of the apostrophe to Venus as the procreator of all things at the beginning of 'De rerum natura' (I, 1–20). The mother goddess, Goethe continues, has no reason to worry over the needs of her creatures, for which she has amply provided (lines 4–9); Lucretius similarly declares: 'for them all the earth herself brings forth all they want in abundance, and nature the cunning fashioner of things' (V, 233–34). Goethe's manner, after this preamble, is expository: there follows a poetic account of some of his theories of animal form. The first of these—'Every animal *is* an end in itself' (line 12) and 'So the shape of an animal patterns its manner of living' (line 25)—is a restatement of Lucretius's repudiation of teleology: animals are not created for a purpose; their purpose is a natural consequence of their shape. As Lucretius expresses it: 'Nothing is born in us simply in order that we may use it, but that which is born creates the use' (IV, 834–35). Constant laws, Goethe adds, govern the development of all natural forms, and these naturally imposed limits are inviolable (lines 14–15 and 31–32):

> All its organs are formed according to laws that are timeless,
> Even a form very rare will hold to its type, though in secret.
> ... Here are the limits no god can alter, honoured by Nature:
> Only a limit enables a form to rise to perfection.[49]

(The term 'type' clearly alludes to Goethe's theory of an osteological 'type' to which all vertebrates conform, but no technical details are supplied here concerning the number and disposition of bones; the formulation remains general, and the emphasis is simply on the law-governed nature of animal growth.) Again, there are comparable passages in Lucretius: 'A limit has been fixed for the growth of things after their kind and for their tenure of life and... it stands decreed what each can do by the ordinances of nature, and also what each cannot do' (I, 584–88; see also V, 923–24 and VI, 65–66). After citing a few examples of harmonious animal organisation, Goethe concludes that the limbs of a given animal are never mutually incompatible (lines 23–24):

> ... and the limbs of each, being vital,
> Never conflicting the one with the other, have life as their function.

---

49 The closeness of these lines (and of lines 50–52) to the sentiments expressed in the sonnet 'Nature and Art' of 1800 (HA, I, 245) provides further evidence for dating the poem to around the turn of the century, rather than to 1806.

He subsequently reinforces this point, declaring that monstrous hybrids such as horned lions are impossible (lines 46–47). For these observations, there are again precedents in Lucretius (V, 878–80 and 918–19): 'But centaurs never existed, nor at any time can there be creatures of double nature and twofold body combined together of incompatible limbs [...] there is no proof that creatures of mixed growth could be made, and limbs of various creatures joined into one.' In the ceaseless battle between forces of destruction and preservation, the latter succeed in holding their own (lines 33–35); for this point too, there are parallels in Lucretius (for example, lines 569–70).

There is indeed scarcely a sentiment in the first three-quarters of Goethe's poem that does not have its counterpart in 'De rerum natura' (although the examples used to illustrate the matching principles are often different). There is also, in the 'Metamorphosis of Animals', that same sense of confidence and certainty which Lucretius derives from the universal rule of natural law. But no less significant than what Goethe includes in his poem is what he excludes from it. For whereas 'The Metamorphosis of Plants' had closely followed the doctrines in Goethe's botanical treatise of the same title, even presenting them in the same sequence (see note 44 above), one of Goethe's most important zoological theories (the vertebral theory of the skull, according to which the vertebrate skull is composed of modified vertebrae) finds no place at all in the zoological poem or in its original draft; and another (that of the osteological 'type' for all vertebrates) is alluded to only in the most general terms (line 15). They are also absent, of course, in Lucretius's poem. But the two principal theories which Goethe does include (that animals and their organs are not teleologically determined, and that specialism in one function rules out specialism in others) both have parallels in Lucretius. The second of these theories, sometimes referred to as the law of 'compensation' or of the 'correlation of parts',[50] is regularly enunciated in Goethe's scientific writings with the help of commercial metaphors: a limited 'budget' (*estate, budget, household*) of resources available to each animal species, within which 'no part can be added to without something being taken from another' (HA, XII, 176). And indeed, such metaphors (*saved, balance, expenditure*) are also

---

50   See, for example, Rudolf Magnus, *Goethe as a Scientist*, new edition (New York, NY: Henry Schuman, 1949), p. 84.

present in the first draft of the 'Metamorphosis of Animals' (WA, I. Abteilung, LIII, 549–52). But significantly, they are absent from the final version of the poem. It would therefore seem that Goethe modelled his poem, at least up to line 49, very closely indeed on Lucretius—so much so that only such ideas and formulations as are compatible with 'De rerum natura' are included, and the rest either omitted or expressed in the most general of terms. And even if it were objected that the poem is, in a sense, a fragment, and that we cannot therefore decide what Goethe might have added to it, there is no evidence to suggest that he at any time planned to include in it any further zoological doctrines: the first draft contains no theories which are not also present in the final version; the opening lines suggest that whatever might have preceded them would have concerned natural forms of a lower order than the vertebrates ('to venture upon the final step'); and the conclusion, as I shall shortly argue, precludes a return to the specifics of zoology. In short, from the initial evocation of the goddess (line 4) to the rejection of monstrous hybrids (lines 44–49), the idiom and substance of Goethe's poem are eminently Lucretian. It is, indeed, a Lucretian poem on modern (Goethean) science—but only in so far as modern science can be made to resemble the science of Lucretius himself.

Yet despite these close affinities, the differences between the two poems are profound. Where Lucretius is expansive and discursive, Goethe is selective and concentrated. He deals not with the entire natural world, as Lucretius had done, but only with zoology; and even his own zoological theories are not comprehensively covered. Nevertheless, his 'Metamorphosis of Animals' is a complete poem—no less complete than that on 'The Metamorphosis of Plants'. For in both of these poems, the function of the main, descriptive section is not to provide a comprehensive account of botany or of zoology, but merely to lay the basis for a broader concluding statement on nature and man—a personal statement of love as a creative principle in the first poem, and a more general statement on law and freedom throughout nature in the second (lines 50–52):

> May this beautiful concept of power and limit, of random
> Venture and law, freedom and measure, of order in motion,
> Defect and benefit, bring you high pleasur...

The first part of the poem contains all that is necessary to support this conclusion, so that further zoological detail would have been superfluous. Goethe then widens the scope of his conclusion even further, to encompass human morality, practical activity, art, and politics (lines 54–56):

> Moral philosophers never attained to a concept sublimer,
> Nor did men of affairs, nor artists imagining; rulers,
> Worthy of power, enjoy their crowns on this account only.

In other words, from his observations on zoology, Goethe has moved at once to the highest level of generalisation on humanity and the universe. But there is no such climactic summation in 'De rerum natura'. Lucretius moves continually to and fro between general principles and empirical illustrations, so that his work attains an epic breadth which is foreign to Goethe's concentrated didacticism. There is also, in the next lines of Goethe's poem, a degree of optimism and jubilant faith in humanity that is absent from Lucretius's sombre reflections on the universal struggle for existence (lines 57–58):

> So be glad of it, Nature's loftiest creature, now feeling
> Able to follow her loftiest thought on her wings of Creation.

The beginning of Goethe's poem certainly seemed to presuppose an earlier section within a longer poem on nature. But the ending, in which the reader is invited to look backwards, not forwards, makes it difficult to imagine how it could have continued beyond this point (lines 59–61):[51]

> Stand where you are, be still, and looking behind you, backward,
> All things consider, compare, and take from the lips of the Muse
>   then,
> So that you'll see, not dream it, a truth that is sweet and is certain.

The first part of this poem (up to line 49) represents Goethe's only sustained attempt at writing Lucretian verse. But in concluding it

---

51   For this reason, I find it difficult to agree with Erich Trunz's remark (HA, I, 585): 'Both the beginning *as well as the end* [my italics] point to connections within a larger work.' The only natural continuation would be further reflections on the place of human beings in the universe. Besides, the reference to the Muse at the end refers back to that in lines 52–53 rather than forward to what the Muse might say in the future.

in the way he did, he denied himself the possibility of developing it into a truly Lucretian work. He opted instead for a shorter analogue of the Lucretian poem, whose structure is foreshadowed in that of 'The Metamorphosis of Plants': a few, largely concrete, observations on the natural world are invested, in an abstract and general conclusion, with symbolic and universal significance. He already shows that predilection for the shorter didactic statement, dealing with a few representative phenomena, which becomes characteristic of his later poetry on nature and science. There are, admittedly, further echoes of Lucretius in his later poems;[52] but they never approximate so closely to the Lucretian model as does the first part of 'Metamorphosis of Animals'. The scientific poems in the sixth book of *Tame Xenia* (1826), for example, are dense, gnomic, and epigrammatic. And most of the philosophical poems in the collection *God and the World*, published in 1827, are far closer in character to the concluding lines of 'Metamorphosis of Animals' than to its earlier, Lucretian section: they are the concentrated utterances of a sage rather than the systematic teachings of a scientific didacticist, and their tone is more often lyrical than expository. Nevertheless, Goethe remains closer in his attitudes to Lucretius than to Brockes, Haller, and the other didactic poets of the earlier eighteenth century in Germany: his world, like that of the Roman poet, is a unitary whole, in which nature and man are one. But as he told Sulpiz Boisserée in 1815,[53] he now believed that a single long poem on nature was impracticable, and contented himself with assembling various of his shorter poems on nature and science into the balanced collection *God and the World*. Thus, although his later ideas on the natural universe did go into his poetry, it was not the poetry of a new Lucretius.

---

52 For example, as Bapp ('Goethe und Lucrez', p. 66) notices, the poem 'In Howard's Honoured Memory', published in 1820, echoes Lucretius's description of cloud shapes (IV, 129–42), and its eulogy of Luke Howard recalls Lucretius's eulogies of Epicurus. T. J. Reed's description, in *The Classical Centre: Goethe and Weimar 1775–1832* (London: Croom Helm, 1980), p. 238, of the 'Classical Walpurgis Night' in *Faust* as 'a new *De rerum natura*' applies to the scope and spirit of the dramatic pageant rather than to its form; the refutation of Anaxagoras by Thales recalls, however, Lucretius's refutation of Anaxagoras in 'De rerum natura', I, 830–920 (see Bapp, p. 66).

53 Conversation with Boisserée, 3 October 1815, in *Goethes Gespräche*, ed. by Wolfgang Herwig, 4 vols (Zurich and Stuttgart: Artemis Verlag, 1965–72), II, 1103.

In 1800, Goethe gave up his plan for a great epic of nature, and made it over to the young philosopher Schelling. He doubtless knew what he was doing: Schelling's poetic gifts were minimal, and what little survives of his neo-Lucretian efforts is eminently undistinguished. This is the case with the poem 'Animal and Plant', probably written in 1800; it is a lame take-off, in elegiac couplets, of Goethe's poem 'The Metamorphosis of Plants', attempting as it does to associate natural history with the relations between man and woman. It is also, as the following lines show, a crass example of male chauvinism, associating woman with vegetable passivity and man with animal freedom:

> And she [nature] gave vegetable nature to woman, whom I call the
>   plant-like
> One among animals, and man among them the animal one.
> More tender is womanly love, more imperative, quiet, and briefer;
> More animal, freer, but also more durable is love in the man.[54]

Further studies of Dante and his verse-form petered out in translations and fragments, and Schelling in turn abandoned the plan (as did the Danish philosopher Henrich Steffens, who also appears to have picked up the idea of an epic on the universe in Weimar in 1799 or early in 1800).[55]

Schelling did attempt, however, to discuss the philosophical and aesthetic implications of the project, and to explain why past initiatives had invariably failed. He does so in his *Philosophie der Kunst* of 1802–03, in the section on the didactic poem.[56] His argument is complicated, but it runs in essence as follows. The didactic poem, which has a specific end, namely to impart knowledge, is not properly an art-form, since art must have universality and not be tied to any particular purpose. But knowledge itself possesses universality if it is total knowledge—that is, if it is a complete reflection of the universe. Thus the only didactic poem which will be truly artistic in this sense will be one, as Schelling

---

54   F. W. J. von Schelling, *Werke*, ed. by Manfred Schröter, 6 vols (Munich: Beck Verlag, 1927), 4. Ergänzungsband (1959), p. 523.

55   On Schelling's plan and its failure, see Rudolf Haym, *Die romantische Schule*, 4th edn (Berlin: Weidmann, 1920), pp. 695–96; Fritz Strich, *Die Mythologie in der deutschen Literatur von Klopstock bis Wagner*, 2 vols (Halle: Niemeyer, 1910), II, 29–37; Aesch, pp. 261–63; and Plath, p. 48. On Steffens, see Plath, p. 45 and Steffens, *Was ich erlebte*, 10 vols (Breslau: Max, 1840–44), IV, 401–02 ('The subject was always too formidable for me').

56   *Werke*, Ergänzungsband (1959), pp. 309–18.

puts it, 'in which directly or indirectly, the universe, as reflected in knowledge, is the object'. He continues: 'Since the universe, in its form and essence, is only One, there can ideally be only One absolute didactic poem, of which all individual examples are mere fragments, namely the poem *on the nature of things*' (p. 315). All didactic poems of the past, including that of Lucretius, are of necessity only partial, since they are based on partial knowledge. Lucretius, for example, reduces the world to material particles, thereby ignoring the dimension of spirit. Schelling then concludes (echoing Schiller's essay *On Naïve and Sentimental Poetry*):[57] 'That didactic poem, then, in which [...] the object represented is itself poetic, is still to be written' (p. 317). In other words, the absolute didactic poem, the modern 'De rerum natura', still lies in the future, for our knowledge of the universe is as yet incomplete.

Schelling now builds into his argument the observation which Herder had made shortly before (see p. 14 above) when he maintained that a complete system of knowledge is itself inherently poetic. Once human knowledge is complete (that is, once it has achieved identity with the universe), the world-spirit will, as it were, itself generate the absolute didactic poem, and a new mythology to go along with it. Schelling concludes (p, 318): 'The origin of the absolute didactic poem or speculative epic therefore coincides as a single whole with the completion of science, and just as science originally emerged from poetry, it is also its most beautiful and final destiny to flow back into this ocean.' Art is thus both the original source and ultimate destination of knowledge (a view which Schiller had already expressed in his didactic poem 'The Artists' of 1789).[58] But what the new mythology which the progress of knowledge will eventually generate will look like, Schelling does not say.

Schelling's argument no doubt made him feel better about his failure to carry out the project that Goethe had handed over to him. But what he says is more than just a personal apology. Whereas Goethe settled for

---

57   See Schiller, *Werke*, Nationalausgabe, XX, 453: 'That didactic poem in which the thought itself were and would remain poetic, is still to be written.'

58   See Schiller's comments on this poem in his letter to Körner of 9 February 1789 in *Briefwechsel zwischen Schiller und Körner*, ed. by Klaus L. Berghahn (Munich: Winkler, 1973), pp. 100–01: 'Thus after the thought [...] that art prepared the way for scientific and ethical culture has been articulated [...] only then may it be said [...] that the perfection of humanity is realised when scientific and ethical culture are resolved into beauty.'

less than the original plan—for a collection of shorter poems on nature and science—Schelling claims that the plan is in principle *impossible* to fulfil, at least for the foreseeable future. He prices it, so to speak, right out of the market. History, of course, has so far proved him right. The closest approximation to the modern epic of nature is perhaps Alexander von Humboldt's *Cosmos*, which reviews all of nature as an organic whole, and pays tribute to Goethe's aspiration to integrate poetry, philosophy, and science.[59] But *Cosmos* is written in prose, not verse, and its formal ancestor is not Lucretius's 'De rerum natura' but Herder's *Ideas on the Philosophy of History*, which tried to present an integral vision of the natural world and human history.

Nevertheless, Schelling's explanation of why the 'absolute didactic poem' has never been written is not, to my mind, either complete or satisfactory. Nor is his secondary argument—of which the Romantics were particularly fond—that it was the lack of a new mythology that hampered modern scientific poets.[60] In the most successful didactic poem of the past, 'De rerum natura', mythology is in fact used quite sparingly, and it is clear that Lucretius regards the classical myths only as poetic figures: he specifically denies that the gods perform any function whatsoever in the natural universe (II, 1090–92). His main subject is the dynamic process of nature itself. (Schelling simply betrays his own failure to appreciate 'De rerum natura' when he declares (p. 316) that only the opening hymn to Venus and the eulogies of Epicurus, which display 'personal enthusiasm', are truly poetic.) One of the nearest things we have to a modern myth of the universe as a self-contained, natural system is that of the 'earth-spirit' (*Erdgeist*) in Goethe's *Faust*, Part I; and some critics have regretted that Goethe did not develop this further, but overlaid it instead with the old dualistic Christian framework of a transcendental God in the 'Prologue in Heaven' (see, for example, Reed, p. 136). It may well be that *Faust* would have been an even more impressive play, more in tune with modern sensibilities, if he had stuck to his original myth. But didactic poetry on scientific themes is a different matter. For good mythology tends to make for bad science,

---

59   See Humboldt, *Kosmos. Entwurf einer physischen Weltbeschreibung*, 5 vols (Stuttgart and Tübingen: Cotta, 1845–62), II, 75; also Plath, p. 74.
60   Some modern critics, in the wake of Fritz Strich (see note 55 above), have continued to adduce this as a major reason for the failure of the scientific epic in modern times: see, for example, Aesch, pp. 250–60.

as Lucretius well realised when he banished his gods from the universe as we know it to remote and inaccessible regions. The reasons for the failure of the modern epic of nature are more complex than this.

Part of the explanation lies in literary history, of course. In so far as the Lucretian poem is a specific case of the didactic poem in general, it was bound to share in that general decline in popularity of didactic poetry which is apparent in the later eighteenth century as the lyrical poetry of personal experience came to the forefront and prose became the main didactic medium. But the failure of the epic of nature also had a lot to do with the way in which science had developed. It is significant that most of the scientific poetry of the eighteenth century deals with natural history rather than with, for example, chemistry or physics. As the exact sciences grew more mathematical and hence more abstract, they became increasingly resistant to poetic expression. Wordsworth, in the preface to his *Lyrical Ballads*, hoped that science might eventually become more accessible to the ordinary run of people, and said: 'If the time should ever come when what is now called science, thus familiarised to men, shall be ready to put on, as it were, a form of flesh and blood, the Poet will lend his divine spirit to aid the transfiguration, and will welcome the Being thus produced, as a dear and genuine inmate of the household of man.'[61] This, of course, was not to be. Science has since grown more abstract still. But it is not just the abstraction of modern science that eludes Lucretian treatment. Its sheer extent and complexity are another insuperable obstacle. Admittedly, Lucretius himself had maintained that the universe is infinite (I, 958–67);[62] the difference is that the known contents of his infinite universe were vastly fewer and simpler than those of the infinite universe of today. Even by 1800, scientific knowledge had developed too far for the Lucretian poem to accommodate it. In fact, such poetry had degenerated into encyclopaedism over fifty years earlier (which casts an ironic light on Schelling's claim that science had not yet developed far enough for the 'absolute didactic poem' to be written).

---

61   William Wordsworth, *Poetical Works*, ed. by Thomas Hutchinson, new edition, revised by Ernest de Selincourt (London: Oxford University Press, 1950), p. 738.

62   Aesch, pp. 253–66, sees the infinity of the modern universe as the other principal reason why the neo-Lucretian epic failed. He seems unaware that Lucretius's universe was infinite too.

But there is more to it than that. The aim of Lucretius himself was *not* primarily to communicate the particulars of the scientific knowledge of his day; he uses these only to illustrate the underlying principles, or rather principle, on which this knowledge is based: namely, the principle that all things are susceptible to explanation in terms of natural causes, without the aid of religion (see Fabian (1968), p. 89). This principle is in turn the basis of his, and Epicurus's, moral philosophy, which promises the deliverance of human beings from fear, and the serenity of philosophical detachment. We are to attain this end not by denying the existence of death, suffering, and evil, but by accepting them as inevitable, and by learning to live with them as best we can through control of the passions, enjoyment of pleasure, and avoidance of pain. The link between Lucretius's view of the universe and his moral philosophy is thus a firm one. Newtonian science offered no such moral reassurance.[63] There were, it is true, systems of thought in the eighteenth century which claimed to encompass both the universe of science and the whole of moral and metaphysical reality: above all, that of Leibniz, which supplied the philosophical foundation of most didactic poems in Germany up to the middle of the century. But the link between Newtonian science and Leibniz's philosophical optimism was neither a close nor a necessary one; his optimism was based not on the progress of physics but on a priori reasoning on the nature of possible worlds. So long as the Leibniz-Wolffian system remained the popular philosophical orthodoxy in Germany, it seemed to go along quite happily with science: teleological reasoning from the wise design of creation helped to preserve the association. But ironically, the very work which the optimists took as their model for the scientific poem, Lucretius's 'De rerum natura', itself contained one of the greatest threats to their optimism in the whole of world literature. For Lucretius's universe is the product of random movements of atoms, which is incompatible with that benevolent providence in which the eighteenth century so much wanted to believe. As a result, much neo-Lucretian poetry was simultaneously anti-Lucretian poetry. Its faith in science drew it towards Lucretius, and its faith in providence drew it away from him. This ambivalent posture merely underlined its internal weakness and its inferiority to its model.

---

63   Even in the eighteenth century, regrets were sometimes expressed that it did not encompass the moral and spiritual world (see Schatzberg, p. 271).

It is no coincidence that the most successful didactic poem of the eighteenth century, Pope's *Essay on Man*, sticks largely to moral philosophy, says little about science (despite its tributes to Newton), and, for all its optimism, is full of caveats on the ability of the human intellect to comprehend the universal purpose: 'Know then thyself, presume not God to scan.' Pope did not expound an integrated philosophical system;[64] his aims were more modest. He simply stated some of the tenets of popular optimism as it was then current, and devoted most of his poem to moral questions. His optimism was associated with, but not demonstrated from, the findings of modern science, and by the end of the century, this association had become even more tenuous. Science simply could not furnish the basis for a moral philosophy on the Leibnizian pattern. Goethe took the logical step of creating a new, anti-Newtonian science of his own in order to preserve the unity between nature as he understood it and individual moral existence.[65] To him and to many of his German contemporaries, the philosophy of Spinoza, which dispensed with a transcendental God, appeared increasingly attractive, supplementing, or even supplanting, the philosophy of Leibniz.

The development of modern science thus goes a long way towards explaining why the eighteenth century never produced a *De rerum natura* to rival the poem of Lucretius. But there is a further reason why it could not have succeeded: Lucretius, as a poet, had certain advantages over his modern successors which it was not in their power to share. In the age of Newton, science made great discoveries. But Lucretius made an even greater one: he discovered science itself. The teachings of the Greek philosopher Epicurus struck the Roman poet with the force of a revelation, and in his poem, he sets out with evangelical fervour to convert his friend Memmius, and by extension all his readers, to the new gospel. His disadvantage as an early Roman poet, operating with a Latin which, as he himself says in apology (I, 136–45), was ill equipped to render the abstractions of Greek philosophical theory,

---

64   As Lessing and Moses Mendelssohn pointed out in their treatise *Pope a Metaphysician!* (see note 34 above); see also Fabian (1979), p. 536, and Peter Michelsen, 'Ist alles gut? Pope, Mendelssohn und Lessing. Zur Schrift *Pope ein Metaphysiker!*', in *Mendelssohn-Studien*, ed. by Cécile Lowenthal-Hensel and Rudolf Elvers (Berlin: Duncker & Humblot, 1979), pp. 81–109.

65   For further examination of this endeavour, see the essay 'The Ethical Foundation of Goethe's Scientific Thought' later in this volume.

became in fact one of his strongest assets: he was compelled to become a linguistic innovator, to deploy in new ways all the resources of archaism, colloquialism, and the down-to-earth concrete vocabulary he had at his disposal, and they lent his verse a vitality and exuberance which an established philosophical terminology could never have achieved.[66] The force of his poetry, what Statius called the *docti furor arduus Lucreti* ('the high passion of the learned Lucretius'),[67] was the force of triumphant assurance. As Herder shrewdly observed, 'Never will a didactic poet write more ardently and forcefully than Lucretius wrote: for he believed what he taught' (SW XIV, 194). Bertolt Brecht, in his remarkable unfinished attempt to render the doctrines of *The Communist Manifesto* in hexameters, shared at least one quality of Lucretius which few of his other imitators possessed, namely his tone of impassioned conviction.[68] That was precisely what Polignac, Wieland, and the eighteenth-century anti-Lucretians lacked. They were dealing in the already well-worn currency of Cartesian and Leibnizian metaphysics, and they were fighting a rearguard action on behalf of a declining faith. In fact, they were themselves already half seduced by the scientific gospel of their Roman predecessor, whose naturalistic tendency was ultimately more in keeping with the spirit of their age than were their own half-hearted compromises between science and religion. By the beginning of the nineteenth century, those who talked of a future epic of the universe had no new wisdom with which to replace the faith they had lost—hence their constant references to an indeterminate future, and to a new mythology yet to come. The Spinozism which some of them espoused was admittedly more consistent with modern science than Leibniz's metaphysical theories had been—not in its legacy of pantheism (which was already archaic), but in its affirmation of the universal rule of natural law. But this could no longer be presented as a new gospel. Europe already took it for granted.

---

66   See Alexander Dalzell's chapter on Lucretius in *The Cambridge History of Classical Literature*, Vol. II, Part 2, 'The Late Republic', ed. by E. J. Kenney (Cambridge: Cambridge University Press, 1982), pp. 33–55 (p. 46).

67   P. Papinius Statius, *Silvae*, II, 7, line 76.

68   Brecht, *Das Manifest*, in *Gesammelte Werke*, 20 vols (Frankfurt a. M.: Suhrkamp, 1967), X, 911–30.

Although the new Lucretius never made his appearance, the whole episode had at least two positive results: the poems on nature and science by Goethe, who wisely settled for less than the original over-ambitious plan; and the splendid hexameter translation of *De rerum natura* by Karl Ludwig von Knebel, who abandoned his own project of a neo-Lucretian poem[69] in order to restore the original to his German contemporaries.

---

69   On Knebel's early project and his reasons for abandoning it, see his letter to Goethe of 2 February 1825, in *Briefwechsel zwischen Goethe und Knebel*, II, 362.

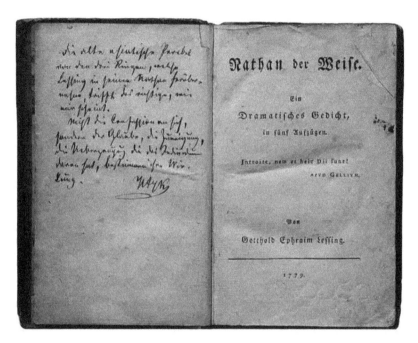

Gotthold Ephraim Lessing, *Nathan the wise. A dramatic poem in five acts* ([no place or publisher information], 1779). © Foto H.-P. Haack, https://commons.wikimedia. org/wiki/File:Lessing_Nathan_der_Weise_1779.jpg

2. On the Rise of Toleration in Europe

Lessing and the German Contribution[1]

If we examine the rise of toleration in Europe, the most prominent documents are easily identified. In Britain, there is John Locke's *Letter concerning Toleration*; in France, Voltaire's *Treatise on Toleration*; and in Germany, Lessing's drama *Nathan the Wise*. The last of these is anomalous: why should a drama acquire such significance for so fundamental a problem in European history?[2] No doubt this is partly because Germany, a disunited country until the second half of the nineteenth century, has traditionally looked to its cultural—and especially literary—achievements to define its national identity, and still habitually consults its classical authors for guidance on present-day problems. But it is also, I think, because Lessing's play, with its parable of the three indistinguishable rings which represent the rival claims of the three monotheistic religions, exemplifies a distinctively German approach to the problem of toleration. Before I look at a selection of German writers to substantiate this claim, I would like to comment

---

1   An earlier version of this chapter was originally published as 'On the Rise of Toleration in Europe. Lessing and the German Contribution', in *Modern Language Review*, 105 (2010) xxviii–xliv (Presidential Address of the Modern Humanities Research Association, delivered on 21 May 2010).

2   See Wolf Dietrich Otto, 'Toleranzkultur und Pädagogik oder: Wie reden deutsche Pädagogen über Toleranz?', in *Kulturthema Toleranz. Zur Grundlegung einer interdisziplinären und interkulturellen Toleranzforschung*, ed. by Alois Wierlacher (Munich: Iudicium, 1996), pp. 565–631 (p. 626): 'It is striking that Lessing figures as the unique point of reference in the German tradition of tolerance.' For Lessing's play, see Gotthold Ephraim Lessing, *Sämtliche Schriften*, ed. by Karl Lachmann and Franz Muncker, 23 vols (Stuttgart, Leipzig and Berlin: Göschen, 1886–1924), III, 1–177 (parable of the rings, pp. 90–95).

   https://doi.org/10.11647/OBP.0180.02

briefly on the two works just mentioned by Locke and Voltaire, in order to highlight some crucial differences between Britain, France, and Germany in their pursuit of toleration.

But first, a note on the word 'toleration' itself. Although I shall shortly refer to some of the edicts and legislative measures governing the practice of toleration in Europe, I shall be chiefly concerned with the theoretical pronouncements of the writers and thinkers who sought to promote it. The link between the theory and practice of toleration is often indirect,[3] for governments are of course influenced by political, economic, and other factors apart from the opinions of theorists.[4] But although practice often lags behind theory, most of the measures demanded by the theorists did eventually find their way into the statute books of the modern western democracies. It should also be noted that, until fairly recent times, toleration meant primarily religious toleration, whereas today, it more often applies to the toleration of cultural and ethnic differences.

John Locke published the first and most important of his four *Letters concerning Toleration* in 1689. He had written it in response to Louis XIV's revocation of the Edict of Nantes in 1685, the edict which, for nearly a century, had granted toleration to the Protestant minority in France. Locke advocates freedom of conscience as a natural right, for which even Jews, Muslims, pagans, and Unitarians are eligible.[5] To that extent, his *Letter* is liberal and rational in spirit. But in denying toleration to atheists (on the ground that they cannot take credible oaths in a court of law) and to Roman Catholics (on the ground that they owe allegiance to a foreign power),[6] he introduces ad hoc political considerations influenced more by his wish to secure the established Church of England and the Protestant succession to the British throne than by any rational principle. Together with the Act of Toleration of 1689, Locke's work helped to secure religious peace in Britain by affirming the supremacy of the established church, and at the same time supporting freedom

3   See Hans R. Guggisberg, *Religiöse Toleranz. Dokumente zur Geschichte einer Forderung* (Stuttgart–Bad Cannstatt: frommann-holzboog, 1984), pp. 9–11.

4   See Joachim Whaley, 'A Tolerant Society? Toleration in the Holy Roman Empire, 1648–1806', in *Toleration in Enlightenment Europe*, ed. by Ole Peter Grell and Roy Porter (Cambridge: Cambridge University Press, 2000), pp. 175–95 (p. 184).

5   John Locke, 'A Letter concerning Toleration' in Focus, ed. by John Horton and Susan Mendus (London and New York: Routledge, 1991); text of *Letter*, pp. 12–56 (p. 51).

6   Ibid., pp. 45–47 and 84–85.

of worship on the part of the Protestant non-conformists. In their characteristically British pragmatism and spirit of compromise, Locke's *Letter* and the act of parliament with which it coincided contrast sharply with their nearest continental equivalents.

In France, appeals for toleration, after the revocation of the Edict of Nantes and the end of toleration for Protestants, have much greater urgency and radicality than Locke's *Letter*, for they were directed both at France's established religion and at the French state itself for encouraging religious persecution. The classic protest is that of Voltaire in his *Treatise on Toleration* of 1763, in which he deploys all his skill in satire and eloquence to denounce the torture and execution of the Protestant Jean Calas, falsely accused of murdering his son to prevent his conversion to Catholicism. Voltaire is fond of citing, as he does here, the example of other countries in which numerous religions and nationalities coexist and work together in harmony, as in the Ottoman empire and the London stock exchange.[7] He does so, however, not because he respects the religions in question, but because he believes that the more of them are allowed to coexist, the more likely they are to neutralise each other and lose the power which a monopolistic religion is able to exercise in France. The logic of his views, and of those of most of his allies in the French Enlightenment, is to require a secular state, tolerant of but indifferent to the diverse religious beliefs and practices of its subjects. Such a requirement was eventually enshrined in Article 10 of the Declaration of the Rights of Man as approved by the French National Assembly in 1789: 'No one shall be disquieted on account of his opinions, including his religious views, provided that their manifestation does not disturb the public order established by law.'

I shall return later to Lessing's drama and its parable of the three rings, but I must point out in advance that, although it is based on an Italian model—namely the story of the three rings in Boccaccio's *Decameron*—Lessing changes the latter in fundamental respects. In particular, although Boccaccio's story leaves it in doubt which of the three rings—or the religions they represent—is the true one, it does not question the basic assumption that only one of them can be exclusively

---

7   Voltaire, *Treatise on Tolerance*, translated by Brian Masters, ed. by Simon Harvey (Cambridge: Cambridge University Press, 2000), pp. 19–22 (Ch. 4); also Voltaire, *Letters on England*, translated by Leonard Tancock (London: Penguin Books, 1980), p. 41 (Letter 6).

true. But in Lessing's case, the claims of all three remain indefinitely open: all three religions have the option of demonstrating, if not their exclusive truth, then at least their relative moral worth, by the conduct of their adherents. In short, Lessing's parable has an inbuilt pluralism which, as I shall attempt to show, is characteristic of a distinctive German tradition. Unlike British pragmatism and French secularism, this pluralistic tradition holds that, since we have no means of knowing whether or not one of the rival religions has an exclusive claim to truth, they should all be tolerated and respected.[8]

So far as I can determine, this pluralistic tradition first emerges in Germany in the late Middle Ages, with Nicholas of Cusa, who took his name from his birthplace of Kues on the River Moselle. He taught at the university of Cologne, and became a Cardinal and diplomat in the service of Rome. In this capacity, he travelled to Constantinople in 1437 and arranged for the Byzantine emperor John VIII Palaeologus to attend a conference in Florence, at which a union of the Greek Orthodox and Roman Catholic confessions was provisionally agreed. Inspired by this ecumenical initiative, Cusa went on to claim that, despite all differences in religious rites and doctrines, religion is ultimately one, for all contradictions are resolved in God, whose divine truth is inaccessible to finite mortals.[9] On receiving the news in 1453 that Constantinople had fallen to the Turks, he at once proceeded to write *On Religious Peace* (*De pace fidei*), which incorporates a dialogue between seventeen representatives of different faiths, all of which embody partial manifestations of divinity.[10] Cusa was probably the first Christian thinker to call for inter-religious harmony and to teach what later became known as 'perspectivism': that is, the doctrine that each religion offers a distinct and partial perspective on the one ineffable truth.[11]

---

8   On the meaning of the term 'pluralism' as used in this essay, see Michael Salewski, 'Europa, der tolerante Kontinent?', in *Religiöser Pluralismus und Toleranz in Europa*, ed. by Christian Augustin, Johannes Wienand and Christiane Winkler (Wiesbaden: Verlag für Sozialwissenschaften, 2006), pp. 12–27 and passim.

9   *Nicholas of Cusa on Learned Ignorance* [*De docta ignorantia*, 1440], ed. by Jasper Hopkins (Minneapolis: Arthur J. Banning Press, 1981). See also the article 'Toleranz' in *Geschichtliche Grundbegriffe*, ed. by Otto Brunner, Werner Conze and Reinhart Koselleck, 8 vols (Stuttgart: Klett, 1972–97), V, 445–605 (pp. 459–61).

10   *Nicholas of Cusa on Interreligious Harmony* [*De pace fidei*, 1453], edited and translated by James E. Biechler and H. Lawrence Bond (Lewiston, Queenston and Lampeter: Edwin Mellen, 1990).

11   Ibid., p. xxv; also *Nicholas of Cusa on Learned Ignorance* pp. 28–29 and 182.

The problem of religious differences became acute in Germany with the coming of the Reformation some sixty years later. Christianity now faced new, internal divisions, with Catholicism, Lutheranism, and subsequently Calvinism all claiming exclusive truth for their doctrines. Their conflict had serious political consequences as the hundreds of German rulers and their states divided their allegiance between the rival confessions. When successive attempts in the 1540s failed to heal the breach between Catholicism and Lutheranism, war broke out and agreement was not reached until the Peace of Augsburg of 1555, which bound the subjects of German states to adopt the confession of their ruler.[12] This was the same disastrous principle of *cuius regio, eius religio* which ended the Thirty Years War nearly a century later, aggravating rather than terminating religious controversy by making the religious faith of millions of people dependent on the whim of their particular head of state.

Not surprisingly, these conflicts inspired many attempts in Germany to eliminate or minimise religious differences. The reformer Martin Bucer, for example, worked tirelessly to unite the warring parties,[13] and the Catholic theologians Georg Witzel and Georg Cassander, with the encouragement of the Habsburg emperors Ferdinand I and Maximilian II, sought to establish common ground between the warring confessions.[14] Several German humanists, including Philipp Melanchthon and Johannes Reuchlin, strove to heal the breach with Rome (and in Reuchlin's case, to secure equal rights for the Jews).[15] The independent theologian Sebastian Franck went further still, declaring— uniquely in the first half of the sixteenth century—'I have my brothers among the Turks, Papists, Jews and all peoples'; Franck also called for universal tolerance, to include even heretics of every description.[16]

In due course, various German rulers began to adopt more tolerant measures, with Brandenburg-Prussia (whose Hohenzollern rulers were not otherwise renowned for their liberal sympathies) leading

---

12   See Francesco Ruffini, *Religious Liberty*, translated by J. Parker Heyes, with a preface by J. B. Bury (London and New York, NY: Williams & Newgate, 1912), pp. 209–10.
13   See Henry Kamen, *The Rise of Toleration* (London: Weidenfeld & Nicolson, 1967), pp. 66–68.
14   Ibid., p. 97.
15   Guggisberg, *Religiöse Toleranz*, pp. 47–48; Kamen, *Rise of Toleration*, pp. 86–92.
16   Guggisberg, *Religiöse Toleranz*, pp. 80–82; Kamen, *Rise of Toleration*, pp. 77–78.

the way. In 1611, the Elector Johann Sigismund granted freedom of worship to the Catholics of East Prussia who had until recently been citizens of Poland;[17] and when he himself converted from Lutheran to Calvinist observance two years later, he refrained from requiring his country to convert along with him. His grandson, the 'Great Elector' Friedrich Wilhelm, recognised all three major confessions in his realm and also tolerated Baptists, Socinians, and Jews.[18] Like their more famous successor Frederick the Great, these rulers were motivated as much by political and commercial considerations as by their own religious convictions (or lack of them); in order to keep the peace in Prussia's widely dispersed territories and to increase its population by immigration and territorial expansion, it made sense to keep religious restrictions to a minimum. Similarly, more than one confession was tolerated, at least on a *de facto* basis, in several imperial cities such as Augsburg, Biberach, and Kaufbeuren, no doubt for commercial reasons. These practical examples, plus the fact that, after the Peace of Westphalia of 1648, three Christian confessions were allowed to coexist within the Holy Roman Empire, could only encourage the advocates of religious pluralism and toleration to continue their efforts.[19]

I am, of course, aware that pluralistic attitudes and ecumenical initiatives were not confined to the German territories in the sixteenth and seventeenth centuries. Towards the end of the sixteenth century, for example, the French philosopher Jean Bodin, in his clandestine treatise *Colloquium Heptaplomeres*, constructed an open-ended dialogue between seven representatives of diverse religions and Christian confessions, in which it remains unclear which of them, if any, is the true one.[20] In the 1640s in England, the independent theologians Henry Robinson and John Goodwin argued that no one can possess the whole of truth, so that error is always possible and divergent opinions should be tolerated.[21]

---

17 Ruffini, *Religious Liberty*, p. 241.
18 See Klaus Deppermann, 'Die Kirchenpolitik des Großen Kurfürsten', *Pietismus und Neuzeit*, 6 (1981), 99–114 (pp. 99, 101, 104 and 113–14).
19 See Wolfgang Wüst, 'An der Toleranzgrenze. Der frühmoderne "Ernstfall" für Aufklärung, Toleranz und Pluralismus', in *Religiöser Pluralismus*, pp. 53–68 (pp. 56–58); also Ursula Goldenbaum, 'Einleitung', in *Appell an das Publikum. Die öffentliche Debatte in der deutschen Aufklärung 1687–1796*, ed. by Ursula Goldenbaum (Berlin: Akademie Verlag, 2004), pp. 1–118 (pp. 8–9 and 81–84).
20 Guggisberg, *Religiöse Toleranz*, pp. 112–121.
21 Kamen, *Rise of Toleration*, pp. 177–78.

And in 1670, the French Huguenot Isaac d'Huisseau published a work entitled *The Reunion of Christianity*, in which he sought common ground between the confessions in a few basic principles conducive to moral rectitude.[22] With the coming of the Enlightenment, the cause of religious tolerance was widely supported in France, for example in the two main works of Montesquieu.[23] But the point I wish to make is that, in countries other than Germany, there is not the same long and continuous tradition of religious pluralism and attempts to reconcile the warring religions; this pluralism was, after all, a response to the political as well as religious diversity of the Holy Roman Empire with its multitude of virtually independent states. The strength of this tradition becomes especially clear in the eighteenth century, above all through the work of Leibniz and his enormous influence on German thought.

Leibniz has the distinction of putting both religious and cultural pluralism on a metaphysical foundation. Already in his *Discourse on Metaphysics* of 1686, he declares:[24]

> Every substance is like a complete world and like a mirror of God, or indeed of the whole universe, which each expresses in its own way, much as one and the same town is represented differently according to the different positions from which it is viewed. Thus the universe is in a sense multiplied as many times as there are substances, and the glory of God is likewise multiplied by as many different representations as there are of his works.

In other words, all simple substances—or what Leibniz would later describe as 'monads'—view the universe from different perspectives; and in his subsequent works, he repeatedly uses this optical image to denote the uniqueness and relativity of all human insights.[25] In keeping with this perspectivism, Leibniz discerns some truth and value in all religious confessions, maintaining that '*it is possible to be saved* in every religion, *provided that one truly loves God above all things*' [Leibniz's

---

22 *La Réunion du Christianisme, ou la manière de rejoindre tous les chrétiens sous une seule confession de foy* (Saumur: René Pean, 1670); see also Ruffini, *Religious Liberty*, pp. 116–17.

23 *Lettres persanes* (1721) and *De l'Esprit des lois* (1748); see also Guggisberg, *Religiöse Toleranz*, pp. 237 and 241.

24 Gottfried Wilhelm Leibniz, *Philosophische Schriften*, ed. by Hans Heinz Holz, 4 vols in 6 (Frankfurt a. M.: Suhrkamp, 1965–92), I, 76–78.

25 Ibid., II/1, 459–61 and II/2, 174 (*Théodicée*, Pt. II, Para. 147 and Pt. III, Para. 357); IV, 464 and 466 (*Monadologie*, Paras. 57 and 60).

italics],[26] and on another occasion, 'I have found that most sects are right in a good part of what they affirm, but not so much in what they deny'.[27] These convictions underlie his protracted but ultimately unsuccessful negotiations, supported by both Protestant and Catholic German rulers, to reunite the Christian confessions.[28]

Leibniz's perspectivism is not entirely original: it is foreshadowed to some extent by Nicholas of Cusa.[29] But Leibniz is original in the way in which he extends it beyond religious differences to different civilisations, notably those of Europe and the Far East, as expressions of the universe from different perspectives.[30] Before the end of the seventeenth century, he made personal contact in Italy with several members of the Jesuit mission to China and corresponded regularly with them in subsequent years. In 1697, he published a series of documents which he had obtained through these exchanges, with the aim of showing that European culture had as much to gain from China as China had from Europe, declaring in his editorial preface: 'they [the Chinese] surpass us [...] in practical philosophy, that is, in the precepts of ethics and politics adapted to the present life and use of mortals'; he also added 'we need missionaries from the Chinese who might teach us the use and practice of natural religion, just as we have sent them teachers of revealed theology'.[31] Leibniz particularly admired the enlightened emperor Kang Xi, a contemporary of Louis XIV, who, unlike the French monarch, promulgated an edict of toleration in which Buddhism, Christianity, and Islam were granted equal rights.[32] When the Christian missionaries

---

26   Leibniz to Duchess Sophie of Hanover, August 1699, cited in Maria Rosa Antognazza, *Leibniz. An Intellectual Biography* (Cambridge: Cambridge University Press, 2009), p. 340.

27   Leibniz to Nicolas Rémond, 10 January 1714, cited in Antognazza, *Leibniz*, p. 500.

28   See Kamen, *Rise of Toleration*, p. 229; also Antognazza, *Leibniz*, pp. 47, 361, 366, 399 and 404–06.

29   See Robert Zimmermann, 'Der Cardinal Nicolas Cusanus als Vorläufer Leibnizens', *Sitzungsberichte der Kaiserlichen Akademie der Wissenschaften*, 8 (Vienna, 1852), 306–28; also Kiyoshi Sakai, 'Leibnizens Chinologie und das Prinzip der Analogie', in *Das Neueste über China. G. W. Leibnizens "Nova Sinica" von 1697*, ed. by Wenchao Li and Hans Poser (Stuttgart: Steiner, 2000), pp. 275–93 (p. 267).

30   See Antognazza, *Leibniz*, p. 360.

31   Gottfried Wilhelm Leibniz, *Writings on China*, ed. by Daniel J. Cook and Henry Rosemont Jr. (Chicago and La Salle, IL: Open Court 1994), pp. 46–47; also Franklin Perkins, *Leibniz and China. A Commerce of Light* (Cambridge: Cambridge University Press, 2004), p. 154.

32   Antognazza, *Leibniz*, p. 361; Leibniz, *Writings on China*, p. 53.

were eventually expelled by Kang Xi's son, it was because of their own intolerance: they disagreed among themselves on doctrinal principles and refused, on the Vatican's insistence, to accommodate Christian liturgy to Chinese rites and terminology.[33]

Leibniz's cultural perspectivism thus accorded equal status to Chinese and European culture: Chinese ethics was superior to European ethics; European science was superior to Chinese science; and while Chinese natural religion was superior to that of Europe, the revealed Christianity of Europe was superior to Chinese religion, which had no transcendental revelation. But while Leibniz's cultural perspectivism confined itself to differences between contemporary cultures, it had nothing to say on historical differences, and so did nothing to counteract the increasingly prevalent view that the modern age was in many ways superior to the earlier phases of history. This omission was made good in 1752 by Johann Martin Chladenius (or Chladni), who argued in a work on the theory of history (*Allgemeine Geschichtswissenschaft*) that our perception of history is relative to the position or point of view (*Sehepunkt* or *Standpunkt*) that we occupy within it.[34] With this insight, Leibniz's metaphysical, religious, and cultural perspectivism was complemented in Germany by a new historical perspectivism.

Another example of religious pluralism, more radical than that of Leibniz, is that of Gottfried Arnold, author of a monumental history of the Christian church with particular reference to heretics (*Unparteiische Kirchen- und Ketzerhistorie*, 1699–1700). Arnold's closest affinity as a thinker is to Sebastian Franck, by whose radical individualism he seems to have been influenced.[35] His rebellion against orthodox Lutheranism—he was himself a Lutheran pastor—becomes an attack on

33 Perkins, *Leibniz and China*, p. 199.

34 See Reinhart Koselleck, *Futures Past. On the Semantics of Historical Time*, translated by Keith Tribe (Cambridge, MA and London: MIT Press, 1985), pp. 136 and 140; also Hinrich C. Seeba, '"Der wahre Standort einer jeden Person". Lessings Beitrag zum historischen Perspektivismus', in *Nation und Gelehrtenrepublik. Lessing im europäischen Zusammenhang*, ed. by Wilfried Barner and Albert M. Reh (Detroit, MI and Munich: Wayne State University Press and edition text + kritik, 1984), pp. 193–214 (p. 210),

35 See Siegfried Wollgast, 'Zu den philosophischen Quellen von Gottfried Arnold und zu Aspekten seines philosophischen Systems', in *Gottfried Arnold (1666–1714). Mit einer Bibliographie der Arnold-Literatur ab 1714*, ed. by Dietrich Blaufuss and Friedrich Niewöhner (Wiesbaden: Harrossowitz, 1995), pp. 301–35 (p. 332).

church authority in general. He teaches a kind of theological anarchism, in which Christ himself figures as the first persecuted heretic.[36] It follows from these premises that religious truth is not to be found in any one place or society, but disseminated among many nations and communities. The lesson which runs throughout Arnold's work is that the only acceptable attitude on the part of religious authority is to allow complete liberty of conscience and to practise universal toleration. Arnold's vast compilation had considerable influence in its time, and was read and respected by Herder, Lessing, and Goethe among others.

Some fifty years after Leibniz's death, there was a sudden revival of interest in his philosophy with the posthumous publication of his *New Essays on Human Understanding* in 1765[37] and the six-volume edition of his works by Louis Dutens in 1768;[38] Herder and Lessing both studied him intensively during the following years. In his notes on Leibniz, Herder twice refers to Leibniz's metaphor of optical perspectives and seeks to develop it further. On the first occasion, in the draft of a letter probably written in 1768 and only recently published, he applies the optical metaphor to history in order to highlight the necessary incompleteness of each individual's historical vision, saying:[39]

> Every human eye has always had its own angle of vision: each projects the object before it in its own way; and at all events, just as little as a complete body can appear as it really is on a flat surface, so perhaps, despite all the abundance of circumstantial memoirs, is it in an ideal sense impossible to construct a complete history of even a *single* thing or event.

And on the second occasion, Herder points to the inadequacy of Leibniz's optical metaphor of the individual monad or soul as a 'mirror' of the universe, arguing that the perceiving subject must add a subjective element of its own in the process of perception:[40]

> So if our soul is a living mirror of the universe, it must not reflect this universe *out* of itself so that it is not *in* itself but *outside* itself with no

---

36   See Guggisberg, *Religiöse Toleranz*, pp. 226–27.
37   In *Oeuvres philosophiques latines et françoises de feu M. de Leibnitz*, ed. by Rudolf Erich Raspe (Amsterdam and Leipzig: Schreuder, 1765).
38   Leibniz, *Opera omnia, nunc primum collecta*, ed. by Louis Dutens, 6 vols (Geneva: De Tournes, 1768).
39   Johann Gottfried Herder, *Ausgewählte Werke in Einzelausgaben. Schriften zur Literatur*, 2 vols (Berlin and Weimar, Aufbau Verlag, 1985–90), II/1, 685.
40   Johann Gottfried Herder, *Sämtliche Werke*, ed. by Bernhard Suphan, 33 vols (Berlin: Weidmann, 1877–1913), XXXII, 226.

communicability between the two [...]. On the contrary, there must be in each soul an internal basis for the presence of that part of the universe which it surveys, and which should not be sought in some third being as the basis of both [as in Leibniz's theory of pre-established harmony—HBN].

Like the individual subject itself, what that subject perceives in history—for example, a particular nation or age—will likewise be unique, or as Herder puts it, 'the genius of human and natural history lives in and with each nation as if the latter were the only one on earth',[41] or again, 'each nation has its centre of happiness within itself, just as every sphere has its own centre of gravity.'[42]

Thus Herder's well known cultural relativism or pluralism has its roots in Leibniz's metaphysics, and he endows each nation or society with a dynamic, organic quality akin to that of Leibniz's monads, each of which has its own sufficient reason within it.[43] As already noted, Herder develops these ideas further. For example, since each nation has its own inherent value, he deplores colonialism with its destruction of indigenous cultures, and the activities of European missionaries in suppressing non-Christian systems of belief.[44] He is, of course, also influenced by Rousseau and other contemporary opponents of Eurocentrism;[45] but Leibniz's cultural perspectivism and the metaphysical pluralism which underpinned it certainly pointed him in the same direction.

A word now about Lessing. I have yet to discuss his play *Nathan the Wise*, but at this point, it should be noted that he was well acquainted with the theory of perspective, both in its literal sense as a branch of optics and in its metaphorical application to denote limited degrees of insight in metaphysics, epistemology, religion, and other areas. Thus, in the ongoing debate in Germany as to whether or not the ancients fully understood the laws of perspective in visual art, he correctly argued that linear perspective was a Renaissance discovery and refuted those who thought otherwise.[46] He also applied the metaphors of perspective

---

41 Ibid., XVIII, 249.

42 Ibid., V, 509; see also V, 455.

43 See H. B. Nisbet, 'Herder. The Nation in History', in *National History and Identity*, ed. by Michael Branch (Helsinki: Finnish Literature Society, 1999), pp. 78–96 (p. 79).

44 Herder, *Sämtliche Werke*, V, 550; also IV, 472, XVIII, 221–24, and 249.

45 See Robert Wokler, 'Multiculturalism and Ethnic Cleansing in the Enlightenment', in *Toleration in Enlightenment Europe*, ed. by Grell and Porter, pp. 69–85 (p. 82).

46 Lessing, *Sämtliche Schriften*, X, 255–56; also Seeba, 'Der wahre Standort', pp. 205–09.

to dramatic theory, declaring that the dramatist must project himself into the points of view of the characters he creates, and at the same time unify these limited viewpoints in a comprehensive view of the action which the reader or spectator is allowed to share.[47] Besides, he knew at least some of the works of Nicholas of Cusa, and there is evidence that he prevailed upon one of his learned associates to translate Cusa's *On Religious Peace*, with its interreligious dialogue, from Latin into German; the manuscript of this translation unfortunately disappeared after Lessing's death.[48] More significantly, his admiration for Leibniz and his major indebtedness to Leibniz's thought are amply documented. In the present context, the main point to note is that, in one of two essays on Leibniz which Lessing published in 1773 after intensive study of his works, he speaks approvingly of Leibniz's ability to discern an element of truth, though never the whole truth, in the most divergent opinions— that is, his perspectivism. In Lessing's own words:[49]

> In his quest for truth, Leibniz never took any notice of accepted opinions; but in the firm belief that no opinion can be accepted unless it is in a certain respect, or in a certain sense true, he was often so accommodating as to turn the opinion over and over until he was able to bring that certain respect to light, and to make that certain sense comprehensible. [...] He willingly set his own system aside, and tried to lead each individual along the path to truth on which he found him.

The main difference between Lessing's perspectivism and that of Leibniz is that Lessing's version incorporates a higher degree of scepticism with regard to obtaining certainty on the truths we believe we possess, not least those of religion. Lessing inherited this scepticism from Leibniz's adversary Pierre Bayle, one of the writers he most admired in his early years and one of the most important progenitors of toleration. Bayle's

---

47   Lessing, *Sämtliche Schriften*, IX, 185 and 371; also Seeba, 'Der wahre Standort', pp. 200–03.

48   See Markus Schmitz, 'Die eine Religion in der Mannigfaltigkeit der Riten. Zur Erkenntnistheorie von Cusanus' *De pace fidei* sowie Lessings *Nathan* als Ausgangspunkt einer Konzeption des friedlichen Miteinanders verschiedener Religionen', in *Lessings Grenzen*, ed. by Ulrike Zeuch (Wiesbaden; Harrassowitz, 2005), pp. 181–95; also Konrad Arnold Schmid to Lessing, 8 and 18 December 1779, in Gotthold Ephraim Lessing, *Werke und Briefe*, ed. by Wilfried Barner and other hands, 12 vols (Frankfurt a. M.: 1985–2003), XII, 293–94 and 298.

49   Gotthold Ephraim Lessing, *Philosophical and Theological Writings*, ed. by H. B. Nisbet (Cambridge: Cambridge University Press, 2005); also in Lessing, *Sämtliche Schriften*, XI, 470.

scepticism had the effect, in Lessing's case, of reinforcing Leibniz's perspectivism by further stressing that all truth is relative, so that no religion can claim exclusive access to it. I have examined these questions in greater detail elsewhere,[50] and I shall simply add here that, once we realise that Lessing's perspectival theory of truth underlies his view of the three monotheistic religions—and of the three rings which represent their rival claims in *Nathan the Wise*—some common misunderstandings of that play and its relation to religious toleration can be avoided.

In the second half of the eighteenth century, a subtle change took place in the discourse of toleration, and Lessing is among the first to exhibit it. What changes is the use and significance of the word 'toleration' (German *Toleranz*) itself, as well as the adjective 'tolerant', which begins to go out of fashion and even to take on negative associations. For example, the word *Toleranz* occurs only twice in all of Lessing's works, in both cases with reference to past ages (the Reformation and the medieval period); and on both occasions, Lessing's aim is not to recommend toleration as a positive value for the present, but to deplore its absence as a minimum requirement in past ages—that is, to condemn *in*tolerance.[51] Similarly, Herder speaks with heavy sarcasm in 1774 of the 'universal international benevolence [*Völkerliebe*] full of tolerant subjugation, extortion, and enlightenment' which characterises the present age;[52] and Kant, in 1784, praises Frederick the Great for declining to accept 'the presumptuous title of *tolerant*'.[53] What has happened here is that the concept of toleration, in its then accepted sense of 'sufferance' or 'putting up with', was seen to imply an act of indulgence by a condescending authority which might at any time withdraw the concession in question. At a time when at least some western governments (the USA in 1776 and 1787 and France in 1789) began to frame legislation guaranteeing basic freedoms to their subjects, the relevant declarations speak not of universal toleration, but of universal and inalienable *rights*.[54] This terminology is

---

50 See H. B. Nisbet, *Gotthold Ephraim Lessing. His Life, Works, and Thought* (Oxford: Oxford University Press, 2013), pp. 123–24 and 511–13.

51 Lessing, *Sämtliche Schriften*, V, 45 and IX, 210.

52 Herder, *Sämtliche Werke*, V, 486.

53 Immanuel Kant, *Political Writings*, ed. by Hans Reiss, 2nd edn (Cambridge: Cambridge University Press, 1991), p. 58; also in Immanuel Kant, *Gesammelte Schriften* (Berlin: Preussische Akademie der Wissenschaften, 1900–), VIII, 40.

54 Thus, in the era of the French Revolution, Mirabeau rejects the concept of toleration in favour of an unrestricted right to religious freedom (Guggisberg, *Religiöse Toleranz*, p. 289), as does Tom Paine (*Toleration in Enlightenment Europe*, ed. Grell and Porter, pp. 16, 46, and 115).

derived from the ancient tradition of natural law, revived and codified in the seventeenth and early eighteenth centuries by such writers as the Dutch theorist Hugo Grotius and the Germans Samuel von Pufendorf and Christian Thomasius (the last of whom recommended toleration of *all* religions).[55] This revival of natural law also marks a step in the direction of secularisation, inasmuch as natural rights extend not just to religion, but to all forms of belief, so long as their observance does not disturb the public peace; and unlike the pluralistic and perspectivist attitudes already mentioned, natural law makes no judgement as to the truth or value of the religious and cultural attitudes to which the right of free expression is granted. The same is true of Kant's theory of freedom: it makes no mention of religion other than as a possible support for morality, and it defines the right to freedom of conscience in purely secular terms as an inherent aspect of individual moral autonomy.[56] As for the word 'toleration', it has in present-day usage acquired a more positive meaning (often denoted in English by the variant noun 'tolerance') to denote respectful recognition of the legitimate beliefs of others which we ourselves do not happen to share.

But where does this leave the German tradition of pluralism and perspectivism as the recognition of religious, cultural, and historical differences? This tradition lives on in various guises, one of which is nineteenth-century historicism, the historical method pioneered by Herder whereby each historical age and culture is seen as a unique and valuable whole, reconstructed by the historian in an act of empathetic understanding.[57] This is what Leopold von Ranke had in mind when he famously declared of the historical process: 'Every epoch has a direct relationship to God, and its value consists not in what it gives rise to, but in its existence itself.'[58]

Closely related to this is another development in German thought, more far-reaching and longer-lived than nineteenth-century historicism, namely hermeneutics. Hermeneutics is a quintessentially German

---

55	See *Geschichtliche Grundbegriffe*, V, 503; also Ruffini, *Religious Liberty*, pp. 218 and 223–27.
56	Kant, *Gesammelte Schriften*, VI, 237.
57	See Friedrich Meinecke, *Die Entstehung des Historismus*, 2 vols (Munich and Berlin: R. Oldenbourg, 1936).
58	Leopold von Ranke, *Über die Epochen der neueren Geschichte*, ed. by Theodor Schieder and Helmut Berding (Munich: Historische Kommission der Bayerischen Akademie der Wissenschaften, 1971), p. 60.

discipline, associated with such names as Friedrich Schleiermacher, Wilhelm Dilthey, Martin Heidegger, and Hans-Georg Gadamer. From its theological beginnings as a guide to interpreting scriptural texts and discovering their supposedly true meaning, it was gradually secularised in the eighteenth century to become a means of discovering the multiple meanings of literary and other texts (Chladenius, already referred to above, was one of those involved).[59] For Schleiermacher and others, the meaning of the Bible becomes progressively enlarged as knowledge of its historical context and the psychology of its writers increases.[60] For Dilthey, such divinatory psychology becomes the basic means of comprehension for the humanities in general.[61] In the hermeneutic enterprise, feeling and imagination play an important part, and for Gadamer, their conclusions are always subject to enlargement and modification. Hermeneutics no longer claims to discover any 'objective' meaning, but rather the individuality of the text and its author as the interpreter's 'horizon' merges with that of the writer under scrutiny.[62] There is no universal viewpoint, only individual perspectives; and since we can never exclude our own preconceptions—or even know how far these are involved in our interpretation—our conclusions must always be provisional.[63] Thus, hermeneutic understanding is an ongoing, open-ended process, in which new experience modifies or negates previous expectations; and as we learn to perceive the historicity of the text or writer studied, we simultaneously become aware of our own historicity.[64] Gadamer's aim and achievement is to distinguish clearly between the objective knowledge provided by science, which is purged of human

---

59 See Johann Martin Chladenius (Chladni), *Einleitung zur richtigen Auslegung vernünftiger Reden und Schriften* (Leipzig: Lankisch, 1742): also Koselleck, *Futures Past*, pp. 136 and 306 and Seeba, 'Der wahre Standort...', p. 210.

60 See Odo Marquard, 'Frage nach der Frage, auf die die Hermeneutik die Antwort ist', in Marquard, *Abschied vom Prinzipiellen. Philosophische Studien* (Stuttgart: Reclam, 1981), pp. 117–46 (pp. 128–31).

61 See Hans-Georg Gadamer, *Wahrheit und Methode. Grundzüge einer philosophischen Hermeneutik*, 4th edn (Tübingen: Mohr, 1975), pp. 173–74; also the article 'Hermeneutik' in *Historisches Wörterbuch der Philosophie*, 13 vols (Darmstadt: Wissenschaftliche Buchgesellschaft, 1971–2007), III, 1061–73 (p. 1064).

62 Gadamer, *Wahrheit und Methode*, pp. 177–80 and 356–59; see also Charles Taylor, 'The Politics of Recognition', in *Multiculturalism. A Critical Reader*, ed. by David Theo Goldberg (Cambridge, MA and Oxford: Blackwell, 1994), pp. 75–106 (pp. 98 and 101).

63 Gadamer, *Wahrheit und Methode*, pp. 374–75.

64 Ibid., pp. 338–40.

values and purposes, and the bilateral understanding of human phenomena furnished by hermeneutics and by every discipline based on hermeneutic principles.[65] In short, modern hermeneutics is another product of the pluralistic, perspectivist tradition from which it first emerged in eighteenth-century Germany.

But while hermeneutic understanding may well be conducive to toleration (in the modern sense of respectful recognition of the Other), the link with toleration is no longer a necessary one as it had been in the religious and cultural pluralism of, for example, Leibniz, Lessing, and Herder. Several factors subsequently intervened to render this link more tenuous. Herder's stress on the uniqueness of national cultures was already capable of two constructions: on the one hand, it could help to foster pluralism and international tolerance, as Herder certainly intended; but on the other, it could encourage nationalism, not always of a tolerant variety. The famous chapter on Slavonic culture in Herder's *Ideas on the Philosophy of History* became a sacred text of pan-Slavism, and his praise of folk culture in his anthology *On German Character and Art* became grist to the mill of German nationalism in the following centuries.[66] At the same time, internal conflicts and differences which had provided a stimulus to pluralistic attitudes in Germany since the Reformation were diminished by other developments, such as the reduction of inter-confessional strife in 1817 with the unification of the two main Protestant churches in Prussia (soon followed by other German territories), the recognition of religious freedom in the constitution of Bismarck's Reich (already foreshadowed in the Prussian legal code of 1794), and the unification of Germany itself in 1871.

Other major developments in nineteenth-century thought undermined pluralism more directly. For instance, both Hegel and Marx saw history as a uni-directional process leading towards uniform political (and by implication cultural) arrangements. More significantly, perspectivism reappears as a central concept in Nietzsche's thought, and it is with Nietzsche that it is now most closely linked. But it no longer has the meaning it had held for its earlier adherents. In both philosophy and theology, perspectivism had hitherto required a

---

65   See Charles Taylor, 'Gadamer on the Human Sciences', in *The Cambridge Companion to Gadamer*, ed. by Robert J. Dostal (Cambridge: Cambridge University Press, 2002), pp. 126–42 (pp. 127–29).

66   Herder, *Sämtliche Werke*, XIV, 277–80 and V, 159–231.

balance to be struck between its positive and negative aspects, between subjectivity and objectivity, between confidence that every perspective affords some degree of truth or value and scepticism as to whether any perspective offers an adequate degree of certainty. With Nietzsche—and with his postmodernist followers—the balance shifts decisively towards the negative, towards subjectivity, towards uncertainty. Like others before him, Nietzsche argues that all our knowledge is perspectival and therefore relative.[67] He also concedes that we can increase our knowledge by acquainting ourselves with as many different perspectives as possible.[68] But since the number of possible perspectives is infinite, our knowledge can never be complete, and we have no way of deciding which, if any, of our judgements concerning truth or value are objectively valid. Indeed, our failure to recognise this fact is a source of weakness, or as Nietzsche puts it, it is 'an expression of the sickness of humanity as opposed to the animals'.[69] Our respect for truth, he maintains, is the result of an illusion, and the world has no underlying meaning [*Sinn*], but countless possible meanings.[70] The most valuable meanings are those we create for ourselves and affirm with all our strength—or rather, with our *will*, as the later Nietzsche never tires of repeating. However inconsistent these arguments—like those of all radical relativists—may be (for example, it is plain that Nietzsche has his own set of values which he considers superior to those of others), it is certain at least that his variety of perspectivism did nothing to further the cause of toleration in Germany. In fact, he has no use whatsoever for toleration, which he sees simply as a cloak for indifference or lack of conviction in one's own ideals.[71]

The catastrophes caused by nationalistic militarism and anti-Semitism in the twentieth century require no discussion here; it is enough to say that, after 1945, the need for religious, ethnic, and cultural toleration in Germany became more obvious than ever before. This need has been further intensified in recent decades by the presence of several millions of Muslims in the Federal Republic. These factors have generated a widespread preoccupation with toleration, witnessed by ongoing public

---

67 See Steven D. Hales and Rex Welshon, *Nietzsche's Perspectivism* (Urbana and Chicago, IL: University of Illinois Press, 2000), p. 35.
68 Friedrich Nietzsche, *Werke in drei Bänden*, ed. by Karl Schlechta (Munich: Hanser, 1965–67), II, 860–61 (*Zur Genealogie der Moral*).
69 Ibid., III, 441 (*Aus dem Nachlass der achtziger Jahre*).
70 Ibid., III, 424 and 903 (*Aus dem Nachlass der achtziger Jahre*).
71 Ibid., I, 246: II, 610, 619, and 1165; III, 516 and 888, etc.

debates and a huge volume of publications on the subject, [72] and it is widely acknowledged that the need for pluralistic attitudes—not only in Germany, but also in other western countries—is currently acute.

To return to Lessing: to what extent is his drama *Nathan the Wise* relevant to the present situation? Given that this drama emerged, as I have shown, from a long tradition of pluralism as a means to religious toleration, it obviously retains its relevance to all inter-religious conflicts. And although inter-religious strife is less of a problem in the present age of secularism and civil rights than inter-cultural friction, the play's depiction of (albeit fleeting) harmony between representatives of Christian, Jewish, and Muslim communities also lends support to multiculturalism as a present-day alternative to social unrest. The suspense of judgement in Nathan's parable regarding the truth claims of the three monotheistic religions—the judge in the parable suggests that a conclusive answer may be found, if at all, some million years hence—is also in keeping with the postmodernist conviction that no concept can have an ultimate, unequivocal meaning.[73] The judge's recommendation that the moral conduct of the three quarrelling sons, rather than their religious beliefs, should be the deciding factor between their claims is in keeping both with Kant's moral philosophy and with the conclusions of Rainer Forst, the author of the fullest German study of toleration in recent times.[74] And in Germany in particular, Lessing's play has a remarkable way of gaining new relevance as events or comments in the play invite comparison with topical equivalents. This applies not only to Germany's current relations with its Muslim minority, but also to the bigoted Christian patriarch's repeated comment on the adoption of a Christian child by a Jew: 'The Jew must be burnt'! ['Der Jude wird verbrannt!'].[75]

---

72   For a full bibliography of works on toleration, mainly but not exclusively in German, from 1945 to 1995, see *Kulturthema Toleranz*, ed. Wierlacher (see note 2 above), pp. 635–70; works published since 1995 can be found in the annual bibliography 'Cannstatter Bibliographie zur Toleranz- und Intoleranzforschung', which is available online.

73   Lessing, *Sämtliche Schriften*, III, 95; on the play's affinities with postmodernism see also Peter Sloterdijk, *Gottes Eifer. Vom Kampf der drei Monotheismen* (Frankfurt a. M. and Leipzig: Insel, 2007), pp. 170–71.

74   Rainer Forst, *Toleranz im Konflikt. Geschichte, Gehalt und Gegenwart eines umstrittenen Begriffs* (Frankfurt a. M.: Suhrkamp, 2003), esp. pp. 596–97, 604, and 642).

75   Lessing, *Sämtliche Schriften*, III, 117.

What, then, are we to make of those critics—some, but by no means all of them Jewish—who dismiss or attack the play as irrelevant, unhelpful, or even pernicious? Some of their objections—for example, the claim that Lessing's intention is to persuade the Jews to abandon their faith and become assimilated to gentile society—are demonstrably out of keeping with Lessing's views, as I have shown elsewhere.[76] But other criticisms are less easy to refute. As a set text in German schools, the play can all too readily become trivialised by over-familiarity, and its message of toleration may be undermined when repeated by less than tolerant teachers.[77] Others find the play's utopian ending unconvincing, when three of the main characters discover that they are all members of one family.[78] More seriously, the noted German writer W. G. Sebald describes the early post-war performances of the play in Germany as 'perfidious tactlessness' in view of the horrendous crimes committed by that country so shortly before.[79] Seen in this context, the lessons of the play may well seem grossly inadequate, or indeed arouse justified suspicions that some of the play's admirers may be using it as an aid to self-exculpation or complacency in relation to events for which they were at least to some extent responsible. Such feelings are certainly present in the Hungarian-Jewish dramatist George Tabori's parody *Nathan's Death* (1991), in which Sultan Saladin flatly refuses to listen to Nathan's parable and Nathan, having retrieved the charred bodies of his children from his burnt-out house, ends up by reciting his parable with no one to hear it and dies alone as a demented, Lear-like figure.[80] Among the most

---

76 See, for example, Hans Mayer, 'Der weise Nathan und der Räuber Spiegelberg' [1973], in *Lessings 'Nathan der Weise'* (Wege der Forschung, 587), ed. by Klaus Bohnen (Darmstadt: Wissenschaftliche Buchgesellschaft, 1984), pp. 350–73 (p. 367); also Nisbet, *Gotthold Ephraim Lessing. His Life, Works, and Thought*, pp. 616–18.

77 See, for example, Navid Kermani's contribution in Angelika Overath, Navid Kermani and Robert Schindel, *Toleranz. Drei Lesarten zu Lessings Märchen vom Ring* (Göttingen: Wallstein, 2003), pp. 33–45 (pp. 36–37).

78 See, for example, Angelika Overath's contribution in ibid., pp. 21–31 (pp. 29–31); also Avishai Margalit, 'Der Ring. Über religiösen Pluralismus', in *Toleranz. Philosophische Grundlagen und gesellschaftliche Praxis einer umstrittenen Tugend*, ed. by Rainer Forst (Frankfurt a. M. and New York, NY: Campus Verlag, 2000) pp. 162–76.

79 W. G. Sebald, 'Die Zweideutigkeit der Toleranz. Anmerkungen zum Interesse der Aufklärung an der Emanzipation der Juden', in *Der Deutschunterricht*, 36, Heft 4 (1984), pp. 27–47 (p. 28).

80 See Silvia Stammen, 'Geschichte der Zerstörung—Zerstörung der Geschichte. *Nathans Tod* im Textvergleich mit *Nathan der Weise*', in *Theater gegen das Vergessen. Bühnenarbeit und Drama bei George Tabori*, ed. by Hans-Peter Bayerdorfer and Jörg

extreme among all the play's critics is the German-Jewish writer Henryk M. Broder, who, in a work entitled *Critique of Pure Tolerance* (*Kritik der reinen Toleranz*), denounces the play in the course of his wider offensive against tolerance in general and tolerance of Islam in particular.[81]

In the light of these differences of opinion, it is no wonder that any performance of *Nathan the Wise*, at least in Germany, is bound to be problematic. If it is performed straight (which it rarely is), it may come across as hackneyed, utopian, and unconvincing—or even, in this age of disillusion, as an involuntary satire on the ideals it is meant to represent; and if it is performed against the grain, it may lose sight altogether of the ideals which inspired it.

Where does this leave us? If we ask whether or not *Nathan the Wise* still has value as an appeal for religious and cultural tolerance, there is no easy answer. But if, in keeping with Gadamer's hermeneutics, we enlarge our horizon to accommodate that of other perspectives and relate the work to the rich and long-lived German tradition of pluralism, it may be possible to conclude that—no less than Locke's *Letter* in Britain and Voltaire's *Treatise on Toleration* in France—Lessing's play still merits its position in Germany as the most significant, though controversial, document on toleration in the German language.

Schönert (Tübingen: Niemeyer, 1997), pp. 283 and 318, for a detailed analysis of Tabori's text.

81   Henryk M. Broder, *Kritik der reinen Toleranz* (2008), 2nd edn (Munich: Pantheon, 2009), pp. 7–8 and 210.

Painting of Gotthold Ephraim Lessing by Anton Graff (1771), Kunstsammlung
der Universität Leipzig, Photograph by Liberal Freemason (2007), Wikimedia,
Public Domain, https://commons.wikimedia.org/wiki/File:Gotthold_Ephraim_
Lessing_Kunstsammlung_Uni_Leipzig.jpg

3. On the Function of Mystification in Lessing's Masonic Dialogues, *Ernst and Falk*[1]

In his late work *The Education of the Human Race*, Lessing suggests that the time may now have come in which the New Testament has outlived its usefulness as a guidebook—at least for the more farsighted among his contemporaries. But anyone who has attained this insight would do well, he adds, to keep it to themselves: 'Take care, you more able individual who stamp and fret on the last page of this primer, take care not to let your weaker classmates perceive what you suspect, or already begin to see! Until they have caught up with you, those weaker classmates!'[2]

This partiality for concealment, and indeed for mystification, is repeatedly evident in Lessing's late writings and conversations, but it is nowhere more conspicuous than in his Masonic dialogues *Ernst and Falk*. There have, of course, been various attempts by Lessing critics to explain the function of secrecy in this work. But the relevant interpretations are often mutually incompatible, and all are in some measure incomplete. A comprehensive explanation of this phenomenon should not, in my

---

1   An earlier version of this chapter was originally published as 'Zur Funktion des Geheimnisses in Lessings "Ernst und Falk"', in Peter Freimark, Franklin Kopitzsch and Helga Slessarev (eds.), *Lessing und die Toleranz* (Detroit, MI and Munich; Wayne State University Press and edition text + kritik, 1986), pp. 291–309.

2   Gotthold Ephraim Lessing, *Sämtliche Schriften*, ed. by Karl Lachmann and Franz Muncker, 23 vols (Stuttgart, Leipzig and Berlin: Göschen, 1886–1924), XIII, 429–30. For the German text of *Ernst and Falk*, see ibid., XIII, 389–411. For an English translation, see Gotthold Ephraim Lessing, *Philosophical and Theological Writings*, ed. by H. B. Nisbet (Cambridge: Cambridge University Press, 2005), pp. 184–216; all references in this essay are to this edition, and are identified by page numbers in brackets within the text.

    https://doi.org/10.11647/OBP.0180.03

opinion, confine itself to the Masonic dialogues, but should view their mystifications in the context of related stylistic elements in other works of Lessing's later years, because they are all, as I shall try to show, part of a wider rhetorical strategy. The aim of this essay is accordingly to examine all past interpretations of the mystifications in *Ernst and Falk*, and to define their function (or functions) within his late works as a whole.

It is not the purpose of this essay to examine the role of the secret societies in eighteenth-century Europe—not least because this topic has been extensively discussed from the later twentieth century onwards.[3] But I may perhaps be allowed some introductory remarks on the relationship of Lessing's dialogues to the secret societies of his time. For it was precisely the intense interest of the contemporary public in these institutions that provided the context which Lessing was able to exploit for his own rhetorical ends.

It would seem at first sight anomalous that these societies enjoyed their greatest popularity in Germany and other European countries at almost the same time as the Enlightenment attained its fullest development. Attempts have been made to explain their remarkable success by contending that, in the age of reason, mysteries acquired a rarity value, and that the secret societies helped, in view of the growing secularism of the times, to fill the vacuum left by the decline in significance of religion and its associated rituals.[4] These circumstances may certainly

---

3   See, for example, J. M. Roberts, *The Mythology of the Secret Societies* (London: Secker and Warburg, 1972); Rudolf Vierhaus, 'Aufklärung und Freimaurerei in Deutschland', in *Das Vergangene und die Geschichte. Festschrift für Reinhard Wittram zum 70. Geburtstag*, ed. by Rudolf von Thadden, Gert von Pistohlkors, and Hellmut Weiss (Göttingen: Vandenhoeck & Ruprecht, 1973), pp. 23–41; R. H. Frick, *Die Erleuchteten. Gnostisch-theosophische und alchemistisch-rosenkreuzerische Geheimgesellschaften bis zum Ende des 18. Jahrhunderts* (Graz: Akademische Druck- und Verlagsanstalt, 1973); Richard van Dülmen, *Der Geheimbund der Illuminaten* (Stuttgart-Bad Cannstatt: Frommann, 1975); ibid., 'Die Aufklärungsgesellschaften in Deutschland als Forschungsproblem', in *Francia*, 5 (1977), pp. 251–75; *Geheime Gesellschaften*, ed. by Peter Christian Ludz (Heidelberg: Schneider, 1979); Ludwig Hammermayer, *Der Wilhelmsbader Freimaurerkonvent von 1782* (Heidelberg: Schneider, 1980); Margaret C. Jacob, *The Radical Enlightenment. Pantheists, Freemasons and Republicans* (London: Allen & Unwin, 1981); *Freimaurer und Geheimbünde im 18. Jahrhundert in Mitteleuropa*, ed. by Helmut Reinalter (Frankfurt a. M.: Suhrkamp, 1986); Jan Assmann, *Religio duplex. Ägyptische Mysterien und europäische Aufklärung* (Berlin: Verlag der Weltreligionen, 2010).

4   See, for example, Roberts, *Mythology*, p. 57 and Ludz (ed.), pp. 170f.

have contributed to the success of the secret societies, especially in Protestant countries. But it is equally certain that the attraction of the societies, at least for progressively minded thinkers, lay largely in their close affinity to the aims and ideals of the Enlightenment itself. And the societies were not slow to exploit this affinity: they made calculated use of the age's enormous thirst for knowledge by creating the impression that initiation into their secrets promised new insights from which the uninitiated were excluded. Lessing himself cherished hopes of this kind when he sought admission to the Freemasons in 1771 in Hamburg. He became a Freemason because he hoped to further his research into the origins of Freemasonry, and he felt drawn to a movement which seemed dedicated to the most progressive social and political values then current.[5] But his disillusionment with the movement followed quickly and comprehensively, and he shared this experience with many other progressive-minded thinkers of the time. Nevertheless, the societies had means of dealing with such negative reactions. The disappointed initiates were promised subsequent admission to higher grades within the order, and when their expectations were again disappointed, other societies such as the Illuminati and the Rosicrucians were available which, in the later 1770s and early 1780s, recruited most of their members from among disillusioned Freemasons. Such organisations fed on each other, taking over and modifying their rivals' rituals, and thereby lured their proselytes with the prospect of ever higher truths and ever more profound secrets. Lessing did not adopt this course. Instead, he found his own highly original course of action by writing *Ernst and Falk*.

Lessing was by no means the first to make literary capital out of the secret societies. The authors of the numerous novels on this theme in the late eighteenth century, among them Schiller and Goethe, followed a similar strategy.[6] But there is an important difference—not only in the literary genre adopted—between Lessing's dialogues and the contemporary prose narratives on related topics, a difference rooted in Lessing's own disillusionment with such organisations. His aim is

---

5   See Heinrich Schneider, 'Lessing und die Freimaurer', in ibid., *Lessing. Zwölf biographische Studien* (Berne: Francke, 1950), pp. 166–97 (p. 168).

6   See, for example, Wilfried Barner, 'Geheime Lenkung. Zur Turmgesellschaft in Goethes *Wilhelm Meister*', in *Goethe's Narrative Fiction*, ed. by William J. Lillyman (Berlin and New York, NY: De Gruyter, 1983), pp. 85–109 (p. 108).

fundamentally distinct, in that he writes not so much about as against the secret societies. He is concerned, in *Ernst and Falk*, to undermine official Freemasonry as he knew it, to reduce its mysteries and obsession with secrecy and redefine it as an open brotherhood of all unprejudiced men (there were, of course, no female Freemasons). His own disillusion is reflected in the disappointment of Ernst, who, soon after his admission to the order, loses patience with the Freemasons and their constant prevarications and promises of higher insights (p. 204). But we are here confronted with a further paradox: if the two speakers, and the author himself, feel so disenchanted with the secret societies, why do secrets and further mystifications play so essential and conspicuous a part in the dialogues?

To answer this question, it is necessary to examine the stylistic devices and turns of phrase which Lessing employs for the purpose of mystification, and to analyse their function. A brief initial outline of the form and structure of the dialogues, and in particular their rhetoric of mystification, may facilitate this end.

The five dialogues fall into two sections, inasmuch as the first three are separated from the final two by a pause during which Ernst leaves his friend to join the Freemasons. The first three dialogues deal with the antithesis between, on the one hand, Freemasonry as it ought to be—that is, the 'true' Freemasonry whose task consists in counteracting the national, religious, and social differences between human beings, and on the other hand, Freemasonry as it is in the existing Masonic lodges, whereby its inadequacies become increasingly conspicuous. Ernst repeatedly confuses these two concepts, which leads him to join a lodge in the hope of obtaining further enlightenment. The final two dialogues examine the present, decadent state of the Masonic order, before concluding with an investigation of its origin and a return to the true historical task of Freemasonry. On a personal level, the first three dialogues depict Ernst's growing curiosity and initiation into some of the Masonic secrets; this reaches its climax with his formal admission to a Masonic lodge. The last two dialogues depict his profound disappointment, which gradually gives way to a renewed conviction in the value of 'true' Freemasonry as Falk further enlightens him on its role in human history.[7]

---

7   On the structure of the dialogues see Peter Michelsen, 'Die "wahren Taten" der Freimaurer. Lessings *Ernst und Falk*', in *Geheime Gesellschaften*, ed. Ludz, pp. 293–324 (p. 294).

Lessing's choice of the philosophical dialogue is well suited to the theme in question, for it functions like a process of initiation[8] in which Ernst (and with him, the implied reader)[9] is gradually introduced to further secrets of Freemasonry. For example, when Ernst begins to grasp the complexity of the questions under discussion, he is informed by Falk that he is already 'half a Freemason' (p. 191). This takes place before he becomes the member of a lodge, which indeed affords him far less insight than his conversations with Falk. The dialogue form—consisting of private conversations in which the confidentiality of the topic and the need to keep it secret are repeatedly emphasised—illustrates and exemplifies the process which is the subject of the conversations, namely the process of individual and collective enlightenment. The role of Freemasonry in history, as Falk describes it, constitutes a parallel to his own role in the personal enlightenment of his friend.[10]

But it would be misleading to speak without qualification of enlightenment and growing insight. For the enlightenment which is imparted to Ernst (and the reader) is only relative enlightenment, not least because the unelucidated mysteries are much more strongly emphasised than those which are clarified. The very title of the work implies an esoteric material: the dialogues are 'for Freemasons'. The dedication, with its metaphor of the unfathomable well of truth and its prophetic tone, is likewise profoundly mysterious (p. 184). The 'Preface by a third party', which is certainly by Lessing himself, already acquaints us with that indirect form of expression which Falk employs almost exclusively throughout the later dialogues. With reference to the subsequent conversations, the preface asks the question: 'Why has no one spoken out so clearly long ago?' (p. 185). The question must, of course, be taken as ironic, for much of what follows will be anything but clear. Besides, no answer is supplied at all, and the preface simply continues: 'This question could be answered in many different ways', before the further, apparently similar, question is raised as to 'why the

---

8 See Ion Contiades, *G. E. Lessing: 'Ernst und Falk'. Mit den Fortsetzungen J. G. Herders und F. Schlegels* (Frankfurt a. M.: Insel Verlag, 1968), p. 129.

9 See Gonthier-Louis Fink, 'Lessings *Ernst und Falk*. Das moralische Glaubensbekenntnis eines kosmopolitischen Individualisten', *Recherches Germaniques*, 10 (1980), pp. 18–64 (p. 24).

10 See Paul Müller, *Untersuchungen zum Problem der Freimaurerei bei Lessing, Herder und Fichte* (Diss. Berne: Haupt, 1965), p. 34.

systematic textbooks of Christianity arose at so late a stage, [and] why there have been so many good Christians who neither could nor would define their faith in an intelligible manner'. These questions likewise remain unanswered, and the preface concludes with the invitation 'Readers may make the application for themselves'.

Right at the beginning of the dialogues proper, Falk evades his friend's questions. When Ernst asks him if he is a Freemason, he at first does not answer the question at all, and when it is repeated, he gives the disconcerting reply: 'I think I am.' It is therefore hardly surprising that, early in the second dialogue, Ernst loses patience with Falk and his refusal to give clearer answers, and is able to pass the judgement on him and all Freemasons that 'they all play with words, and invite questions, and answer without answering' (p. 190). In the third dialogue, Falk confirms that the ways of the Freemasons are anything but straight, because he rejects Ernst's conclusion that they 'counteract' the evils of constitutional states as far too definite. Instead, he says that the Freemasons help other people in an indirect way to become aware of such deficiencies: '"To counteract" can here mean at most to activate this awareness in them from afar, to encourage it to germinate, to transplant the seedlings and remove the weeds and superfluous leaves' (p. 199). He is at the same time describing here his own tactics towards his friend, as also evinced when he speaks in riddles and paradoxes—for example, when he tells him that the good deeds of the Freemasons are 'good deeds aimed at making good deeds superfluous' (p. 190), or when, instead of providing unambiguous explanations, he asks rhetorical questions (e.g. on pp. 196f.). He repeatedly teases his friend with Socratic irony, pretending to know less than he really knows. When Ernst becomes irritable and declares that he wants to hear nothing more about Freemasonry, Falk tells him that he is indeed willing to tell him more about them (pp. 191f.); but as soon as Ernst again becomes curious, Falk resumes his evasive tactics: he even claims to have forgotten their earlier discussion (p. 197). Among other things, this leads to a position where, by the final dialogue, Ernst has come so fully to terms with Falk's evasive behaviour that he hesitates to ask any further direct questions. He would like to ask how it came about that the Freemasons derived so much of their symbolism from architecture, but says instead: 'Shall I guess, or may I ask?' Falk reacts in characteristic style and declares that Ernst could have guessed the answer if he had asked a different question, so that Ernst now has to guess what that other question might have been (pp. 212–13).[11]

Falk's tactics of mystification, as his own comments confirm, are akin to the language of the Freemasons. This becomes especially clear if we consider the symbols and metaphors used in the dialogues, for they are for the most part borrowed from Masonic terminology. Among them are, for example, the image of flames and smoke which the two speakers first use with reference to the advantages and disadvantages of civil society, and later to those of the Masonic order itself (pp. 195 and 203), as well as the images of sunrise and sunset, which are used in their literal sense at the beginning of the dialogues but acquire a symbolic meaning at the end (pp. 452, 209, and 216). Falk twice uses alchemical images, thereby alluding to the occultism of some contemporary lodges, but since he employs them to denote the progressive role of 'true' Freemasonry in history, he invests them with a positive sense. Just as sodium nitrate must be present in the air before it can settle on walls as saltpetre, so must unprejudiced people be present in society before they can address the tasks of true Freemasonry; and just as the alchemist who is able to make silver deals in old scrap silver to conceal his secret, so may the Freemasons publicise some of their intentions in order to distract attention from their real activities (p. 201). And the word *Arbeit* ('work' in English) which official Freemasonry uses to designate the business of the order is used more than once by the two speakers to designate the business of 'true' Freemasonry (p. 198).[12] Nearly all of these symbols and expressions, in keeping with the theme of the dialogues, are associated with the realm of mystery.

It can therefore hardly be denied that the dialogues consistently make use of rhetorical mystification. Although some of the secrets of 'true' Freemasonry are aired as Falk gradually enlightens his friend, it remains a peculiarity of this work that nearly every secret that is revealed is balanced by a new, unresolved secret. For example, as soon as Falk has reported that the work of the Freemasons includes the

---

11 On Falk's evasiveness, see Wolfgang Heise, 'Lessings *Ernst und Falk*', in *Weimarer Beiträge*, 11 (1979), pp. 5–20 (pp. 11f.).

12 James Anderson, *The Constitutions of the Ancient and Honourable Fraternity of Free and Accepted Masons*, rev. edn, ed. by John Entick (London: J. Scott, 1767), p. 314

task of combatting ethnic, religious, and social prejudices, he at the same time emphasises that this task is only 'part of their business'. He repeats this comment: 'I say *part* of their business' (p. 197), and thereby indicates that they are also concerned with further, unknown business. And when Ernst is somewhat later convinced that Falk has named all the social evils that the Freemasons are concerned to remove, Falk at once qualifies his earlier statement: 'I have named only a few of them as examples. Only a few of those which are evident to even the most short-sighted observer' (p. 199); there are accordingly further, unnamed evils that must also be resisted. Even towards the end of the dialogues, after Falk has introduced his friend into some secrets regarding the origin of Freemasonry, he adds with reference to further information he has yet to communicate: 'Hear me now simply as one hears the first rumour of some major event: it stimulates one's curiosity more than it satisfies it' (p. 214). The concluding 'Note' to the reader also mentions a sixth dialogue, which Lessing did not write (and probably had no intention of writing).[13] His reference to a further conversation simply serves to emphasise the fragmentary nature of the work and the provisionality of the thoughts it contains: Lessing thereby hints at further unresolved secrets and insights into the nature of 'true' Freemasonry.

The dialogues accordingly leave a great deal open. The number of unanswered questions and resolved mysteries is roughly equal.[14] Lessing has also made the mystification tactics of the secret societies not just the object, but also the formal principle of his dialogues and thereby produced the effect of raising the curiosity of his readers to the highest pitch. It remains to be asked what purpose this device is meant to serve.

In the wake of Reinhart Koselleck's study *Kritik und Krise. Ein Beitrag zur Pathogenese der bürgerlichen Welt* (*Critique and Crisis. Enlightenment and the Pathogenesis of Modern Society* (Freiburg: Karl Alber Verlag, 1959; English edition Cambridge, MA: MIT Press, 1988)), it became widely accepted by Lessing scholars that Lessing's mystifications and the role of the secret societies in his dialogues must have a political explanation. The political interpretation of the secrecy practised by the Freemasons

---

13   See Karl S. Guthke, 'Lessings "Sechstes Freimaurergespräch"', *Zeitschrift für deutsche Philologie*, 86 (1966), 576–97.

14   Peter Michelsen (see note 7 above), pp. 309 and 312, in my view exaggerates the extent to which the fifth dialogue resolves the enigmas which arose in the previous dialogues.

and similar societies in the eighteenth century is, of course, much older than Koselleck's book. Well over a century ago, Hermann Hettner, for example, declared that the secret societies of the Enlightenment were 'a product of the general immaturity and oppression which stifled any vigorous expression of public life. [...] What [...] in a despotic state is a secret society is under freer circumstances a free alliance and public association.'[15] The political theory of the secret societies did, of course, gain a great deal in the way of breadth and complexity from the work of Koselleck and his followers, and it is largely due to him that interest in Lessing's Masonic dialogues has grown so strongly over the last half century. This has led to the recognition that *Ernst and Falk* is a significant political document and Lessing's political testament. According to Koselleck, the secret societies of the Enlightenment functioned as proto-democratic organisations which prepared the way for the emancipation of the bourgeoisie. Secrecy was for them a political necessity, because, in the absolutist state, the new and potentially revolutionary ideals of individual freedom and equal rights could be rehearsed only in the private sphere. At the same time, the fact that most Masonic lodges—in contrast, for example, to the Illuminati—disclaimed any involvement in politics[16] constituted an implicit criticism of the political world on which they turned their backs.

The application of this theory to Lessing's Masonic dialogues has led to the often repeated claim that his tactics of mystification are a symptom of political caution, or even that they served as a cloak for revolutionary attitudes.[17] But the claim that Lessing held revolutionary

---

15 Hermann Hettner, *Geschichte der deutschen Literatur im achtzehnten Jahrhundert*, ed. by Georg Witkowski, 4 vols (Leipzig: Paul List Verlag, 1928), II, 213 (first published in 1856–70).

16 See Anderson, *Constitutions*, p. 316: 'we are also of all *Nations, Tongues, Kindreds*, and *Languages*, and are resolved against all *Politicks*, as what never yet conduced to the Welfare of the *Lodge*, nor ever will.'

17 See, for example, Ehrhard Bahr, 'The Pursuit of Happiness in the Political Writings of Lessing and Kant', *Studies on Voltaire and the Eighteenth Century*, 151 (1976), 167–74 (p. 174): 'It now becomes clear that the anonymity of the dialogues' publication was due as much to their political implications as to considerations of Masonic secrecy. In order to have any chance for discussion and eventual application, German political theory was forced to hide behind the acceptable secrecy of the Freemasons'. See also Klaus Bohnen, *Geist und Buchstabe. Zum Prinzip des kritischen Verfahrens in Lessings literaturästhetischen und theologischen Schriften* (Cologne: Böhlau, 1974), p. 184, and Manfred Durzak, 'Gesellschaftsreflexion und Gesellschaftsdarstellung bei Lessing', *Zeitschrift für deutsche Philologie*, 93 (1974), 546–60 (p. 558).

political views is demonstrably untenable. As Gonthier-Louis Fink has shown in detail,[18] his political ideals in *Ernst and Falk* are related to those of early German liberalism—as in the thought of the young Fichte, for example, or that of Wilhelm von Humboldt—with no hint of any threat to the existing state. Besides, these ideals are propounded quite openly in the first two dialogues. Anyone who maintains that the metaphor of the anthill, which Ernst and Falk praise as a model of peaceful anarchy, anticipates the Marxist-Leninist doctrine of the overthrow of class society overlooks important contrary evidence;[19] for Lessing's remark, as reported by Friedrich Heinrich Jacobi, that 'in a conversation I had with him, he became so heated that he declared that *civil society* must be abolished completely',[20] remains an isolated outburst out of keeping with the views expounded in the Masonic dialogues. The two speakers conclude regretfully that the analogy of the anthill will never be applicable to human society, and they are in agreement that the social differences which the state entails are necessary evils. The Freemasons must, of course, resist the state-sanctioned disunity among the populace, but 'without detriment to this state or these states' (p. 200). The evils inherent in civil society must indeed be resisted, but no one should try to eliminate them completely,' for one would simultaneously destroy the state itself along with them' (p. 199). And civil society and the state, despite all the evils associated with them, are much to be preferred to the state of nature (p. 195). The highest aim of Lessing's Freemasons is therefore not to abolish the state, the church, or class distinctions, even if they employ the concepts of harmonious anarchy and perfect human equality as regulative, utopian ideas. They are in no way revolutionaries, for they disapprove of the American Revolution and the alleged participation of the Freemasons in it (p. 209).[21]

But this is not to deny that Lessing's dialogues contain progressive and even radical sentiments. There are examples of these firstly, in Falk's pronouncement in the second dialogue that any happiness of the state whereby even the smallest number of individual members

---

18   Fink, 'Lessings *Ernst und Falk*', pp. 37–49 and 59–62.
19   See, for example, Heise, 'Lessings *Ernst und Falk*', pp. 5f.
20   *Lessing im Gespräch*, ed. by Richard Daunicht (Munich: Wilhelm Fink, 1971), pp. 519f.
21   See on this Michelsen, 'Die "wahren Taten"', p. 307, who convincingly refutes the exaggerations of the Koselleck party.

suffers is simply a cloak for tyranny (p. 191), and secondly, in Ernst's attacks on class prejudices, antisemitism, and elitist attitudes within the Masonic order (p. 207). Similarly, Lessing's liberal individualism, as in Falk's declaration that the state is not an end in itself but only a means to individual happiness, does not amount to an implicit attack on the absolutist state such as the Prussia of Frederick the Great, in which there could be no question of individual freedom as an end in itself.[22] I merely wish to point out that firstly, the political radicalism of this work has all too often been exaggerated, whereas its tendency can be described as subversive only in the sense of a belief in gradual and peaceful progress; and secondly, that the political content of the dialogues is not alone enough to explain their consistent mystification and secretiveness. Only a few years later, Kant, as a Prussian citizen, had no hesitation in openly defending liberal individualism in his essay *What is Enlightenment?* (1784) and supporting the thesis that the only just laws are those which a people could impose on itself. And Lessing himself was in no way irresolute when it came to broadcasting radical opinions, as he did in theological matters in 1777 when he published the truly explosive 'Fragments' of Reimarus, in which it was claimed, among other things, that the apostles secretly disinterred the body of Christ and invented the story of the resurrection.

Besides, Falk distinguishes two kinds of secret: 'mystifications', which could in principle be expressed directly if it were appropriate or desirable to disclose them, and 'the secret', which cannot be expressed at all (p. 205). Radical political ideas plainly belong to the former category; but Falk insists the 'true' Freemasonry has to do not with 'mystifications', but with 'the secret'—and that, of course, is quite a different matter.[23]

The claim that Lessing resorted to mystification for fear of censorship[24] can be refuted on similar grounds, for although he was forbidden in July 1778 to publish further writings without the approval of the Brunswick censors, he had already completed *Ernst and Falk* (apart

---

22   This is not contradicted by Lessing's reply of 1769 to a letter from Nicolai in which he vehemently rejects the latter's praise for the supposed freedom of speech enjoyed in Prussia; this was a private response provoked by Nicolai's manifestly excessive claims, and would never have been made in any public statement: see Lessing to Nicolai, 25 August 1769, in Lessing, *Sämtliche Schriften*, XVII, 298.

23   As Karin Hüskens-Hasselbeck, *Stil und Kritik. Dialogische Argumentation in Lessings philosophischen Schriften* (Munich: Fink, 1978), convincingly argues.

24   See, for example, Müller, *Untersuchungen*, p. 25.

from the dedication and prefaces) in the previous year. And even if the prohibition had been imposed at an earlier date, there is no reason to assume that he would have paid any more attention to it than he did during his later theological polemics, when he without hesitation published unapproved writings even after the prohibition.

The attempt has also been made to explain the secrecy observed by Lessing's Freemasons as a moral necessity. Thus Gonthier-Louis Fink, for example, maintains that an action can only be described as virtuous if it is not publicised, for publicity would allow pride and self-regard to operate as motives, so that the moral autonomy of the action might be jeopardised.[25] But although Falk maintains that the 'true deeds' of Freemasonry are a secret in the sense that they cannot be expressed in words, he also indicates that they do become known to outside observers inasmuch as they can be learnt and imitated by example (pp. 186–87). This fact somewhat reduces the credibility of the moral explanation of the secret, for it appears that such deeds are taken note of by at least a select public. But a further objection can be formulated to the moral interpretation: deeds that are kept secret for moral reasons must by definition be capable of communication, but this is clearly not the case with the 'true deeds' of the Freemasons; for according to Falk, they *cannot* be made known by the 'true' Freemason, even if he wished to do so. In other words, the 'true deeds' of the Freemasons are either known to some other Freemasons, in which case they are at least in part lacking in moral autonomy; or they are in principle incapable of disclosure, in which case the secrecy which surrounds them cannot be imposed by moral considerations. It therefore follows that the moral interpretation provides at most only a partial explanation for the secrecy in which Lessing's Freemasons enshroud their activities.

The most obvious explanation for the mystifications in *Ernst and Falk* is, of course, that the work deals with Freemasonry—and not just the ideal, utopian kind of Freemasonry which Falk attempts to define, but also with the real Masonic order. And Lessing, as an official member of that order, was bound by oath not to divulge any Masonic secrets. I have already mentioned that the form of the work is entirely appropriate to its subject, and that some of its symbols and images are associated with Masonic practice. There is also no doubt that Falk does allude to certain

---

25   Fink, 'Lessings *Ernst und Falk*', pp. 55f.

Masonic secrets—especially in the last two dialogues, in which there are various references to the origin, rituals, and symbolism of Freemasonry. In addition, Ludwig Hammermeyer's research on the Strict Observance branch of the movement has shown that Lessing's dialogues contain, among other things, a commentary on the contemporary crisis within that system, and that Lessing was concerned to influence the present course of events: his attack on the Templar legend in the fourth dialogue equates precisely with the aim of the Grand Master of the Strict Observance, Duke Ferdinand of Brunswick-Lüneburg (to whom the first three dialogues are dedicated), namely to discredit the Templar legend, while his publication of the last two dialogues constitutes one of the first public refutations of the doctrine that the modern Freemasons are the direct successors of the Knights Templar. Before their publication, Duke Ferdinand circulated the manuscript of these two dialogues among the office-bearers of the Strict Observance to further his reforming plans.[26]

Nevertheless, the main tendency of the dialogues is to play down such secrets of contemporary Freemasonry as its alchemistic experiments, conjuration of spirits, and Templar legend, which are among those 'mystifications' which could easily be expressed in words. (Besides, all the main secrets of institutional Freemasonry have been exposed at various times, as had already happened in France in the first half of the eighteenth century.)[27] Falk even says that such mysteries, once they have fulfilled their purpose in the history of Freemasonry, have no need of further secrecy. He says, for example, of the relationship between the historical Knights Templar and the Freeemasons: 'It should rather be stated openly, so long as one defines the specific point which made the Templars the Freemasons of their time' (p. 205). But characteristically, he does not define this relationship specifically, and merely tells his friend that he would be able to guess the answer to this question himself if he were to read the history of the Templars more closely. Falk is speaking of something which may once have been a true 'secret', but which has meanwhile fulfilled its historical function, so that it can now be understood correctly and made public. But among those Freemasons who have not

---

26   See Hammermeyer, *Der Wilhelmsbader Freimaurerkonvent*, pp. 26f.
27   See Hans-Heinrich Solf, 'Die Funktion der Geheimhaltung in der Freimaurerei', in *Geheime Gesellschaften*, ed. Ludz, pp. 43–49, (p. 44).

yet grasped the historical significance of the Templar order, its memory survives only in the 'mystifications' of the Templar legend.

It is nevertheless remarkable that Falk's own mystifications concern not only the inexpressible 'secret' of 'true' Freemasonry, but also some of the 'mystifications' of the contemporary Masonic order. Is it meant to be merely ironic when he states that a person who discovers the philosophers' stone will at that same instant become a Freemason? Or when he says that spirits will heed only the voice of a Freemason (p. 204)? It seems as if Lessing wishes to leave open the possibility that an as yet unrecognised rational sense might underlie even the most ridiculous ploys of contemporary Freemasons.[28] For Falk expressly declares of such delusions: 'It's enough [...] that I can already discern in their toys the weapons which the men will one day wield with a steady hand' (p. 206).[29]

The above reflections show that the mystifications in Lessing's dialogues are partly due to the fact that secrets are the subject of the dialogues, above all that 'secret' that underlies the workings of 'true' Freemasonry in history, but also those 'mystifications' of contemporary Masonic lodges which could in principle be expressed directly and publicised. But that by no means exhausts the problem. The mystifications in *Ernst and Falk* are part of a wider tendency, indeed a strategy, which can be detected throughout Lessing's later works (although it finds its most prominent expression in *Ernst and Falk*).

Lessing was inclined throughout his life to maintain a certain reserve towards even his closest friends, and especially in his later years, it became his habit to keep his philosophical speculations to himself, to express them only indirectly, or to try them out in conversation with younger acquaintances such as Karl Wilhelm Jerusalem, Johann Anton Leisewitz and Friedrich Heinrich Jacobi. But the decisive factor which transformed this habit from a personal idiosyncrasy into a conscious principle of his thought was his growing conviction (probably

---

28   It is possible that he is here alluding to the case of a Jewish Freemason, alchemist, and spiritualist called Samuel Jacob Falk (from whom Lessing's Falk no doubt takes his name), who was expelled from Brunswick territories in the 1730s and later lived on in London as an important but shadowy figure in international Freemasonry; for further details, see H. B. Nisbet, *Gotthold Ephraim Lessing. His Life, Works, and Thought* (Cambridge: Cambridge University Press, 2013), pp. 597–98.

29   Cf. Falk's earlier remark (p. 204) 'that I see in all these fantasies a quest for reality, and that one can still deduce from all these false directions where the true path leads to'.

strengthened by his intensive studies of Leibniz in the years 1772 and 1773) that language—and particularly fixed traditional concepts—imposes limits on the emergence and recognition of new ideas, limits which creative thought must seek to overcome.[30]

Lessing's changed attitude towards the possibilities of linguistic expression is particularly conspicuous if we compare his remark in the *Letters on Literature* of 1759: 'Language can express everything which we think clearly'[31] with the following exchange between Ernst and Falk:

> Ernst: If I have a concept of something, I can also express it in words.
> Falk: Not always, and often not in such a way that others derive
>   exactly the same conception from the words as what I have in
>   mind. (p. 187)

Falk is here referring specifically to the concept of Freemasonry. Why, one might ask, should it be so difficult, or even impossible, to express its meaning in words? The problem becomes no easier to solve since Falk uses the word 'Freemasonry' in two distinct senses—firstly, to denote the real Masonic order, then also in the ideal, utopian sense of what he calls 'true' Freemasonry. But it can only be this second sense that is particularly difficult to define.

Peter Michelsen has tried to overcome this difficulty in the following manner: the true significance of Freemasonry as it appears in the final dialogue, he says, is simply friendship, which is able to transcend all the limitations of nations, religions, and classes. Friendship, however, cannot possibly be understood by means of its conceptual definition, but only through personal experience—through the experience of brotherly interaction between human beings.[32] There is indeed a close association in the records of the secret societies between friendship and secrecy. In the original constitution of English Freemasonry, for example, it is stated that there are areas of Masonic life which cannot be explained in words, and can only be understood by means of personal contact: 'All Preferment among *Masons* is grounded upon personal Worth and

---

30 On Lessing's doubts in his later years concerning the capacity of language to express ideas, see paragraph 73 of *The Education of the Human Race*: 'I am perhaps not so much in error as that language is inadequate for my concepts': Lessing, *Philosophical and Theological Writings*, ed. Nisbet, p. 235.

31 Lessing, *Sämtliche Schriften*, VIII, 132.

32 Michelsen, 'Die "wahren Taten"', pp. 297 and 314.

personal Merit only [...]. Therefore no *Master* or *Warden* is chosen by Seniority, but for his Merit. It is impossible to describe those Things in Writing, and every Brother must attend in his Place, and learn them in a Way peculiar to his *Fraternity* [...]'.[33]

These words, however, tend to suggest that the experience of friendship—or fraternal collaboration—is rather a means of understanding Freemasonry than the aim of Freemasonry itself: a means of recognising and appreciating the personal worth of other Freemasons. The decisive insight indicated here is not so much the experience of fraternal interaction in itself (although this experience is entirely necessary), but the fact that recognition of individual merit can only be based on the attitudes and actions of the individual in question, which give him the right to be a Freemason. In Lessing's case, it is in my view no different. His partners in the dialogues were already close friends before their conversations begin (they address each other by the familiar 'Du'), so that it can scarcely be the experience of friendship into which Ernst needs to be initiated; he must rather be led to an understanding of those personal attitudes and actions which turn individuals into true Freemasons of the kind Falk has in mind, and whose collective expression is the world-historical achievement of Freemasonry.

It may be helpful to consider in this context Wieland's ideas on friendship and secret societies. For there is a striking similarity between Lessing's definition of Freemasons and Wieland's definition of the 'Cosmopolitan Order' of his own invention, as described in his novel *The History of the Abderites* of 1781[34] and in more detail in his essay *The Secret of the Cosmopolitan Order* of 1788.[35] Just like Lessing, Wieland distances himself from the actual secret societies of his time and contrasts them with the utopian model of a fraternity of enlightened men whom he describes as 'Cosmopolitans': 'There is a kind of mortals who call themselves *Cosmopolitans* and who, without formal arrangement, without badges of membership, without lodge meetings, and without being bound by sworn oaths, constitute a fraternity which is more firmly united than any other order in the world, including Jesuits and Freemasons'. They, too, have a secret which cannot be expressed in words, for it is:

---

33   Anderson, *Constitutions*, p. 313.
34   Christoph Martin Wieland, *Werke*, ed. by Fritz Martini and Hans Werner Seiffert, 5 vols (Munich: Hanser, 1964–65), II, 230–32.
35   Wieland, *Werke*, III, 550–75.

not a secret that depends on the silence of its members or on their care not to be overheard, but a secret over which nature itself has cast its veil. For the Cosmopolitans can without hesitation let it be trumpeted to the world at large; and they may be sure that, apart from themselves, no human being would understand it.

According to Wieland, the Cosmopolitans are friends from the moment they first meet, and their friendship is based 'on the need to love ourselves in those who most resemble us'.

These extracts from Wieland are not, however, just an interesting parallel to Lessing's dialogues. It is also quite conceivable that they influenced the latter, for the version from which I have quoted in translation appeared already in 1774 in a continuation of his novel *The History of the Abderites* in his journal *Der Teutsche Merkur*[36]—that is, before *Ernst and Falk*, at least in its present form, was written. Lessing had closely followed Wieland's career as a writer since the 1750s, and he regularly refers to his works (and in a very positive tone in the 1770s). In 1775, he declined an invitation from Wieland to contribute to the *Der Teutsche Merkur*,[37] and his essay *On a Timely Task* of 1776 is conceived as an answer to a question which Wieland had posed in that journal.[38] It is therefore very likely that Lessing knew Wieland's observations of 1774 on the 'Cosmopolitans', and it cannot be ruled out that he received the initial inspiration from Wieland's novel for his plan to contrast the actual secret societies of his time with an ideal kind of fraternity.

Friendship therefore constitutes an essential part of that secret which surrounds Wieland's Cosmopolitan Order. This was implicit in his version of 1774, and in the essay of 1788 on the same subject he expressly writes: 'The entire secret lies in a certain natural relationship and sympathy which manifests itself between similar beings in the universe'.[39] No one outside the Cosmopolitan Order can partake in the secret, because they have no share in the friendship which exists between the Cosmopolitans. But significantly, it is not their friendship which makes them Cosmopolitans: it is rather their Cosmopolitanism which makes them friends. What is implicit in the 1774 version is formulated explicitly in the later essay, in which Wieland states: 'One

---

36   *Der Teutsche Merkur*, VII/2 (May, 1774), 125–65 (pp. 149–51).
37   Lessing to Wieland, 8 February 1775, in Lessing, *Sämtliche Schriften*, XVIII, 129.
38   See Nisbet, *Gotthold Ephraim Lessing. His Life, Work, and Thought*, p. 525.
39   Wieland, *Werke*, III, 560.

does not become a Cosmopolitan by acceptance and instruction: but one finds oneself in their society because one is a Cosmopolitan'.[40] In other words, the essence of Wieland's Cosmopolitanism—and of Lessing's ideal Freemasonry—does not consist in friendship itself (although it does express itself in friendship), but in those personal qualities and attitudes which one must first possess before one can count as a Cosmopolitan—or a Freemason. Friendship is the means of preserving the secret of the Cosmopolitans or ideal Freemasons and simultaneously makes it possible to share their secret; but the secret they share is their Cosmopolitanism, or Freemasonry, itself.

To return to Lessing's dialogues: Falk quickly passes on from the concept of Freemasonry to the 'deeds' of the Freemasons. Since the essence of Freemasonry cannot be communicated in words, it is communicated by means of deeds, which therefore function in this context as a substitute for words. But it soon emerges that the concept of 'deeds', like that of Freemasonry before it, has a double sense: it applies not only to the philanthropic actions of the actual Masonic order (the foundation of schools, orphanages, and the like), but also to the 'true deeds' of ideal Freemasonry. And just as in the earlier case, it is this second, utopian sense which, according to Falk, can be defined only with difficulty, or not at all:

> Falk: [...] Their true deeds are their secret.
> Ernst: Aha! so they can't be explained in words either?
> Falk: Probably not!—I can and may tell you only this much: the true deeds of the Freemasons are so great, and so far-reaching, that whole centuries may elapse before one can say 'This was their doing!' (p. 189)

Thus the concept of Freemasonry can only be expressed through deeds; but the deeds themselves cannot be defined simply either. The reason for this seems to consist not in the fact that, as deeds, they can only be recognised by means of experience, but in the fact that the historical consequences which lend the deeds their full significance can only be understood later as parts of a meaningful process (perhaps within a providential framework). The secret therefore contains more than just the experience of friendship.

---

40   Wieland, *Werke*, III, 554.

Nevertheless, a further ambiguity still remains. Falk says 'I can and may tell you only this much'. The 'may' creates the impression that he could say more if he were permitted to do so. A similar ambiguity occurs on several occasions in the dialogues, for example in Falk's comment that true Freemasonry is 'something which even those who know cannot say' (p. 186). It remains uncertain whether those who know about the secret cannot express it because of the inadequacy of language, or whether they have decided for particular reasons to remain silent about it. The line between 'mystifications' and the 'secret' seems to be anything but clear-cut.[41]

All of this suggests that more than one reason is possible as to why the concepts of 'Freemasonry' and the 'true deeds' of the Freemasons must remain mysterious and indefinable. Perhaps it is in fact impossible to express them adequately in words, but even if it were possible, it might not be advisable; and the historical repercussions of the Masonic deeds may be so far-reaching that it becomes possible only long afterwards to understand their significance, and hence to define the deeds themselves accurately.

The dialogues do, however, contain some indications which allow us to conclude why Falk considers language inadequate to grasp the nature of Freemasonry fully. The task of the Freemasons does not consist in directly combatting those necessary evils which divide states, religions, and social classes. It is rather a matter of altering the attitudes of people by promoting in them an awareness of these evils—a process which can naturally succeed only very gradually: '"To counteract" can here mean at most to activate this awareness in them from afar' (p. 199.) It is therefore a feeling, an altered awareness, that must be propagated here—and not, for example, a new doctrine. This passage furnishes an indication of what Falk must have meant earlier when he rejected Ernst's claim that it must surely be possible to convey at least an approximate conception of Freemasonry by means of words: 'An approximate conception would in this case be useless or dangerous. Useless if it didn't contain enough, and dangerous if it contained the slightest amount too much' (p. 187). That is, if a particular definition of Freemasonry were to understate the

---

41 See also these words from the second dialogue: 'Falk: [...] you already recognise truths which are better left unsaid. / Ernst: Although they *could* be said. / Falk: The wise man *cannot* say what is better left unsaid.' (p. 191)

historical task of the Freemasons in moderating the necessary evils of society (for example, by reducing the role of the Freemasons merely to charitable initiatives), it would be useless; but if it were to exaggerate that task (for example, by representing it as a revolutionary undertaking), it would be dangerous inasmuch as it might call into question the continued existence of the state itself. It follows from this that all linguistic definitions should be handled with the utmost caution. Even if it is in principle possible to formulate such definitions (and that will not always be the case, for example with the experience of friendship), such definitions will be at best deficient. This unceasing awareness of the inadequacy of language—not just, for example, in conveying the experience of friendship, but also in conveying human convictions and ideals in general—is characteristic of Lessing's Masonic dialogues and of his later philosophical and theological writings in general. And in my opinion, it is above all this awareness which accounts for the consistent tactics of mystification that are so conspicuous in *Ernst and Falk*.

What Falk, and with him Lessing, sets his face against is the tendency, inherent in all established concepts, to reinforce those very socio-political divisions which he seeks to relativise and deactivate. In her book *Die List der Kritik* (*The Cunning of Criticism*) Marion Gräfin Hoensbroech provides perhaps the best analysis to date of that 'communicational scepticism' of Lessing whereby he seeks to subvert entrenched linguistic conventions with a view to neutralising the traditional patterns of thought which tend to promote social and political disunity.[42] She illustrates how Lessing, on the one hand, expands the conventional definition of Freemasonry as an exclusive philanthropic organisation and liberalises it in the spirit of its original constitution, and on the other hand, calls into question those prejudices inherent in such concepts as 'happiness', 'nature', or 'fatherland' which contemporary political theory exploited. No one who has recognised the negative social consequences of such concepts can continue to use them in the same way as someone who uses them with all their conventional implications. But instead of seeking to replace them with new concepts or doctrines—for these new concepts and doctrines would entail exactly the same risk of exclusivity and intolerance as the older ones—the true Freemason continues (to

---

42   Marion Gräfin Hoensbroech, *Die List der Kritik. Lessings kritische Schriften und Dramen* (Munich: Fink, 1976), p. 24.

borrow Falk's alchemistic metaphor) to deal publicly in the 'scrap silver' of the old concepts while secretly augmenting it with the new silver of that dynamic, and hence elusive, sense which he has discovered beneath the old ones.[43]

That is therefore the main reason why Lessing refuses to supply any unambiguous or conclusive definitions of the central concepts in his dialogues. He deals in the same way with the positive 'spirit' of religion in contrast to its ossified 'letter' in his theological writings, and with the mysteries of Christian revelation in *The Education of the Human Race*. This also gives us the answer to the question he posed in the preface to *Ernst and Falk*: 'why have there been so many good Christians who neither could nor would define their faith in an intelligible manner?' (p. 185). For even if the doctrines of Christianity can be (albeit inadequately) defined, it still remains advisable to regard such definitions as at best provisional and inconclusive. The mystifications and ambiguities in *Ernst and Falk*, as in other later writings of Lessing, are thus part of a well-considered strategy. They are in no way a symptom of unclear thinking, as one Marxist critic claims;[44] this would imply that Lessing would have replaced his mystifications by unambiguous concepts if he had known the writings of Marx. But it should by now be clear that Lessing rejects all ideologically binding definitions—whether new or old—for the simple reason that, by virtue of their fixed form, they consolidate prejudices and one-sidedness. Instead, he rightly regards them all as provisional and incomplete. This is the main source of that liberating influence which emanates from his writings even today. Nothing repelled him so much as intolerance, including that associated with unquestioned traditional assumptions.[45]

The principal factor responsible for the mystifications and evasions in *Ernst and Falk* is therefore neither political caution, fear of censorship, respect for the moral autonomy of virtuous actions, the Masonic oath of secrecy, the inexpressibility of individual experience, the imponderability of history, nor imprecise thinking on Lessing's part—although several of these elements, along with the pleasure he always took in keeping

---

43   Ibid., pp. 36–48.

44   Heise, 'Lessings *Ernst und Falk*', p. 18.

45   See, for example, Gerhart Schmidt, 'Der Begriff der Toleranz im Hinblick auf Lessing', *Wolfenbütteler Studien zur Aufklärung*, 2 (1975), 121–36 (p. 133).

his friends and readers guessing, doubtless played a minor part. The explanation lies to a far greater extent in his growing perception that all institutionalised concepts, especially those with a normative content, are at best provisionally valid and at worst liable to confirm existing prejudices and to prevent the development of new and more constructive ideas. To a certain extent, all linguistic formulas are for him at the same time falsifications. The cumulative effect of the mystifications in the Masonic dialogues therefore consists in casting doubt on all doctrinal systems, of which the system of institutional Freemasonry is only one example—but an example which, in view of the secrets associated with it, is extraordinarily suitable for Lessing's purposes.

It has often been observed that the Masonic dialogues have a pedagogic element.[46] That is certainly correct, and Falk's mystifications are closely linked to the work's didactic intention. Education consists, for Lessing, not in passing on existing knowledge, but in the endeavour to develop the pupil's own capacities. Falk's evasive manoeuvres, riddles and subtleties are designed to awaken Ernst's curiosity and so to lead him towards independent thinking. This is also the explanation for the paradoxical juxtaposition of mystification and the ideals of the Enlightenment which we encounter so often in Lessing's later writings: for the tactics of mystification in the dialogues are not primarily designed to mystify, but rather to stimulate the will to enquiry and discovery more effectively than could ever be achieved by direct and intensive preaching of the gospel of Enlightenment. As the preface of the work puts it, 'Readers may make the application for themselves' (p. 185). Right from the first page of the work, Lessing generates, by economical means, that aura of the mysterious, the adventurous, the forbidden, which in 1771 had made it so enticing for him to become a Freemason before disillusionment took over. But he separates these negative impressions from the Masonic order itself by redefining Freemasonry in a new, open sense, so that Ernst's (and the reader's) curiosity and intellectual excitement are transferred to Falk's subversive and constructive ideas on human progress.

After the crisis of the Strict Observance movement around 1780, the prohibition of the Illuminati in 1785, and the rise of the Rosicrucians as a

---

46   See, for example, Müller, *Untersuchungen*, p. 26 and Fink, 'Lessings *Ernst und Falk*', p. 26.

reactionary interest group in the later 1780s, the secret societies had lost their appeal in Germany—at least for progressive thinkers. Adolf von Knigge, who had formerly belonged to the inner circle of the Illuminati, declared in 1788 with some bitterness that the secret societies were 'useless [...], because there is no need in our times to conceal any kind of important instruction in secrecy [...]. It is pointless for individual people to try to speed up the process of enlightenment; for they cannot do so, and if they can, it is their duty to do so in public'.[47] Wieland, in his essay of 1789 on the concept of enlightenment, had likewise said that the way to enlightenment must be a public way, and that the old penal laws against 'secret conventicles and covert fraternities' ought to be renewed.[48] And in his own Masonic dialogues of 1793, Herder advocated the abolition of all secret societies in favour of an international and public community of thinking people in the spirit of the old 'republic of scholars'.[49] Lessing did not live to experience these developments. But in his own way, he had already gone beyond them. For he did not confine himself to rejecting the negative aspects of the secret societies of his time. He went one step further in turning the model of the secret society and its rhetoric of mystification into an effective medium for his own emancipatory thinking.

---

47   Adolf von Knigge, *Sämtliche Werke*, ed. by Paul Raabe, 24 vols (Nendeln, Liechtenstein: KTO Press, 1978–93), III, 194f.

48   Wieland, 'Sechs Fragen zur Aufklärung', in *Was ist Aufklärung? Thesen und Definitionen*, ed. by Ehrhard Bahr (Stuttgart: Reclam, 1974), pp. 23–28 (p. 27).

49   Johann Gottfried Herder, *Sämtliche Werke*, ed. by Bernhard Suphan, 33 vols (Berlin: Weidmann, 1877–1913), XVII, 129f.

Giovanni Battista Tiepolo, *Pope St Clement Adoring the Trinity* (1737–1738), oil on canvas, Alte Pinakothek, Munich. Photograph by Bot (Eloquence) (2005), Wikimedia, Public Domain, https://commons.wikimedia.org/wiki/File:Giovanni_Battista_Tiepolo_016.jpg

4. The Rationalisation of the Holy Trinity from Lessing to Hegel[1]

The subject of this essay is the rationalisation of religious mysteries, especially that of the Holy Trinity, in German thought between the early Enlightenment and the later stages of philosophical Idealism.[2] The wider context of this development is, of course, the perennial debate on the nature of the Trinity which runs throughout the Christian era. But its more immediate context is that transitional period in early modern thought during which philosophers as well as theologians made considerable efforts to construct speculative, rational explications of the central doctrines of the Christian religion.

Rational (or natural) theology has, of course, played a significant part in Christian thinking since Patristic times. The attempts of the Church Fathers to explicate the nature of the divine being drew freely on secular philosophy, especially that of Plato and Neo-Platonism. But all such attempts—unless they were prepared to incur the risk of heresy—stopped short of trying to demonstrate the truth of such mysteries as the Trinity or the Atonement by rational means. There was, on the other hand, never any problem with such basic truths of natural religion as the existence of God and the immortality of the human soul; the Aristotelian theology of the Middle Ages, for example, was always ready to supply rational demonstrations of these. But for orthodox believers, Church authority and Scriptural revelation, rather than rational explanation, remained the principal guarantors of the truth of the central mysteries.

---

1   An earlier version of this chapter was originally published as 'The Rationalisation of the Holy Trinity from Lessing to Hegel', in *Lessing Yearbook*, 31 (1999), 115–35.

2   I am grateful to Professor Douglas Hedley for advice on some of the theological issues discussed in this essay, and to Professor Laurence Dickey for new insights into Hegel's philosophy of religion.

   https://doi.org/10.11647/OBP.0180.04

In the seventeenth and eighteenth centuries, however, as secular criteria of truth asserted their claims ever more vigorously and cosmological proofs of God's existence in the Aristotelian tradition came under increasing attack,[3] rational theology in the Platonic (or ontological) mode underwent one of its periodic revivals; it was redeveloped by various thinkers from the Cambridge Platonists to the German Idealists in order to place the central Christian doctrines on a sounder philosophical basis and to defend them against secular attitudes which were perceived as implicitly or explicitly hostile to Christianity.[4] Such initiatives invariably involved some degree of accommodation or compromise with secular thought, and the risk of relapsing into time-honoured heresies such as pantheism was never far away. In these developments, as this essay will argue, Lessing's reflections on the Holy Trinity mark a crucial stage. They point ahead to the natural theology of German Idealism and to the philosophy of history of Hegel.

Since its official adoption by the Council of Nicaea in AD 325, the doctrine of the Holy Trinity (*tres Personae in una Substantia*) has repeatedly been a focus of controversy.[5] This is hardly surprising. Not only does it deal with such fundamental theological issues as the essential nature of God and his relationship with the world; it also presents itself as a mystery, but at the same time, by employing concepts associated with familiar areas of experience and regularly encountered in rational discourse (person, father, son, spirit, and the related term *logos*), it has seemed from the beginning to invite philosophical analysis. The Trinitarian controversies which form the immediate background to Lessing's interest in this topic occurred during the seventeenth and

---

3   On the distinction between 'cosmological' and 'ontological' approaches to natural theology see Paul Tillich, 'Zwei Wege der Religionsphilosophie', in Tillich, *Gesammelte Werke*, ed. by Renate Albrecht, 14 vols (Stuttgart: Evangelisches Verlagswerk, 1959–75), V, 122–37).

4   On the types of argument involved and their role in the natural theology of German Idealism see Werner Beierwaltes, *Platonismus und Idealismus* (Frankfurt a. M.: Klostermann, 1972).

5   On the doctrine of the Trinity in general, see Leonard Hodgson, *The Doctrine of the Trinity* (London: Nisbet, 1943); *Essays on the Trinity and the Incarnation*, ed. by A. E. J. Rawlinson (London: Longmans, 1928); article 'Trinität' in *Religion in Geschichte und Gegenwart*, 3rd edn, 7 vols (Tübingen: Mohr, 1957–65), VI, 1025; Emerich Coreth, *Trinitätsdenken in neuzeitlicher Philosophie*, Salzburger Universitätsreden, 77 (Salzburg: A. Pustet, 1986); Jürgen Moltmann, *History and the Triune God. Contributions to Trinitarian Theology* (London: SCM, 1991). On the early controversies, see especially Hodgson, *The Doctrine of the Trinity*, pp. 99 et seq.

eighteenth centuries, and involved the Socinian, Arian, and Unitarian heresies.[6] These controversies became acute in Germany during Lessing's lifetime as both critics and apologists of religion applied the methods and concepts of philosophical rationalism to traditional Lutheran theology. Since the relationship between philosophy and theology was one of Lessing's chief preoccupations throughout his life, he followed the relevant debates with interest and formulated his own views on the Trinity on several occasions. The first stage of this enquiry will be to examine his main observations on the subject, with brief comments on their specific context in the history of German thought.

Lessing's earliest surviving reference to the Trinity is an oblique one, in the fragment *Thoughts on the Moravian Brethren* of 1750. He declares: 'I consider Christ [here] merely as a teacher illuminated by God. But I reject all the dreadful consequences which maliciousness might deduce from this statement.'[7] As his disclaimer indicates, he is fully aware that the view he expresses is unorthodox; with its implicit denial of Christ's equality of substance with the Father, it in fact embodies the Arian (or Unitarian) heresy, and implicitly calls the Trinity itself into question.

But Lessing—himself the son of a clergyman—took theology much too seriously to stop at this point. For not long afterwards, he made a systematic attempt to demonstrate the doctrine of the Trinity with the help of Wolffian and Leibnizian metaphysics. His conclusions are embodied in the posthumously published fragment *The Christianity of Reason*, which was probably written in 1753.[8] It has been suggested that this fragment was influenced, among other things, by his reading of Johann Thomas Haupt's work on the Holy Trinity, a substantial volume which, from a position of Lutheran orthodoxy, enumerates and seeks to refute all rational explanations of the Trinity from the Scholastic period to the present.[9] This little-known work, which is an important source

---

6   On these controversies, see Hodgson, pp. 219–24 and J. Hay Colligan, *The Arian Movement in England* (Manchester: Manchester University Press, 1913).

7   Gotthold Ephraim Lessing, *Sämtliche Schriften*, ed. by Karl Lachmann and Franz Muncker, 23 vols (Stuttgart, Leipzig and Berlin: Göschen, 1886–1924), XIV, 158; subsequent references to this edition are identified by the abbreviation LM.

8   The evidence for this date is contained in a letter of 1 December 1753 from Lessing's friend Christian Nicolaus Naumann to Theodor Arnold Müller, in which the content of the fragment is accurately summarised. The letter is reproduced in Richard Daunicht, *Lessing im Gespräch* (Munich: Fink, 1971), pp. 58f.

9   See Alexander von der Goltz, 'Lessings Fragment *Das Christentum der Vernunft*. Eine Arbeit seiner Jugend', *Theologische Studien und Kritiken*, 30 (1857), 56–84 (esp. pp.

on philosophical debates of the Trinity in mid-eighteenth-century Germany, was favourably reviewed in the *Berlinische Privilegierte Zeitung* of 28 December 1751, and the review, which has traditionally been attributed to Lessing, appears in all major editions of his works. But as Karl S. Guthke has shown, there is no evidence whatsoever that this review—like most other reviews of the early 1750s included in editions of Lessing's works—was in fact written by him; and even if he did write it, there is no indication that he read more than the first few pages of the book, for the review consists almost entirely of near-verbatim extracts from the author's preface.[10]

Be that as it may, the young Lessing was undoubtedly familiar with the attempts of at least some writers to rationalise the Trinity. Leibniz, in his *Théodicée*—which Lessing appears to have studied by 1754 at the latest[11]—refers to two of these, while himself defending the orthodox Lutheran view that the central mysteries of Christianity are above, but not contrary to, reason. That is, they can be shown to be free from internal contradiction, even if their truth cannot be conclusively demonstrated. The passage in question runs as follows:[12]

> he who proves something *a priori* explains it by the efficient cause; and he who can furnish such reasons in an exact and sufficient manner is also in a position to comprehend the thing in question. That is why the scholastic theologians blamed Raymond Lull for undertaking to demonstrate the Holy Trinity by means of philosophy. [...] and when Bartholomew Keckermann, a well-known reformed author, made a very similar attempt on the same mystery, he was no less blamed by some modern theologians. Thus those who seek to explain this mystery and render it comprehensible will be blamed, whereas praise will attach to those who attempt to defend it against the objections of its adversaries.

74–80). The work in question is Johann Thomas Haupt, *Gründe der Vernunft zur Erläuterung und zum Beweise des Geheimnisses der Heiligen Dreieinigkeit* (Rostock and Wismar: J. A. Berger and J. Boedner, 1752).

10   Karl S. Guthke, 'Lessings Rezensionen. Besuch in einem Kartenhaus', *Jahrbuch des Freien Deutschen Hochstifts* (1993), 1–59 (esp. pp. 38–40). For the review itself, see LM IV, 382f. The fact that Lessing makes no reference, in *The Christianity of Reason*, to various rationalisations of the Trinity described by Haupt which are not unlike his own, and that he presented his conclusions to his friend Naumann as 'a new system', might well suggest that he knew little or nothing of Haupt's work.

11   See the various references to this work in Lessing's and Mendelssohn's treatise *Pope a Metaphysician!*, written in 1754 (LM VI, 411–45).

12   Gottfried Wilhelm Leibniz, *Philosophische Schriften*, ed. by Hans Heinz Holz and other hands, 4 vols in 6 (Darmstadt: Insel Verlag, 1965–92), II/1, p. 158.

The rationalisations of Lull and Keckermann to which Leibniz refers
follow a pattern which was first established in the *De Trinitate* of St
Augustine. Augustine insists that the nature of the Trinity is ultimately
incomprehensible, but (not unlike Leibniz) he also maintains that
it is both possible and necessary to defend it against unbelievers or
detractors.[13] He therefore tries, with the help of images and analogies
based on the operations of the human mind, to render it at least to
some extent intelligible, and formulates his conclusions with the help
of Aristotelian logic and concepts drawn from Neo-Platonic philosophy.
For example, the mind consists of the separate faculties of memory,
understanding, and will; yet all three—like the Trinity—are one.[14]
Or as he puts it on another occasion, 'there is a certain image of the
Trinity: the mind itself, its knowledge, which is its offspring, and love
as a third; these three are one and one substance. The offspring is not
less, while the mind knows itself as much as it is; nor is the love less,
while the mind loves itself as much as it knows and as much as it is.'[15]
A few theologians (including those mentioned by Leibniz)[16] are more
ambitious, and attempt—at the risk of being condemned as heretics—to
develop Augustine's formulas into a full deductive demonstration of the
Trinity. The basic outline of such deductions, which change little (except
in frequency) from the Scholastic period to the eighteenth century, is
as follows. God's understanding being necessarily perfect, must have
a perfect object; and since God is infinitely good, he must also will the
objective existence of his own perfection, which he 'eternally begets' in
the form of the Son. The Holy Spirit—regularly described since Patristic
times as the *vinculum* or bond of love between Father and Son[17]—is then
defined in terms of the necessary relation between these two Persons as
the subjective and objective manifestations of God.

---

13 St. Augustine, *The Trinity*, translated by Stephen McKenna, The Fathers of the
Church, 45 (Washington, D.C.: Catholic University of America Press, 1970), pp.
175f., 467ff., 513, 521, etc.

14 Ibid., p. 311.

15 Ibid., p. 289; on the philosophical affinities of Augustine's doctrine, see the article
'Augustine', in *The New Catholic Encyclopedia* (New York, NY: McGraw-Hill, 1967), I,
1053.

16 On the Trinitarian deductions of Lull and Keckermann see the article 'Raymundus
Lullus', in the *Realencyclopädie für protestantische Theologie und Kirche*, 3rd edn (Leipzig:
Hinrichs, 1896–1913), XI, 712–14 and the article 'Bartholomäus Keckermann', in
ibid., X, 196; cf. also Haupt, *Gründe der Vernunft*, pp. 291ff.

17 Cf. Hodgson, *The Doctrine of the Trinity*, p. 68.

In Lessing's early years, a deduction of this kind had been tentatively suggested by the leading Wolffian among Lutheran theologians, Siegmund Jacob Baumgarten (the elder brother of the aesthetician Alexander Gottlieb Baumgarten). Like most rationalist philosophers of the time, Baumgarten took it for granted that God's existence as a necessary and perfect being can be deduced by reason. But he then further argued that the cognitive and conative aspects of God's self-consciousness, namely 'God's most perfect conception of himself' and 'God's most perfect inclination towards himself' acquire objective existence as the Son and the Holy Spirit respectively:[18]

> For if the complete inclination or determination of the divine will gives reality or existence to the objects conceived of, while God necessarily has a conception of himself and is also necessarily wholly inclined towards himself, it follows that this conception and inclination of God will appear to exist in its own right, because it would otherwise, without the reality of both these objects, not be the most perfect possible.

Baumgarten was nevertheless careful not to offend Lutheran orthodoxy; for he pointed out that, although he did claim demonstrative certainty for his deduction of God's necessary existence, he made no such claim for his deduction of the Trinity, which he regarded as purely speculative and in no way as a substitute for revelation.[19] It is highly probable that the young Lessing was familiar with these ideas, not only in view of his intensive studies of Wolffian philosophy during his early years,[20] but also because his friend Christian Nicolaus Naumann explicitly refers to Baumgarten in the letter of 1753 in which he summarises the content of Lessing's fragment *The Christianity of Reason*.[21]

    The main elements of Lessing's deduction of the Trinity are contained in the following extract from that work (Lessing's paragraph numbers are omitted for the sake of readability):[22]

---

18   Siegmund Jacob Baumgarten, *Theologische Lehrsätze von den Grundwahrheiten der christlichen Lehre* (Halle: Gebauer, 1747), p. 82; cf. ibid., *Evangelische Glaubenslehre*, 3 vols, ed. by Johann Salomo Semler (Halle: Gebauer, 1759–60), I, 570. On Baumgarten's views on the Trinity, see also Haupt, *Gründe der Vernunft*, pp. 184f. and Reinhard Schwarz, 'Lessings Spinozismus', *Zeitschrift für Theologie und Kirche*, 65 (1968), 271–90 (esp. pp. 275–83).

19   Baumgarten, *Theologische Lehrsätze*, p. 81; cf. *Evangelische Glaubenslehre*, I, 565.

20   Cf. H. B. Nisbet, 'Lessings Ethics', *Lessing Yearbook*, 25 (1993), 1–40 (pp. 3, 5, and 13).

21   See note 8 above.

22   LM V, 175–78; for a complete English translation of the work, see Gotthold Ephraim Lessing, *Philosophical and Theological Writings*, translated by H. B. Nisbet

To represent, to will, and to create are one and the same for God. One can therefore say that everything which God represents to himself, he also creates.

God can think of himself in only two ways; either he thinks of all his perfections at once [...] or he thinks of his perfections discretely [...]

God thought of himself from eternity in all his perfection; that is, God created from eternity a being which lacked no perfection that he himself possessed.

This being is called by Scripture the *Son of God*, or what would be better still, the *Son God* [...]

The more two things have in common with one another, the greater is the harmony between them [...]

Two such things are God and the Son God, or the identical image of God; and the harmony which is between them is called by Scripture *the spirit which proceeds from the Father and Son*. [...][23]

God thought of his perfections discretely; that is, he created beings each of which has something of his perfections [...]

All these beings together are called the world.

The most novel feature of Lessing's argument—apart from his substitution of the Leibnizian concept of 'harmony' for the traditional *vinculum* of love, with its more affective associations, between Father and Son—is that he deduces not only the generation of the Son, but also the creation of the universe, from his initial premise that thought and creation are identical for God. One of the implications of this premise is that God's actions are governed by some kind of metaphysical necessity; and this, of course, is difficult to reconcile with the orthodox doctrine of the absolute freedom of the divine will (especially in the act of creation). Leibniz was aware of this difficulty, and he duly distinguished between the *moral* necessity underlying God's choice of the best of possible worlds and the *metaphysical* necessity inherent in deterministic systems like that of Spinoza, from which, in keeping with his frequent professions of orthodoxy, he always took care to distance himself. But determinism is never far away from his, or Wolff's, metaphysical optimism; and Lessing, who was himself to draw deterministic conclusions from it in his later years,[24] already brings out some of these implications in *The Christianity*

(Cambridge: Cambridge University Press, 2005), pp. 25–29.

23   John XV.26 and XVI. 27.

24   See, for example, LM XII, 298; also Nisbet, 'Lessing's Ethics', pp. 21–24.

of Reason.[25] This can be seen not only from the frequency with which the verbs *müssen* ('must'), and *können* ('can') with a negative, appear in the fragment.[26] It is even more evident from the fact that Lessing attributes the same kind of necessity to the (temporal) creation of the universe as he does to the (eternal) generation of the Son. This near-equation of the two processes, as will become apparent later, is a step of major significance for philosophical interpretations of the Trinity after Lessing's death.

All of these developments are the inevitable result of the attempt to demonstrate the doctrine of the Trinity by rational means. For logical necessity, when applied to physical or metaphysical realities, becomes indistinguishable from physical or metaphysical necessity; and if the same mode of necessity applies to both transcendental and immanent realities, the distinction between transcendence and immanence—itself essential to that distinction between the divine and human aspects of Christ with which Lessing had struggled as early as 1750—becomes increasingly difficult to sustain.

We do not know for certain why Lessing failed to complete *The Christianity of Reason*. It is, however, probable that Moses Mendelssohn, whom he first met in 1754, dissuaded him from doing so (as Lessing indicates in a letter to his old friend twenty years later).[27] It may well be that Mendelssohn, as a Jew, defended his own Unitarian conception of God with enough eloquence to persuade Lessing to abandon his own Trinitarian deduction—at least for the time being.[28] Lessing does, however, return to his idea of a necessary relation—or even identity—between God's thoughts and their object in the fragment *On the Reality of Things outside God*, probably composed in Breslau in 1763 in the course of his studies of Spinoza. From this necessary relation, he draws the following inference (which clearly has some affinity with Spinoza): 'if, in the concept which God has of the reality of a thing, everything is present that is to be found in its reality outside him, then the two

---

25 On the possible influence of Spinoza on Lessing's early thought see Karl S. Guthke 'Lessing und das Judentum', *Wolfenbütteler Studien zur Aufklärung*, 4 (1977), 229–71 (pp. 252ff.); cf. also Benedict de Spinoza, *Ethics*, Part I, Propositions 17 and 33. As a Jew, Spinoza , of course, has no place for Christian theology in his system.

26 Namely in Paragraphs 1, 2, 4, 9, 12, 17, 18, 20, 22, 24, 26, and 27.

27 Lessing to Mendelssohn, 1 May 1774, in LM XVIII, 110.

28 Cf. Mendelssohn's humorous critique of the doctrine of the Trinity in his letter of 1 February 1774 to Lessing (LM XXI, 6).

realities are one, and everything which is supposed to exist outside God exists in God.'[29] It is true that there is no mention on this occasion of the Holy Trinity. But the fragment of 1763 plainly reinforces that tendency which was already present in *The Christianity of Reason* to regard the created universe as no less necessary a consequence of the divine nature than the latter's internal divisions.

Lessing's views on the Trinity during the twenty years between *The Christianity of Reason* and *Andreas Wissowatius's Objections to the Trinity* of 1773 (in which he gives a favourable assessment of Leibniz's defence of the Trinity against the Socinian heresy) are difficult to determine, because the evidence is extremely scant. It is safe to say, however, that they are unlikely to have been any more orthodox than before. It is common knowledge, however, that his views on Lutheran orthodoxy, and on the doctrine of the Trinity in particular, underwent a major change in 1771—probably as a result of his studies of Leibniz soon after his move to Wolfenbüttel.[30] (He may also have been anxious, of course, to establish his credentials as a sincere Christian in advance of his publication of the notorious 'Fragments' of Reimarus.) Consequently, when he edited and republished Leibniz's orthodox defence of the Trinity against the Socinian Wissowatius in 1773, he expressed wholehearted admiration for it.[31] He admired it, moreover, not just for its philosophical acumen, but also, as he now declared, because he had come to believe that the orthodox defence of the Trinity as a mystery not fully accessible to reason, yet free from internal contradiction, is a more defensible philosophical position than the half-baked Socinian doctrine that Christ, though merely human and not consubstantial with God, nevertheless deserves to be worshipped. His respect for orthodoxy—especially as defended by Leibniz—was undoubtedly increased around that time by his polemical engagement with the so-called Neologists or rational theologians such as Eberhard, Teller, and Töllner;[32] these theologians, while still claiming to be Christians, either played down the doctrine of

---

29   LM XIV, 292 (for a complete translation of this work, see Lessing, *Philosophical and Theological Writings*, pp. 30–31); cf. Spinoza, *Ethics*, Part I, Propositions 15 and 35.

30   On some of these developments see Henry E. Allison, *Lessing and the Enlightenment* (Ann Arbor, MI: University of Michigan Press, 1966), pp. 121–61.

31   See LM XII, 90 and 93–99; also Lessing to Mendelssohn, 1 May 1774, in LM XVIII, 110 and Georges Pons, *G. E. Lessing et le Christianisme* (Paris: Didier, 1964), p. 267.

32   See LM XVI, 251–53 (against Töllner and Teller); also Schwarz, 'Lessings Spinozismus', pp. 283f.

the Trinity or rejected it altogether as incapable of rational proof. Lessing had much less respect for theologians of this complexion than for the Unitarian Adam Neuser, whose conversion from Christianity to Islam he defended in 1774.[33] In all of these cases, his regard for intellectual honesty and philosophical rigour seems a more important factor in his assessment of Trinitarian thinking than any personal commitment to orthodox Lutheranism—despite the fact that he continues to treat the latter with respect throughout the rest of his life.

Lessing's views on the Trinity during his last years, like his views on religion in general, are marked by ambiguity, scepticism, and experiment. It is nevertheless likely that, when he describes the doctrine of the Trinity as 'complete nonsense' in a letter to Mendelssohn in 1774,[34] this extreme formulation is at least in part a concession to the anti-Trinitarian views of his Jewish friend; for he was soon to try once again, in *The Education of the Human Race*, to rationalise the Trinity in a manner similar to his early attempt in *The Christianity of Reason*. The main cause of his uncertainty, of course, is not so much the doctrine of the Trinity as such; it is the difficulty he had always had, since his earliest statement on the subject in 1750, in relating it to the historical personage of Jesus Christ and the latter's claim to consubstantiality with the deity.[35] All of his remarks on the Trinity in the later 1770s—with the notable exception of *The Education of the Human Race*—relate to this difficulty, which underlay his intensive studies of the origins of the gospels in 1777–78. His main work on the subject, the posthumous *New Hypothesis on the Evangelists Considered as Purely Human Historians*, concludes that the earliest versions of the gospels, and the testimony they contained of those who knew Christ personally, presented him merely as a human being (albeit a very remarkable one): 'Indeed, even if they [i.e. those who knew Christ personally] regarded him as the true promised Messiah, and called him, as the Messiah, the Son of God: it still cannot be denied that they did not mean by this a Son of God who was of the same essence as God'.[36] Only the theological interpretation placed on Christ's activities at a later date by the last of the evangelists, namely St John, could justify the claims which were subsequently made

---

33   LM XII, 203–54.
34   LM XVIII, 110
35   Cf. Pons, *Lessing et le Christianisme*, p. 397.
36   LM XVI, 389; English translation of this work in Lessing, *Philosophical and Theological Writings*, pp. 148–71.

for his divine significance;[37] and Lessing's scepticism concerning this gospel is made abundantly clear in *The Testament of St John* of 1777.[38] His final verdict on Christ's divine status, as expressed in his *First Supplement* [...] *to the Necessary Answer* of 1778, is accordingly that there is no reliable evidence whatsoever for it in the Scriptures, and that the Church Fathers relied rather on oral tradition than on the Bible when they formulated the doctrine of the Trinity during the fourth century: 'Anyone who does not bring the divinity of Christ into the New Testament, but seeks to derive it solely from the New Testament, can soon be refuted [...]. They [the Church Fathers] did not claim that their doctrine was a truth clearly and distinctly contained in Scripture, but rather a truth derived directly from Christ and faithfully passed down to them from father to son.'[39] But like the evidence of the Bible, that of oral tradition is no more than historical; and this, of course, gives rise to the famous crux in *On the Proof of the Spirit and of Power* (1777) concerning 'the broad and ugly ditch' which separates historical evidence from demonstrable rational truth:[40]

> if I have no historical objection to the fact that Christ raised someone from the dead, must I therefore regard it as true that God has a Son who is of the same essence as himself? What connection is there between my inability to raise any substantial objection to the evidence for the former, and my obligation to believe something which my reason refuses to accept?

It is essential to note once again that it is not the doctrine of the Trinity itself which Lessing here finds incompatible with reason, but only the identification of the historical Christ with the second person of the Trinity. This doubt still besets him in what is perhaps his last pronouncement on the subject, the short reflection *The Religion of Christ*, probably of 1780, in which 'the Christian religion', defined as that religion which treats Christ himself as divine, is described as 'so uncertain and ambiguous that there is scarcely a single passage which any two individuals, throughout the history of the world, have thought of in the same way'.[41]

---

37   LM XVI, 390.
38   LM XIII, 9–17; English translation of this work in Lessing, *Philosophical and Theological Writings*, pp. 89–94.
39   LM XIII, 373 and 376.
40   LM XIII, 6; English translation of this work in Lessing, *Philosophical and Theological Writings*, pp. 83–88.
41   LM XVI, 519; English translation of this work in Lessing, *Philosophical and Theological Writings*, pp. 178f.

The scepticism of these late writings is not, of course, Lessing's only response to religious ideas in his final years. It goes along with that growing interest in intellectual experiment, in rational speculation, which finds its fullest expression in *Ernst and Falk* and *The Education of the Human Race*.[42] In contrast to his defence, in 1773, of Leibniz's orthodox assertion that the central mysteries of Christianity cannot be resolved by reason, he now returns, in *The Education of the Human Race*, to a position close to that of *The Christianity of Reason*, and expressly defends his right to unchecked speculation:[43]

> Let it not be objected that such speculations on the mysteries of religion are forbidden. [...] the development of revealed truths into truths of reason is absolutely necessary if they are to be of any help to the human race. [...]
>
> It is not true that speculations on these things have ever done damage and been disadvantageous to civil society [...]
>
> On the contrary, such speculations—whatever individual results they may lead to—are unquestionably the *most fitting* exercises of all for the human understanding [...]

In his renewed attempt in this late work to explore the rational potential of the Christian mysteries—especially that of the Trinity—Lessing introduces an important new factor which had not, so far as I am aware, played any significant part in Trinitarian thought during the Enlightenment, or indeed since the Reformation, namely history. In doing so, he follows a twofold strategy. On the one hand, he looks to historical reality for a rational sense akin to that revealed in the mysteries; and on the other, he tries once more to deduce from the mysteries a rational meaning which might help to make further sense of historical reality. The aim of this dual approach is to demonstrate not only that reason and revelation coincide, but also that both have an objective correlate in human history. Lessing's aim, in short, is to overcome 'the broad and ugly ditch' which separated historical from rational truth, no longer by direct inference from the former to the latter (for he had concluded, with Leibniz, that this was impossible), but by a novel attempt *to detect parallel patterns in both*. It will shortly be argued that this attempt was to

---

42   See my discussion of these features in Chapter 3 above.

43   LM XIII, 431f.; English translation of this work in Lessing, *Philosophical and Theological Writings*, pp. 217–40.

have far-reaching significance for later German thought; but something must first be said about the Trinitarian content of Lessing's philosophical treatise. His relevant observations are as follows:[44]

> Must God not at least have the most complete representation of himself, i.e. a representation which contains everything which is present within him? But would it include everything within him if it contained only a representation, only a possibility of his *necessary reality*, as well as of his other qualities? [...] Consequently, God can either have no complete representation of himself, or this complete representation is just as necessarily real as he himself is, etc. [...] and this much at least remains indisputable, that those who wished to popularise the idea could scarcely have expressed themselves more comprehensibly and fittingly than by describing it as a *Son* whom God begets from eternity. [...] What if everything should finally compel us to assume that God [...] chose rather to give [man] moral laws and to forgive him all transgressions in consideration of his *Son*—i.e. in consideration of the independently existing sum of his own perfections, in comparison with which and in which every imperfection of the individual disappears—than not to give him them and thereby to exclude him from all moral happiness, which is inconceivable without moral laws?

The affinity between Lessing's reflections on the Trinity in *The Education of the Human Race* and those in *The Christianity of Reason* is obvious and has frequently been noted. Just how close the link between the two works is becomes even clearer when we realise that a particular topic which, according to Naumann's letter of 1753, was to have been dealt with in the final, unwritten section of *The Christianity of Reason*—namely 'the origin of evil'[45] —is in fact taken up in *The Education of the Human Race*.[46] But despite such affinities, there are significant differences in the treatment of the Trinity in the two works. For in the first place, Lessing now claims—with an oblique acknowledgement of a similar, but more mystical scheme in the work of Joachim of Fiore and other medieval writers—that history itself displays a tripartite progression of increasing rationality, the third phase of which is yet to come:[47] that is, the structure

---

44 LM XIII, 430f.
45 See note 8 above.
46 In Paragraph 74 of that work: LM XIII, 431.
47 Paragraphs 86–88, LM XIII, 433f.; on Joachim's doctrines, see Herbert Grundmann, *Studien über Joachim von Floris* (Leipzig: Teubner, 1927) and Moltmann, *History and the Triune God*, pp. 91–109. It is, however, important to note that Joachim does not

of the ultimate model of rationality, namely the Trinity, is reflected in the objective creation of the three-personed creator. And secondly, Lessing's rational deduction of the Trinity itself no longer distinguishes between the eternal generation ('from eternity') of the Son and the temporal, but equally necessary, creation of the universe.[48] On the contrary, while the 'necessary reality' of God's conception of himself (corresponding to the necessary identity of thought and creation for God in *The Christianity of Reason*) refers on this occasion only to the Son and not to the universe as well, this Son is himself defined in terms much more suggestive of the created universe than of the Son of Scripture and of the Athanasian Creed; and just as in the early fragment, no attempt whatsoever is made to identify this Son with the historical Christ. Friedrich Heinrich Jacobi was certainly in no doubt that the first two persons of Lessing's Trinity were simply coded expressions for the creator and creation as understood in Spinoza's metaphysics. For in response to Lessing's suggestion in Paragraph 73 of *The Education of the Human Race* 'that his [i.e. God's] unity must also be a transcendental unity which does not exclude a kind of plurality', Jacobi commented: 'But considered solely in this transcendental unity, the deity must be absolutely devoid of that reality which can only be expressed in particular individual things. This, the reality, with its concept, is therefore based on *Natura naturata* (the Son from eternity); just as the former, the possibility, the essence, *the substantiality of the infinite*, with its concept, is based on *Natura naturanti* (the Father).'[49] And when, in Paragraph 75, Lessing describes the Son as 'the independently existing sum of his own [i.e. God's] perfections, in comparison with which and in which every imperfection of the individual disappears', his words are undoubtedly suggestive of the created universe—though not so much that of Spinoza as that of Leibniz, in which the apparent imperfection of individual elements is as nothing when compared with the perfection of the whole.[50] It is also

---

assimilate the Trinity itself to the historical process, as was to happen in varying degrees in the so-called 'process theology' of more recent times.

48   LM XIII, 430f.

49   Friedrich Heinrich Jacobi, *Werke*, 6 vols (Leipzig: G. Fleischer, 1812–25), IV/1, pp. 87f. Panajotis Kondylis, *Die Aufklärung im Rahmen des neuzeitlichen Rationalismus* (Stuttgart: Klett-Cotta, 1981), p. 612, similarly concludes that Lessing identifies the Son with the created world in this passage.

50   LM XIII, 431; the use of 'in which' in addition to 'with which' is significant: it suggests that the imperfections are to be found *within* the Son, which would scarcely make sense if the Son were distinct from the created world.

significant that, in the last few references to God after the deduction of the Trinity in *The Education of the Human Race*, only one (on the God of Joachim and his medieval contemporaries) directly employs the word 'God' (Paragraph 88), which is replaced by 'nature' on two other occasions (Paragraphs 84 and 90). And as for the traditional distinction between the supra-temporal existence of the Trinity (including the Son) 'from eternity', and the finite and temporal existence of creation, Lessing seems to be at pains to efface it: in his vision of the future course of history and of the transmigration of souls within the present world, he presents this process not as finite but as eternal, as the concluding sentence of the entire work emphasises: 'Is not the whole of eternity mine?'.[51] Finally, it is a curious fact that the Holy Spirit, which had featured in the deduction of the Trinity in the *Christianity of Reason*, does not appear at all in the parallel deduction in the *Education of the Human Race*. This serves to reinforce that parallel between history and revelation (or reason) which Lessing tries to establish with the help of Joachim of Fiore's chiliastic interpretation of history: just as the third age (of the Spirit) has still to come, so too does the self-realisation of reason (or the rational deduction of dimly perceived truths by the human intellect) remain at present unfinished.

It must be emphasised that the assimilation of the Trinity to the temporal universe and to human history in *The Education of the Human Race* is by no means complete. In keeping with the experimental, allusive strategy of his late works, Lessing offers no systematic theology of history: the precise status of the Son remains ambiguous, and no rational deduction of the Holy Spirit is supplied. It is true that, in Christian theology, there had always been some kind of link between the second person of the Trinity and the temporal universe—at least since Origen formulated his doctrine of eternal generation; and while orthodoxy has always insisted that Father and Son are co-eternal, it has long been acceptable to believe that 'the Father represents the Eternal Source of created Time, the Transcendent Origin, and the Son represents the Eternal Agent, immanent in the Time-process'.[52] But as soon as creation itself is deduced as a necessary consequence of God's being, pantheistic implications are difficult to avoid; for as one authority puts it: 'The heart

---

51   LM XIII, 436.
52   F. H. Brabant, 'God and Time', in Rawlinson (ed.), *Essays on the Trinity*, pp. 354f.

of pantheism is to be found in the abolition of particularity because the world and everything in it becomes reduced to a logical implication of the being of God.'[53] In this very general sense—and without seeking to re-open the time-honoured debate concerning Lessing's supposed Spinozism—we may certainly detect pantheistic overtones in Lessing's Trinitarian deductions. But in his case, the balance is already shifting away from all three persons of God to the created world: his rational deduction of the Trinity is complemented by an inductive review of history within a Trinitarian framework. In fact, the assimilation of the universe to God in the pantheism of the early modern period is merely a prelude to the assimilation of God to the universe, and Lessing's doctrine of the Trinity marks a crucial stage in this progression. He is the first, so far as I can determine, to relate the Trinity simultaneously to the self-realisation of reason as a divine or ideal principle and to the created universe (and more specifically to human history). The consequences of this development for subsequent German thought will be discussed in the remainder of this essay.

Lessing's (at least partial) assimilation of God to the created universe and to human history did not pass unnoticed among his contemporaries. It is one of the central themes in the so-called *Spinozastreit* ('Spinoza Quarrel') of the 1780s, and probably helped to shape the theology of Herder's dialogues *God* of 1787.[54] But the full implications of Lessing's Trinitarian speculations were to be realised not in the works of Herder, but in the writings of the next generation.

From an early stage in his career, the philosopher Schelling was familiar with Lessing's speculative construction of the Trinity in *The Education of the Human Race*. He refers explicitly to it in his *Lectures on the Method of Academic Study* of 1802, saying of the doctrine of the Trinity:[55]

> Reconciliation, through God's own birth into finitude, of the finite realm which has fallen away from him is the first thought of Christianity

---

53   Colin E. Gunton, *The One, the Three and the Many* (Cambridge: Cambridge University Press, 1993), p. 56.

54   See Marion Heinz, 'Existenz und Individualität. Untersuchungen zu Herders *Gott*', in *Kategorien der Existenz. Festschrift für Wolfgang Janke*, ed. by Klaus Held and Jochem Hennigfeld (Würzburg: Königshausen & Neumann, 1993), pp. 160–78 (p. 173).

55   F. W. J. von Schelling, *Sämtliche Werke*, ed. by K. F. A. Schelling, 14 vols (Stuttgart: Cotta, 1856–61), I. Abteilung, V, 294.

and the completion of its whole view of the universe and its history in the idea of the Trinity, which for that very reason is absolutely necessary to it. It is well known that Lessing, in his work *The Education of the Human Race*, attempted to reveal the philosophical significance of this doctrine, and what he said about it is perhaps the most speculative element in all his writings. But his view still lacks the connection of this idea with the history of the world, which consists in the fact that the eternal Son of God, born from the being of the Father of all things, is the finite realm itself as it is in the eternal contemplation [*Anschauung*] of God, and which appears as a suffering God subordinated to the vicissitudes of time and, in the culmination of its appearance, in Christ, closes the world of finitude and opens that of infinity, or the domain of spirit.

Perhaps in order to magnify the originality of his own Trinitarian speculations, Schelling is unfair to Lessing on two counts here. For despite Schelling's denial, Lessing had indeed established close links between the Trinity and human history in *The Education of the Human Race* (as described in detail above); and he had also implied that a strong affinity, or even identity, exists between the Son of the Trinity and the finite world as a whole (Schelling's 'finite realm itself as it is in the eternal contemplation of God'). The only significant difference between the two thinkers here is that, while Lessing offers allusive hints rather than dogmatic propositions, and detects a structural parallel between human history and the Holy Trinity without explicitly assimilating the former to the latter, Schelling presents a systematic deduction of a kind that Hegel was later to develop more fully, in which human history and its phases appear as necessary consequences of the self-realisation of the divinity. Schelling gives no indication, however, whether he was familiar with Lessing's earlier reflections on the Trinity in *The Christianity of Reason*. He does continue, in his later works (see p. 103 below), to speculate further on the Trinity; but these later thoughts are neither as fully developed nor as closely related to those of Lessing as are those of his friend Hegel, whose Trinitarian thought and its relationship to that of Lessing will now be examined.

Hegel's debt to and affinities with Lessing have never been adequately investigated, and only a few scholars have noted specific influences. These include Henry E. Allison, who suggests that the central thesis of the young Hegel's fragmentary essay *The Positivity of the Christian Religion* (1795–96) echoes Lessing's distinction, in his posthumous fragment

The Religion of Christ, between the religion of Christ as a purely ethical faith, and the Christian religion with all its positive doctrines.[56] Wulf Köpke also notices a close familiarity with *Nathan the Wise* in Hegel's early writings,[57] and Johannes von Lüpke detects 'the determining influence of Lessing' in the writings of Hegel's Berne and Frankfurt periods.[58] Other Lessing scholars not infrequently point to similarities between *The Education of the Human Race* and Hegel's philosophy of history; but they tend simply to note that both thinkers present history as a teleological process governed by an immanent providence,[59] or to describe Lessing's essay as the first of a series of increasingly secular philosophies of history continued by Hegel, Marx, and others.[60]

Hegel scholars, on the other hand, have long been aware that the young Hegel was profoundly influenced by Lessing, and that he even looked up to him as something of a hero.[61] Schelling, after all, addressed him in 1795 as 'Lessing's intimate';[62] and although Hegel's early excerpts from Lessing's works have not survived,[63] various scholars have noted that he was closely familiar with, and indebted to, several of Lessing's works, including *Nathan the Wise*,[64] *The Education of the Human Race*[65]

---

56 Allison, *Lessing and the Enlightenment*, pp. 193f.; see also Hegel, *Werke*, ed. by Eva Moldenhauer and Karl Markus Michel, 20 vols (Frankfurt a. M.: Suhrkamp, 1970), I, 104–229: Hegel cites Lessing on several occasions in this essay.

57 Wulf Köpke, 'Der späte Lessing und die junge Generation', in *Humanität und Dialog. Lessing und Mendelssohn in neuer Sicht*, ed. by Ehrhardt Bahr and other hands (Detroit, MI and Munich: Wayne State University Press and edition text+kritik, 1982), pp. 211–22 (pp. 211 and 215f.).

58 Johannes von Lüpke, *Wege der Weisheit. Studien zu Lessings Theologiekritik* (Göttingen: Vandenhoeck & Rupprecht, 1989), p. 28.

59 See, for example, Wilm Pelters, *Lessings Standort. Sinndeutung der Geschichte als Kern seines Denkens* (Heidelberg: L. Stiehm, 1972), pp. 97–100.

60 See, for example, Arno Schilson, *Geschichte im Horizont der Vorsehung. G. E. Lessings Beitrag zu einer Theologie der Geschichte* (Mainz: Matthias Grünewald Verlag, 1974), pp. 291 and 293.

61 For detailed evidence, see the references to Lessing in the index to H. S. Harris, *Hegel's Development. Toward the Sunlight 1770–1801* (Oxford: Clarendon Press, 1972), especially those on pp. 43, 99, 101–03, 140f., 174n., and 189.

62 Schelling to Hegel, 4 February 1795, in *Briefe von und an Hegel*, ed. by Johannes Hoffmeister, 5 vols (Hamburg: Meiner, 1952–54), I, 21.

63 See Harris, *Hegel's Development*, p. 48.

64 Ibid., pp. 37, 141, 174, 329, etc.

65 Ibid., pp. 99 and 213n; also Laurence Dickey, *Hegel. Religion, Economics, and the Politics of Spirit 1770–1807* (Cambridge: Cambridge University Press, 1987), pp. 160 and 284.

and *Ernst and Falk*.[66] In addition to these works, he was almost certainly familiar—as already mentioned—with the posthumous fragment *The Religion of Christ*, which Lessing's brother Karl published in 1784 in the volume *G. E. Lessing's Posthumous Theological Papers* and again in 1793 in Volume 17 of Lessing's *Complete Works*. But if this is the case, then it is equally likely that the young Hegel also knew Lessing's early fragment *The Christianity of Reason*, which appeared posthumously in the same two volumes, and which—together with Paragraphs 73 and 75 of *The Education of the Human Race*—constitutes Lessing's main attempt to rationalise the mystery of the Holy Trinity. Whether or not Hegel studied and ruminated on the writings in question—and there is a strong probability that he did—the remainder of this essay will argue that there is a striking continuity between his own Trinitarian reflections and those of his early hero Lessing: the logic of the earlier thinker's ideas is amplified and completed in the work of his more systematically-minded successor.

It has rightly been said that Christianity 'is the most direct route to the heart of Hegel's philosophy'.[67] And the one aspect of Christianity which is absolutely central to his thinking is the doctrine of the Holy Trinity, which he sees as the archetypal model of spirit (*Geist*) in general. All spirit or thought, for Hegel, is a dynamic process, and the structure of the Trinity is in his view essentially dynamic. It is for him the supreme example of spirit's self-comprehension and self-realisation, and hence of universal reason as it progressively actualises itself throughout creation, and in particular in human thought and history. As he puts it in his *Lectures on the Philosophy of History*:[68]

> Spirit, therefore, is the product of itself. The most sublime example is to be found in the nature of God himself [...]. the older religions also referred to God as a spirit; [...] Christianity, however, contains a revelation of God's spiritual nature. In the first place, he is the Father, a power which is abstract and universal but as yet enclosed within itself. Secondly, he

---

66 Jacques d'Hondt, *Hegel Secret. Recherches sur les sources cachées de la pensée de Hegel* (Paris: Presses universitaires de France, 1968), pp. 267–80; also Harris, *Hegel's Development*, p. 105.

67 Duncan Forbes, Introduction to Hegel, *Lectures on the Philosophy of World History. Introduction: Reason in History*, translated by H. B. Nisbet (Cambridge: Cambridge University Press, 1975), p. ix.

68 Hegel, *Lectures on the Philosophy of World History* (as in note 67 above), p. 99.

is his own object, another version of himself, dividing himself into two so as to produce the Son. But this other version is just as immediate an expression of him as he is himself; he knows himself and contemplates himself in it—and it is this self-knowledge and self-contemplation which constitutes the third element, the Spirit as such. [...] It is this doctrine of the Trinity which raises Christianity above the other religions. [...] The Trinity is the speculative part of Christianity, and it is through it that philosophy can discover the Idea of reason in the Christian religion too.

Hegel's Trinitarian reflections are, of course, much more central to his thought, and much more fully developed, than Lessing's.[69] But as the above quotation shows, they plainly have much in common with them. In particular, both thinkers regard the Trinity as a model for the process of human history, which displays a pattern parallel to the internal dynamics of reason itself: just as the divine nature is progressively realised in rational creation, so also does human reason progressively develop to ever higher degrees of insight (which Lessing associates primarily with the development of morality, and Hegel primarily with that of freedom). Hegel, of course, goes far beyond Lessing's simple tripartite model of the three ages of man, and provides a long and circumstantial account of the whole of world history, including its geographical basis and the rise and fall of all major cultures of the past as known in his time. Nevertheless, his basic premise that history is itself a rational process, and that the archetypal model of this process is the Trinity, reveals a fundamental affinity between his *Lectures on the Philosophy of History* and Lessing's *Education of the Human Race*.[70]

If we now turn to the theological significance of Lessing's and Hegel's thoughts on the Trinity, the continuity between the two is again conspicuous. Hegel attempts, for example (again in his *Lectures on the Philosophy of History*), to deduce both the Son and the created world from the nature of God as spirit or universal reason, much as Lessing had done in *The Christianity of Reason*; he does so by distinguishing between two

---

69   Hegel's fullest discussion of the Trinity appears in his *Lectures on the Philosophy of Religion*: see Hegel, *Werke*, XVII, 221–40. For a general account of his Trinitarian thought and its development see Jörg Splett, *Die Trinitätslehre G. W. F. Hegels* (Freiburg and Munich: Alber, 1965); also Dale M. Schlitt, *Hegel's Trinitarian Claim. A Critical Reflection* (Leiden: Brill, 1984).

70   I accordingly cannot agree with Schilson, *Geschichte im Horizont der Vorsehung*, p. 274, who says that neither Lessing's early nor late discussions of the Trinity in any way anticipate Hegel's Trinitarian construction of the philosophy of history.

discrete aspects of the spirit's self-expression, namely as pure Idea (the Son) and as finite particularity (the world) respectively. As in Lessing's two modes of divine self-conception ('at once' and 'discretely'), these two aspects are parallel and equally necessary expressions of God:[71]

> the spirit sets itself in opposition to itself as its other [...] The other, conceived as pure idea, is the Son of God, but this other in its particularity is the world, nature, and finite spirit: the finite spirit is thereby itself posited as a moment of God. Thus man is himself contained in the concept of God, and this containment can be expressed as signifying that the unity of man and God is posited in the Christian religion.

But his Trinitarian deduction is at the same time more comprehensive than Lessing's, in that Hegel also finds a place in it for the Incarnation of the Son—i.e. the coming of the historical Christ, whom Lessing had found it impossible to accommodate in his rational deduction of the Trinity: '"*When the fullness of the time was come, God sent forth his Son*", says the Bible.[72] This simply means that self-consciousness had raised itself to those moments which belong to the concept of spirit, and to the need to grasp these moments in an absolute manner.'[73] What we have here is in fact the full and systematic exposition of ideas which were adumbrated in Lessing's writings in fragmentary and experimental form, and briefly enlarged upon by the young Schelling.

But apart from the fact that they are more fully and systematically developed than Lessing's, Hegel's Trinitarian deductions would appear at first sight to differ from Lessing's in a more fundamental respect, in that he consistently seems more anxious—not unlike Leibniz and Wolff—to show that his interpretations of Christian mystery are entirely compatible with orthodox Christian doctrine. This is obvious, for example, in the care he takes to give separate rational explanations of the Son as part of the Trinity and the historical Christ as the embodiment of the Son in time, i.e. in history. The same concern is evident when he explicitly warns, in his *Lectures on the Philosophy of Religion*, against any direct identification—such as Lessing had seemed to hint at in *The Education of the Human Race*—of 'the eternal Son' with the created universe.[74]

---

71   Hegel, *Werke*, XII, 392.
72   Galatians IV.4.
73   Hegel, *Werke*, XII, 386f.
74   Ibid., XVII, 245.

Why Hegel should be more concerned than Lessing often was to accommodate his religious ideas to orthodox doctrines is an interesting question. His apparent respect for orthodoxy has, I believe, much more to do with philosophical, indeed secular considerations than with any profound theological conformity, or with any desire to preserve the Christian mysteries from full rational explication—for he is no less committed than Lessing was to doing precisely that. The apparent difference between Hegel and Lessing in the matter of Christian orthodoxy is due above all to the systematic character of Hegel's thought, as opposed to Lessing's love of experiment and his insouciance over any real or apparent philosophical contradictions he might find himself in. For Hegel's fundamental philosophical endeavour is to defend the unity and mutual compatibility of all expressions of the human mind, and of the various elements of his own system in particular. That is, in its fully developed form, religion, as well as art, must ultimately embody the same truths as philosophy. The truths which art and religion embody can therefore in principle be fully expressed in philosophical terms, and in practice, Hegel claims to have so expressed them in his own system. In short, there is no ultimate mystery about existence which philosophy—or reason—cannot resolve.[75]

Hegel accordingly says of Lutheran Protestantism, which is for him the supreme and most developed form of Christianity: 'Protestantism requires us to believe only what we know'.[76] And it is here that his position as an heir to the Enlightenment, and his close affinity with Lessing, becomes most obvious (although he also exhibits an *esprit de système* which has more in common with early eighteenth-century rationalism than with the later phases of the Enlightenment). In his early years, Lessing had set out, very much in the spirit of Wolffian rationalism, to construct a 'Christianity of Reason', but soon abandoned it in a half-finished state. When he resumed it in *The Education of the Human Race*, his conclusions are even more tentative and fragmentary—but this

---

75   It is precisely the claim to have rationalised all mystery out of Christianity that rendered Hegel's system unacceptable to various philosophically inclined Christians such as Coleridge: see Douglas Hedley, 'Coleridge's Intellectual Intuition, the Vision of God, and the Walled Garden of "Kubla Khan"', *Journal of the History of Ideas*, 54 (1998), 115–34 (p. 134).

76   Hegel, *Werke*, ed. by Phillip Marheineke and other hands, 18 vols (Berlin: Duncker und Humblot, 1832–45), XII/1, p. 246.

time by design, as the older Lessing is more interested in destabilising existing systems than in creating new ones. [On this feature of the older Lessing's thought, see Chapter 3, pp. 77–78 above]. But Hegel began where Lessing left off, and completed the project of a 'Christianity of Reason' more comprehensively—if I am not mistaken—than any other thinker before or since. His logical analysis of the Spirit and its Trinitarian structure is a much more circumstantial development of Lessing's rational deduction; his rationalisation of the Son achieves what Lessing had vainly aspired to, and comprehensively embraces the second person of the Godhead, the historical Christ, and the created universe; his philosophy of history—as already mentioned—is a more detailed and impressive rational account of the historical process as the realisation of spirit (again with strong Trinitarian implications) than Lessing's simple Joachite scheme; and his presentation of revealed religion and its mysteries as an embodiment of truth at a less developed level than that of rational philosophy is an impressive fulfilment of Lessing's demand for 'the development of revealed truths into truths of reason'. This is not for a moment to suggest that Lessing's writings on the Trinity were the direct source or inspiration of Hegel's philosophical system, whose origins are far more complex than that. All that I wish to argue is that Lessing's reflections on the Trinity represent a critical stage in the application of philosophy to Christian theology, and open up possibilities which various others, and Hegel in particular (probably in conscious awareness of Lessing's earlier efforts) were later to exploit.

In conclusion, a few words may be said on later developments in Trinitarian thought, and on the significance of Lessing's and Hegel's contributions to it as viewed in historical retrospect. Speculative constructions of the Trinity reappear in the works of various writers after Hegel, and many of them are plainly indebted to him. The late Schelling, for example, in his 'philosophy of revelation' of the 1840s and 1850s, renews the Joachite model of the three ages of history,[77] and cites Leibniz and Lessing as major philosophical interpreters of the Trinity in the modern period.[78] Clearly indebted to Hegel, Schelling repeats the latter's denial that the Son can be identified with the created world,

---

77 Schelling, *Werke*, ed. by Manfred Schröter, 6 vols (Munich: Beck, 1965; reprint of 1927 edition), V. 463f.

78 Ibid., VI, p. 314.

but nevertheless proceeds to interpret the Persons of the Trinity as 'cosmic, demiurgical powers' which progressively realise themselves in temporal reality.[79] Related ideas, again obviously influenced by Hegel, can be found in the works of such nineteenth-century philosophers and theologians as Anton Günther (1783–1863),[80] Christian Hermann Weisse (1801–66),[81] and Aloys Emanuel Biedermann (1819–85).[82]

It is possible, however, that Hegel's philosophical analysis of the Trinity took this particular line of enquiry as far as it could go, for few philosophers have attempted to take it any further. His legacy is to be found not so much among philosophers as among theologians, especially the exponents of that so-called 'process theology' which presents God as developing in time and influenced by temporal events.[83] In orthodox quarters, the reception of this aspect of his thought in recent times has, of course, remained predominantly critical. It was already apparent to Leibniz that philosophical deductions of the Trinity are fraught with difficulty, and he and other defenders of orthodoxy in the eighteenth century were not convinced by them. Johann Thomas Haupt pointed out in 1752 (following Porphyry's critique of Christianity in the third century) that attempts to deduce the second person of the Trinity from the first readily lead to an infinite regress: for even if we conclude that God's 'representation of himself' necessarily has an independent objective existence as the Son, equal and parallel to that of the Father, the Son's 'representation of himself' must in turn have an independent objective existence, and so on *ad infinitum*: in short, there is no rational ground for limiting the number of persons in the Trinity to three.[84]

This difficulty is removed, of course, as soon as the Son is identified with the created universe, which can be represented not as a mirror-image of the Father but as a gradual unfolding of the Father's perfections in the temporal process. But this construction is no less fraught with difficulties than the previous one. Even Hegel's formulation—although

---

79   Ibid., VI, 314 and 339f.
80   See Bernhard Osswald, *Anton Günther. Theologisches Denken im Kontext einer Philosophie der Subjektivität* (Paderborn and Munich: Schoningh, 1990, esp. pp. 179–229.
81   See the article on Weisse in *Allgemeine deutsche Biographie* XLI, 590–94 (p. 591).
82   See the article on Biedermann in *Allgemeine deutsche Biographie*, XLVI, 540–43 (p. 541).
83   Cf. Schlitt, *Hegel's Trinitarian Claim*, p. 1.
84   Cf. Haupt, *Gründe der Vernunft* (see note 9 above), pp. 170, 185, 198f., and 294.

it is far more sophisticated than its eighteenth-century predecessors—attributes a metaphysical necessity of an impersonal kind to the expression of the Absolute in the world of appearances, a necessity which is incompatible with the action of a consciously intelligent, free, and omnipotent creator of the universe of space and time; for unlike Christian orthodoxy, it implies that the created universe (including human history) is a necessary 'moment' of the divine nature, essential to the being of God as the vehicle of his developing consciousness, rather than the free product of his will.[85] As one theological critic of German Idealism puts it:[86]

> The Father 'eternally begets and loves the Son through the Spirit'. But this activity of God is not the same as the Time process. The eternal begetting of the Son is not the same as the creation of the world, through which God comes to self-consciousness. This is to make us necessary to God, and in fact to make us the Second Person of the Trinity.

But the main weakness of Hegel's construction of the Trinity, like Lessing's and every other speculative deduction before and since, is that it is ultimately incommensurable with the empirical nature of the revelation which it purports to explain. In the last resort, Lessing's 'broad and ugly ditch' remains as unbridgeable as ever. No rational deduction can demonstrate that the self-revelation of God necessarily took place specifically in Jesus of Nazareth as distinct from any other individual,[87] nor can it prove the identity of the latter with that Son whom the Nicene Creed describes as 'begotten of his Father before all worlds', and of whom St Paul declares 'he is before all things, and by him all things consist'.[88]

Lessing was conscious of these difficulties. But he did not abandon his efforts to rationalise the Trinity and other Christian mysteries, because he was convinced of their heuristic potential—even if whatever rational sense they might yield bore little relation to the historical basis of Christianity. As he puts it in Paragraph 77 of *The Education of the Human Race*: 'And why should we not nevertheless be guided by a religion whose historical truth, one may think, looks so dubious, to better and

---

85 Cf. Hodgson, *Doctrine of the Trinity*, pp. 130–33 and 190.
86 F. H. Brabant in Rawlinson (ed.), *Essays on the Trinity*, p. 349.
87 Cf. Moltmann, *History and the Triune God*, p. 82.
88 Colossians I.17.

more precise conceptions of the divine being, of our own nature, and of our relations with God, which human reason would never have arrived at on its own?'[89]

What Lessing suggests here is, I think, absolutely right—more right (or at least potentially more productive) than what he says in Paragraph 4 of the same work, which notoriously appears to contradict the later statement just quoted from Paragraph 77: 'revelation [...] gives the human race nothing which human reason, left to itself, would not also arrive at; it merely gave it, and gives it, the most important of these things sooner.'[90] This latter passage reflects his own earlier endeavours, as in *The Christianity of Reason*, to provide a conclusive rational demonstration of one of the main Christian mysteries. Paragraph 77, however, represents his later, more fruitful insight that the source of an idea (and this is as true in philosophy as it is in science) is in itself unimportant. It is its potential to generate further thought that counts. I have tried to show how some of that potential was realised, not just in theology but also in the philosophy of history; for in conjunction with Herder's cultural relativism, Hegel's assimilation of the Trinity, as universal, self-realising reason, to history supplied the basis for the most influential philosophical account in modern times of the historical process and its internal dynamics.

---

89   LM XIII, 482.
90   LM XIII, 416. See, however, Karl Eibl, '"kommen würde" gegen "nimmermehr gekommen wäre". Aufklärung des "Widerspruchs" von § 4 und § 77 in Lessings *Erziehung des Menschengeschlechts*', *Germanisch-Romanische Monatsschrift*, 65 (1984), pp. 461–64, who makes an interesting case for the view that the two paragraphs are not in fact in contradiction.

La Matrone d'Éphèse, etching and engraving from *Contes et nouvelles en vers par Jean de La Fontaine* (Paris: de l'imprimerie de P. Didot, 1795), Metropolitan Museum of Art, Harris Brisbane Dick Fund, 1933, Photograph by Pharos (2017), Wikimedia, CC0 1.0, https://commons.wikimedia.org/wiki/File:La_Matrone_d%27Ephese,_ from_Contes_et_nouvelles_en_vers_par_Jean_de_La_Fontaine._A_Paris,_ de_l%27imprimerie_de_P._Didot,_l%27an_III_de_la_R%C3%A9publique,_1795_ MET_DP813934.jpg

5. Lessing and Misogyny

Die Matrone von Ephesus[1]

The story of the widow of Ephesus is recorded in innumerable versions, from Europe to China and from antiquity to the present day.[2] But the most familiar version, at least in European literature, is that in the *Satyricon* of Petronius.[3] A young widow, renowned for her fidelity, vows to starve herself to death in her husband's tomb. One night, a soldier on guard nearby over the corpses of some crucified thieves notices a light in the tomb and discovers the widow, with her maidservant in attendance. Encouraged by the maidservant, he prevails upon the widow first to share his meal, and subsequently to respond to his amorous advances. Meanwhile, a relative of one of the crucified thieves removes the unattended corpse and takes it away for burial. The soldier, on discovering the loss, resolves to commit suicide rather than face execution for neglecting his duty. But the widow proves equal to the emergency: reluctant to lose her lover, she offers her husband's body as a substitute for the one stolen from the cross.

My aim in this essay is to examine Lessing's unfinished comedy on this subject, *Die Matrone von Ephesus*, and in particular to explain why he abandoned it when it was almost completed. This question has been

---

1   An earlier version of this chapter was originally published as 'Lessing and Misogyny. "Die Matrone von Ephesus"', in *Texte, Motive und Gestalten. Festschrift für Hans Reiss*, ed. John L. Hibberd and H. B. Nisbet (Tübingen: Niemeyer, 1989), pp. 13–31.

2   See Peter Ure, 'The Widow of Ephesus. Some Reflections on an International Comic Theme', *Durham University Journal*, 49 (1956–57), 1–9; M. Dacier, 'Examen de l'Histoire de la Matrone d'Éphèse', *Mémoires de littérature, tirés des Registres de l'Académie Royale des Inscriptions*, 41 (1780), 523–45; and Eduard Grisebach, *Die Wanderung der Novelle von der treulosen Witwe durch die Weltliteratur*, 2., vermehrte Ausgabe (Berlin: Lehmann, 1889).

3   Petronius, Gaius, *Satyricon*, and Seneca, L. Annaeus, *Apocolocyntosis*, Loeb Classical Library, rev. edn (London: Heinemann, 1956), pp. 228–35.

        https://doi.org/10.11647/OBP.0180.05

discussed before, but none of the explanations so far advanced strikes me as satisfactory. Before I turn to the fragment itself, however, I should like to say something about the misogynistic associations of the story and Lessing's attitude to them, for this will have a bearing on my later attempt to explain why the play remained a fragment.

The attitude of misogyny is closely associated with the story of the widow, but its scope and expression vary considerably from one version to another. Over the centuries, these versions move along a scale between two extreme positions: between misogynistic condemnation of female infidelity on the one hand, and good-humoured tolerance, or even approval, of the widow's change of heart on the other. Lessing described Petronius's story as 'undoubtedly the most bitter satire ever written on female frivolity',[4] and it certainly does imply a cynical and negative judgement on womanhood (which is hardly surprising in the context of a work in which most of the male characters are paederasts). Nevertheless, Petronius's version is a long way from the extreme of misogyny. This extreme is reached in the versions of monkish compilers in the Middle Ages, some of whom conclude with diatribes on female depravity, and even aggravate the widow's offence by having her mutilate her husband's body to make it more closely resemble the corpse of the crucified thief.[5] But in modern times, the movement is all in the opposite direction. In La Fontaine's influential verse-tale *La Matrone d'Éphèse* of 1682, the humorous element is predominant,[6] as it is in almost all versions written in the eighteenth century, when the story achieved its greatest popularity.[7] Most writers are, of course, aware of the misogynistic potential of the tale; but they generally qualify it or tone it down considerably,[8] even to the extent of making the main figure a man instead of a woman. In short, a more tolerant attitude than ever

---

4   Gotthold Ephraim Lessing, *Sämtliche Schriften*, ed. by Karl Lachmann and Franz Muncker, 23 vols (Stuttgart, Leipzig and Berlin: Göschen, 1886–1924), IX, 333; for the text of Lessing's (incomplete) dramatic version, see ibid., III, 439–66. Subsequent references to this edition are identified by the abbreviation LM.

5   See, for example, Ure, p. 2 and Elisabeth Frenzel, *Stoffe der Weltliteratur* (Stuttgart: Kröner, 1962), pp. 666–69.

6   Jean de La Fontaine, *Contes et Nouvelles en vers*, ed. by Georges Couton (Paris: Garnier, 1961), pp. 341–45.

7   See Roseann Runte, 'The Matron of Ephesus in Eighteenth-Century France. The Lady and the Legend', *Studies in Eighteenth-Century Culture*, 6 (1977), 361–75.

8   See Michael M. Metzger, *Lessing and the Language of Comedy* (The Hague: Mouton, 1966), pp. 164ff.

before is taken towards the widow's lapse. In so far as her return to life is prompted by natural feelings—and in the age of sensibility, the voice of the heart has great moral authority—it merits approval rather than condemnation.[9] Nevertheless, her abrupt conversion from obsession with the dead to passion for the living becomes a frequent object of satire prose and verse narrative, fable, comedy, farce, and even opera.

Such good-humoured satire on female fickleness is prominent in the dramatic versions with which Lessing was most familiar, namely Houdar de La Motte's *La Matrone d'Éphèse*[10] and Christian Felix Weisse's *Die Matrone von Ephesus*.[11] The idiom of these comedies, unlike that of Lessing's own fragment, is not yet that of the age of sensibility, but the robuster and more cynical humour of the Rococo period. The cruder of the two plays, La Motte's prose comedy, in fact contains a good deal of knockabout farce, with servants blundering into each other in the darkness of the tomb, and the widow subjected to the advances not only of the soldier, but also of the soldier's seventy-year-old father. There is, admittedly, a virulent denunciation of female perfidy towards the end;[12] but it cannot be taken seriously, since it comes from the jealous old man when he discovers that his son has beaten him in the competition for the widow's affections. In fact, this same old man pleads with the widow soon afterwards to substitute her husband's body for the missing corpse and to marry his son to save him from suicide. And this, of course, helps to diminish the widow's responsibility for the gruesome act which follows.

The comedy of Lessing's friend Weisse is very much in the Anacreontic mode. Its morality is that stylised and ironic hedonism which is typical of Rococo poetry and the widow is easily won over by the conventional *carpe diem* arguments of the soldier and the maidservant. Within these

---

9   See Runte, pp. 363 and 367; also Wilhelm Heinse's remark of 1773, quoted in Grisebach, *Die Wanderung der Novelle von der treulosen Witwe*, p. 119: 'Just set yourself in the position of the widow! You will find nothing unnatural about her.'

10   Houdar de La Motte, *Oeuvres*, 10 vols (Paris: Prault, 1753–54), V, 463–510; though not published until 1754, the play was first performed in 1702 (see Metzger, *Lessing and the Language of Comedy*, p. 167).

11   Christian Felix Weisse, *Weissens Lustspiele*, 3 vols (Karlsruhe: Schmieder, 1778), I, 209–60; rev. edn, in Weisse, *Lustspiele* 3 vols (Leipzig: Dykische Buchhandlung, 1783), I, 365–422.

12   La Motte, *Oeuvres*, V, 505: 'Henceforth, all women are for me so many monsters that I abhor! They are nothing but frivolity, inconstancy, dissimulation, perfidy, and all the vices in the world together.'

Rococo conventions, women are, of course, primarily a source of erotic pleasure, and the institution of marriage tends to elicit misogynistic comments, as in Weisse's lines 'I know that many would gladly pay double the fare/ If Charon would take the wife away promptly.'[13] When the subject of corpses is mentioned in this play, it is treated quite literally with gallows humour as in the maidservant's remark on the removal of the thief's body: 'Oh you accursed thief, who stole the thief away/ May the devil take you and the corpse along with you!'[14] But here, as in the widow's own suggestion concerning her husband's body, the black humour has no undertones of moral criticism, and the play's Anacreontic frivolity gives it an unreality which takes the edge off its satire on the heroine.

The misogynistic humour which sometimes occurs in these dramas is also to be found in Lessing's works, especially in his early years. It appears most often in his epigrams, many of which are modelled on those of Martial, and which are frequently directed at the institution of marriage. The following are typical:[15]

> The world contains at most a single evil wife:
> It's sad that every man thinks his one fits the role.
>
> A wife—God spare me this!—is useful only twice—
> Once in the marriage bed, and once when she is dead.

There are numerous other examples of acerbic wit at the expense of women in Lessing's early poems, many of them in the Anacreontic idiom;[16] and the early comedy *The Old Maid* contains only slightly less virulent satire on an old maid who is desperate to catch her man.[17] (Such satire, it must be added, is not directed solely and specifically at women: in the same year as *The Old Maid*, Lessing wrote another satirical comedy, *The Misogynist*, this time at the expense of men.)

It is against this background that we must assess Lessing's interest in the story of the widow of Ephesus, which began during his friendship with Weisse when the two were students in Leipzig, and continued at least until the end of his Hamburg period. We do not know what his

---

13   Weisse, *Lustspiele* (1783), I, 369.
14   *Weissens Lustspiele* (1778), I, 258.
15   LM I, 12 and 43.
16   See, for example, LM I, 161f.
17   LM III, 201–34.

earliest sketches were like.[18] But when he did most of his work on the play—namely in Hamburg—he was concerned above all to modify or neutralise the misogynistic element in the story, and there is little sign in the surviving fragments of the venomous satire on women which we find in his early poetry. Indeed, with Lessing's version of the story, we reach the opposite extreme to that of the medieval misogynists: it marks the culmination of the eighteenth-century tendency to depict the widow in as favourable a light as possible. Lessing makes every effort to retain our sympathy for the widow, and to present her change of heart as fully understandable. His main reason for doing so, as he indicates in the *Hamburg Dramaturgy*, is to bring the play into line with his own theory of comedy as it had now developed—that is, as a realistic form of drama which evokes sympathetic laughter at human weakness, without forfeiting the audience's respect for the comic hero.[19]

As Lessing puts it, anyone who attempts to dramatise the story faces a peculiar difficulty, a difficulty which previous dramatisations, such as La Motte's, had failed to overcome. The problem is that, in a dramatic version, it is much more difficult to take a tolerant view of the widow's behaviour than it is in the narrative form. For in the narrative version, our distance from the events and our delight at the story's ironic twists make us able to accept, or even excuse, the widow's final stratagem to save her lover, namely the surrender of her husband's body: 'her weakness seems to us to be the weakness of the entire sex; [...] what she does, we believe almost any woman would have done'.[20] But on the stage—especially if the characters are realistically drawn—it is difficult to make the widow's act, when we experience it at first hand, seem anything other than a revolting crime, and the widow herself as meriting anything less than the death penalty: 'And the less artistry the poet employs in her seduction, the more she seems to us to merit this

---

18   They may well have differed considerably from the surviving fragments, as a letter from Weisse to Karl Wilhelm Ramler on 21 July 1768 suggests. Weisse writes: 'He [Lessing] showed me the plan of his *Widow of Ephesus* several years ago: in his version, if I remember rightly, the widow's husband comes to life again' (cited in Waldemar Oehlke, *Lessing und seine Zeit*, 2 vols (Munich: C. H. Beck, 1919), I, 438). This suggests that Lessing intended to diminish the widow's guilt by revealing at the end that the husband was not after all dead—a device employed in various versions before his time (cf. Ure, 'The Widow of Ephesus', p. 4 and Runte, 'The Matron of Ephesus', p. 364).

19   See LM IX, 333f. and 302ff. (*Hamburg Dramaturgy*, §§36 and 28f.).

20   LM IX, 334

punishment; for we then condemn in her not women's frailty in general, but a preeminently frivolous and dissolute female in particular.'[21] In other words, what Lessing objects to most of all in the earlier dramatisations of the story is their failure to retain our sympathy and respect for the widow. And he blames this shortcoming on the dramatists' failure to motivate her change of heart convincingly, and to eliminate the offensive aspects of the ending: 'In short, if Petronius's tale is to be transferred successfully to the theatre, it must both retain the same ending and not retain it; the widow must go so far and not go so far. The explanation of this on another occasion!' He is clearly alluding here to the solution he adopted in his own uncompleted play: he makes the report of the stolen corpse an invention of the soldier's servant, thus obviating the need for the substitution to be carried out at all.[22] Nevertheless, the widow still has to go so far as to agree to the substitution before it is shown to be unnecessary; and it is shortly before this point is reached that Lessing's final draft of *The Widow of Ephesus* breaks off. As a result, most critics have concluded that he abandoned the work because he was unable to present the widow's agreement to the substitution convincingly or acceptably—that is, to avoid making her seem vicious or depraved.[23]

I do not believe that this is the reason why he failed to complete the play. But in order to prove my point, I must first ask what measures he adopted to solve the problem he himself identified—that of motivating the widow's final actions convincingly and presenting them so as not to forfeit our sympathy. To accomplish this end, he employed two distinct strategies: he set about raising the level of the principal characters and their dialogue, making them more refined and sophisticated than in any previous version of the story and eliminating the coarser elements almost completely; and he worked out the widow's motivation to the last

---

21   Ibid.

22   LM III, 443.

23   See, for example, F. J. Lamport, *Lessing and the Drama* (Oxford: Oxford University Press, 1981), p. 156: 'after the seriousness with which Antiphila and her grief are portrayed it is hard to imagine her being convincingly cured to the point even of agreeing to such a scheme', and T. C. van Stockum, 'Lessings Dramenentwurf *Die Matrone von Ephesus*', *Neophilologus*, 46 (1962), 125–34, (p. 131): 'we may well assume that Lessing finally gave up the experiment as psychologically impossible'; see also Robert Petsch, '*Die Matrone von Ephesus*. Ein dramatisches Bruchstück von Lessing', *Dichtung und Volkstum*, 41 (1941), 87–95 (p. 88); Jürgen Schröder, *Gotthold Ephraim Lessing. Sprache und Drama* (Munich: Fink, 1972), p. 303; and Peter Pütz, *Die Leistung der Form. Lessings Dramen* (Frankfurt a. M.: Suhrkamp, 1986), p. 72.

detail, building up a series of pressures which leave her little alternative but to act as she does, and render her behaviour wholly understandable.

In the first of these strategies, Lessing was merely carrying further the tendency of his age to portray the widow in an increasingly sympathetic light. Thus, La Fontaine, La Motte, and others had made the suggestion concerning the substitution of the corpse come not from the widow, as in Petronius, but from her servant,[24] and, as a concession to religious sensibilities, they described the thief as hanged rather than crucified. Besides, the widow's admission of love for the soldier now usually came *after* his threat of suicide instead of before.[25] Lessing's draft for the ending of the play shows that he planned not only to adopt such earlier mitigations of the widow's conduct, but also—as already mentioned— to add the significant new device of making the report of the stolen corpse an invention of the soldier's servant, thereby eliminating the grisly ending altogether. The soldier himself has also become an officer and—at least in some respects—a gentleman. Furthermore, as critics have noticed,[26] Lessing's efforts to raise the tone of the play from farce to more serious comedy can be detected even from one draft of his play to the next. For example, in the earlier of the two longer fragments, the first thought of the widow Antiphila on waking from her sleep is food; in the final version, it is of her departed husband. And whereas the officer Philokrates, in the earlier version, invents the story of an ambiguous oracle which had prophesied that 'he would find the best woman among the dead', this misogynistic joke is deleted in the later version. In fact, all the coarser and misogynistic humour that remains is relegated to Philokrates's servant Dromo, as when he declares that he believes in women's fidelity just as he believes in ghosts, or when he echoes the earlier promise of the widow's maidservant Mysis that they will witness 'an example of marital love [...] such as [...] the world sees every day'.[27]

---

24 See La Fontaine, *Contes et Nouvelles*, p. 345 and La Motte, *Oeuvres*, V, 509.

25 See, for example, Weisse (1778 edition), I, 257. All this, of course, is part of a wider process of growing refinement throughout the eighteenth century; cf. John McManners, *Death and the Enlightenment* (Oxford: Oxford University Press, 1981), p. 451.

26 See, for example, Petsch, '*Die Matrone von Ephesus*', p. 90 and Karl S. Guthke (ed.), postscript to G. E. Lessing, *D. Faust; Die Matrone von Ephesus* (Stuttgart: Reclam, 1968), p. 76.

27 LM III, 444. This rejoinder appears only in the penultimate version of the fragment; but since the initial cue for it is retained in the final version (LM III, 450), it is clear

It is, however, going too far to suggest that Lessing has so ennobled the main characters as to remove the element of satire entirely.[28] The jokes of the servant Dromo are aimed at female weakness in general; but they are also a commentary on the widow's weakness in particular. Besides, the widow Antiphila herself swears the superbly ironic oath never to leave the tomb 'without my soul's beloved'. But this delightful touch does not merely ironise her own supposed fidelity; it is also an ingenious device to prevent her from committing perjury, and thus helps to temper the force of the satire. Her very name 'Antiphila' (which Lessing takes over from Weisse, although he adopts no other names from the latter's play) casts an ironic light on her chastity, since it means 'returner of love'.[29] What Lessing has done, then, is to strike a balance between refining the widow's character on the one hand to make her more sympathetic, and retaining an element of satire—albeit mild and good-humoured satire—on her weakness on the other.

But it is to the second of his strategies—that of providing a flawless motivation for the widow's conduct—that Lessing devotes most attention. As he had pointed out in the *Hamburg Dramaturgy*, her culpability increases 'the less art the poet has employed on her seduction'. Accordingly, he develops the widow's psychology in far greater detail than any previous writer, and employs every conceivable device to make her seduction plausible and convincing.

For example, we are told by her servant near the beginning that she has been convulsed with grief for forty-eight hours, and has finally fallen asleep through exhaustion. There can thus be no doubt about her affliction; but is it also clear that its most critical phase is over. Tears, as Kant points out in his *Anthropology*, have a restorative effect in such situations: 'A widow who, as they say, will not let herself be comforted (i.e. will not let her tears be prevented), looks after her health without knowing or actually wishing it.'[30] And sleep doubtless

---

that Lessing intended to supply the punchline in the (unwritten) revised version of the scene in question.

28   This is the drift of Metzger's interpretation, which takes a wholly positive view of the main characters and represents the play as a serious comedy in the same vein as *Minna von Barnhelm* (Metzger, *Lessing and the Language of Comedy*, pp. 171–74).

29   Metzger (see previous note) takes her name to mean 'against love', which makes no sense in the light of Philokrates's description of it as 'a lovely, flattering name' (Metzger, p. 170).

30   Immanuel Kant, *Gesammelte Schriften* (Berlin: Preussische Akademie der Wissenschaften, 1900–), VII, 262.

plays its part too. For although, when the widow awakens, she launches into despairing tirades and takes her solemn oath never to leave the tomb without her beloved, she is at least able to talk about her situation now without breaking down. And when she suddenly learns from her servant that a soldier has been there while she slept and is about to return with his commanding officer, it is clear that her consciousness of her femininity has also returned. For although she is forced to feign sleep again to escape the officer's attentions, the stage-direction tells us that she throws herself on her husband's coffin 'in a negligent but alluring posture'.[31] Forcing her to feign sleep is one of Lessing's most ingenious additions to the plot: for the widow is thereby compelled to listen to the enraptured officer's praises of her beauty, delivered with passionate eloquence, whereas this would have been out of the question if she admitted to being awake. When she is eventually obliged, by the ardent officer's touching her hand, to abandon her pretence, his abject plea for shelter from the storm outside, followed by respectful praise for her fortitude and resolution, is not easy to dismiss. But even so—and despite the maidservant's growing intervention on behalf of the officer—she resolves to flee the tomb as soon as he goes off to fetch provisions (thereby revealing an impulsive tendency which casts doubt on the seriousness of her oath). She is prevented from leaving only by the officer's immediate return. When, on realising her intention, he suddenly and nobly capitulates and agrees to leave himself, she is momentarily caught off balance; this allows him to regain the initiative, which he promptly does by claiming, at the mention of her husband, to have been her husband's bosom friend and comrade-in-arms in earlier days. This ruse is Lessing's second major innovation, and it is as ingenious as the previous one of forcing the widow to feign sleep. For the officer is now able to gain the widow's confidence, and to appear to share her grief; and she, very understandably, now retreats from her insistence that he leave at once. The more he commiserates with her and magnifies their common loss, the more she likes it—and him—until he suddenly remembers his duty.

This is where Lessing's final fragment breaks off. The widow's motivation up to this point is complete. All that remained to be written

---

31 An earlier draft is more explicit: 'in a not unpractised posture'.

was one short scene with the false report concerning the stolen corpse, followed by the officer's suicidal despair and the widow's agreement to save him. With the widow now facing a new catastrophe which she must associate intimately with the first—the loss of her husband's friend and the sharer of her grief—it is not straining credibility unduly to suppose that she is not likely to resist for long her servant's insistence that, as a matter of life and death, the only way to save the officer is by surrendering her husband's corpse. This grim prospect would have been removed immediately, however, by the confession of the officer's servant that he had invented the story of the theft to further his master's designs; and after the officer's stern rebuke, the comic atmosphere would have returned with the final scene, essentially complete in draft, between the two servants.

One further device should be mentioned which Lessing employs in order to make the widow's change of heart acceptable. Although he was able, by the ambiguous wording of the widow's oath, to prevent her committing perjury, this does not excuse her morally from breaking the vow she *believed* she was making. But even here, he retains our sympathy for her by making this vow the product of extreme, indeed excessive grief, which has plunged her into religious despair and caused her to question providence and even to denounce the gods.[32] We know, however, from the crises of faith of Tellheim in *Minna von Barnhelm* and the hero of *Nathan the Wise* that such doubts of providence are, for Lessing, signs of temporary emotional imbalance in people who have reached the end of their tether. It is incumbent on the dramatist to counteract such doubts and to reaffirm the world-view of theodicy, of metaphysical optimism.[33] The widow's denial of the gods, and the oath she swears in her state of despair, are a sign that her grief has gone too far. If there is a providence—and its existence is axiomatic for Lessing—she will surely, and rightly, be prevented from carrying out the oath she thought she was making. In short, this oath itself was an aberration; and conversely, her violation of it will confirm that she has returned to normality.[34]

---

32 LM III, 452.
33 See LM, X, 120f. (*Hamburg Dramaturgy*, §79).
34 Cf. Lamport, *Lessing and the Drama*, p. 156 and Metzger, *Lessing and the Language of Comedy*, p. 173.

Never was what Friedrich Schlegel described as Lessing's 'dramatic algebra' put to more rigorous use than it is in *The Widow of Ephesus* to make the heroine's motivation comprehensible in terms of realistic psychology. Never before had so diverse, subtle and devastating an accumulation of pressures been brought to bear so tellingly against the widow's resistance, or her capitulation been made to seem so inevitable. Some measure of Lessing's success can be obtained if we compare it with his attempts shortly afterwards to solve the related problem of motivation in *Emilia Galotti*,[35] in which the heroine has to confess, immediately after her bridegroom's murder, that she may not be able to resist the advances of a seducer—a seducer whom she has every reason to suspect of complicity in the murder. In *The Widow of Ephesus*, we witness in detail how the widow's seduction is put into effect and her resistance overcome. In *Emilia Galotti*, on the other hand, our knowledge of the heroine's psychology depends largely on hearsay and on her own concluding statements, for we have not seen enough of her behaviour at first hand to form an independent assessment of her motives.[36] But this is too familiar to need elaboration. All I wish to point out is that Emilia's motivation is much less transparent, and much more problematic, than the widow's motivation for her change of heart towards the officer. And if this is so, it must seem improbable that Lessing's dissatisfaction with the widow's motivation was the reason why he failed to complete *The Widow of Ephesus*, as several critics maintain,[37] although he successfully completed *Emilia Galotti* soon afterwards.

It has also been suggested that the widow's final action—her agreement to surrender her husband's corpse—was potentially too offensive for Lessing to be able to complete the play.[38] He had, of course,

---

35   The affinities between the two plays, including verbal echoes of *The Widow of Ephesus* in the later play, have often been noticed: compare, for example, the maidservant's words at the end of Lessing's draft of the eighth scene of his comedy (LM III, 444) and the closing words of the prince at the end of *Emilia Galotti*; also the officer's enumeration of the identifying traits of the widow's late husband (LM III, 463) and the dialogue between the prince and Marinelli in Act I, Scene 6 of *Emilia Galotti*.

36   This point is well made by G. A. Wells, 'What is Wrong with *Emilia Galotti*?', *German Life and Letters*, 37 (1983–84), 163–73.

37   See note 23 above.

38   See Erich Schmidt, *Lessing. Geschichte seines Lebens und seiner Schriften*, 4th edn, 2 vols (Berlin: Weidmannsche Buchhandlung, 1923), I, 559: 'Even as a mere *jeu d'esprit*, this wanton transposition of bodies resists theatrical treatment, for one plays no games with corpses'.

already eliminated the most offensive aspect of the traditional ending by making the substitution of the corpse unnecessary. And there is a further factor which helps to make the widow's consent to this proposal acceptable, as comparison with *Emilia Galotti* will again confirm. Both plays are based on prose narratives of classical antiquity. But *Emilia Galotti* is given a modern, contemporary setting, whereas *The Widow of Ephesus* retains its setting in ancient times. The change of setting created serious problems with the former play, whose tragic ending—the father's killing of his daughter to save her virtue—became much less plausible in a modern context than in the context of family honour and threatened enslavement in ancient Rome.[39] Such problems do not arise in *The Widow of Ephesus*, however, for it presupposes a society in which a widow can publicly decide to starve herself to death in her husband's tomb and in which a soldier can face execution for allowing a dead man's body to be removed by his relatives for burial. But once we have accepted such customs as these, the need for the substitution of a corpse, and the widow's consent to this under extreme pressure also become easier to accept than they would have been in a modern setting. As in *Nathan the Wise*, the psychology is realistic, but the setting gives us a certain distance from the events depicted.

Besides, one must not exaggerate the eighteenth century's squeamishness over such matters as references to corpses on stage.[40] The sheer number of dramatisations of the story suggests that the subject-matter in itself was not considered unacceptable,[41] and the positive reception of Lessing's fragment when it appeared posthumously in 1784 indicates that its content as such was not regarded as offensive.[42] This is hardly surprising, when we consider that much more gruesome

---

39 See Wilfried Barner and other hands, *Lessing: Epoche–Werk–Wirkung*, 5th edn (Munich: C. H. Beck, 1987), p. 364; also Lamport, *Lessing and the Drama*, pp. 177f.

40 Erich Schmidt's reaction to this question (see note 38 above) is more characteristic of his own times than of Lessing's (his Lessing biography was first published in 1884–92).

41 Oehlke, *Lessing und seine Zeit*, I, 468, cites the *Bibliothèque des Théâtres* of 1784 as stating 'Chaque théâtre a sa Matrone d'Éphèse'; see also Ure, 'The Widow of Ephesus', pp. 5f.

42 See, for example, the review in the *Litteratur- und Theaterzeitung of 1784* cited in G. E. *Lessing, Werke und Briefe*, ed. by Wilfried Barner and other hands, 12 vols (Frankfurt a. M.: Deutscher Klassiker Verlag, 1985–2003), VI, 791f.: 'A marvellous, marvellous play!' [etc.].

material than this was currently appearing on the German stage. In Gerstenberg's *Ugolino* of 1768, which was successfully performed in Berlin in 1769 and sympathetically received by Lessing[43] and Herder,[44] two coffins are brought on to the stage, one containing Ugolino's dying son and the other his dead wife; another of the sons subsequently has to be restrained from making a cannibalistic attack on his mother's corpse. [45] There is nothing remotely like this in *The Widow of Ephesus*, whose potentially gruesome aspects are eliminated entirely or reduced to an absolute minimum. Their presence therefore does not explain why Lessing left the work unfinished.

It has also been suggested that he failed to complete the play for reasons of time or pressure of work on *Emilia Galotti*.[46] But this play in particular, which is by far the most complete of his dramatic fragments, needed very little work indeed to finish it: the final scene was complete in draft., and only the penultimate scene, whose outlines had also been established, remained to be written. And to say that his interest shifted to *Emilia Galotti* is to state the consequence, not the cause, of his loss of interest in the earlier play. Some reports in fact suggest that he actually did complete it. For example, Boie claims on 28 May 1771, after a visit to Lessing, that the play was complete but that Lessing refused to show it to him, and Eschenburg reports in 1785 that a complete text of the play was among the box of papers which Lessing lost in 1775 in Leipzig.[47] But even if the play was complete in 1771, we still have to explain why Lessing did not publish it or show it to anyone in the following years, although he had no such inhibitions about *Emilia Galotti*, which he published as soon as it was completed.

---

43 See Lessing, *Werke und Briefe*, XI/1, 470 and 503–07, Lessing to Nicolai, 4 August 1767 and Lessing to Gerstenberg, 25 February 1768. The widow's dream, as recounted in the penultimate fragment of Lessing's play (LM III, 441), is in fact modelled on Gaddo's dream in *Ugolino*, as Schröder, *Gotthold Ephraim Lessing*, p. 298, points out.

44 See Herder's extensive review in Johann Gottfried Herder, *Sämtliche Werke*, ed. by Bernhard Suphan, 33 vols (Berlin: Weidmann, 1877–1913), IV, 308–20.

45 Heinrich Wilhelm von Gerstenberg, *Ugolino*, ed. by Christoph Siegrist (Stuttgart: Reclam, 1966), pp. 31 and 58f.

46 See the respective editors' remarks in Lessing, *Werke und Briefe*, VI, 792 and LM III, p. xiii.

47 See *Lessing im Gespräch*, ed. by Richard Daunicht (Munich: Fink, 1971), pp. 303 and 392; see also the report of Johann Anton Leisewitz on p. 574 of the same volume. Lessing was, however, in the habit of declaring that he had completed a play as soon as he had drafted a complete scenario, as C. F. Weisse reports (Daunicht, *Lessing im Gespräch*, p. 29).

Thus, none of the explanations advanced for Lessing's failure to complete or publish *The Widow of* Ephesus—the problem of the widow's motivation, the difficulty of coping in a dramatic version with the coarser and potentially distasteful aspects of the story, lack of time, or the pressure of other work—is wholly adequate. The decisive factor is altogether more obvious—so much so that this may explain why no one, so far as I can see, has suggested it before.

We do not know precisely when Lessing abandoned his fragment, but it is generally agreed that he must have done so at some time between 1769 and 1771.[48] During this time, a series of events occurred which decisively affected his personal life, and which had an unforeseen bearing on the play he was working on. The first of these was the death of a friend. In December 1769, his friend Engelbert König died in Venice in the course of a business trip to Italy, and the news reached Lessing in January 1770 in Hamburg.[49] In April of that year, Lessing moved to Wolfenbüttel; and in June, he began an affectionate correspondence with Eva König, the widow of his deceased friend and his own wife-to-be. Life had suddenly caught up with art: the courtship of a widow had become the centre of Lessing's own emotional existence.

But is there any evidence of more specific parallels between the real-life situation and that in the play, and if so, of whether Lessing was ever aware of them? Such evidence does indeed exist, and it is to be found in his correspondence with Eva König.

On 21 September 1770, on her way from Hamburg to Vienna to settle her late husband's affairs in that city, Eva wrote to Lessing from Salzburg. Although she had experienced bouts of grief and depression over her recent bereavement during earlier stages of her journey, there is no trace of it in this letter: she has had a busy week, her health has improved, she has met numerous friendly people, she has been sightseeing, and she gives Lessing news of the local theatre. But she also tells him of an

---

48   See, for example, LM III, p. xiii; Schmidt, *Lessing,* I, 560; and Lessing, *D. Faust,* ed. Guthke, p. 76. This dating is confirmed by echoes in the text of Lessing's *Wie die Alten den Tod gebildet,* completed in 1769 (cf. Metzger, *Lessing and the Language of Comedy,* p. 180 and Schröder, *Gotthold Ephraim Lessing,* p. 301), and by the echoes of *Die Matrone von Ephesus* in *Emilia Galotti* (completed winter 1771–72; cf. note 35 above).

49   See Gert Hillen, *Lessing-Chronik. Daten zu Leben und Werk* (Munich: Hanser, 1979), p. 60.

unfortunate incident with her maidservant which has deprived her of sleep on the night before her journey is due to resume:[50]

> My maid, in the company of the valet of a count whose lodging is opposite mine, has got so terribly drunk that she has done nothing all night but vomit. I am her attendant [...] A pleasant occupation!—given that there is in any case nothing in the world that I find more repulsive than a drunkard. She has just fallen asleep, and I only wish that, when she awakens, she will be in a state that allows us to depart.

Her next letter, written nine days later from Vienna, is very different in tone. Suddenly plunged into her late husband's business affairs, she can no longer suppress her grief, and writes: 'Whenever someone speaks to me, I have tears in my eyes: [...] But how can it be otherwise? Everything reminds me of my past happiness'.

Lessing replies to both of these letters on 25 October. And the remarkable thing about his reply is that it rolls the situations in Eva's two separate letters into one. He writes:[51]

> Your maid was as good as no maid at all, if not worse than none. But who knows? In the end it was probably better that the miserable creature had her own activities, that she loved and drank the best available wine with the best available fellow—than if she had been a good and sensitive soul who did not let her mistress out of her sight and wept no less than she did. In the former case, you were forced to abandon your own thoughts; in the latter, your grief would have been intensified. You will say that I have a particular gift for discovering something good in something bad. I do indeed have this gift, and I am prouder of it than of anything I know or can do.

The situation, as Lessing imagines it, has become that of the widow of Ephesus, whose maidservant's flirtation with the officer's servant was the first step in the widow's return to life and love. And instead of blaming the maid for keeping Eva, who was in precarious health, up all night, he commends her for helping to distract her from her grief and restore her to life. He is applying the psychology of his drama to the real-life situation, and echoing his own attempts to portray the widow's recall to life in a favourable, even providential

---

50 *Meine liebste Madam. Lessings Briefwechsel mit Eva König 1770–1776*, ed. by Günter and Ursula Schulz (Munich: C. H. Beck, 1979), p. 22.

51 Ibid., pp. 32f.

manner. But once these connections had been made, it would have been unthinkable for him to resume work on the incomplete play, or to publish it if he had already completed it; for in it, the widow's recall to life is coupled with a betrayal of her deceased husband's memory, and her suitor's claim to have been her late husband's friend is shown up as a calculated falsehood. For different reasons, it would have seemed to both Eva and Lessing like a sick joke. Instead, Lessing abandoned the play for another long-standing dramatic project, namely *Emilia Galotti*, which he could complete with an easier conscience. For although its view of female psychology is akin to that of *The Widow of Ephesus*—for the heroine confesses to the same kind of weakness as that to which the widow succumbs—Emilia does not betray the memory of her deceased fiancé, but chooses to die instead.

Although Eva may have known of Lessing's interest in the theme in his Hamburg years, it is unlikely that he ever showed her the dramatic fragment. For she was only too ready to look for connections between his writings and his personal life. For example, a few weeks before their engagement in September 1771, she writes urging him to join her in Hamburg, and mentions that she has just been reading his recently reprinted epigrams, with their biting misogynistic humour:[52]

> I have just put down your *epigrams*, and am now confirmed in my long-held opinion—that you are an arch-*misogynist*. But is it not quite godless of you to put us down in this way at every opportunity? You must have come up against some desperately wicked women. If this is the case, I forgive you; but otherwise, you must really be punished for all the malice you treat us to.

Her tone is teasing and light-hearted, but she has clearly been taken aback. It is not difficult to imagine how she would have reacted to the far more subtle satire on feminine weakness, with its embarrassing closeness to her own situation, which Lessing had just come so near to completing.

I therefore believe that it was primarily external circumstances, rather than failure to solve the internal problems he had identified in the story, which prevented Lessing from completing or publishing *The Widow of Ephesus*. And I could end this discussion here, were it not that I have

---

52   Ibid., p. 82 (10 August 1771).

so far said nothing about the feminist perspective and what it can tell us about the play. So far as I can see, the feminists have not yet turned their attention to this work, although there has been a fair amount of feminist criticism of other dramas by Lessing, and one feminist essay has been written on the theme of the widow of Ephesus in eighteenth-century France.[53] The line taken in these accounts is predictable: women are inherently good, and any shortcomings they display are the result of their oppressed position in a male-dominated society. The essay on the widow of Ephesus is no exception: it argues that most French versions of the theme after 1700 glorify the widow as a champion of natural feeling over social injustice and an inequitable custom.[54] This line of interpretation certainly fits Lessing's fragment too, inasmuch as Lessing does not condemn the widow, but portrays her change of allegiance as understandable and excusable. There is, however, no suggestion in Lessing's fragment that the widow is a victim of social injustice or an unjust custom, for her decision to starve herself to death, though not resisted by her fellow-citizens, is not encouraged by them either. Nevertheless, there is an element of male egotism and male injustice in Lessing's play. And I should be sorry if this element were not given due recognition. For firstly, the officer Philokrates is an unabashed male chauvinist, as his dialogue with the widow's maidservant Mysis reveals when he announces that he has come to comfort the widow:[55]

> Philokrates: I come to comfort her.
> [...] Mysis: She is sleeping.
> [...] Philokrates: So much the better! Then I can see whether she's worth comforting [...] I'll gladly let her go back to sleep if she disappoints my expectations.

His pity, in other words, is entirely dependent on the widow's sexual attractiveness. And secondly, Philokrates's story that he was a close friend of her late husband is an unscrupulous invention, designed merely to further his ulterior end. In short, if the widow's return to life and love is a positive step, we must not forget that it is made possible

---

53 See note 7 above.

54 Runte, 'The Matron of Ephesus in Eighteenth-Century France', p. 367; see also p. 369: 'She [the widow] rose from the depths of mysogenic [*sic*] satire [...] to the heights of goodness (when Good is equated with Natural).'

55 LM III, 455.

by the relentless pressure of a predatory male who avails himself of all the seducer's arts. It would therefore seem that, on some occasions at least, even the male chauvinist has his uses.

But this brings me to what I think is the real internal weakness of Lessing's play, a weakness exacerbated by his very success in overcoming the problem he had set out to solve, namely that of the widow's motivation. Lessing's widow is subjected, at her most vulnerable moments, to an overwhelming series of pressures, beginning with flattery she cannot escape, appeals to her pity, praise of her fortitude, apparent compliance with her wishes, professed friendship for her late husband, and feigned commiseration, culminating in an all-too-genuine threat of suicide. These pressures are so great, and they are applied with such finesse and timing, that her momentary consent to the macabre proposition that was to have been put to her would have been both understandable and excusable. But the very magnitude of these pressures means that her decision to abandon her oath cannot be wholly free. She overcomes the tyranny of her husband's memory only by surrendering to another dominant male; whereas only a free decision to return to life, taken without external harassment, could fully restore her dignity. Yet such a decision is not possible within the framework of the traditional story—not, at least, if it is to remain credible in terms of realistic psychology. For the story itself contains an element of misogyny which no amount of manipulation on Lessing's part could expunge. The problem is that, the freer an agent the widow is, the more vicious she will appear; and the less free she is, the more she will appear a passive victim of male domination. The story, in other words, can be varied to emphasise either the widow's fickleness or her weakness; but in neither case will she appear in a favourable light. Lessing chose to retain our sympathy for her by diminishing her responsibility. But as her responsibility diminishes, so too does her moral autonomy. And even if he found this view of female psychology more acceptable than most of us would do today,[56] it is doubtful whether he could have been entirely happy, after writing *Minna von Barnhelm*, with a heroine as passive as his widow eventually

---

56   Compare his remark in the *Hamburg Dramaturgy* (LM IX, 334) on the widow's seduction in Petronius's story: 'her weakness seems to us the weakness of her entire sex; [...] what she does, we think just about any woman would have done'.

became. The fact that he went on to complete *Emilia Galotti* is perhaps significant; for Emilia asserts her moral autonomy to avoid falling victim to the weakness to which she confesses herself susceptible.

There is in Lessing a streak of cynical humour which at times assumes misogynistic or even misanthropic forms[57]—although he was certainly no misogynist in his personal views, as his letters and conversations amply testify.[58] It was, I suspect, to this side of his humour that the story of the widow of Ephesus first appealed in his student days in Leipzig. And although he did all he could to mitigate the morally offensive aspects of the story, and although his version stands historically at the opposite extreme to the misogynistic diatribes of the medieval monks, he could not eliminate its misogynistic content entirely without destroying the story's structure, and with it the main source of its humour. Whether or not he had such considerations in mind when he decided to abandon his comedy, it is impossible to say. But it is certain that, around the time at which he stopped work on it, he was confronted with a real-life situation which must have shown up the play's latent misogyny in all its harshness. And that was enough to ensure that it would never be published in his lifetime.

---

57 See, for example, the searing witticisms in his famous letter on the death of his son to Eschenburg (31 December 1777, in LM XVIII, 259), at which Eschenburg was understandably horrified, and Lessing's subsequent explanation (7 January 1778, in LM XVIII, 261): 'And my fault is not despair, but rather levity, which at times only expresses itself in a somewhat bitter and misanthropic manner'.

58 See, for example, his letter of 29 November 1770 to Eva König (*Meine liebste Madam,* p. 39) in which he takes exception to a recently published play with the title *Die Hausplage* (*The Domestic Plague:* feminine) on the grounds that a domestic plague could just as easily be a man as a woman; see also Daunicht, *Lessing im Gespräch,* p. 440 for his defence of a prostitute on whose death dismissive remarks had been made.

Portrait of Thomas Amory by Joseph Blackburn, photograph by Okita2 (2012), Wikimedia, Public Domain, https://commons.wikimedia.org/wiki/File:Thomas_Amory_1760_Joseph_Blackburn.jpg

6. The German Reception of an Irish Eccentric

The Controversy over Thomas Amory's
The Life of John Buncle, Esq. (1778–79)[1]

Apart from his published works—of which *The Life of John Buncle, Esq.* was easily the most successful—little is known of Thomas Amory, described in the *Dictionary of National Biography* as an 'eccentric writer'. The son of one Councillor Amory who accompanied William III to Ireland and acquired extensive property in County Clare, he was probably born in 1691. He may have been born in London, to which he returned after spending a substantial period in Dublin; he subsequently pursued his work as a writer and became a virtual recluse. He died at an advanced age in 1788, survived by his only son.

The Life of John Buncle, Esq. is a novel in autobiographical form,[2] and there are some similarities between the career of the eponymous hero and that of the author. As the hero tells us, 'I was born in London and carried as an infant to Ireland, where I learned the Irish language, and became intimately acquainted with its original inhabitants' (I,vii). He spent his childhood, we are told, 'at Bagatrogh Castle, my father's seat

---

   https://doi.org/10.11647/OBP.0180.06

in Mall-Bay, on the coast of Galway' (II, 525) and studied for five years in Dublin, at Trinity College (I, 4 and II, 146), before embarking on an extended tour of northern England, the account of which occupies most of the novel. After marrying seven wives[3] in quick succession and losing each in turn through illness or accident, he goes off on a voyage of circumnavigation—of which no details are supplied in the novel—and finally settles in London to write his memoirs.

Buncle's expeditions over the fells of Westmorland, Durham, and Yorkshire follow a recurrent pattern with only minor variations. After traversing previously unscaled crags, terrifying abysses. bottomless lakes, blazing outcrops of bitumen, and tortuous potholes, he arrives in a secluded and idyllic valley where he encounters one or more women of exceptional beauty, erudition, and affluence, usually associated with a religious community dedicated to a Unitarian faith opposed to both Anglican orthodoxy and Roman Catholicism.[4] After an interval of elegant living and dining, during which Buncle holds forth at length on theology in particular—although he is equally capable of discoursing on such diverse subjects as algebra, microscopy, ethics, bibliography, medicine, conchology, and politics—he marries his hostess and enjoys a brief period of bliss, which is abruptly terminated by his wife's untimely death. The hero, now enriched by his deceased partner's fortune, then resumes the cycle of mountaineering, learned discourse, matrimony, and bereavement. During his travels, he repeatedly chances upon acquaintances from his Irish past, most of whom, like Buncle himself, are decidedly eccentric.

It is not at first sight obvious why this curious work, when it became known in Germany during the 1770s, should have provoked responses

---

3   The German commentators speak of eight, presumably because Friedrich Nicolai cites this number in his preface to the German translation: *Leben Bemerkungen und Meinungen Johann Bunkels nebst den Leben verschiedener merkwürdiger Frauenzimmer. Aus dem engländischen übersetzt*, 4 vols (Berlin: Nicolai, 1778). On the history of this work's publication and the identity of the editor (Hermann Andreas Pistorius) and translator (Raimarus von Spieren) see Alexander Košenina, 'Zur deutschen Übersetzung zweier Romane Thomas Amorys und der sich anschliessenden Fehde zwischen Wieland und Nicolai', *Daphnis* 18 (1989), 179–98. The second novel included in this translation, Amory's *Leben verschiedener merkwürdiger Frauenzimmer*, will not be considered here, since it played no significant part in the controversy over the main novel.

4   Miss Maria Spence is typical of these women, possessing (in addition to considerable wealth) 'the head of Aristotle, the heart of a primitive Christian, and the form of Venus de Medicis' (II, 162).

ranging from delight and admiration to indignation and contempt. On the one hand, it was the main inspiration of Friedrich Nicolai's novel *Sebaldus Nothanker* (1773–76),[5] and Moses Mendelssohn recommended it with enthusiasm to Lessing, who was sufficiently impressed to consider translating it himself. A translation by another writer was subsequently commissioned by Nicolai, with sixteen engravings by the celebrated Daniel Chodowiecki, and published, after considerable publicity and a highly successful subscription, in 1778.[6] On the other hand, Christian Garve found Buncle's learned disquisitions so unoriginal and platitudinous that he had difficulty finishing the book, and the plot likewise failed to capture his interest.[7] Wieland, for his part, was so incensed by the novel that he published a circumstantial denunciation, in five instalments, in his *Der Teutsche Merkur;*[8] this elicited a bitter counter-attack from Nicolai,[9] to which Wieland duly responded,[10] and a further counterblast from Nicolai appeared shortly afterwards (1779).[11] The dispute between the two writers became the object of a feeble satire by August Friedrich Cranz (1779),[12] and a satirical sequel to the novel itself, published anonymously by Andreas Stein, appeared a few years later.[13]

---

5   See Richard Schwinger, *Friedrich Nicolais Roman 'Sebaldus Nothanker'* (Weimar: Felber, 1987), p. 264) and Lawrence Marsden Price, *The Reception of English Literature in Germany* (Berkeley, CA: University of California Press, 1932), pp. 225f.

6   See Košenina, 'Zur deutschen Übersetzung [...]', pp. 192f.

7   Garve to Nicolai, 9 February 1771 (quoted from the unpublished original by Košenina, 'Zur deutschen Übersetzung [...], p. 182).

8   Christoph Martin Wieland, 'Die Bunkliade', in *Der Teutsche Merkur* (1778), Drittes Vierteljahr, 77–90 and 165–72; Viertes Vierteljahr, 55–75, 158–73, and 248–60.

9   Friedrich Nicolai, [advertisement and call for subscriptions] in *Allgemeine Deutsche Bibliothek*, 31 (1777), unpaginated notices at end of this volume, pp. [1] and [3]; 'Ein paar Worte betreffend Johann Bunkel und Christoph Martin Wieland', (Berlin and Stettin: no publisher named, 1779); this also appeared in 1778 in a supplementary volume to the *Allgemeine Deutsche Bibliothek*.

10   Wieland, 'Abgenöthigter Nachtrag zur Johann-Bunkliade', *Der Teutsche Merkur* (1779), Erstes Vierteljahr, 154–72.

11   Nicolai, 'Nachricht', in *Allgemeine Deutsche Bibliothek*, 37 (1779), Erstes Stück, pp. 295–316.

12   [August Friedrich Cranz], 'Fragment eines Schreibens über den Ton in den Streitschriften einiger teutschen Gelehrten und Schöngeister' (no author, place of publication or publisher named, 1779); the British Library holds a copy of this wordy and puerile performance, which begins with satirical allusions to Amory's novel and Nicolai's German edition, but soon loses all contact with them. Košenina, 'Zur deutschen Übersetzung [...]', p. 194 lists two supplementary pieces by Cranz, published in 1779 and 1781 respectively, which I have been unable to consult.

13   [Andreas Stein], *Geschichte einiger Esel oder Fortsetzung des Lebens und der Meynungen des Weltberühmten John Bunkels*, 3 vols (Hamburg and Leipzig: no publisher named, 1782–83).

The dispute between Nicolai and Wieland was exacerbated by an earlier disagreement, and not least by the fact that Wieland's *Der Teutsche Merkur* and Nicolai's *Allgemeine Deutsche Bibliothek* were currently engaged in a circulation war. Nevertheless, real issues of literary criticism were involved, and Wieland's polemic embodies a serious, if one-sided, reading of Amory's novel. The aim of the present essay is to examine briefly the main arguments involved, with a view to defining more precisely the literary status of this problematic novel and the reasons why it met with such divergent reactions in Germany.

The most obviously contentious feature of the novel was, of course, its unorthodox treatment of religion. Buncle's hostility towards the Athanasian Creed and its doctrine of the Trinity—a hostility which, ironically enough, he seems to have absorbed from his tutor at Trinity College Dublin (I, 379)—his obsessive advocacy of Unitarianism,[14] his opposition to supernaturalism and defence of natural religion, and his evident debt to the English and French freethinkers of the seventeenth and early eighteenth centuries[15] doubtless account for much of the novel's appeal to the Berlin *Aufklärer*. Mendelssohn, for example, regarded the Trinity as logically absurd, and held that Unitarianism was closely akin to his own Jewish faith.[16] Lessing's positive response to the novel when he first read it (in English) in 1771 was certainly influenced by the same factors, but his enthusiasm waned, as he explained to Nicolai eight years later, when he began to take Christian orthodoxy more seriously during the ensuing period, and to find Unitarianism (or Arianism) unsatisfactory in spite of its superficially greater rationality.[17] These writers would also have found little to quarrel with in Buncle's

---

14   Or, more precisely, of Socinianism: he recognises Christ as an object of worship, but denies his divinity (II, 247f. and 255f.).

15   He names Locke as his chief intellectual mentor (I, 6), but his long discussion of contradictions in the gospels (I, 451–94) shows familiarity with works by Toland, Morgan, Collins, Simon and many others. His bibliographical references should be treated with caution, however, since some of his authorities—for example, 'the Rev. Athanasian Bigot' (II, 528) are plainly fictitious.

16   See his letter to Lessing of 1 February 1774 in Gotthold Ephraim Lessing, *Sämtliche Schriften*, ed. by Karl Lachmann and Franz Muncker, 23 vols (Stuttgart, Leipzig and Berlin: Göschen, 1886–1924), XXI, 6 and Moses Mendelssohn, *Gesammelte Schriften. Jubiläumsausgabe*, ed. by Michael Brocke and other hands, c. 38 vols (Stuttgart/Bad Cannstatt: frommann-holzboog, 1971–), VII, 102 and 106.

17   See Lessing's letter of 30 March 1779 to Nicolai, in Lessing, *Sämtliche Schriften*, XVIII, 312; also G. L. Jones, 'Lessing and Amory', *German Life and Letters*, 20 (1966–67), 298–306.

fulminations against Catholicism—'the diabolism of popery' (I, 344), with its worship of 'the tiny god of dough' (II, 491)—even if Nicolai and Pistorius (the editor whom Nicolai appointed to supervise the translation of the novel) considered it politic to delete or tone down the more extreme anti-Catholic passages in order to secure the imperial privilege for the work's publication. Nicolai still felt able, however, to reassure potential subscribers in respect of Buncle's religious views: 'They are to be highly recommended to all readers who are prepared to reflect seriously on religious matters.'[18]

Wieland's objections to the novel, however, had little to do with its religious unorthodoxy. He was, after all, a product of the *Aufklärung* himself and—at least in his mature years—sympathetic towards liberal opinions in theology. Buncle's liberal attitudes were in accord with Wieland's in other respects too, as in the following passage on women's intellectual capacities and education: 'Learning and knowledge are perfections in us not as we are men, but as we are rational creatures, in which order of being the female world is upon the same level as the male [...]. And if women of fortune were so considered, and educated accordingly, I am sure the world would soon be the better for it' (II, 281; cf. also I, 273f.). Nevertheless, Buncle's attitude towards women is fundamental to Wieland's criticism of the novel—and indeed to any interpretation of the work. It accordingly calls for further discussion here.

Buncle has two obsessions in life, one of which is Unitarian theology. The other is women. In his own words (II, 483f.):

> As I was born with the disease of repletion, and had made a resolution not to fornicate, it was incumbent on me to have a sister and companion, with whom I might lawfully carry on the succession [...] And if [...] I was to live for ages, and by accidents lost such partners as I have described; I would with rapture take hundreds of them to my breast, one after another, and piously propagate the kind.

As a modern editor of the novel comments, 'John Buncle is a Mormon born out of due time':[19] his repeated marriages are as close as he can

---

18 Nicolai [advertisement and call for subscribers], in *Allgemeine Deutsche Bibliothek*, 31 (1777), Zweites Stück, p. [3] of unpaginated notices at end of volume.

19 Baker, Ernest A., Introduction to his edition of Thomas Amory, *The Life and Opinions of John Buncle Esquire* (London: Routledge, 1904), p. ix.

get to polygamy without violating legal and religious prohibitions, and death is always at hand to ensure a brisk turnover of spouses. The novel is full of erotic suggestion, often of a polygamous kind, as when Buncle discovers the beautiful Azora at the head of a religious community consisting solely of women, a plague having carried off all the men. Such episodes recall *The Isle of Pines* of 1668, with its polygamous narrator on his desert island.[20] The absence of effective male competition adds relish to Buncle's enjoyment, and his encounter with the lovely widow Imelda gains piquancy from the thought of her deceased husband, 'Sir Loghlin Fitzgibbons, an old Irish knight, who was immensely rich, and married her when he was creeping on all fours, with snow on his head, and frost in his bones, that he might lie by a naked beauty, and gaze at that awful spot he had no power to enjoy' (II, 185). The private medical studies which Buncle subsequently takes up suggest to him a more ingenious way of overcoming the restrictions of monogamy when he happens to dissect a woman of unusual anatomy: as he tells us, 'there was found two vaginas, and a right and left uterus' (II, 445). He decides, however, that the risk of superfetation would outweigh any advantages which such a wife might offer, and concludes 'I should not chuse to marry a woman with two vaginas, if it was possible to know it before wedlock'. (Nicolai's editor, the clergyman Pistorius, understandably omitted this passage from the German translation.)

All this is squarely in the Rabelaisian tradition,[21] of course (although Amory's novel, unlike the work of Rabelais, has no satirical element, and the narrator himself is without any sense of humour or irony), and it would not have shocked the broader-minded among eighteenth-century readers unduly. Wieland, who often sailed close to the wind himself in his treatment of erotic subjects, was nevertheless scandalised by Buncle's behaviour. But what offended him was not so much Buncle's polygamous inclinations as his unconvincing attempts to lend them moral and religious respectability. One of Buncle's objections to Catholicism, for example, is to its requirement of priestly celibacy, and he points out in one of his learned digressions that many priests, and

---

20 See Paul Ries, '*Die Insel Pines*: Philosophie, Pornographie oder Propaganda?', in *Literatur und Volk im 17. Jahrhundert*, ed. by Wolfgang Brückner and other hands (Wiesbaden: Harrassowitz, 1985), pp. 753–76.

21 Cf. William Hazlitt's remark, cited in Baker, Introduction, p. v: 'The soul of Francis Rabelais passed into John [*sic*] Amory.'

even saints, of the early Church—including St Peter himself—were married (II, 128ff.). He also resorts to the most questionable variety of casuistry in his (inevitably successful) attempts to talk the reluctant beauty Statia into matrimony: 'Oppose not the gospel covenant [...]. I will pour out my spirit upon thy seed, and my blessing upon thine offspring [...] it must be a great crime, to deprive children of this intailed heavenly inheritance, by our resolving to live in a state of virginity. In my opinion, it is a sin greater than murder' (II, 46f.). Wieland, who describes this argument as 'the most perfect ideal of impertinence and insanity that was ever shaken out of a human brainbox', concludes: 'The most infamous thing about this is that religion always has to serve as a figleaf to cover the nakedness of his goatish old Adam'.[22]

There can be no doubt that, especially in the second volume of the original novel (which was published ten years after the first), Buncle's high moral tone and habitual concern with outward respectability progressively diminish. He is less fastidious in his choice of company, and some of the Irish friends from his student days whom he encounters on his travels are plainly delinquents (and, one suspects, representatives of Buncle's own half-repressed inclinations). These include Jack Gallaspy, whose exploits he recounts with evident relish ('He debauched all the women he could, and many whom he could not corrupt, he ravished') and Tom Gollogher, who 'left nineteen daughters he had by several women a thousand pounds each. This was acting with a temper worthy of a man' (II, 150 and 155f.). During a stay in London, he tours the brothels in the company of the bookseller and pornographer Edmund Curll (one of several real personages who make a disconcerting appearance in the novel). His excuse for such visits—that they were made only 'on account of the purity of the wine, and the stillness of the house' (II, 388)—will convince few readers; his real interest, of course, is in the inmates, and his long narrative of the career of Carola Bennet, a reformed prostitute (II, 384–400), reads like an extract from John Cleland's *Memoirs of a Woman of Pleasure*.

The nadir of Buncle's moral development is reached, however, when he abducts two attractive wards of Old Cock, a wealthy curmudgeon, in order to recoup his gambling losses (II, 201), and later elopes with

---

22 Wieland, 'Die Bunkliade', in *Der Teutsche Merkur* (1778), Viertes Vierteljahr, pp. 66 and 73.

another miser's daughter in order to boost his fortune (II, 411f.). These lapses, together with the priggish and pharisaical way in which he seeks to exonerate his own conduct while censuring the moral shortcomings of others (apart from his old cronies) are among the most frequent targets of Wieland's criticism, summed up in his description of Buncle as 'neither more nor less than a selfish anti-trinitarian idler, lecher, and libertine, of no use to God or the world'.[23]

But the main reason for Wieland's indignation, and for the lengths to which he goes in order to justify and express it, is not so much the novel itself as the contrast between it and the claims which Nicolai had made for it in his advertisement to potential subscribers. For Nicolai had emphasised '[the] goodheartedness, good humour, and noble philanthropy which runs throughout the work' and described the hero as a man who looks back on his life 'with a good conscience and complete awareness of having been irreproachable and useful'.[24] Such claims, Wieland contends, amount to a brazen misrepresentation, a ploy to increase the sales of a worthless book: 'From his [Nicolai's] hand we have the repugnant changeling of an Irish non-conformist crossbreed of zealot and freethinker in place of a pleasant, useful, witty and edifying work.'[25]

Ought we therefore to conclude that the appeal of Amory's novel to such readers as Nicolai, Mendelssohn, and Lessing consisted exclusively in its liberal views on religion, and that it was otherwise, as Wieland suggested, devoid of all poetic as well as moral merit? Such a verdict would be premature, above all because it takes insufficient account of the novel's literary qualities. It is with these that the remainder of this essay will be concerned.

Nicolai, like any enterprising publisher, spared no effort to present his product in the most favourable light possible. In order to do so, he emphasised the novel's affinities with as many famous writers and popular tendencies in literature as he could. He knew from the start, of course, that the prestige of English literature was currently such that almost any hitherto untranslated novel could expect reasonable sales; but if it could also be shown to bear comparison with the works

---

23   Wieland, 'Die Bunkliade', in *Der Teutsche Merkur* (1778), Drittes Vierteljahr, p. 167.
24   Nicolai, as in note 17 above, pp. [1] and [3].
25   Wieland, 'Die Bunkliade', in *Der Teutsche Merkur* (1779), Erstes Vierteljahr, p. 166.

of the greatest English writers, its commercial success was effectively guaranteed. He accordingly wrote in his advertisement of 1777:[26]

> He [i.e. Buncle] is perfectly unique in himself, and as original in his own way as Shakespeare or Samuel Richardson, although with this difference, that their perfections stem solely from an innate uncultivated genius, whereas Buncle's sublime peculiarity seems to be the fruit of a genius and imagination that have been heated and led to sprout, as if in a hothouse, by a romantic nature and religious zeal.

All the signals were there for the fashionable German readership of the 1770s, from the names of the most idolised English writers to such catchwords as 'original', 'genius', and 'sublime peculiarity';[27] and for good measure, Nicolai's translator rendered the novel's title *The Life of John Buncle, Esq.* as *Life, Observations and Opinions of John Buncle*, with its echo of Sterne's immensely popular *Life and Opinions of Tristram Shandy* (and of Nicolai's own successful *Life and Opinions of Sebaldus Nothanker*, on whose format and outward appearance those of the new translation were modelled).

This comparison with Shakespeare and Richardson was, of course, grossly inflated, and it was duly ridiculed by Wieland. Nevertheless, it did not originate with Nicolai, for as his advertisement makes clear, this particular passage is a quotation, translated from the remarks of an anonymous English critic in the *Monthly Review* of 1766.[28] This evidence that Amory's novel had its admirers in England as well as in Germany should at least be borne in mind before Nicolai's positive judgement is dismissed as purely self-interested; in fact, even his favourable view of Buncle's moral character has its counterpart in another passage which he translated from the same English review: 'For all his oddity, he always displays the character of an honest man, full of earnest desire to promote the welfare of his fellow men and eagerly in pursuit of what he considers to be the cause of truth.'[29] The association with Sterne, moreover, is not entirely gratuitous (although the two novelists are plainly of a very different calibre). The autobiographical form, the constant digressions, the personal hobbyhorses and the eccentricity of

---

26 Nicolai, as in note 18 above, p. 133.
27 Cf. Košenina, 'Zur deutschen Übersetzung [...]', p. 192.
28 Nicolai, as in note 18 above, p. 133; *Monthly Review*, 35 (1766), p. 34.
29 Nicolai, ibid.

the characters are genuine points of similarity, even if the differences—such as Amory's complete lack of irony—are fundamental. (It is perhaps worth adding that there can be no question of *Tristram Shandy* having influenced Amory's novel significantly, for its first volume appeared more than four years after the first volume of *The Life of John Buncle, Esq.* was published.)

Apart from the novel's affinities with specific English writers, Nicolai was also at pains to emphasise its realistic aspects, no doubt in view of the fact that realism in fiction had grown in popularity since the time of Fielding, in Germany no less than in Britain. There are indeed certain realistic features in Amory's work, such as its genuinely autobiographical elements (for example, the narrator's account of his studies), its description of various identifiable localities, its portraits of low life in London, and its observations on science and natural history. For much of the time, however, Amory's love of the bizarre and the fantastic, together with his addiction to hyperbole, relegate such tendencies to a subordinate position. Nicolai nevertheless did his utmost to magnify them, explaining the more conspicuous oddities of personality and behaviour as characteristic of English provincial society. Thus, he accounts for the omnipresence of erudite young women in Stainmore Forest and the valleys of Westmorland by pointing out 'that in England, an understanding of many truths important to mankind is more widely distributed, and less confined to major cities and exalted circles than in other countries', and he attributes the remarkable fondness of such ladies for theological speculation to the wild and 'romantic' nature of their mountainous surroundings.[30] This insistence on the work's realistic character (*wahrscheinlich* is the term Nicolai uses), is no doubt also designed to reinforce his contention that the novel is full of practical educational value.[31]

Such were Nicolai's principal claims in that advertisement to which Wieland took such exception. It certainly contains exaggerations and distortions, particularly with regard to the novel's moral significance and its standing in English literature (although there were precedents for such judgements in earlier criticism); and Nicolai's endeavours to associate the work with such different types of literature as realistic

---

30   Nicolai, as in note 18 above, p. 133.
31   Ibid.

fiction, autobiography, the picturesque tour, and the novel of religious edification and moral instruction sound very much like an attempt to make it seem all things to all men. Nevertheless, there is evidence that his lack of precision is, at least to some extent, the result of genuine uncertainty as to how to classify an idiosyncratic text which incorporates characteristics of a whole series of literary forms. He accordingly describes it as 'a novel, if one will', and admits that 'this story [...] does not have the profile of a formal novel intended to follow a single main action through in accordance with a consciously devised plan'; he then proceeds to note its affinities with autobiography.[32] He might also have added, with equal justification, that it contains elements of other types of fiction as well, including the erotic novel, the literature of fantasy (like the memoirs of Baron Munchhausen, published a few years later), and above all the picaresque novel; but none of these forms was sufficiently respectable to accord with the high moral claims which Nicolai wished to make for the work. Interestingly enough, Wieland was just as uncertain as to the precise literary category to which Amory's novel belonged. But instead of attributing this uncertainty to the originality and uniqueness of the work, he argued more harshly that the work was worthless by any literary definition, and finally described it as a 'rhapsody', a term indicative of disorder and formlessness:[33]

> That John Buncle's life and opinions, as delivered to us by the bookseller Nicolai, is in every respect—whether as a true life-history, a philosophical and Christian novel, a work of genius, wit or taste, or as a moral book written to instruct and teach by example—a highly insipid scrawl and a rhapsody filled with ill-reasoned ratiocinations, false principles and offensive examples; [...] all this requires no other proof than that someone to whom God has given reason and five senses should also pray for the measure of patience needed in order to read this book [...].

Thus, just as there was no agreement about the novel's literary merit, so also was there no agreement about its literary form—nor has there been any since. An interesting more recent attempt to define its place in literary history is that of Ian Campbell Ross, who suggests that the main reason why the novel has on the whole been ignored by historians

---

32 Ibid.
33 Wieland, 'Abgenöthigter Nachtrag' (see note 10 above), pp. 163f.

of English literature is that it lies outside the English literary tradition: 'It is, rather, an early attempt at a novel in English by an Irish writer: a novel founded on anecdote, one which exploits a rich and rewarding seam of fantasy and which, in addition, throws some light on the origins of Irish fiction.'[34] According to Ross, its ancestry is to be found not so much in earlier fiction by English authors as in the Irish *seanchas*, in the oral tradition of fantastic storytelling in which the narrator insists on the story's truth. This interpretation has much to recommend it, because Buncle is indeed a compulsive raconteur, his stories are usually fantastic, he insists on their complete veracity, and the flimsiness and—quite literally—rambling nature of the plot are just what one might expect if its function were merely to link a series of anecdotes loosely together. But not even this reading is entirely satisfactory, because the greater part of Buncle's narrative does not consist of anecdotes at all—or indeed of any other mode of fiction—but of a succession of learned harangues and disquisitions (including self-contained written treatises) on theology, ethics, and numerous different subjects, sometimes attributed to other characters whom Buncle encounters, and often embodying lengthy inventories of facts, from chemical formulae and medical bibliographies to episodes in Church history. As one editor of the novel puts it, 'It is, in fact, such a paradox of a book that it tempts one to fly into paradoxes'[35]

It may therefore be possible to understand why some critics have dismissed this strange composition as totally absurd, of even as the product of a deranged mind. Thus the anonymous notice in the *Critical Review* of 1766—the same year in which the *Monthly Review* likened the author to Shakespeare and Richardson—consisted of the single sentence: 'This is an irreviewable performance because the nonsense we encounter in perusing it, is insufferable.'[36] Over a century later, the *Dictionary of National Biography*, in its article on Amory, declared that some of the episodes in the novel 'suggest the light-headed ramblings of delirium', and added 'Amory was clearly disordered in his intellect'.

Whichever way one looks at it, *The Life of John Buncle, Esq.* is a strange and anomalous production. It is of an indeterminate and composite

---

34 Ian Campbell Ross, 'Thomas Amory, *John Buncle*, and the Origins of Irish Fiction', *Éire—Ireland*, 18/3 (1983), 71–85 (p. 72).

35 Baker, Introduction, p. vi.

36 Anon., *Critical Review*, 21 (1766), p. 470; also quoted in Ross, 'Thomas Amory [...]', p. 85.

genre, and it is difficult to see why many of its parts were included at all; it is repetitive and digressive, and most of its dialogues are really monologues of the hero to which his collocutors meekly listen and assent; the learned discourses are long-winded and derivative, and often shallow and platitudinous; the plot is fantastic and incredible; and the whole composition, as Wieland remarked, is lacking in coherence. It is, in fact, a kind of literary montage in which the degree of unity prescribed by the classicistic poetics of its time, and encountered in the vast majority of novels until the fictional experiments of modernism, is altogether absent. Such unity as it does possess lies in the personality of its hero and narrator, in whose mind and life-history the disparate elements of the work converge. But since the hero's personality is itself riven by a fundamental contradiction which is neither resolved nor relativised by any higher authorial perspective, even this unity is fragile and imperfect.

Despite all those moral shortcomings to which Wieland took such exception, there is nevertheless a positive quality about John Buncle which is central to the work's appeal. There is something engaging, even wholesome, about his unflagging zest for life and that boundless self-confidence which enables him to ignore the contradictions in his own personality. He is never malicious, he is simply led by his passions; and his pedantic attempts to assert his moral disinterestedness while constantly betraying his real and far from disinterested motives are not without their involuntary humour. He is, for all his intellectual pretensions and theological learning, basically naïve. He lives by his impulses—especially his sexual impulses—and imagination, and most of his intellectual effort is aimed at justifying and sanctifying their promptings. He is also filled with a naïve curiosity and eagerness to learn about all manner of subjects; but despite his five years at Trinity College, this curiosity is marked by the indiscriminate zeal and arbitrary enthusiasms of an untrained mind.[37]

What, then, did the controversy between Nicolai and Wieland contribute to the understanding of Amory's novel? The answer must be: very little indeed. Nicolai presented it as an edifying work of moral

---

37 It is worth mentioning that there is apparently no record of Amory himself having studied at Trinity College (see Ross, 'Thomas Amory [...]', p. 73) or, for that matter, at any other university.

realism in the autobiographical mode, and tried to relate it, not very convincingly, to the mainstream of English literature. Wieland, in his entertaining polemic, had no difficulty in refuting these claims, and presented it instead as a mixture of literary trash and moral humbug. Both of these approaches, however, miss the true source of the work's appeal, because they take the hero—and particularly his ideological protestations—much too seriously. The kind of criteria which Nicolai and Wieland apply are simply not appropriate to one who ends his preface (written by Amory in the persona of Buncle) with the following valediction to the literary critics: 'I have only to add, that I wish you all happiness; that your heads may lack no ointment, and your garments be always white and odoriferous' (I, viii). One of these critics has since concluded that Amory's novel is 'impossible to understand [...] outside of an Irish context'.[38] This may well be so; and if it is, there could clearly be little hope for either Nicolai or Wieland, both of whom were German and knew virtually nothing of Ireland or Irish culture.[39] One may not have to be Irish oneself, of course, in order to appreciate Amory's writings—but it probably helps.

---

38   Ross, 'Thomas Amory [...]', p. 85.

39   On the widespread ignorance of Ireland in eighteenth-century Germany see Eda Sagarra, 'Die "grüne Insel" in der deutschen Reiseliteratur. Deutsche Irlandreisende von Karl Gottlob Küttner bis Heinrich Böll', in *Europäisches Reisen im Zeitalter der Aufklärung*, ed. by Hans-Wolf Jäger (Heidelberg: Carl Winter, 1992), pp. 182–95.

Portrait of Johann Gottfried Herder by Gerhard von Kügelgen (1809), oil on canvas,
Tartu University Library, Photograph by Trzęsacz (2018), Wikimedia, Public Domain,
https://commons.wikimedia.org/wiki/File:Herder_by_K%C3%BCgelgen.jpg

7. Herder's *The Oldest Document of the Human Race* and his *Philosophy of Religion and History*[1]

A perplexing feature of Herder's *Älteste Urkunde des Menschengeschlechts* (*The Oldest Document of the Human Race*) of 1774–76 is its fundamental ambivalence regarding the legitimacy of natural and supernatural modes of explanation. On the one hand, he denies that the creation story in the book of Genesis has anything more than limited temporal and geographical significance for our understanding of nature. But on the other hand, he attributes to that same creation story, and particularly to what he calls its 'hieroglyphic' form, a supra-temporal significance for the development of human knowledge, including natural science. The aim of this essay is firstly, to examine the two sides of this ambivalence, and secondly, to trace the historical influences which underlie Herder's conviction that the Mosaic 'hieroglyph' served as a basic key to understanding nature in the past, and even retains this function in the present.

In the earliest drafts of *The Oldest Document*, the above-mentioned ambivalence is not yet apparent. Herder's antipathy towards all interpretations of the Bible in the light of modern science and vice versa is strongly marked: the Bible and science, he believes, should be kept strictly separate. He writes, for example, of the prophecy of the Flood to Noah: 'In truth, [...] a geographical or physical report was not God's intention'; and then, more generally on nature as understood by

---

1   An earlier version of this chapter was originally published as 'Die naturphilosophische Bedeutung von Herders "Ältester Urkunde des Menschengeschlechts"', in Brigitte Poschmann (ed.), *Bückeburger Gespräche über Johann Gottfried Herder 1988* (Rinteln: Bösendahl, 1989), pp. 210–26.

   https://doi.org/10.11647/OBP.0180.07

an inhabitant of the ancient East: 'He had not been on voyages with Maupertuis and Condamine. He had not weighed the earth and heavenly bodies with Newton'.[2] The world of modern science, he later continues, is disproportionately more complex than that of the ancient Hebrews: 'Our world is not the creation of heaven and earth; it is composed of suns and earths, of planets and comets, of spiral galaxies and milky ways'.[3] It is consequently mistaken to look in the Mosaic creation story for revelations concerning the basic truths of modern science: 'Oh, it is one of the weakest infirmities of the human spirit to expect a supernatural physics and metaphysics of creation from the divine understanding, or even to contemplate it for a single moment'.[4]

Besides, Herder leaves us in no doubt as to why he regards all attempts to harmonise the Bible and modern science as absurd. There are three major reasons for his negative attitude. Firstly, and especially in his early drafts of the years 1768 and 1769, he adopts a fundamentally secular approach: he views all supposedly supernatural influences with distrust, and condemns all those who seek to limit scientific freedom by religious dogma: 'To claim to discover *Galileo's* and *Torricelli's* and *Newton's* physics in an ancient song of the Sabbath—is strange enough! But to be compelled to find it? to compel it to be there if it does not freely present itself? [...]—that is Gothic ignorance and barbarous Gothic distortion! It suppresses the human spirit and hampers free invention [...]'.[5] And although such virtually freethinking sentiments are considerably toned down in the final version of 1774 and the discoveries of modern science are even described—albeit metaphorically—as 'revelations', he still insists that these discoveries should not be judged by the yardstick of Mosaic cosmology: '*Descartes* and *Newton, Newton* and *Euler*! Emissaries of God to the human race, why should their revelations be expurgated in the light of an ancient oriental composition?'[6]

The second reason why Herder resists all attempts to harmonise the Bible and natural science is his conviction that the creation story is primarily a poetic document rather than a philosophical or scientific

---

2   Johann Gottfried Herder, *Sämtliche Werke* (henceforth SW), ed. by Bernhard Suphan, 33 vols (Berlin: Weidmann, 1877–1913), VI, 49; cf. VI, 205ff.

3   SW VI, 46.

4   SW VI, 86f.

5   SW VI, 85.

6   SW VI, 207; cf. SW VI, 89.

treatise. Thus he writes in his early fragments entitled *Archaeology of the Orient*: 'And I maintain that a physical system [...] will never provide the key to Moses. The whole piece is obviously nothing but a poem, an oriental poem, built entirely on sensuous appearance, on the opinions of the national faith, and even on utterly false opinions'.[7] Although the implicit critique of supernaturalism that still clings to such early pronouncements is absent in the 1774 version, Herder still emphasises the poetic character of the creation document as a *'commemorative song'*[8] or *'a portrait of dawn, an image of the break of day'.*[9] In this respect, the document in question is accordingly much more accessible to aesthetic intuition than to the scientific understanding.

The third and final reason why Herder wishes to keep the Bible and science strictly separate is that historicism which distinguishes so many of his early works on literature and history. It is simply inconceivable for him that the ancient Israelites, in their own historical and cultural context, could have held the same views on nature as the scientists of the eighteenth century:[10]

> Since in the earliest times the true composition of air, the atmosphere, and the formation of rain, hail, snow, clouds, thunder and lightning was unknown to them or not yet as familiar as it is to us, their ecstatic, image-filled eyes created for them a world as they saw it, or thought they saw it. Thus the sky was for them at one moment a great, widespread tent, at another a blue, solid vault, at another even the floor of God and his thunder-horses and thunder-chariot.

To summarise the conclusions so far: from the earliest to the final version of *The Oldest Document*, Herder's arguments against the application of modern science to the first book of Moses and vice versa play a major part. They are particularly prominent in the final version of 1774, for they are discussed right at the beginning of the work and occupy nearly the first twenty pages.[11] The entire project of physico-theology, whereby attempts were made in the first half of the eighteenth century to reconcile the most diverse areas of science with the Bible and

---

7   SW VI, 32f.
8   SW VI, 325.
9   SW VI, 258.
10   SW VI, 13.
11   SW VI, 197–217.

Christian dogmatics, is dismissed as an aberration. In Herder's words, '*Scheuchzer*'s, *Nieuwentyt*'s and other works of this kind are mostly good or excellent in their physical sections, but lamentable in their theological, and especially their *interpretative* parts'.[12]

One might therefore expect that *The Oldest Document* would have little positive to offer in respect of natural science and natural philosophy, let alone that the author would himself attempt to attribute any scientific significance to the Mosaic creation story. But precisely the opposite is the case. In fact, Herder begins between 1770 and 1774 to modify his views on this entire range of questions; but instead of abandoning his original arguments against scientific interpretations of Genesis, he simply lets them stand and increasingly applies the same methods which he had previously condemned in other interpreters.

Such contradictions are, of course, by no means uncommon in Herder's works. In the present case, the explanation is not difficult either, because we can follow step by step how the plainly secularising approach of his *Archaeology of the Orient* of 1768–69 is gradually superseded by the much more ambivalent attitude of *The Oldest Document* of 1774–76.

This development is, of course, connected with his apparent turn to revealed religion and his increasingly close relationship with the Christian fideist Hamann. The effects of this change of outlook in *The Oldest Document* of 1774 include, for example, the fact that the creation story is now described as a '*divine revelation*',[13] and that naturalistic interpretations of the earliest phase of human history by Voltaire, Hume, Maupertuis and others are circumstantially rejected.[14] In addition to revelation by natural means, Herder now expressly speaks of 'the *voice of a teacher* [...], for which *no one but God* was present at the beginning of time'. [15] Despite his earlier pronouncements, he now seems to suggest that the first human beings gained through divine revelation insights into nature and cosmogony which they could not have attained by natural means.[16]

---

12   SW VI, 202.
13   SW VI, 258.
14   SW VI, 265f., 309, etc.
15   SW VI, 265f.
16   Cf. Rudolf Haym, *Herder*, 2nd edn (Berlin: Aufbau Verlag, 1954), 2 vols, I, 592: 'Thus Herder's view fluctuates in mystical vagueness between the natural and the miraculous.'

But along with this apparent new piety, there is a second and more important factor which caused Herder, despite his own counter-arguments, to assume a positive scientific content in the creation story. This factor is his conviction, already emerging in his years in Riga, that the explanation of any phenomenon must be sought above all in its origin or first manifestation—in other words, that its later stages of development are already present in its earliest state and can perhaps already be detected there. This conviction is expressed as follows in his early *Fragments on Recent German Literature*: 'In the seed lies the plant with all its parts; in the embryonic animal the creature with all its limbs: and in the origin of a phenomenon the whole wealth of elucidation through which its explanation becomes *Genetic*'.[17] As this sentence suggests, Herder's so-called 'genetic method'[18] seems to be related to the preformation theory of eighteenth-century biology, a theory to which Herder subscribed until at least his Bückeburg period.[19] If one applies this 'genetic method' to the first emergence of science—and these beginnings, for Herder, are to be found in that very document which he and most of his contemporaries regarded as the oldest surviving description of the origin of the world, i.e. the initial chapters of the Bible—one must logically conclude that the discoveries of modern science must at least implicitly be contained in this 'oldest document'. And this is precisely what Herder's theory of the Mosaic 'hieroglyph' maintains. In short, Herder's predilection for 'genetic' explanation led him to revive and reformulate a much older concept, still current in the seventeenth century, namely the concept of a *prisca sapientia*, or original wisdom of the first human beings, in which all the scientific discoveries of later centuries were implicitly or explicitly foreshadowed.[20]

This concept of a *prisca sapientia* is merely the philosophical and scientific version of a much more comprehensive theory of religious

---

17 SW II, 62.

18 This expression is used, for example, by Max Rouché, *La philosophie de l'histoire de Herder* (Paris: Société d'édition: Les Belles Lettres, 1940), p. 21.

19 Cf. H. B. Nisbet, *Herder and the Philosophy and History of Science* (Cambridge: MHRA, 1970), pp. 65f. and 201f.; also Hans Dietrich Irmscher, 'Grundlagen der Geschichtsphilosophie Herders', in *Bückeburger Gespräche über Johann Gottfried Herder*, ed. by Brigitte Poschmann (Rinteln: Bösendahl, 1984), pp. 12–19.

20 The concept of a *prisca sapientia* is discussed in detail in the important article by J. E. McGuire and P. M. Rattansi, 'Newton and the "Pipes of Pan"', *Notes and Records of the Royal Society*, 21–22 (1966–67), 108–43 (pp. 115 and 123).

history—the theory of a *prisca theologia* or original revelation of all the main truths of religion to the first human beings.[21] The following outline of the *prisca theologia* and *prisca sapientia* may serve to furnish a better understanding of Herder's hypothesis of a 'hieroglyph', particularly in its scientific connotation; and at the same time, Herder's 'genetic method' will be applied to his own thought.

The conception that all religions and mythologies of early antiquity are based on a single original revelation, of which the Old Testament version is merely the oldest and most reliable record, was already current in antiquity. It was first developed and expounded in detail by several Church Fathers, above all Lactantius, Clement of Alexandria, and Eusebius. These Church Fathers supported their theory by reference to various supposedly ancient texts of the pagan religions, for example the hermetic and Orphic writings and Pythagorean 'Carmina aurea'. (In fact, most of these writings were nor composed until the first centuries AD.) They took the view that all these texts, albeit with many later falsifications, reflected a single prototheology which contained such articles of faith of the Judaeo-Christian tradition as monotheism, the Holy Trinity, and the creation of the world out of nothing. It was also believed that traces of the original revelation could be discerned in Platonic philosophy. The main object of these reinterpretations of heathen texts was, of course, apologetic: they were meant to convince the heathens that their own religious and philosophical writings were merely corrupt versions of the oldest sacred writings of Christianity, and that the only authentic record of the original revelation was that in the Bible. If they could once be convinced that this was the case, there was no further obstacle to their conversion to Christianity.

The history of this theory of a *prisca theologia* from the Church Fathers and Neo-Platonism to its revival in and after the Renaissance by various thinkers from Ficino to Cudworth was largely illuminated in 1972 by D. P. Walker in his essay collection *The Ancient Theology. Studies*

---

21 On the concept of a *prisca theologia*, see especially D. P. Walker, *The Ancient Theology. Studies in Christian Platonism from the Fifteenth to the Eighteenth Century* (London: Duckworth, 1972). Although Walker (p. 1) claims to have first introduced the term *prisca theologia*, it occurs in several works within the tradition he himself discusses, e.g. in one of the passages he cites (p. 20) from Ficino, and in Paul Ernst Jablonski, *Pantheon Aegyptiorum*, 3 vols (Frankfurt an der Oder: Christian Kleyb, 1750–52), III, p. iv.

in Christian Platonism from the Fifteenth to the Eighteenth Century. One of the most interesting insights which Walker provides is that of the central role which ancient Egypt, and particularly the Egyptian God Thoth or Theut (who is sometimes identified with Hermes Trismegistus), played in the transmission of the original revelation.[22]

Herder is actually one of the last proponents of this ancient theory. He first discovered the outlines of the *prisca theologia* chiefly from ancient sources, as his letter of 15 October 1770 to J. H. Merck indicates: he cites in it a list of authors he has read in connection with his 'hieroglyph' hypothesis, namely 'Jablonsky, Philo, Clement [of Alexandria], Eusebius, Orpheus, Porphyry, Jamblichus, and the Pythagoreans of Gale'.[23] The Church Fathers and Neo-Platonists listed here were all indebted to the tradition of the *prisca theologia*. Jablonski, who is named in *The Oldest Document* as an authority on the Egyptian religion, was also an adherent of the *prisca theologia*, as were Thomas Hyde, Ralph Cudworth, and other commentators on the religions and philosophies of antiquity with whose work Herder became acquainted between his Riga and Bückeburg periods. Herder's library, in which oriental works were particularly numerous, also contained a remarkable number of works directly related to the *prisca theologia* tradition.[24]

It may at first sight seem surprising that this theory of the *prisca theologia* could still be taken seriously around 1770 despite its drastic simplification and generalisation of ancient religious history. It owed its enduring credibility above all to the short Biblical chronology which—apart from a few sceptics—was still generally taken as authoritative, although it was increasingly called into question by geological discoveries. If the earth was less than 6,000 years old, all the religions of antiquity must have arisen within a relatively short time among peoples

---

22   Walker, *The Ancient Theology*, pp. 16, 18f., and 101; cf. McGuire and Rattansi, 'Newton and the "Pipes of Pan"', p. 128.

23   Johann Gottfried Herder, *Briefe. Gesamtausgabe 1763–1803*, ed. by Karl-Heinz Hahn, Wilhelm Dobbek and Günter Arnold, 10 vols (Weimar: Böhlau, 1977–2001), I, 261. The work by Gale cited by Herder is presumably the *Opuscula mythologica physica et ethica, graece et latine*, ed. by Thomas Gale (Amsterdam: Henricus Wetsteinius, 1688); it contains an item entitled *Ex quorundam Pythagoreorum libris fragmenta, in quibus de Philosophia Morali agitur* (pp. 657–752).

24   *Bibliotheca Herderiana* (Weimar: privately printed, 1804): No. 600, *Das Platonisch-Hermetische Christentum von Colberg*; No. 1062, *Ursinus de Zoroastre, Hermete Trism. Sanchoniathone*. Norimb. 1661; No. 2927, Ath. Kircheri *Oedipus Aegyptiacus*. Rom 1652; etc.; cf. Walker, *The Ancient Theology*, pp. 231ff.

whose common origin was still recent. And if the Old Testament—or at least the five books of Moses—dated from the earliest times, it was quite probable that the oldest writings of all the other early religions were in some way indebted to them or related to them via a common source. Already in the seventeenth century, this theory was also applied to science. This application seemed particularly appropriate, since the first chapter of the Bible had the origin of the world as its subject and since cosmogony occupied a central place in nearly all the religions of antiquity. As part of the original revelation, the Mosaic creation story therefore seemed to be the model for all the later creation stories; and if its truth was supposedly beyond doubt, as it still was in seventeenth-century Europe, then all parts of modern science which dealt with the origin of the world must necessarily be in accord with the Mosaic account.

One did not need to subscribe to the *prisca theologia* theory in order to accept that the Bible and science were compatible, since this was in any case an article of faith for all the Christian churches. But the extended version of this theory, that of the *prisca sapientia*, went much further. This theory assumed that the original revelation contained a greater number of truths concerning nature and the universe than those recorded in the Bible. Newton, for example, was of the opinion that not only the Copernican theory of the planets, but also his own theory of gravity was among these truths, which had subsequently been lost but already rediscovered by some thinkers in antiquity.[25] There are even some indications that Newton saw the main purpose of his own scientific work as that of rediscovering the pure and unadulterated truths of the original divine revelation, and that he for a time had the intention of incorporating his thoughts on this problem in a new edition of his *Principia Mathematica*.[26]

This conception of science as a rediscovery of truths from the earliest times is, of course, very different from the usual picture of modern science and its development from Galileo to Newton as a progressive and secularising movement which turned its back on all received wisdom and tradition. But in more recent times, it has become ever clearer that

---

25   See McGuire and Rattansi, 'Newton and the "Pipes of Pan"', p. 109; also Walker, *The Ancient Theology*, p. 243.

26   See McGuire and Rattansi, 'Newton and the "Pipes of Pan"', p. 121.

the ideological premises of science, right down to the present day, have been by no means as uniform and straightforward as previously assumed.[27] Even by the time of the Enlightenment, we still encounter all kinds of archaic elements and relics of mystical and hermetic wisdom, and not just in the thought of such outsiders as Swedenborg and Lavater, but also in the work of Leibniz, Newton, and other leading thinkers.[28] There were, of course, great differences, both between individuals and national traditions. For example, French natural philosophy since the time of Descartes emphasised its originality and superiority to all earlier disciplines more strongly than was the case in other countries, and showed little interest in looking for precursors of its own theories in the earliest times.[29] In England, however, the case was quite otherwise: scholars as different as Francis Bacon, whose work *De sapientia veterum* presented ancient mythology as an allegorical expression of opinions closely related to his own theories,[30] and the Cambridge Platonists More and Cudworth, along with the experimental scientists Boyle and Newton,[31] considered many—if not all—modern discoveries as rediscoveries of ancient truths. This constant retrospection on the most distant past certainly contributed to that preoccupation with first beginnings and original circumstances that became characteristic of the eighteenth century, and is encountered in the works of Leibniz, Rousseau, Buffon, and Kant—as well, of course, as Herder.[32]

These were accordingly the traditions which Herder took up when he applied his 'genetic method' to the so-called 'oldest document of the human race'. The end result was that his Mosaic 'hieroglyph' became a universal means of explanation, and threatened to supplant that historical relativism which was still dominant in the early versions of

---

27 Cf. J. V. Golinski, 'Science in the Enlightenment', *History of Science*, 24 (1986), pp. 411–24; I am indebted to Robert Iliffe of the Department of History and Philosophy of Science, University of Cambridge, for the reference to this article and to Newton's interest in the *prisca sapientia* in his unpublished papers.

28 Cf. Rolf Christian Zimmermann, *Das Weltbild des jungen Goethe. Studien zur hermetischen Tradition des deutschen 18. Jahrhunderts*, 2 vols (Munich: Fink, 1969–79), I, 139f.

29 See Walker, 'Newton and the "Pipes of Pan"', pp. 195f.

30 On Herder's familiarity with such ideas of Bacon see H. B. Nisbet, 'Herder and Francis Bacon', *Modern Language Review*, 62 (1967), pp. 267–83 (pp. 268f.).

31 See McGuire and Rattansi, 'Newton and the "Pipes of Pan"', pp. 132–36.

32 Cf. Frank E. Manuel, *The Eighteenth Century Confronts the Gods* (Cambridge, MA: Harvard University Press, 1959), p. 132.

his work. The 'hieroglyph' was now not only intended to serve as a key to the wisdom of the earliest human societies, but was also endowed with a supra-temporal significance for modern science.

Herder's growing belief in the authority of the Bible, even in relation to science, is most prominently expressed in the fourth part of *The Oldest Document*, published in 1776: the story of Adam is here interpreted with the help of the theories of Haller and Buffon.[33] For it is now Herder's intention to prove that the truths of revelation have been confirmed by modern science—the very hypothesis which he had condemned in the first part of his work two years earlier. But it is significant that nearly all the scientific references of 1776 are to Haller's physiology, whereas the equivalent theories of other contemporary thinkers and scientists such as Helvétius, Moscati, La Mettrie and de Maillet are unceremoniously rejected.[34] What Herder particularly likes about Haller's reflections is their vitalistic tendency: all biological processes are reduced to invisible 'forces' (*Kräfte*), which Herder so often employs as a means of avoiding the appearance of contradiction between naturalistic and supernaturalistic modes of explanation; in contrast with this approach, the methods of Helvétius and the other rejected theorists are unambiguously mechanistic and materialistic. Thus, Herder can appeal to Haller when he declares: 'The breath of God is within us, a *collection of invisible, powerful* and *so diverse vital forces combined* only in vapour'.[35] But this solution to the conflict between opposite methods of explanation is only apparent: it leaves untouched that deeper ambivalence which runs through *The Oldest Document*, and which derives from Herder's characteristic wish to employ both relative and absolute standards in the explanation of natural and historical processes.

Let us finally turn to the scientific and philosophical significance of Herder's 'hieroglyph'. When this theory first appears in the drafts of 1768 or 1769, its claims to validity are still modest. For example, the 'hieroglyph' still has nothing to do with nature and natural science; it purports to be no more than a structural feature of the creation story, a complex of symmetries and parallelisms in the Mosaic description of

---

33   SW VII, 11f., 17f., 24, 80, 90f., etc.
34   SW VII, 71–76; cf. also SW, VII, 114: the name 'Telliamed' cited here is a reversal of his own name used by de Maillet as a pseudonym.
35   SW VII, 13.

the seven days of creation which Herder describes as a 'hieroglyph'.[36] Its significance at this stage is purely formal and poetic. The first indication that Herder accords a wider scope to his theory occurs in his letter to Merck of 15 October 1770, in which he tells his friend: 'I have made a strange discovery in recent days, that the hieroglyph which I have long since noticed in the first book of Moses, Chapter I and Chapter II to verse 3 [...] is as certainly basic throughout the entire Egyptian pantheon, secret rituals, wise teachings of Thoth or Theut, etc. as my name is Herder.'[37] He further asserts—just like the advocates of the *prisca sapientia*—that the creation story must have arisen before the time of Moses, because the Egyptians seem to have acquired it from an earlier source. This lends a higher degree of probability to his suppositions that the original revelation contained many more truths than Moses records, and that the 'hieroglyph' implies far more extensive knowledge than the Bible explicitly mentions.

When the first volume of *The Oldest Document* appeared in 1774, the scope of Herder's theory had become wider still. The 'hieroglyph', he claims, was the basis not just of the Egyptian religion, but also of all the arts and sciences of early times: 'now all *human writing and symbolism* had taken shape *around it and in it*, the oldest, *most important arts and sciences of human society, physics and chronology, astronomy* and what was called *philosophy* emerged from it'.[38] Towards the end of the first part of the work, such claims become even more exaggerated, inasmuch as the 'hieroglyph' now counts as something 'which was to engage *all the senses and forces of the human being*, exert pressure on and guide *his entire soul* for *eternities of his race*'[39]—and hence fulfils a permanent heuristic function; in short, it was the *origin* of *everything that exists!*'[40]

Thus Herder now claims for his 'hieroglyph' a cognitive content which goes far beyond the limits of our knowledge of nature. The scope of this content also exceeds everything I could find in the main sources on which he drew for *The Oldest Document*, although the 'hieroglyph' is in this respect merely a logical extension of the ancient notion of a

---

36   SW VI, 38f.
37   Herder, *Briefe. Gesamtausgabe*, I, 261.
38   SW VI, 290.
39   SW VI, 319.
40   SW VI, 323.

prisca sapientia. Herder's immediate source seems to have been Paul Ernst Jablonski (whose name is, incidentally, the first in the list of sources mentioned in his letter to Merck). One reads in Jablonski, for example, that Thoth or Theut was originally not a god but only the name of a monument on which all the elements of Egyptian religion were inscribed (no doubt in hieroglyphic script).[41] What Herder says about the scientific content of his 'hieroglyph' is likewise largely based on Jablonski, to whom he owes many of his remarks on chronology and the seven planets, the seven primary colours, the seven metals, the seven musical notes, etc. as basic elements of Egyptian natural history.[42] That the number seven in *The Oldest Document* became almost an obsession for him is again partly due to Jablonski.[43] Herder's choice of the word 'hieroglyph' to designate the symmetrical structure of the creation story is, however, due to Hamann;[44] but it cannot be ruled out that the extensive literature on the Egyptian hieroglyphs listed in the catalogue of Herder's library may also have played a part—for example, the work entitled *Hieroglyphica sive de sacris Aegyptiorum* (Basle, 1556) by J. P. Valeriano, who emphasised that Moses had gained his education in Egypt and described his manner of writing as 'hieroglyphic'.[45]

But before I leave these reflections, I should like to draw attention to an interesting parallel to Herder's 'hieroglyph'—a parallel which was perhaps known to him and which, like his own equivalent, is closely related to the tradition of the *prisca theologia*. In the last years of the seventeenth century, the French Jesuit Joachim Bouvet, a missionary in China who had immersed himself in the wisdom of the ancient Chinese, claimed to have discovered an important secret. He believed that he had unravelled the mystery of the *Y-King*, a work supposedly written by the

---

41   Jablonski, *Pantheon Aegyptiorum* III, iv.

42   SW VI, 376 and 382; cf. Jablonski, *Pantheon Aegyptiorum*, III, liiif.

43   See Jablonski, *Pantheon Aegyptiorum*, III, xxiv: 'numerus septenarius Orientalibus sanctus erat'.

44   See Sven-Aage Jørgensen, in *Bückeburger Gespräche über Johann Gottfried Herder 1988*, ed. by Brigitte Poschmann (Rinteln: Bösendahl, 1989), p. 104.

45   See also Walker, *The Ancient Theology*, p. 102 and *Bibliotheca Herderiana* No. 2651: Jo. Pier. Valeriani *Hieroglyphica*, Francof. 1678; No. 1650: *Hieroglyphica Horapollinis* a Dav. Hoeschelio. Aug. Vind. 1595; No. 2676: Athan. Kircheri *Prodromus Aegypticus*, Rom. 1636; etc.; on the history of the hexagonal figure described by Herder as a 'hieroglyph', whose origins lie not in Biblical studies but in the magical and alchemistic literature of the Middle Ages, see Gershom Scholem, 'The Curious History of the Six-Pointed Star', *Commentary. A Jewish Review*, 8 (1949), 243–51.

mythical emperor Fohi, which played an important part in the thought of Taoism. The *Y-King* contains a long series of hexagrams, i.e. squares composed of six parallel lines, one or more of which may be interrupted in the middle. These hexagrams had been used for prophecy since ancient times, but Bouvet believed he had discovered a much more profound sense in them, namely the lost wisdom of the first Biblical patriarchs who had visited China in early times, and which they then recorded in symbolic form in the *Y-King*. (The intention which underlay his efforts, of course, was to convert the Chinese to Christianity.) He said in summary of his conclusions: 'The figure in the system of FOHI was like a universal symbol, invented by some extraordinary genius of antiquity like *Hermes Trismegistus*, in order to render visible the most abstract principles of all the sciences.'[46] Bouvet further remarked on the *Y-King*: 'this kind of writing seems to me to embody the veritable idea of the ancient hieroglyphs and the Cabbala of the Hebrews',[47] and concluded that the study of this work offered an opportunity 'to recover the ancient and universal system of the sciences'.[48] He also declared that the Chinese script was derived from the Egyptian hieroglyphs, and that the emperor Fohi was presumably none other than Hermes Trismegistus, Enoch, or Zoroaster.[49]

These ideas first became known in Europe through Bouvet's correspondence with Leibniz. This correspondence, in which Leibniz showed a keen interest in Bouvet's research and himself attempted a mathematical interpretation of the hexagrams, lasted from roughly 1697 to 1702; it was published in extract in 1734[50] and included in 1768 in the major Leibniz edition compiled by Louis Dutens.[51]

There is no evidence that Herder knew this correspondence. But we do know that he was reading ancient Chinese writings during the

---

46 G. W. Leibniz, *Opera omnia*, ed. by Louis Dutens, 6 vols (Geneva: Fratres de Tournes, 1768), IV/1, pp. 147f. (letter of Bouvet to le Gobien, 8 November 1700, forwarded by le Gobien to Leibniz on 10 November 1701). On this entire episode see Walker, *The Ancient Theology*, pp. 221–29 and Joseph Needham, *Science and Civilisation in China*, vol. II (Cambridge: Cambridge University Press, 1956), pp. 340–45.

47 Leibniz, *Opera omnia*, IV/1, pp. 154f.

48 Ibid., IV/1, p. 168.

49 Ibid., IV/1, pp. 160 and 158.

50 G. W. Leibniz, *Recueil de diverses Pièces sur la Philosophie*, ed. by Christian Kortholt (Hamburg: publisher unknown, 1734), pp. 70ff.

51 Leibniz, *Opera omnia*, IV/1, pp. 145–68.

preparation of *The Oldest Document*. For example, he borrowed in June 1772 through his friend Christian Gottlob Heyne another sacred text from the Göttingen library,[52] namely the *Shu-King*, in an edition which also included an essay on the *Y-King*;[53] extracts from this essay and from the *Shu-King* itself are still present in his posthumous papers.[54] The author of the essay on the *Y-King* was a colleague of Bouvet, who refers to the latter's theory on the common ancestry of the Chinese and Christian religions, but without going into any detail. However that may be, Herder also possessed a work by Johann Thomas Haupt on the *Y-King*, in which the questions discussed by Bouvet and Leibniz are mentioned;[55] it remains to be seen whether he already possessed this book at the time of writing *The Oldest Document*. But even if Herder knew nothing of Bouvet's correspondence with Leibniz at the time of *The Oldest Document*, it is unlikely that the similarity between his 'hieroglyph' and Bouvet's theory of the Chinese hexagrams was simply coincidental. For the similarity must be due at least in part to the fact that Bouvet and the other French Jesuits in China were working within the framework of the same tradition that Herder encountered through other sources—the tradition of the *prisca theologia* and the *prisca sapientia*.

Finally, another important question remains unanswered. What did Herder mean when he declared that the 'hieroglyph' was the origin of all the sciences, and that it was destined to guide human beings 'for eternities of [their] race'?[56] That the 'hieroglyph' may have hinted at a few basic elements of the oldest theories of nature, especially if it concerned simple groups of seven planets, notes, metals, etc., is conceivable and comprehensible. But in what sense could it also have foreshadowed discoveries of *modern* science?

In the first part of his *Ideas on the Philosophy of History* of 1784, Herder develops a theory which was to play a significant part in nineteenth-century biology—the theory of an animal 'type', according to which

---

52   Herder, *Briefe. Gesamtausgabe*, II, 183, Herder to Heyne, June 1772.

53   *Le Chou-King, un des livres sacrés des Chinois*, ed. by Joseph de Guignes (Paris: N. M. Tilliard, 1770).

54   See Hans Dietrich Irmscher and Emil Adler, *Der handschriftliche Nachlass Johann Gottfried Herders. Katalog* (Wiesbaden: Harrasowitz, 1979), p. 235.

55   *Bibliotheca Herderiana*, No. 2813: Joh. Thom. Haupts *Auslegung des kayserl. Buchs Ye Kim*, Rostock 1753.

56   SW VI, 319.

all the vertebrates, and perhaps even other creatures and natural forms, were constructed on a single model.[57] In the same connection, he cites similar ideas from Buffon's works on comparative anatomy, which probably influenced his own theory.[58] Despite this anatomical connection, I am not convinced that Herder's concept of an organic 'type' was derived from his anatomical reflections; it arose rather, I believe, from the 'hieroglyph' of *The Oldest Document*. The two theories have numerous points of contact. For example, Herder calls his 'hieroglyph' the *'type of creation'*;[59] and on another occasion, he compares it to the human figure and calls it a 'microcosm',[60] just as, in an early draft of the *Ideas*, he associates his concept of 'type' with that of a microcosm.[61] Even the theological expressions he uses to characterise the 'hieroglyph' recur in the *Ideas* when he defines the 'type' as follows: 'this one type, i.e. the basic inner laws of this single active force through which the creative and productive deity reveals himself'.[62] But more important than these verbal affinities is the conceptual relationship between the two theories. When Herder draws attention to the parallelisms in the creation story in order to elucidate his 'hieroglyph', he refers more than once to the fact that Moses groups together the creatures of the water and the air. In view of the anatomical similarities between the two classes of animals, he maintains that this association is entirely justified: 'The parallel of the two oceans, air and water! Here the fish fly, as it were, on their winged fins, and there the birds swim on their wings'. [63] Within the framework of comparative anatomy, he reverts in the *Ideas* to the same parallel with a reference to Moses.[64] In other words, even the anatomical content of the 'type' theory recalls the 'hieroglyph' of *The Oldest Document*.

But there is an even closer connection between the 'hieroglyph' and the 'type', which Herder only hints at in his later works, as for example in the following sentences from an early draft for the *Ideas*: 'One and the

---

57   SW XIII, 66–69; cf. SW XIII, 274 and SW XIV, 590. For further details on this theory, see H. B. Nisbet, 'Herder, Goethe and the Natural "Type"', *Publications of the English Goethe Society*, 37 (1967), pp. 83–119.

58   SW XIV, 624 and 693.

59   SW VI, 485.

60   SW VI, 314f. and 419.

61   SW XIII, 68n.

62   SW XIII, 274.

63   SW VI, 245; cf. SW VI, 53f.

64   SW XIII, 424.

same form repeats itself in all earthly beings. Where formation begins, from the snowflake and the crystal [...] up through all the structures of plants and animals, only one prototype seems to be present'.[65] And he says many years later in his *Adrastea*: 'The laws of formation of creative nature are everywhere the same; the flower of winter, the snowflake, reveals to you the secret of emerging worlds'.[66] The answer to the question as to why the snowflake in particular should be the key to this secret lies, of course, in the form of the snow crystal, which represents a hexagonal star and is therefore identical with Herder's 'hieroglyph'.

If Herder still has in mind the 'hieroglyph' of *The Oldest Document* in such passages from his late works, and if the concept of the 'type' in the *Ideas* arose out of it, why does he not explicitly refer to his earlier theory? It probably is not mentioned for the same reason that it is not referred to in the section of the *Ideas* on ancient Egypt, where one might most readily have expected it: after the negative reception of his mystical speculations in *The Oldest Document*, Herder hesitates to renew these speculations in works or contexts where the progress of the empirical sciences is the focus of discussion.[67] In his later works, his natural philosophy is based largely on Spinoza, and his scientific thought mainly on the results of recent research. But it can be seen from *The Oldest Document* that some of his ideas on natural philosophy go back to a very much older tradition.

---

65   SW XIV, 590.

66   SW XXIII, 533; cf. SW XXII, 88.

67   Cf. Ulrich Faust, *Mythologien und Religionen des Ostens bei Johann Gottfried Herder* (Münster: Aschendorff, 1977), p. 102: 'The chapter on Egypt in Herder's *Ideas* indirectly indicates that he has taken back those [earlier] empty and vague speculations on the history of Egyptian religious history.'

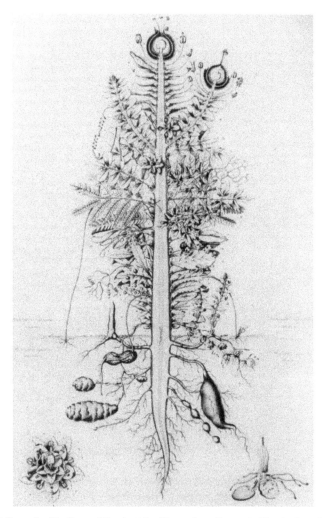

Darstellung der Urpflanze. Woodcut by Pierre Jean François Turpin based on a concept by Johann Wolfgang von Goethe (1837), scanned from Anita Albus, *Die Kunst der Künste. Erinnerungen an die Malerei* (Frankfurt am Main: Eichborn Verlag, 1997). Photograph by JuTa (2010), Wikimedia, Public Domain, https://commons. wikimedia.org/wiki/File:Urpflanze.png

8. The Ethical Foundation of Goethe's Scientific Thought[1]

From the scientific revolution of the seventeenth to the end of the nineteenth century, the main opposition to science came from religion. During the twentieth century, this opposition was largely replaced—at least in the Western world—by a new polarisation of science and the humanities, culminating in the so-called 'two cultures debate', unleashed by the famous lecture of 1959 by C. P. Snow on 'The Two Cultures and the Scientific Revolution'.[2] Snow's central claim was that science and the humanities had by this time parted company to such an extent that they now constituted two separate, and fundamentally incompatible cultures. We have since come to think of this opposition as essentially a feature of modernism, and of the twentieth century in particular.

It is less often remembered that a particularly extreme version of this conflict took place in the late eighteenth and early nineteenth centuries in the work of Goethe, who set up his own version of science in open hostility to that of Newton. In his *Colour Theory* of 1810, he describes Newton's *Optics* as 'a model of sophistical distortion of nature, [...] which only an extraordinary mind like that of Newton, whose wilfulness and obstinacy were the equal of his genius, was capable of constructing'.[3] He continues with a metaphor from gambling, presenting Newton

---

1 An earlier version of this chapter was originally published as 'Die ethische Grundlage von Goethes Naturwissenschaft', in Thomas Jung and Birgit Mühlhaus (eds.), *Über die Grenzen Weimars hinaus—Goethes Werk in europäischem Licht* (Oxford, Berne, Berlin, etc.: Peter Lang, 2000), pp. 171–83.

2 C. P. Snow, *The Two Cultures and the Scientific Revolution*, The Rede Lecture, 1959 (Cambridge: Cambridge University Press, 1959); new edition, with an introduction by Stefan Collini (Cambridge: Cambridge University Press, 1993).

3 Goethe, *Die Schriften zur Naturwissenschaft*, ed. by the Deutsche Akademie der Naturforscher (Leopoldina) (henceforth LA), I. Abteilung, 17 vols (Weimar: Böhlau, 1947–70); II. Abteilung (Weimar: Böhlau, 1959–), LA I. Abt., V, 86.

https://doi.org/10.11647/OBP.0180.08

as a 'cardsharper' who boosts his winnings by deceptive means,[4] and describes Newton's optical theories alternately as 'dishonest', 'shameless', 'scandalous', 'distorted' and 'foolish'.[5] What we have here is an extraordinary spectacle: the greatest European poet of the eighteenth and early nineteenth centuries, who was not otherwise addicted to polemics, denounces the most respected scientist in the world as a liar and swindler, and declares that one of his greatest works in physics is fundamentally false.

How could it come to this extremity? The cause, in my opinion, lies not simply in Goethe's difference of opinion with Newton on the nature and production of colour. For Goethe's above-quoted condemnations plainly show that his objections to Newton's optics were at least as much ethical as scientific in nature, given his contention that Newton's whole way of thinking was ethically suspect or erroneous. And if one wishes to explain how Goethe reached this conclusion, and what assumptions underlie it, one must consult not just his *Colour Theory*, but also his scientific thought in general—and especially the way in which this thought developed from his first scientific observations in the early 1780s.

Goethe's scientific research was much more than a hobby or pastime. His scientific writings occupy thirteen volumes of the Weimar edition of his works, and in the second half of his life, around a third of his working time was devoted to science. He also declared in his final years that he considered his *Colour Theory* a greater achievement than his entire poetic works.[6] This judgement may strike us as extravagant or incomprehensible; but for Goethe, it was justified inasmuch as he regarded his scientific works as a central component of his life's work as an author. They were, for him, an expression of his most profound metaphysical, aesthetic, and not least ethical convictions.

It is not possible in the space of a short essay to discuss the entire corpus of Goethe's scientific writings. I shall therefore confine myself to considering its basic principles. This task is made easier by the fact that his entire work is based on only a few fundamental discoveries

---

4   LA I. Abt., V, 157.
5   LA I. Abt., V, 82, 118, 184f., 187.
6   *Goethes Gespräche mit Eckermann*, ed. by Franz Deibel (Leipzig: Insel-Verlag, 1921), p. 457 (19 February 1829).

or insights which he attained within a very short time—roughly between 1784 and 1790; his later research consists almost exclusively in consolidating and applying these initial insights. I shall therefore begin with a brief survey of these insights, before attempting to define their significance for Goethe's thought in general.

Goethe began his scientific work in the early 1780s with comparative anatomy, and discovered the so-called intermaxillary bone in human beings.[7] This discovery was prompted by the fact that various anatomists had denied that the bone in question, which is present in all other mammals and contains the upper incisors, can be distinguished in human beings from the other bones of the upper jaw.[8] From this circumstance, it was inferred that the absence of this bone, together with other exclusively human qualities such as the capacity for speech and the hope of immortality, is an important distinguishing feature of the human species. Goethe, however, succeeded in distinguishing this bone—of rather the joints or sutures which separate it from the adjoining bones—in human embryos, and later also in hydrocephalic and other malformed skulls.[9] There was, he concluded, no fundamental osteological difference between man and the animals.

The historical context of this discovery was the debate in the second half of the eighteenth century on the classification of plants and animals. Goethe associated himself with that group of scientists such as Buffon who attempted to construct a so-called 'natural system' in which all organisms might be classified by their degree of similarity, in gradual transitions, with other forms in the hierarchy of beings.[10] A natural system of this kind would not be guided by superficial or fortuitous differences, as was the case with the 'artificial' (i.e. arbitrary) system of the Swedish botanist Linnaeus, who classified flowering plants according to the number of their stamens and pistils. The 'natural' classes of plants and animals which Goethe, Buffon and others sought to distinguish were, of course, not yet evolutionary classes in the Darwinian

---

7   Cf. Goethe to Herder, 27 March 1784, in *Goethes Werke*, Weimar edition (henceforth WA), 133 vols (Weimar: Böhlau, 1889–1919), IV. Abteilung, VI, 258.

8   Goethe names in particular the anatomists Camper and Blumenbach.

9   The relevant essays can be found in LA I. Abt., IX, 154–86.

10 LA I. Abt., X, 326f. and 331; see also Goethe's *Italian Journey*, 27 September 1786, in WA I. Abt., XXX, 89f.; cf. also H. B. Nisbet, *Goethe and the Scientific Tradition* (London: Institute of Germanic Studies, University of London, 1972), p. 8.

sense, for the state of knowledge was at that time quite insufficient to form the basis of a Darwinistic theory of common descent. Their aim was simply to distinguish larger groups of living organisms by means of structural similarities. For Goethe, the decisive feature of his discovery of the intermaxillary bone was ultimately its metaphysical significance: it confirmed man's essential membership of nature as a whole, within which all natural forms were related to one another via gradual transitions.[11]

Goethe's next discovery supplied a further proof of the unity of nature, in this case of the flowering plants in particular. In the year 1786, on a visit to the botanic gardens in Padua, he came up with the idea 'that one can perhaps derive all botanical forms from a single example'.[12] This hypothetical basic form, which he soon began to describe as the 'Urpflanze' (archetypal plant), was in his own words a 'model' with which 'one might then invent further plants in an infinite series [...] which, even if they do not exist, at least could exist'.[13] Whether he hoped to find a real plant to match this model (as he maintained in later years)[14] remains uncertain; but his subsequent investigations in Palermo at least led him to a further insight, which rapidly superseded his theory of the 'Urpflanze'. As he compared the many unfamiliar plants, he became convinced that all the main organs of the stem (for example, stem leaves, bracts, sepals, petals, stamens, etc.) are homologous—that is, that they are all modified leaves (as suggested by their names in German, nearly all of which end in '–*blätter*').[15] This insight becomes the central thesis of his main botanical work, the essay 'The Metamorphosis of Plants' of 1790 (which, strictly speaking, ought rather to be called 'The Metamorphosis of the Leaf'). Thus, if Goethe had not succeeded in finding the archetypal plant, he had at least found, to his own satisfaction, the archetypal form of most organs of the flowering plants. The unity of nature was once again confirmed.

Goethe's next two discoveries, inspired by his work on comparative anatomy in the early 1780s but not put into written form until 1790,

---

11   Cf. Goethe to Knebel, 17 November 1784 in WA IV. Abt., VI, 389f.

12   *Italian Journey*, 27 September 1786, in WA I. Abt., XXX, 89; cf. Goethe to Frau von Stein, 9 July 1786, in WA IV. Abt., VI, 242.

13   *Italian Journey*, 17 May 1787, to Herder, in WA I. Abt., XXXI, 239f.

14   *Italian Journey*, 17 April 1787, *in* WA I. Abt., XXXI, 147 (compiled between 1815 and 1817).

15   Cf. the history of his botanical theories, in LA I. Abt., X, 334; also *Italian Journey*, July 1787, in WA I. Abt., XXXII, 44 and LA I. Abt., IX, 8f. and 59.

are the osteological counterparts to the botanical theories of the archetypal plant and the leaf as the archetypal organ of plants. The so-called 'osteological type'[16] (which Goethe also refers to in later years as the 'Urtier' or archetypal animal)[17] corresponds to the archetypal plant as the ideal model for the skeleton of animals: for Goethe now claims to have established that the same osteological units are present, in the same arrangement, in all mammals, from the mole to the elephant and the walrus to human beings.[18] (He was the first to describe the comparative study of these forms in their endless variations as 'morphology', the term still in use for this procedure today.) In osteology, the counterpart of the botanical theory of the leaf as archetypal organ of plants is the so-called 'vertebral theory of the skull' which Goethe formulated in 1790 after finding the broken skull of a sheep that seemed to him to prove that all the main bones of the vertebrate skull are modified vertebrae.[19] The vertebra must therefore, he argued, be regarded as the archetypal organ not only of the spine, but also of the skull. In these two anatomical theories of 1790, a deeper unity or homology was therefore once again basic to the apparently most diverse natural forms.

Goethe's last important insight as a scientist was gained at around the same time, probably in the first months of 1790.[20] He himself relates how he had tried in Italy to discover the basic laws of form and composition in painting.[21] But on the nature of colour in particular, he had been unable to discover anything significant, either from the painters he had met in Rome or from the textbooks and paintings themselves,[22] so that he finally decided to investigate the problem, on his return to Germany, from first principles. The standard work on optics at that time was, of course, Newton's *Optics*, and Goethe therefore undertook to study

---

16 LA I. Abt., IX, 13; see also H. B. Nisbet, 'Herder, Goethe and the Natural "Type"', *Publications of the English Goethe Society*, 37 (1967), 83–119.

17 LA I. Abt., X, 78.

18 LA I. Abt., X, 142.

19 Cf. Diary, 22 April 1790, in WA III. Abt., II, 19; *Tag- und Jahreshefte* 1790, in WA I. Abt., XXXV, 15; also letters to Frau von Kalb, 30 April 1790 and Caroline Herder, 4 May 1790, in WA IV. Abt., IX, 202 and 204 and LA I. Abt., IX, 208, 309 and 357f.

20 On the precise date, cf. LA II. Abt., III, xvif and *Goethes Werke*, Hamburg edition (henceforth HA), ed. by Erich Trunz, 14 vols (Hamburg: Christian Wegner, 1948–64), XIII, 613.

21 See Goethe's *History of Colour Theory*, in LA I. Abt., VI, 415ff.

22 See the preface to his *Contributions to Optics* (1791) in LA I. Abt., III, 12.

Newton's theory and repeat its central experiments.[23] When he was briefly prevented from conducting the experiments, he took a quick look through a prism he had borrowed at the white wall of his room, and expected, on the strength of dimly recollected lectures from his student days in Leipzig, to see the entire surface of the wall resolved into all the colours of the spectrum. He of course noticed at once that this was not the case, and describes his astonished reactions in the following famous words of his *Colour Theory*:[24]

> How amazed I was when the white wall that I looked at through the prism remained white as before, and that a more or less definite colour showed up only where it bordered on a dark object. The window frames ultimately appeared in the most vivid colours, whereas no trace of colour was visible in the pale grey sky outside. It required no long reflection for me to realise that a limit was necessary to produce colours, and I at once said aloud to myself, as if by instinct, that the Newtonian theory was false.

Over the next two decades, Goethe repeated all of Newton's experiments and supplemented them by many others. But he never withdrew his original conclusion that Newton's theory was false, and remained convinced as before that the colours were not, so to speak, contained in the white light and then extracted from it by refraction, but were only produced when light and dark images were superimposed. In other words, clearly defined images of different brightness and darkness are a necessary condition of colour production.[25] From this original opposition, this polarity of light and darkness, Goethe derives all possible kinds and combinations of coloured images that arise under different circumstances, and orders them in series with gradual transitions.[26] He outlines, as it were, a morphology or 'natural system' of colours which is closely linked to those series of typical forms whose 'metamorphoses' he had earlier attempted to classify in botany and zoology.[27] But the unifying element in his continuous series of coloured images is neither a conceptual generalisation nor an abstract, mathematically based

---

23   LA I. Abt., VI, 417–21.
24   LA I. Abt., VI, 420; also *Tag- und Jahreshefte* 1790, in WA I. Abt., XXXV, 13f.
25   Cf. LA I. Abt., VI, 424f.
26   Cf. LA I. Abt., VIII, 314f. (*The Experiment as Mediator between Object and Subject*).
27   Cf. Neil M. Ribe, 'Goethe's Critique of Newton. A Reconsideration', *Studies in the History and Philosophy of Science*, 16 (1985), 315–55 (p. 325).

theory in the manner of Newton, who derived the colours from the different refractive indices of light, but a concrete image, which Goethe now begins to describe as an 'Urphänomen' (archetypal phenomenon) on the model of his earlier archetypal plant and osteological type. The archetypal phenomenon of chromatics is the production of coloured images when light or darkness are viewed through a turbid medium (for example, when the setting sun is viewed through progressively denser layers of the atmosphere).

It is therefore clear that Goethe's colour theory is closely connected to his earlier morphological studies. The biology of his age still consisted largely of natural history, i.e. the description and classification of plants and animals according to their similarities and differences; the functional aspects of biology, such as physiology, embryology, and genetics, were still in their initial stages. Goethe also approached the physical sciences as a natural historian, so that the science of chromatics was for him primarily a natural history of colour. When he was disappointed in his expectations, he attributed the absence of a colour theory of this kind to the enormous prestige and—as it now seemed to him—fraudulent machinations of Isaac Newton. For he did not simply believe that Newton had drawn the wrong conclusions from some specific experiments. He quickly realised that the entire methodology of Newtonian physics was uncongenial to him. I shall mention only two reasons for his misgivings before I examine their ethical implications.

In the first place, Goethe objected to the application of mechanics to nature beyond its function of explaining the simplest kinds of movement. The model of the machine, which the rationalists of the Enlightenment applied not just to the movement of the heavenly bodies, but also to the processes of life itself, was already inimical to him in his early years, because machines are activated by external forces, whereas Goethe believed by 1770 at the latest that nature has its own life force within itself. He prefers to view the earth itself as an organism rather than as a machine. Indeed, despite the Newtonian theory of gravity, he goes so far in a late essay on meteorology as to attribute to the earth a periodic expansion and contraction which he likens to the breathing in and out of a living organism.[28]

---

28   LA, I. Abt., XI, 244–68.

Newton's mechanical optics was also repugnant to him because he regarded chromatics in principle not as a part of physics, but primarily as a science of perception with close links to physiology.[29] Prisms and angles of refraction are, of course, objective entities accessible to physical analysis; but colour only appears when it is perceived by the eye. In other words, mechanics has little relevance to a colour theory whose main aim is to study human perception.

A second fundamental objection of Goethe to Newton concerns the application of mathematics to the study of nature. Physical measurements, as in Newton's optics, in Goethe's opinion yield only a superficial picture of the relevant natural phenomena and miss the main point altogether. In Goethe's words, 'Number and measurement in their vacuity eliminate form and banish the spirit of living contemplation'.[30] The impermissible simplification of nature of which he also accuses mechanics and causal explanation, is for him, in the case of mathematics, particularly serious, because mathematics is a kind of language and Goethe, as a poet, is acutely aware of the inability even of ordinary language to do justice to the plenitude, complexity, and intangibility of natural phenomena.[31] Even poetic language—and at least in this area, he really was an expert—is not completely adequate to this task, and it comes closest to doing so when it employs concrete images, symbols, and metaphors. (One need only think of his novel *The Elective Affinities*, in which the inadequacy of conceptual language becomes a major theme.) In comparison, the language of mathematics is totally inadequate.

In sum, we may conclude that all Goethe's objections to Newtonian science are directed at a single feature, namely its abstraction.[32] For Newton's procedure always concentrates on *one* dimension of nature which corresponds to a particular human need, and therefore necessarily

29   Cf. Gernot Böhme, 'Ist Goethes Farbenlehre Wissenschaft?', in Böhme, *Alternativen der Wissenschaft* (Frankfurt a. M.: Suhrkamp, 1980), pp. 123–53.

30   LA I. Abt., IX, 367.

31   Cf. Karl J. Fink, *Goethe's History of Science* (Cambridge: Cambridge University Press, 1991), p. 46; also Nisbet, *Goethe and the Scientific Tradition*, p. 66.

32   Cf. LA I. Abt., IV, 5; also HA XII, 417 and 432 (*Maxims and Reflections*, nos. 386 and 487); and John Neubauer, '"Die Abstraktion, vor der wir uns fürchten". Goethes Auffassung der Mathematik und das Goethebild in der Geschichte der Wissenschaft', in *Versuche zu Goethe. Festschrift für Erich Heller*, ed. by Volker Dürr and Géza von Molnár (Heidelberg: L. Stiehm, 1976), pp. 305–20; also Manfred Wenzel, '"Die Abstraktion, vor der wir uns fürchten". Goethe und die Physik', *Freiburger Universitätsblätter*, 35, Heft 133 (1996), 55–79.

affords an incomplete or excessively simple image of observed reality; and if abstraction is taken to be a definitive reflection of that reality, superior to sensuous intuition, the result is a one-sided and potentially dangerous misapprehension of nature. It is above all this aversion to abstraction that lends Goethe's science its distinctive character, which rapidly gained him the reputation of an outsider and dilettante among the specialists, and the physicists in particular.

But Goethe's mistrust of abstraction is not just the naïve reaction of a non-mathematician to exact sciences which he was unable to understand. The same mistrust is a feature of his entire thinking, present long before his disagreements with Newton. He repeatedly distances himself from philosophical abstractions, especially in metaphysics,[33] and accepts only particular propositions in the metaphysics of Spinoza, Kant, or Schelling which he feels are in keeping with his own pre-existing convictions. His judgement of didactic poetry is in general negative, because it contains too much abstraction,[34] and his own philosophical poems are distinguished by concrete images and metaphors. His attitude to abstractions in theology,[35] for example, or political theory,[36] is no different. It is accordingly not surprising that he was likewise averse to scientific abstractions. The greatest problem he had to grapple with in the 1790s as he attempted to define his own experimental methodology was consequently how to make generalisations about nature without lapsing into abstraction. For a time, he felt attracted to the inductive philosophy of Francis Bacon, because it is based on sensuous experience; but it did not ultimately satisfy him, since Bacon's inductions also end in abstract generalisations, as for example his famous definition of heat as 'expansive movement of the particles of bodies'.[37] Goethe's own solution to the problem emerged from his earlier theories of the archetypal plant and the osteological type, with the new concept of the 'Urphänomen' or archetypal phenomenon, whose main feature is that is can be observed

---

33 Cf. his reaction to Holbach's metaphysics in *Poetry and Truth*, in WA I. Abt., XXVIII, 68ff.

34 Cf. his essay on didactic poetry, in WA I. Abt., XLI (2), 225ff.; also my essay on Lucretius in the present volume, pp. 1–33, (p. 13).

35 Cf. the article 'Unerforschliches' in the *Goethe-Handbuch*, ed. by Bernd Witte and other hands, 5 vols (Stuttgart: Metzler, 1996–99), IV/2, 1072–74.

36 Cf. Hans Reiss, *Formgestaltung und Politik. Goethe-Studien* (Würzburg: Königshausen & Neumann, 1993), p. 292.

37 Cf. Nisbet, *Goethe and the Scientific Tradition*, p. 36.

in the concrete individual instance, and at the same time incorporates the shared qualities of all similar instances.[38] It is, in other words, a concrete generalisation.

It is tempting to conclude that the distinctive character of Goethe's science, namely its aversion to abstraction, is simply that he is not primarily a scientist but a poet and artist. That is indeed the case, inasmuch as concrete images and visible forms are for him the basic material of both art and science, and he is convinced that the language of art can often convey more about nature than the language of science.[39] But his main objections to Newton are not aesthetic in character, and aesthetic considerations relatively rarely have a direct influence on his scientific observations. Much more important is the fact that, in the course of his morphological observations, he gained the insight—very rare among his contemporaries—that there is no generally valid paradigm for all sciences in all ages, and that not only each individual science, but the scientific method itself is constantly changing and developing in the course of history. He consolidated this insight by detailed historical investigations and implements it convincingly in his most important historical work, the *History of Colour Theory*. In this work, he shows how colour theory has undergone profound changes on the basis of different theoretical premises from one historical epoch to the other. He also discerns a cyclic movement in the development of this science,[40] whereby periods of inductive research are succeeded by periods of theoretical reflection in which the theories in turn solidify into dogmas, until these again are undermined by the emergence of new opinions and assumptions and inductive work again supervenes. Thus Goethe manages to discover forerunners of his own methods and theories in earlier ages—for example, in Greek antiquity. In short, there are different kinds of science, and some are more fertile than others.

This historical relativism makes a very modern impression.[41] But unlike most historians of science today, Goethe ascribes a much more important role to the individual personalities of leading scientists such

---

38   LA, I. Abt., IV, 71.
39   Cf. Goethe to Riemer, 28 October 1821, in WA IV. Abt., XXXV, 158.
40   LA I. Abt., VI, 94'; cf. *Goethe-Handbuch* III, 737.
41   On the relationship of Goethe's theory of the history of science to the corresponding theories of Thomas Kuhn and other modern thinkers, cf. Fink, *Goethe's History of Science*, pp. 85–90; also Dennis Sepper, *Goethe contra Newton. Polemics and the Project*

as Bacon, Descartes, and Newton than, for example, to economic and cultural influences.[42] This psychological mode of explanation leads him to conclude, for instance, that the optical theories of Newton, or at least some of their underlying features, must reflect Newton's personal character. This thought at last leads me back to the question I posed at the beginning of this essay, namely why Goethe's aversion to Newton appears to be influenced more by ethical than by scientific considerations, since Goethe takes the view that Newton's stubborn and deceitful character led him to defend false scientific opinions, even after he had recognised them as such,[43] and that his gullible followers blindly recited his pronouncements as infallible truths.[44]

The problematic aspect of this explanation is that Goethe has not the slightest evidence for Newton's alleged duplicity apart from Newton's scientific writings themselves. In other words, it is not a perceived moral weakness of Newton that leads Goethe to condemn his optical theories, but an alleged weakness of these optical theories that leads him to condemn Newton's moral character. It is basically Newton's whole conception of nature that seems ethically questionable to Goethe, because it in his opinion both does violence to nature and calls Newton's character itself into question. For Goethe belonged to a generation for which the concept of nature was by no means value-free, but loaded with moral implications. From Shaftesbury's nature enthusiasm to the vogue for literary sensibility, the glorification of nature, which steadily increased in the course of the eighteenth century, was familiar to Goethe from an early date. Not only his early literary successes such as *Götz von Berlichingen* and *The Sorrows of Young Werther*, but also his passion for botany in the early 1780s owed much to the works of Rousseau, in which

---

for a New Science of Color (Cambridge: Cambridge University Press, 1988), pp. 18f. and 186f.

42 Cf. LA I. Abt., VI, 87: 'The conflict of the individual with direct experience and indirect tradition is indeed the history of the sciences.' This view is in keeping with the fact that Goethe's favourite form of historiography is the biographical or autobiographical narrative.

43 Cf. LA I. Abt., VI, 295f.: 'It will surely be conceded that many scientific enigmas can only become comprehensible by means of an ethical solution'; see also LA I. Abt., VI, 252f. (on Newton's alleged moral deficiencies).

44 On Goethe's employment of theological categories and metaphors in his polemics against Newton, cf. Albrecht Schöne, *Goethes Farbentheologie* (Munich: C. H. Beck, 1987).

nature is praised as the highest ethical authority and its neglect equated to decadence or corruption.[45]

But the works which Goethe consulted at the time when he was studying Newton's optic theories in the early 1790s play a considerable part in these developments. There is evidence that his first closer acquaintance with Newton's colour theory was derived not from the English or Latin text of the *Optics*, but from German editions of textbooks such as Erxleben's *Elements of Physics*[46] and a German translation of Priestley's *History of Optics*.[47] The difference in languages is in this case decisive. For whereas the English technical terms for the behaviour of light in optical experiments (for example, 'refraction', 'diffraction', 'inflexion', 'dispersion', etc.) sound merely learned and Latinate, the corresponding German expressions like *Brechung, Beugung, Spaltung, Zerstreuung, Zerlegung*, etc. convey an impression of drastic intervention in nature which Goethe was bound to find deeply offensive. He took particular exception to the sixth experiment in Newton's *Optics*, in which light is passed through two small apertures and two prisms to demonstrate that light is composed of rays of different refrangibility which correspond to different colours. Newton called this experiment the *experimentum crucis*, i.e. the experiment of the cross, or decisive experiment. But Goethe at once fastens on to the origin of this metaphor, and writes:[48]

> This is the so-called *experimentum crucis*, in which the researcher subjected nature to torture in order to force it to confess what he had already made up his mind about. But nature is like a steadfast and noble-minded person who sticks to the truth, even under every kind of torment.

To put it differently, Newton's procedure violates the integrity and unity of the object, which is nature. But Goethe is also convinced that

---

45   On Rousseau's influence on Goethe's botanical studies, cf. LA I. Abt., X, 327–30; see also Goethe to Karl August, 16 June 1782, in WA IV. Abt., V, 347f.

46   On Goethe's use of Erxleben and other German textbooks cf. LA I. Abt., III, 15 (*Beiträge zur Optik*, 1791) and LA I. Abt., VI, 418 (*Geschichte der Farbenlehre*); HA XII, 403f. (*Maxims and Reflections*, no. 278); Sepper, *Goethe contra Newton*, p. 28; and Jeremy Adler, '*Eine fast magische Anziehungskraft*'. *Goethes 'Wahlverwandtschaften' und die Chemie seiner Zeit* (Munich: C. H. Beck, 1987), pp. 77f.

47   On Priestley, cf. HA XIV, 226f. and 335f.; on Goethe's borrowing of Priestley's *History* in Klügel's German translation, cf. Elise Keudell, *Goethe als Benutzer der Weimarer Bibliothek* (Weimar: Böhlau, 1931), p. 5 (5 July 1791); on his first borrowings of works of Newton, cf. ibid., 5 October 1791 and 26 June 1792.

48   LA I. Abt., V, 45.

this procedure at the same time endangers the integrity of the subject, i.e. the researcher himself. From the 1790s onwards, he laments the increasing specialisation of science and the harmful effect which this specialisation must have on the development of the individual. He declares, for example, that 'this is precisely the greatest evil of recent physics, that it has, as it were, divorced the experiments from humanity and seeks to recognise nature only in what artificial instruments reveal of it'.[49] The human being is gradually alienated from nature, inasmuch as all his reactions are excluded apart from abstract thought.

But even these anxieties are not enough to explain the violence, untypical of Goethe, with which he directs his polemics against Newton. To understand his reaction correctly, one must look back on those six extraordinarily productive years he experienced before, during, and immediately after his Italian journey. This was the time in which his views on nature and science fully matured, and in which he also believed he had discovered the basic classical rules of art. He came up with the idea that nature and art are parallel spheres,[50] and that both are characterised by elementary forms, by unity in variety, and by organic wholeness and harmonious proportions. In this sense, his view of nature was no less 'classical' than his view of art. His disappointment in the professional scientific world had begun in 1784, when his essay on the intermaxillary bone had met with incomprehension on the part of the anatomists, and he finally began to lose courage when his treatise on 'The Metamorphosis of Plants' was ignored almost completely.[51] When his classical views on art were called into question by the Romantics, his criticism of the latter on account of their one-sided subjectivity was the counterpart of his polemics against Newton in the sphere of science.[52] But towards the end of the polemical section of his *Colour Theory*, he seems to have had an uneasy feeling that he had perhaps gone too far in his attacks on Newton, and refers, by way of apology, to

---

49 Goethe to Zelter, 22 June 1808, in WA IV. Abt., XX, 90; on the need to employ all one's mental powers and skills in the contemplation of nature, cf. Goethe to C. W. M. Jacobi, 16 August 1799, in WA IV, 153.

50 Cf. WA I. Abt., XXXII, 77f.

51 On these disappointments see *Goethe-Handbuch*, III, 744f. and 754f.

52 Cf. Hans Joachim Schrimpf, 'Über die geschichtliche Bedeutung von Goethes Newton-Polemik und Romantik-Kritik' in *Gratulatio. Festschrift für Christian Wegner*, ed. by M. Honeit and M. Wegner (Hamburg: Grossohaus Wegner, 1963), pp. 62–82.

the turbulent times he has lived through.[53] (He had indeed begun work on the polemical section of his work shortly before the Battle of Jena and the French invasion of Weimar.) He felt even more isolated than before after Schiller's death in 1805, and feared that the philosophy of nature and man which he had constructed in the final years of the *ancien régime* was under threat from all sides.

Was Goethe then merely an outsider and eccentric in the sphere of science? So it seemed to most professional scientists in the first half of the nineteenth century, and in optics, almost into the present day.[54] But in more recent decades, relativistic models in the history of science have encouraged more interpreters to see in Goethe's scientific writings an idiosyncratic but defensible view of nature, even if his individual theories have long been superseded; and at the same time, studies of perception have increasingly recognised the physiological section of his *Colour Theory* as a pioneering achievement.[55]

Goethe's biggest mistake as a scientist was his belief that it is impossible to be a specialist in the exact (i.e. mathematical) sciences and at the same time to hold a comprehensive vision of nature as a whole. It simply did not occur to him that Newton's methods and his own view of nature might complement each other. But his scientific writings are still of some value today. His conviction that nature is an organic whole, of which human beings are an essential part, and that we should not pursue our immediate ends without heeding their consequences for the whole, is more relevant and necessary today than in the eighteenth century; it is therefore no coincidence that Goethe has often, and rightly, been cited in recent years as an advocate of environmentalism and a forerunner of green politics.[56] This does not, of course, mean that he shared that

---

53   LA I. Abt., V, 193.

54   On the reception of Goethe's scientific studies in professional circles, cf. Christoph Gögelein, *Zu Goethes Begriff von Wissenschaft auf dem Wege der Methodik seiner Farbstudien* (Munich: Hanser, 1972), pp. 170–200; Felix Höpfner, *Wissenschaft wider die Zeit. Goethes Farbenlehre aus rezeptionsgeschichtlicher Sicht* (Heidelberg: Winter, 1990); Karl Robert Mandelkow, *Goethe in Deutschland. Rezeptionsgeschichte eines Klassikers*, 2 vols (Munich: C. H. Beck, 1980–89), I, 173–98 and II, 39–48.

55   Cf., for example, Ribe, 'Goethe's Critique of Newton', p. 334, and Sepper, *Goethe contra Newton*, pp. 14ff.

56   Cf., for example, Böhme, 'Ist Goethes Farbenlehre Wissenschaft?'; also several contributors (including Gernot Böhme and Klaus Michael Meyer-Abich) to the volume *Goethe und die Verzeitlichung der Natur*, ed. by Peter Matussek (Munich: C. H. Beck, 1998).

hostility to technology that has been voiced by some opponents of scientific progress in recent decades.[57] He expresses his approval, in a late essay, of attempts to harness the elements, even on a large scale; but significantly, he adds that we must be guided by the ordering principles of nature itself before we attempt to control it.[58] In one of his best known poems, he illustrated the disastrous consequences that ensue if we fail to do so: I refer, of course, to the ballad of the magician's apprentice, who unleashes natural forces which he can no longer control.[59] What the apprentice and his present-day successors lack is that all-embracing and unitary conception of nature as a whole, which in Goethe's view ought to underlie all activities informed by scientific knowledge.

---

57 On Goethe's generally positive attitude towards industry and technology, see the *Goethe-Handbuch* IV, 104–07 (mining); 458ff. (handicrafts); 531–35 (industry); 686–89 (machinery).

58 LA I. Abt., XI, 264 (on meteorology); on my article on this topic see *Goethe-Handbuch*, III, 778–85.

59 This poem was written at the same time (1797) as Goethe began the first intensive work on his *Colour Theory*.

Portrait of Immanuel Kant by Johann Gottlieb Becker (1768), oil on canvas, Schiller-Nationalmuseum, Marbach am Neckar, Germany. Photograph by UpdateNerd (2018), Wikimedia, Public Domain, https://upload.wikimedia.org/wikipedia/commons/f/f2/Kant_gemaelde_3.jpg

9. Natural History and Human History in Goethe, Herder, and Kant[1]

The relationship between natural history and human history has played a decisive part in the rise of modern science and the modern historical consciousness. On the one hand, the application of historical thought to nature—i.e. its 'temporalisation'[2]—towards the end of the eighteenth century led to a radical reappraisal of nature as a whole. It was then no longer seen as a timeless hierarchy of unchanging forms, but as a developmental process in which first the physical, and subsequently the biological world were understood as the product of a natural evolution from simple to ever more complex forms.[3] On the other hand, the tendency to view human history increasingly as part of nature and hence as an object of scientific enquiry led to novel attempts to discover historical laws and thereby to predict, or even influence, the future course of history. A central figure in these developments was Goethe; and no less important were his contemporaries Herder and Kant, whose thoughts on nature and history influenced Goethe's thinking (although they also contradicted it in significant respects). A comparison of their views on nature and history may not only lead to a better understanding of Goethe's own views, but also provide a greater insight into one of the

---

1   An earlier version of this chapter was originally published as 'Naturgeschichte und Humangeschichte bei Goethe, Herder und Kant', in Peter Matussek (ed.), *Goethe und die Verzeitlichung der Natur. Goethe-Sonderband in der Reihe Kulturgeschichte der Natur* (Munich: C. H. Beck, 1998), pp. 15–43.

2   See Arthur O. Lovejoy, *The Great Chain of Being* (Cambridge, MA: Harvard University Press, 1933), esp. Chapter 9.

3   See Dietrich von Engelhardt, *Historisches Bewusstsein in der Naturwissenschaft* (Freiburg: Karl Alber, 1979), pp. 44–101.

          https://doi.org/10.11647/OBP.0180.09

most important developments in the scientific and historical thought of the modern era.

All three thinkers were influenced in different ways by the growing tendency of their times to interpret nature as a historical, evolutionary process, and they themselves contributed to it. This essay will first consider their views on the history of the earth and its living organisms, before comparing the theoretical premises of the views in question. Secondly, their views on human history will be examined, and their thoughts on the relationship between nature and history will in turn be compared. The development of their ideas on these topics will be discussed in sequence, from Kant to Herder and finally to Goethe.

Natural History: Empirical Aspects

Theories of nature as a chronological process first appeared in the context of the physical sciences, and particularly that of astronomy. The belief that the physical world, and indeed nature as a whole, has developed over the course of time in a causal process is not, of course, a modern invention: it was already formulated by Democritus, Epicurus, and other atomists of antiquity. It found its most complete expression shortly before the Christian era in Lucretius's didactic poem *De rerum natura*. But not until the scientific revolution of the seventeenth century did this doctrine receive a scientific foundation, for example in the work of Descartes and Leibniz, and not least in Kant's epoch-making treatise of 1755, the *Universal Natural History and Theory of the Heavens*. The preface to this work clearly shows that Kant found himself in some embarrassment over the obvious affinity between his own cosmogony and that of the ancient atomists, because it was well known that the views of the latter were in contradiction to the doctrines of the church; he is therefore at pains to stress the compatibility of his own view concerning the mechanistic theory of the earth's origin with the doctrine of divine creation.[4] With reference to Newton's mechanistic theory of gravitation, he explains the development of the solar system and the universe at large out of an original chaos of scattered material to its present state,

---

4   Immanuel Kant, *Werkausgabe* (henceforth WW), ed. by Wilhelm Weischedel, 12 vols (Frankfurt a.M.: Suhrkamp, 1968), I, 233ff.

in which new galaxies, suns and planets continue to be created through the interaction of gravitational and centrifugal forces.

As soon as it was realised that the physical world as a whole had arisen through natural causes, there were grounds for concluding that its individual components might have arisen in the same way. The main reason why only a few eighteenth-century scientists managed to take this step was that the generally recognised length of the earth's history (itself based on Biblical chronology) was much too short to accommodate even the most cautious estimates of the time needed for so numerous and complex organisms as those already present to evolve through natural causes. Besides, there were numerous indications that these organisms had not undergone any substantial alterations during the last three or four millennia (that is, around half of the earth's supposed age of some six thousand years). There was accordingly a pressing need to look more closely at earth history in order to answer the question as to how the development of the earth itself could have taken place in so short a time. It naturally soon became clear that an incomparably greater length of time had to be postulated. One of the first works to draft a new chronology was Buffon's *Époques de la nature* of 1778. Admittedly, the length of Buffon's geological epochs was again unbelievably short by present-day standards, although he reckoned with tens of thousands instead of just thousands of years. But his work did at least provide an incentive for other scientists to view earth history as a long and complex process.[5]

As far as the universe itself was concerned, Kant was quite prepared to contemplate a really long period of development. He writes, for example, in his *Universal Natural History*: 'Perhaps a whole series of millions of years and centuries elapsed before the sphere of organised nature in which we find ourselves attained its present stage of perfection; and perhaps an equally long period will elapse until nature takes as great a further a step out of chaos.'[6]

Kant's early essay *The Question of whether the Earth is Growing Old Considered in Terms of Physics* (1754) treats earth history, albeit only sketchily, as a very long process.[7] He further develops this draft with reference to Buffon and other earlier theorists in various subsequent

---

5   Cf. Wolf Lepenies, *Das Ende der Naturgeschichte* (Munich: Hanser, 1976), p. 43.
6   Kant, WW I, 334.
7   Immanuel Kant, *Gesammelte Schriften* (henceforth AA), ed. by the Preussische Akademie der Wissenschaften (Berlin: Reimer, 1902–), I, 193–312.

writings, for example his *Physical Geography*[8] and the essay *On the Volcanoes on the Moon*.[9] And although his geological theories, given the limitations of contemporary knowledge, are highly speculative, he constantly strives to base them on natural causes and on natural laws that retain their validity today. He invokes, for example, earthquakes, subsidence, volcanoes, etc. in order to explain the formation of the earth's surface over long periods of time. (The Lisbon earthquake of 1755 had made a deep impression on him.) But the important role which he, like Buffon and other predecessors, ascribes to the sea and its supposed coverage of the earth in early times already looks forward to the neptunistic theories which gained wide acceptance in Germany towards the end of the eighteenth century.

It is therefore not surprising that, in view of the pronounced historical tendency of Kant's vision of nature, he even considers the possibility that all living organisms may be linked by descent from common ancestors. In a well known passage in his *Critique of Judgement* (1790), he observes that the anatomical similarity between many animal species might suggest such a relationship; but he adds 'A hypothesis of this kind might be described as an adventure of reason, and there can be few natural scientists, including the most acute among them, whose minds it has not on occasion crossed.'[10]

There is already a reference in Kant's review of Herder's *Ideas on the Philosophy of History* to such hypotheses, but Kant considers them 'so monstrous [...] that reason shies away from them',[11] and in another work from that same decade he describes the constancy of natural species as a 'law of nature'.[12] But his resistance to the theory of evolution had nothing to do with religion; like many other Enlightenment thinkers, he simply found the empirical evidence so inadequate and the necessary timescale so long that the theories in question seemed ultimately incredible or at best unproven. At any rate, he did not yet feel able, on the basis of such daring hypotheses, to contemplate that 'monstrous' revision of the

---

8   First as a lecture series between 1756 and 1796, then as a book in 1802; cf. AA XIX, 153–436 (esp. pp. 206 and 296–305).
9   1785; AA VIII, 67–76.
10   WW X, 375.
11   WW XII, 792.
12   WW IX, 145.

traditional view of nature which would result from the recognition of an evolutionary relationship between the animals and man.[13]

Herder's views on the history of nature and the origin of species show many similarities with those of Kant. He had attended Kant's lectures on physical geography in Königsberg and was also familiar with his scientific writings. Since I have dealt in detail with Herder's scientific writings elsewhere,[14] I shall confine myself here to a brief outline.

Herder's *Ideas on the Philosophy of History* is one of the best examples of that eighteenth-century tendency, already mentioned above, to establish a connection between nature and history. For he envisages the history of the earth and its living creatures as a continuous process of which human history is a natural sequel. In other words, even the structure of his work presupposes that nature has its own history, and that human history is a part of nature.

Herder was very well read in the scientific literature of his time, and his cosmological reflections in the *Ideas* are many-sided and eclectic.[15] Even more than Kant, who, like Buffon, significantly influenced the initial chapters of the *Ideas*, Herder was attracted to drastic theories of earth history, and speculates at length on geological upheavals and convulsions, for example a shift of the earth's axis, in order to explain the earliest development of the earth. Some of the most extreme reflections of this kind were deleted or omitted (probably on the advice of Goethe, who collaborated closely with Herder during the composition of the first parts of the *Ideas*).[16] The published version of the *Ideas* stresses the influence of the sea, out of which the earth's earliest mountains crystallised; and like Goethe, Herder identified himself increasingly with the neptunism of Abraham Gottlob Werner in his later years.

But much more important than Herder's individual theories is the fact that his conception of nature is fundamentally historical. It is also significant that, despite his tenure of a senior office in the Lutheran church, he takes the view that the earth has developed by purely

---

13   On other evolutionary theories of the late eighteenth century see Engelhardt, *Historisches Bewusstsein*, pp. 82–89.

14   See H. B. Nisbet, *Herder and the Philosophy and History of Science* (Cambridge: MHRA, 1970).

15   Cf. ibid., pp. 167–80.

16   Cf. Johann Gottfried Herder, *Sämtliche Werke* (henceforth SW), ed. by Bernhard Suphan, 33 vols (Berlin: Weidmann, 1877–1913), XIII, 470–84; also Nisbet, *Herder and the Philosophy*, pp. 174–76.

natural causes from its primitive elements: he explicitly states 'that [...] creation [...] animates itself through organic forces implanted within these elements'.[17] Such statements as this, along with the then widely held view that certain simple forms of life have arisen spontaneously and that new varieties of plants and animals can be produced by climatic influences,[18] led various Herder scholars, particularly in the later nineteenth century, to present Herder as a precursor of Darwin. This claim has long since been refuted:[19] for example, Herder explicitly denies in the *Ideas* that man is genetically linked to the apes and that any species can depart from its original genetic character.[20] Nonetheless, he is often involuntarily led in the direction of the theory of evolution, as Kant rightly noticed.[21] His often expressed belief that nature is animated by dynamic, monad-like forces which work their way upwards through the hierarchy of beings from simple to ever higher forms[22] does indeed look forward, on an ideal level, towards that evolutionism which was later confirmed empirically by the palaeontological and genetic discoveries of the nineteenth century. As Arthur O. Lovejoy demonstrated, such hypotheses of idealistic genetics were a necessary stage in that temporalisation of the so-called 'chain of being' which prepared the way for the later, empirically grounded theory of a real evolution of species.[23]

Goethe's theories of earth history have many common features with those of Kant and Herder—features which largely go back to the time of his collaboration with Herder in the early 1780s.[24] But in contrast to those of Kant and Herder, Goethe's ideas are marked by a reluctance to speculate on the earliest phases of earth history. He refuses to go further back in history than the evidence of the earth's present surface and in particular of the oldest granite mountains permit, and declares: 'My spirit has no wings to soar back to those first beginnings. I stand firmly on the granite,

---

17   SW XIII, 422.
18   Cf. Nisbet, *Herder and the Philosophy*, pp. 214f. and 223ff.
19   See esp. Max Rouché, *Herder précurseur de Darwin? Histoire d'un mythe* (Paris: Imprimerie Nouvelle Thouars, 1940); cf. Nisbet, *Herder and the Philosophy*, pp. 210–39.
20   SW XIII, 256f. and 415.
21   WW XII, 792.
22   SW XIII, 167 and 177–81.
23   See Lovejoy, *The Great Chain of Being*, passim.
24   Cf. George A. Wells, 'Goethe's Geological Studies', *Publications of the English Goethe Society*, 35 (1965), 92–137.

and ask it [...] how the mass from which it arose was constituted'.[25] This aversion is doubtless connected with his dislike of theories which seek to explain the origin of the earth by violent forces, and he also declares that 'the dynamic' of slow, quasi-organic development seems more important to him than 'the atomistic and mechanical' which is active in the dissolution and deposition of elements that are already present.[26] For similar reasons, he was particularly drawn to neptunism,[27] because it regarded the slowly acting effect of water on the earth's surface as more fundamental than the spectacular but ultimately insignificant outbursts of volcanoes and earthquakes. In his later years, he is equally convinced that many geological events are initiated by imperceptible chemical processes.[28] In all these cases, he is much more strongly interested in those phenomena which are still active in the present than in completely different phenomena which were allegedly active in a hypothetical primeval era. This scepticism towards hypotheses imposes limitations on Goethe's historical understanding of nature, and his reflections on earth history are consequently markedly different from those of Kant and Herder. Since he considers only the more recent, empirically evident phases in the earth's history as a developmental process in time, his view of nature can be described only in a qualified sense as historical.

Goethe's views on the origin and development of living organisms are subject to similar qualifications. Here again, he distrusts abstract speculation and confines his attention to existing phenomena. Like Herder, he emphasises the effects of climate and environment on living organisms, and adds that 'the animal is shaped by circumstances to circumstances'[29] and 'the genus [...] can change to the species, the species to the variety, and this in turn can change again in infinite ways as a result of other conditions'.[30] But the changes he has in mind—for example, the development of the horse or ox from antiquity to the

25 Goethe, *Die Schriften zur Naturwissenschaft*, ed. by the Deutsche Akademie der Naturforscher (Leopoldina) (henceforth LA), I. Abteilung, 17 vols (Weimar: Böhlau, 1947–70); II. Abteilung (Weimar: Böhlau, 1959–): LA I. Abt., I, 62f.
26 LA I. Abt., I, 378 (1811).
27 Cf. LA I. Abt., I, 95ff. (1785).
28 See LA I. Abt., I, 348 (1807).
29 LA I. Abt., IX, 126 (1795).
30 LA I. Abt., X, 334 (1831).

present[31]—are relatively superficial, and just like Herder, he doubts whether there is a genetic relationship between man and the apes. He writes, for example, 'one cannot (or scarcely can) say that we are related to the apes through the Moors'.[32] The qualification 'or scarcely can' is characteristic of his scientific thought: where the hitherto available empirical evidence does not permit an unambiguous answer, he simply leaves the question open (even though in this particular case, he was fully familiar with the anatomical relationship between man and the animals, as his essay on the intermaxillary bone in man demonstrates).[33] When he reflects, in a later essay, on the origin of the giant sloth, he adds the following qualification to his provisional observations: 'May we be permitted some poetic expression, since prose in general may not be adequate in this instance.'[34] And although in 1823 he publishes a work by the botanist Ernst Heinrich Friedrich Meyer in which the latter declares: 'It is impossible for one species to arise out of another', Goethe neither affirms nor denies this proposition;[35] here again, the question must remain open. As far as evolution is concerned, Goethe's thinking is therefore akin to that of Kant and Herder: he is in principle prepared to understand the development of life and living organisms as a historical process, but the empirical evidence for a fully fledged theory of evolution still strikes him as inadequate.

We may therefore conclude that Kant, Herder, and Goethe were equally convinced of the historicity of the earth and nature as a whole—a natural history governed by natural laws. All three are in this respect true representatives of the European Enlightenment, whose basic convictions included the rule of natural law in all spheres of reality. But the most pronounced difference between their positions—and hence also the originality of Goethe's concept of nature—becomes really apparent only when we consider their methodological premises and their understanding of those processes and mechanisms through which nature develops over time and thereby acquires a historical dimension. A comparative account of the methods and principles which underlie the views of these three thinkers on scientific modes of explanation, and

---

31   LA I. Abt., IX, 254–60 (1822).
32   LA II. Abt., IXA, 201.
33   LA I. Abt., IX, 154–61 (1786).
34   LA I. Abt., IX, 247 (1821).
35   LA I. Abt., IX, 300 (1823).

on causation and change in nature, will therefore conclude the first part of this enquiry.

Theoretical Aspects: Kant

In comparison with those of Herder and Goethe, Kant's theoretical pronouncements on nature and natural history are much more differentiated, thorough, and systematic. Kant was an established philosopher who had addressed scientific themes in whole or in part in his earliest writings as well as in several of his major works. His theory of science was from the start associated with Newtonian physics, and it owed many of its insights to Kant's intimate knowledge of contemporary physical theories, including their mathematical and technically most demanding aspects. Neither Herder's nor Goethe's knowledge of mathematical physics and its philosophical implications bears comparison with that of Kant.

This difference had a profound influence on the ways in which the three thinkers sought to understand and explain natural processes. For Kant, mathematical physics remained the supreme model of scientific explanation.[36] It is even a primary support of his critical idealism, for the authority of Newtonian mechanics and its laws of motion stands for him on a higher intellectual level than that of merely empirical rules. He notes, for example, in the *Critique of Pure Reason*, that such laws are *a priori* necessary, whereas the necessity of principles of empirical observation is only indirect and dependent on contingent circumstances.[37] In the *Metaphysical Foundations of Science* he declares 'that every particular theory of nature contains only as much *genuine* science as mathematics is present in it.'[38] Thus by this definition, only mathematical physics can count as genuine science; and although the theory of gravitation, for example, is partly based on empirical observations,[39] it can count as scientifically sound only in so far as it is based on a mathematical formula in keeping with the inverse square law. Even chemistry, not

---

36 See Michael Friedman, 'Causal Laws and the Foundations of Natural Science', in *The Cambridge Companion to Kant*, ed. by Paul Guyer (Cambridge: Cambridge University Press, 1992), pp. 161–99 (p. 165f.).

37 Cf. WW III, 201–03; also Friedman, 'Causal Laws', pp. 165 and 174.

38 WW IX, 14.

39 WW II, 574f.

yet subject to mathematical treatment in Kant's time, is in his opinion 'no more than a systematic art, or experimental doctrine, but never a genuine science'.[40]

Kant's aim in his own writings on the empirical study of nature is always that of causal explanation in accordance with recognised laws of nature. In an essay of 1785 on earth history, for example, he condemns any appeal to supernatural agencies and says 'in all natural epochs, since no one of these can be defined in a world of the senses as absolutely the first, we are therefore not exempt from the obligation to search as far as possible among universal causes and to follow its chain, as long as the links hang together, in accordance with already established laws'.[41]

Here, the venerable image of the chain, in use since antiquity as a metaphor for the hierarchy of beings in space, is unambiguously temporalised: Kant's view of nature is fundamentally historical. In another work from the same decade (*On the Use of Teleological Principles in Philosophy*), he likewise notes that the term 'natural history' is misleading, because natural history has hitherto dealt almost exclusively with the systematic description of presently existing natural forms; in its place, he outlines as follows a new, genuinely historical definition of its task as that of linear causal explanation: 'to trace the connection between the present conditions of nature and their causes in earlier times, in accordance with laws of action which we do not invent, but derive from the forces of nature as it presents itself to us now, and follow it back only as far as analogy permits—that would be a *natural history*'.[42]

Where the empirical evidence is lacking, the second-best method is in Kant's opinion the heuristic use of analogies. Or, as he had put it in an earlier work, our conjectures would gain in probability 'if one drew on the help of analogies, which must guide us in such cases where our understanding lacks the thread of infallible proof'.[43] It will later be seen that this recommendation of analogical thinking was taken up by Kant's pupil Herder, even if Herder did not always employ this method with the critical circumspection of his teacher.

Basic to Kant's theory of science is the opposition between rational and empirical methods, as for example in his distinction between

---

40   WW IX, 15.
41   AA VIII, 76.
42   WW IX,142.
43   WW I, 336.

explanations by means of *a priori* necessary mathematical laws, and explanations by means of merely empirical rules.[44] The boundary between these two modes of explanation does, of course, shift in the course of Kant's philosophical development. For example, in his late *Opus postumum*, he endeavours to ground further areas of science—above all chemistry—on a secure *a priori* foundation, but the dualistic distinction remains in principle valid. A parallel distinction between physical and biological modes of explanation is equally present in various works of Kant, but even here, the boundary between the two is fluid, although the distinction is never abolished. In the *Universal Natural History*, he defines it as follows:[45]

> No one should take exception if I venture to suggest that it should be possible to understand the formation of all the heavenly bodies, the cause of their motion, and in short, the origin of the entire present constitution of the universe before it will be possible to explain clearly and completely the production of a single herb or caterpillar on mechanical principles.

In this early work, Kant still clings to the traditional belief that the apparently purposive organisation of plants and animals should be explained not only by a special, non-mechanical (namely teleological) kind of causality, but should also be derived from the intentions of a rational creator.[46] The same distinction between mechanical and biological spheres again appears in the *Critique of Judgement* of 1790 in the following statement: 'absolutely no human reason can [...] hope to understand the production of even a blade of grass by purely mechanical causes.'[47] But this time, the teleological mode of explanation is no longer associated with the assumption of a higher reason. All scientific explanations must, according to the older Kant, be based on natural causes,[48] although in the case of organic life, these must be supplemented by a teleological judgement which presupposes a purposive causality—but without

---

44   WW III, 180; cf. Karen Gloy, *Die Kantische Theorie der Naturwissenschaft* (Berlin: De Gruyter, 1976), pp. 19f., 31f., and 183.; see also Hans Schimank, 'Der Aspekt der Naturgesetzlichkeit im Wandel der Zeiten', in *Das Problem der Gesetzlichkeit*, ed. by the Joachim-Jungius-Gesellschaft der Wissenschaften, Vol. II (Hamburg: Richard Meiner, 1949), pp. 139–86 (p. 140).
45   WW I, 237.
46   Ibid., 232 and 234f.; cf. Michael Friedman, *Kant and the Exact Sciences* (Cambridge, MA: Harvard University Press, 1992), p. 12.
47   WW X, 364.
48   Ibid., p. 331.

claiming that such purposes have any objective existence outside the teleological judgement of the viewer.[49] The highest aim of science remains, as before, that of 'mechanical' explanation: that is, even organic processes are based on physical and chemical agencies.[50] But where this mode of explanation is inadequate or impossible because of incomplete knowledge, the 'regulative' use of teleology comes to its aid. Thus, just as in physics, Kant's views in biology on the limits of scientific explanation also become somewhat more flexible in his later years, although the distinction in principle between rigorous and less rigorous modes of explanation is never abandoned. What cannot yet be explained is now no longer automatically consigned to the sphere of theology, but referred to a supplementary, regulatory mode of explanation which in biology, for example, must remain in use until a 'mechanical' causality is discovered in this area too.

The last aspect of Kant's theory of scientific explanation which calls for mention here concerns the nature of natural causes themselves. His attitude to this question alters considerably over the years. In his early works, for example, he still subscribes to Leibniz's metaphysics: the Leibnizian monads as simple, dynamic units are for him the basic constituents of the universe.[51] But even in his earliest works, he dispenses, in scientific contexts, with speculations on the inner nature of those forces (such as attraction and repulsion) which he holds responsible for all natural processes in the physical world. Here, as in so many cases, he doubtless follows the example of Isaac Newton, who rejected all speculation on the inner nature of gravitational force with his famous statement 'hypotheses non fingo'.[52] By the time of his *Inaugural Dissertation* of 1770, he no longer makes any connection between the spatio-temporal world of science and its supposed metaphysical substratum.[53] And in his critical phase, he recognises natural forces only in mathematical formulations and without any anthropomorphic associations. In his late period—that is, in his *Opus postumum*—he admittedly no longer lays as much stress on the mathematical as on

---

49 Ibid., pp. 369f.
50 Ibid., p. 371; cf. Clark Zumbach, *The Transcendental Science. Kant's Conception of Biological Methodology* (The Hague: Martinus Nijhoff, 1984), pp. 80–83.
51 See, for example, his *Monadologia physica* (1756), in WW II, 516–63.
52 Cf. Schimank, 'Der Aspekt der Naturgesetzlichkeit', p. 172; also WW VIII, 805.
53 Cf. Friedman, *Kant and the Exact Sciences*, p. 34.

the dynamic side of Newtonian physics, but without any intention of rehabilitating Leibniz's metaphysics:[54] Kant's dynamism is still entirely phenomenological, and he has no interest in the metaphysical character of natural forces, but only in the scientifically grounded laws of their effects. To this extent, he holds the same opinion as most physicists towards the end of the eighteenth century, whose view is encapsulated, for example, in the definition of natural law in Gehler's *Physikalisches Wörterbuch* (*Dictionary of Physics*) of 1787–95:[55]

> In reality, only the particular effects are present in nature, and the laws exist only in the ideas of natural scientists or the system of physics. Hence the knowledge of natural laws is also not yet a knowledge of the efficient causes and the mechanism whereby the phenomena are produced in time. The laws teach us only what is happening, not why and how it does so.

It is clear from this evidence that Kant's views on natural history and the dynamics of natural processes were decisively influenced by his knowledge of the exact sciences since Newton. His cosmogony, for example, is based almost exclusively on Newton's celestial mechanics, and even his theories of earth history are to a large extent dependent on mechanical laws, in order to explain, for example, the process of erosion and deposition through rain, rivers and sea.[56] It seems at first sight as if the ideas of his pupil Herder on such questions are closely related to his; but on closer inspection, it emerges that Herder's theoretical views, particularly his theories of scientific explanation, natural laws, and causality, are completely different from those of Kant.

Theoretical Aspects: Herder

Neither Herder's cosmogony nor his theory of natural law shows that marked affinity to Newtonian physics which was characteristic of Kant's thinking. Admittedly, there are frequent references in Herder's works to mathematical concepts, laws of motion, and other aspects of mechanics.[57] But unlike Kant, he employs such concepts and principles less in their

---

54   AA XXI, 479; cf. ibid., p. 226.
55   Gehler, III. Teil, cited by Schimank, 'Der Aspekt der Naturgesetzlichkeit', p. 144.
56   See, for example, AA IX, 296ff. (*Physische Geographie*).
57   Cf. Nisbet, *Herder and the Philosophy*, pp. 86–90 and 92–98.

original scientific sense than as metaphors or analogies, as will shortly be seen, in order to describe non-physical processes such as the course of world history or the moral development of human beings. This tendency is already evident in his admission to an astronomer friend: 'I lack [...] the use of higher mathematics, in which, as I suspect, there must at least be excellent *analogies* to enable us to reach higher levels in philosophy.'[58]

Herder's theory of natural laws is also quite different from that of Kant. Like Francis Bacon, whose writings he greatly valued, he regards such laws as inductive generalisations from experience, without any *a priori* components.[59] In 1769, for example, he writes: 'All laws of attraction are nothing other than observed qualities which we rearrange among themselves until a basic principle emerges [...]. The further we can generalise these [principles], the fewer and simpler the laws become, and the nearer we come to a single concept, i.e. the basic concept of the area in question.'[60]

Herder's natural laws are therefore by no means the same as the mathematical laws which play so great a part in Kant's critical philosophy, but rather akin to those empirical regularities which Kant usually describes as 'rules'. For Herder, the mathematical formulation of such laws is in any case irrelevant; in his attempts to refute the critical philosophy, he also indicates that he considers mathematical knowledge not as knowledge *a priori*, but as empirical.[61] And as for the three laws of motion which Kant regards as *a priori* necessary truths, they are for Herder nothing more than identical propositions; the truth of such propositions may well be necessary, but their necessity is merely that of tautologies without any empirical content.[62] It follows from this that Herder's definition of natural laws is much more open, more comprehensive, and looser than that of Kant, so that he does not hesitate to designate numerous phenomena outside the sphere of the exact sciences as 'natural laws', for example in world history or the moral development of mankind.

---

58 Johann Gottfried Herder, *Briefe. Gesamtausgabe 1763–1803*, ed. by Karl-Heinz Hahn, Wilhelm Dobbek and Günter Arnold, 10 vols (Weimar: Böhlau, 1977–2001), III, 109.

59 See H. B. Nisbet, 'Herder and Francis Bacon', *Modern Language Review*, 62 (1967), 267–83 (pp. 271f.).

60 SW IV, 465; cf. also SW XXI, 228f.

61 See, for example, SW XXI, 32f.

62 Ibid., 37f.

There is a similar divergence between Herder's and Kant's views on the role of teleology in natural science. It is true that, in the chapters of the *Ideas* on natural history, Herder tends to avoid a purely anthropocentric teleology as well as any reference to the supposed intentions of God. He writes, for example: 'The philosophy of final causes has been of no benefit to natural history';[63] and we also know that he was strengthened in this opinion not only by the anti-teleological attitude of, for example, Spinoza, Bacon, and Buffon, but also by the objections of his friends Goethe and Knebel to certain teleological passages in the first draft of the *Ideas*.[64] He is, indeed, much less consistent in his treatment of teleology than the critical Kant. He makes no clear distinction, for example, between physical phenomena, which Kant believes can only be explained by mechanical principles, and biological processes, which are sometimes intelligible only with the help of teleology;[65] on the contrary, in keeping with his Neo-Platonic, Leibnizian metaphysics of nature, he is always at pains to avoid any abrupt distinction between different realms of nature. He is also concerned, in his dual role as theologian and secular thinker, to leave open the choice between teleology and mechanical causality by describing the same phenomena both as natural events and as a consequence of divine intentions.[66] But he sometimes falls back on unmistakably teleological models, without any critical reservations;[67] and his opposition to Kant reaches its climax in his later years, when he condemns even the mechanical cosmogony of Kant's *Universal Natural History* which had influenced his own cosmogony so profoundly in the *Ideas*, and instead praises the teleologically flavoured description of the universe as an expression of divine wisdom in Johann Heinrich Lambert's *Cosmological Letters*.[68]

On the real nature of natural causes, Herder again thinks quite differently from Kant. That Leibnizian doctrine of monads which Kant himself had recognised in his early years becomes in Herder's case the foundation of a comprehensive metaphysics of nature in the Neo-Platonic tradition. Nature is for him a continuous hierarchy of

---

63   SW XIV, 202.
64   Cf. Nisbet, *Herder and the Philosophy*, p. 54.
65   Cf. ibid., pp. 46f.
66   Cf. ibid., pp. 49ff.
67   Cf. ibid., p. 53.
68   SW XXIII, 525f.

forms, created, preserved, and transformed by indwelling forces.[69] (He speaks rather of 'forces' than of monads, no doubt because the former expression sounds more down-to-earth and therefore more acceptable in a scientific context.) His concept of forces makes it possible for him to operate with at least terminological consistency between metaphysical, physical, biological and even psychological spheres; but this kind of dynamism is fundamentally different from the purely phenomenological dynamism of the older Kant, who rejects all speculation on the inner essence of natural forces. Herder does, it must be said, sometimes speak with a certain sympathy of the metaphysical scepticism of Hume and the phenomenological reservations of Newton and Kant;[70] but in other cases, he equates the concept of causes to his own concept of forces and turns it into an animistic or spiritual subject. Thus he declares, for example, '[We] rightly conclude that an active force, hence a subject, is basic here'.[71] The whole of nature, for Herder, is therefore filled with dynamic elements which he at times describes as quasi-personal causal forces. When he adduces this principle in order to explain natural processes, his language, despite some similarities with the language of science, recalls neither that of exact Newtonian science nor that of modern natural philosophy, but rather that of Neo-Platonic metaphysics.

Theoretical Aspects: Goethe

Goethe's view of scientific explanation is markedly different from that of Kant. But it has many points of contact with that of Herder (which is scarcely surprising in the light of his close collaboration with Herder around the time of the latter's *Ideas*). But there are nevertheless considerable differences between Herder's and Goethe's understandings of nature. This may help to answer the question of why Goethe's views on nature—in contrast to those of Kant and Herder—have remained so attractive to many people down to recent times.[72]

---

69   Cf. Nisbet, *Herder and the Philosophy*, pp. 8–16.
70   See, for example, SW VII, 381; VIII, 177; XIII, 10, 47, 161, 358, etc.
71   SW XV, 533; cf. also SW XXI, 152.
72   For a range of examples of this positive reception see most of the contributions to the volume *Goethe und die Verzeitlichung der Natur*, ed. by Peter Matussek (Munich: C. H. Beck, 1998).

Goethe's aversion to mathematical physics and Newtonian mechanics is so well known that it requires no further detailed examination here.[73] But this aversion is at least in part responsible for the fact that Kant's *Critique of Pure Reason*, with its uncompromising dualism and close relationship to Newton's physics, appealed much less to Goethe than did his *Critique of Judgement*, which treats art and nature as parallel realms.[74] Goethe's concept of natural law is also fundamentally different from that of Kant. He often speaks, like Herder, of natural laws not only in the physical world, but in the biological sphere too; in comparative anatomy, for example, he discovers 'the law [...] that nothing can be added to one part without a corresponding diminution of another, and vice versa',[75] and he regards the spiral tendency of plants as a 'basic law of life'.[76] It is plain that such laws are for Goethe—and for Herder—are rather general observations of regularities in the empirical world than *a priori* necessary basic laws on the Kantian model. The terms 'law' and 'rule' indeed seem to be almost identical in meaning for Goethe,[77] although the second suggests a simple regularity, whereas the first, with its juristic associations, also calls to mind duress and limitation (often in contrast to arbitrariness, contingency or immoderacy). The word 'law' has for Goethe—again like Herder—a much broader sense than in Newtonian physics. He speaks, for example, of 'the universal law of separation and convergence, rise and fall, alternate balancing movements' in various spheres of nature,[78] and on one occasion defines the beautiful as 'a manifestation of secret natural laws';[79] but in this case again, he is thinking of empirical regularities of a very general kind, and not of precise means of explanation and prediction of natural processes on the model of exact science.

---

73 On Goethe's natural philosophy in its historical context, see H. B. Nisbet, *Goethe and the Scientific Tradition* (London: Institute of Germanic Studies, University of London, 1972).

74 Cf. LA I. Abt., IX, 90–94.

75 LA I. Abt., IX, 124 (1795).

76 LA I. Abt., I, 10 and 346, etc. (1831); cf. also LA I. Abt., I, 9 and 23 (1790); LA I. Abt., I, 9 and 62 (1817); LA I. Abt., I, 9 and 111 (1820); LA I. Abt., I, 10 and 393, etc. (1830).

77 Cf. LA I. Abt., I, 10 and 387 (1830); LA I. Abt., I, 9 and 341 (1824); LA I. Abt., I, 4 and 71 (1808).

78 LA I. Abt., I, 4 and 220 (1808).

79 *Goethes Werke*, Hamburg edition (henceforth HA), ed. by Erich Trunz, 14 vols (Hamburg: Christian Wegner, 1948–64), XII, 467.

This aspect of Goethe's concept of law is perhaps most clearly in evidence in his writings on optics, particularly in his *Colour Theory*. The word 'law' is often used in the *Colour Theory* as a general description of periodically recurring natural processes, for example, in Goethe's reference to 'the first basic law, already familiar to the ancients, that the eye is drawn together and contracted by darkness and conversely released and expanded by brightness'.[80] Goethe proposes the new term *Urphänomen* (archetypal phenomenon) as a more appropriate description of the fundamental colour phenomenon—probably because he wishes to distance himself from the current Newtonian associations which the term 'law' had acquired in the context of physics. For as he says, there are 'higher rules and laws, which do not, however, reveal themselves through words and hypotheses to the understanding, but [...] through phenomena to the intuition. We call them archetypal phenomena, because nothing lies above them in the world of appearance'.[81]

It therefore follows that Goethe's conception of natural law as an empirical generalisation is very close to that of Herder—except that, in Goethe's case, the process of generalisation does not lead to an abstract concept, but to a visual intuition.[82] He distances himself much more decisively than Herder, however, from the belief that the goal of scientific generalisation is the *explanation* of natural processes, and declares: 'One should not look for anything behind the phenomena. They themselves are the theory',[83] or again: 'we do not ask for causes here, but for the conditions under which the phenomena appear'.[84] His view of nature is therefore fundamentally descriptive, and hence closer to older natural history than to modern science. For this reason, he is also much less interested than Kant and Herder in the oldest epochs of earth history, and he leaves the question of the natural evolution of living forms open; his aim is to describe natural processes which are still active, without trying to determine their causes or genetic stages in earlier eras which are no longer accessible to observation. He therefore states that his morphology seeks 'only to represent, and not to explain';[85] and although

---

80   LA I. Abt., VII, 4 (1810).
81   LA I. Abt., IV, 71 (1808).
82   Cf. Nisbet, *Goethe and the Scientific Tradition*, pp. 36–44.
83   HA XII, 432.
84   LA I. Abt., XI, 40 (1798).
85   LA I. Abt., X, 140 (1795).

he often speaks of the 'metamorphosis' of natural organisms, he does not have in mind the descent of such organisms from earlier organisms which are no longer extant, but only the diverse manifestation of constant basic forms in each individual organism (such as the basic form of the leaf in different organs of the plant) or the morphological differences between diverse species (for example, in the skeletons of vertebrates).

Goethe's rejection of teleology is much more consistent and thorough than that of Herder, so that he is able to welcome Kant's discussion of teleology in the *Critique of Judgement*.[86] But his objections to teleological interpretations of nature are not only indebted to the arguments of Kant, Spinoza, and others against the projection of human intentions and attributes into nature; he rejects them also for the same reason that he rejects all explanations of natural processes by mechanical or causal agencies, because such explanations artificially detach a linear series of causes and effects from the unitary, multi-dimensional whole of nature, in which all individual entities mutually condition each other. As he himself puts it, 'if so many beings interact with one another, where are we able to gain the insight in order to decide what is dominant and what is subordinate, what is destined to lead and what is obliged to follow?'[87] And although, like Herder, he sometimes appeals (for instance in some of his late pronouncements on human immortality) to Leibnizian dynamism as a metaphysical system,[88] he usually takes care not to explain natural processes as the effect of invisible forces. He says, for example, 'the word "force" denotes primarily something physical or even mechanical', and takes the view that anthropomorphic growth forces in biology are only inadequate aids to help us to form some conception of what is in fact incomprehensible.[89] His conception of natural forces—at least in scientific contexts—is therefore basically phenomenological, like that of Kant.

For all these reasons, it is plain that Kant, Herder, and Goethe tried to solve the problem of the historicity of nature in different ways, and that Goethe in particular diverges from the others—and from his age as a whole—inasmuch as he is prepared only with major reservations

---

86 LA I. Abt., IX, 92 (1817)

87 LA I. Abt., XI, 245

88 See, for example, *Goethes Gespräche mit Eckermann*, ed. by Franz Deibel (Leipzig: Insel-Verlag, 1921), p. 524 (3 March 1830).

89 LA I. Abt., IX, 99f. (1820).

to apply historical models and linear models of explanation to nature; this is true not only of his thoughts on the evolution of living organisms, but also of his reflections on cosmogony and earth history as well as of his own theory of science. His relative indifference to the temporal dimension is reminiscent not so much of modern science as of earlier natural history, whose main task was to describe an unchanging hierarchy of natural forms. Herder's view of nature, of course, is likewise in some respects old-fashioned—especially his belief in that Neo-Platonic metaphysics of nature which Kant had already rejected in his pre-critical period and which Schelling and other Romantics vainly tried to rescue around the turn of the century. But Herder is also decidedly modern in his consistently historical outlook, which he develops above all in his pronouncements on human history. For him, as also for Kant and Goethe, human history is in a certain sense a natural process. In conclusion, this essay will examine the attempts of these three thinkers to define more closely the relationship between nature and human history.

Human History: Kant

The continued growth of secularisation in the eighteenth century reinforced the tendency to look on world history as a natural process governed by natural laws and at least to some extent capable of explanation by scientific methods.[90] This tendency begins with Dubos and Montesquieu, and reaches its climax in the deterministic systems of the nineteenth century such as those of Marx, Comte, and Taine. Kant, and above all Herder, played a significant part in this development; Goethe was affected to a much lesser degree. The relevant statements of all three thinkers on history are almost exclusively of a theoretical nature. It will therefore be unnecessary to retain there that distinction between empirical and theoretical pronouncements which served to articulate the first part of this essay.

Kant's short essay *Idea for a Universal History from a Cosmopolitan Point of View* (1784) is his most important attempt to understand human

---

90   See the article 'Gesetz' in *Geschichtliche Grundbegriffe*, ed. by Otto Brunner, Werner Conze, and Reinhart Koselleck, 8 vols (Stuttgart: Klett-Cotta, 1972–92), II, 875ff.

history with the help of scientific methods.[91] Herder is not mentioned in it, but the title and theme of the essay recall his *Ideas for the Philosophy of History*; the first part of the latter, published a few months before Kant's essay, was in fact known to Kant before he published his own essay.[92] Both works expressly present history as a natural process and consider the possibility of treating it as an object of scientific analysis. But since Kant published two highly critical reviews of Herder's *Ideas* soon afterwards, it is entirely possible that he intended to show in his essay of 1784 how the philosophy of history might be conducted in a more rigorous manner than he believed it had been in the work of his former pupil.

The main difficulty which Kant encountered in his presentation of history as a natural process was his own dualistic conception of human nature; for in Kant's moral philosophy, man is not only a natural being, but also a free moral subject. He attempts to solve the resulting problem by arguing that the behaviour of humans as natural beings (who are consequently determined by natural laws) gradually enables them to develop a rational consciousness of their own moral freedom, and so to emancipate themselves from the control of nature. But even before they reach that stage, human beings, in contrast to animals, are already free beings to the extent that they can choose between different kinds of behaviour (irrespective of whether the choice they make is morally good or evil).[93] But even if the human will is in this sense inherently free, the actions it initiates are nevertheless for Kant 'natural events'. As he explains, 'hence the *phenomena* to which it [i.e. the human will] gives rise, namely human actions, are determined, just like any other natural event, by general laws of nature'.[94]

But it is clear from the examples cited by Kant that the actions in question are not in the same sense natural as mechanical processes in inanimate nature, because such actions are always guided by conscious and unconscious intentions;[95] they are 'natural' only in the sense that

---

91   WW XI, 33–50.

92   See Rudolf Haym, *Herder*, ed. by Wolfgang Harich, 2 vols (Berlin: Aufbau Verlag, 1954), II, 275.

93   See Erich Adickes, *Kant als Naturforscher*, 2 vols (Berlin: De Gruyter, 1924–25), I, 463.

94   WW XI, 33; on the concept of nature for Kant and his contemporaries cf. Robert Spaemann, 'Genetisches zum Naturbegriff des 18. Jahrhunderts', *Archiv für Begriffsgeschichte*, 11 (1967), 59–74.

95   See, for example, WW XI, 34.

they are motivated by natural desires and impulses such as ambition, greed,[96] aggressiveness,[97] competitiveness,[98] etc. As an expression of selfishness, such impulses are, of course, potentially antagonistic. But according to Kant, this very antagonism between individuals or states, in combination with their mutual dependence for the satisfaction of their needs, constitutes a natural mechanism which drives the development of human capabilities and ultimately compels the individuals or states in question to establish, in their own interests, a peaceful national or international system to guarantee the further development and security of all.[99] This natural process is in the course of time confirmed and accelerated by the insight of reason (for after all, reason itself is, for Kant, in a certain sense an 'implanted' natural proclivity of human beings)[100] until the opposition between nature and reason is finally overcome.[101]

It can clearly be seen from Kant's remarks that he certainly does not regard the supposed natural laws which govern this process of political progress as equivalent, for example, to the laws of mechanics. They must rather be of a statistical character, for he compares the events in which they can in his opinion be detected to those statistical regularities which are manifest in births, marriages, and deaths or in meteorological observations.[102] He presumably believes that similar statistical data (for example, on the increasing rarity of wars, the spread of republican constitutions, the growing interdependence of various states in world commerce, etc.) provide a firm basis for laws which have yet to be discovered and will eventually confirm the progressive direction of history. The laws in question will therefore be of the same kind as, for example, the statistically based laws of supply and demand, which were already beginning to be formulated in eighteenth-century economics.[103]

---

96   WW XI, 38.
97   WW XI, 42.
98   WW XI, 46.
99   WW XI, 37f. and 42.
100 WW III, 158.; see also Hans Werner Ingensiep, 'Die biologischen Analogien und die erkenntnistheoretischen Alternativen in Kants Kritik der reinen Vernunft B, §27', *Kant-Studien*, 85 (1994), 381–93 (p. 392).
101 Cf. WW XI, 38, 41, 46f. and 50.
102 WW XI, 33f.
103 Cf. Joseph A. Schumpeter, *History of Economic Analysis*, ed. by Elizabeth Boody Schumpeter (London: Allen & Unwin, 1954), pp. 209–12; cf. also Hegel's *Rechtsphilosophie*, §189, Zusatz.

Kant nevertheless also cites the discoveries of recent astronomy in his essay on the philosophy of history—if only as an analogy to describe the discoveries he hopes for in the social sciences. He says, for instance, of the creative activity of nature: 'Thus it produced a *Kepler*, who subjected the eccentric orbits of the planets to specific laws in an unexpected way, and a *Newton*, who explained these laws as the result of a universal natural cause.'[104] And although he does not explicitly say so, that natural antagonism between selfish and constructive social tendencies which he regards as the driving force of history is obviously conceived by analogy to the forces of attraction and repulsion of his own *Universal Natural History* and Newton's celestial mechanics.[105] The scientific background becomes clearer when he compares the search for a long-term progressive tendency in world history to the attempts of the astronomers to track the barely perceptible path of the sun and its satellites through the galactic system.[106] Again by analogy with mechanics, the mechanism of human selfishness will finally compel human beings to identify 'a law of equilibrium' between states and to base on it an international system which 'can automatically maintain itself'.[107]

These efforts of Kant to discover gradual political progress in history with the aid of scientific models can scarcely be contested on grounds of method, even if the empirical evidence he hopes for is still incomplete. But his further contention that a 'plan of nature' is visible in history,[108] his conviction that nature has the 'intention' to develop all human capacities and establish a liberal law-governed state,[109] and his replacement of the word 'nature' towards the end of his essay by the word 'providence'[110] all seem to belong to an earlier period in the history of philosophy. They recall rather the optimistic teleology of Leibniz than the *Critique of Pure Reason*. But we must not forget that these objections apply only to supplementary arguments in support of Kant's main thesis, which is itself based on purely naturalistic premises. The very title of Kant's essay indicates that his teleological interpretation of the causal mechanism of history is only a regulative 'idea' of reason, i.e. a working hypothesis

---

104 WW XI, 34.
105 Cf. AA XV, 590f. where this analogy is more prominently expressed.
106 WW XI, 45.
107 WW XI, 43f.
108 WW XI, 34.
109 WW XI, 39.
110 WW XI, 49.

designed, among other things, to promote the alleged progress in history; it should therefore on no account be mistaken for a constitutive principle. The function of this regulative idea is also, not least, rhetorical: it is meant to prove itself as a self-fulfilling prophecy by gaining the reader's cooperation in implementing it. As so often in Kant's writings on empirical topics—such as nature and history—his methodological circumspection and consistency, i. e. the systematic reservations with which he underpins his main thesis, are much more impressive than his empirical deductions which, in keeping with the state of then existing knowledge, are based on highly selective experience.

Kant's reflections on the philosophy of history are in this respect much more impressive than those of Herder's *Ideas*. This, of course, is partly due to the fact that his short essay sets itself a much more modest aim than Herder's wide-ranging work. Kant's pronouncements are scientifically more plausible because he chooses a very precise causal connection and a linear mode of explanation on a scientific model in order to furnish a proof that the dialectic of conflict and interdependence, of competition and need in human society, must generate a quite specific long-term tendency in political history. Herder's aim is much more comprehensive and ambitious. He, too, attempts to apply concepts and models of scientific origin to the study of history; but the results of this attempt are unconvincing, and his real achievement as a philosopher of history relies on quite different methods to those of science. (His first work on the philosophy of history, *Another Philosophy of History* (1774), is not considered here because natural history and scientific models play a much more limited part than in the later—and much more extensive—*Ideas*.)

Human History: Herder

Unlike Kant's philosophy, Herder's holistic view of nature in the *Ideas*, which is significantly influenced by Spinoza's monism, makes no abrupt distinction between the realm of natural necessity and that of human freedom. Both realms are part of a single continuum in which all transitions are gradual. For him, too, man is also 'a free creature' and 'the first *emancipated being* in creation';[111] but his primary concern in

---

111 SW XIII, 146f.

the *Ideas* is to present human history as a natural process, as he himself admits: 'The whole of human history is a pure natural history of human forces, actions, and impulses in time and place.'[112] In contrast to Kant, he makes no explicit attempt to resolve the tension in his work between natural causality and free human intentions.[113]

Generally speaking, Herder follows two complementary strategies in applying models derived from science and natural history to human history. Firstly, he uses his knowledge of natural history and physical geography—that is, of the environment in the widest sense—in order to throw light on the characteristic qualities of numerous human societies in past and present, and thereby to explain their distinctive contributions to history as far as possible by natural causes. This strategy, which forms the core of his 'historicism', is highly successful and had a profound effect on the philosophy of history and historiography of the nineteenth century.[114] But its main concern is with the internal development of individual nations rather than their interaction and succession in the world-historical process. In his treatment of world history proper, he employs the second of his main strategies to explain historical events by propounding historical laws which have a certain similarity to familiar laws of physics and mechanics. This strategy is less successful than the previous one, for reasons that will now be considered further.

Herder speaks, particularly in the *Ideas*, so often of 'laws' and 'natural laws' in connection with human actions and human history that the concept of law is obviously of fundamental importance to his thought.[115] But the significance of this concept is so wide and at the same time so variable that its precise sense in particular contexts is often difficult to determine. For example, it is often unclear whether Herder intends to discover similar or identical laws in nature and history, or whether, in employing the word 'natural law' and related expressions, he is merely borrowing them from science as analogies and metaphors in order to denote roughly comparable regularities in human life. Sometimes, he

---

112 SW XIV, 145.

113 Cf. Frederick M. Barnard, *Self-Direction and Political Legitimacy. Rousseau and Herder* (Oxford: Clarendon Press, 1988), p. 187.

114 Cf. H. B. Nisbet, 'Goethes und Herders Geschichtsdenken', *Goethe-Jahrbuch*, 110 (1993), 115–33.

115 See, for example, SW XIII, 116, 120, 160, 182, 234, 333; XIV, 53, 83, 86, 117, 203, 207, 213ff., 218, 225, 235, 248, 250, etc.

seems to take the view that identical laws are at work in both areas, as when he declares: 'Thus, one and the same law extends from the sun, and from all suns, to the smallest human action. What preserves all beings and their systems is only One: *the relation of their forces to periodic rest and order.*'[116]

But in other cases, he seems to speak not of an identity, but an analogy, as when he envisages the possibility of a 'physics of history',[117] whose laws are allegedly active on a higher level than that of physics proper, or when he suggests that 'mind and morality are also physics, and serve the same laws, which are all ultimately dependent on the solar system, but in a higher order'.[118] Besides, since Herder regards the whole of nature, including human society, as a unitary whole, he is always anxious to detect similarities between its different areas, and to discover analogous processes on different levels.[119] This is no doubt one of the reasons why he uses the term 'natural law' in so wide a range of senses and why it is often difficult to determine whether he considers the relevant parallels as identities or only as analogies.[120] His historical laws are for the most part commonplaces, for example when he mentions an alleged law 'which creates order out of chaos'[121] or when he speaks of 'laws of a disturbed balance' in both nature and history.[122] The concepts which he uses in such cases are general enough to include both areas; but for the same reason, they are rarely specific enough to have an intelligible relation to concrete situations (as with his favourite concept of a 'nemesis' or 'Adrastea' in history, which he employs both in a mythological and in a physical or mechanical sense).[123]

---

116 SW XIII, 234; cf. also SW XIII, 16.

117 SW V, 558.

118 SW XIII, 20; cf. SW XIV, 248.

119 Cf. Hans Dietrich Irmscher, 'Beobachtungen zur Funktion der Analogie im Denken Herders', *Deutsche Vierteljahrsschrift für Literaturwissenschaft und Geistesgeschichte*, 55 (1981), 64–97.

120 Cf. Hans Dietrich Irmscher, 'Aneignung und Kritik naturwissenschaftlicher Vorstellungen bei Herder', in *Texte, Motive und Gestalten der Goethezeit. Festschrift für Hans Reiss*, ed. by John L. Hibberd and Hugh Barr Nisbet (Tübingen: Niemeyer, 1989), pp. 33–63 (p. 53).

121 SW XIV, 215.

122 SW XIV, 218.

123 Cf. Wulf Köpke, 'Nemesis und Geschichtsdialektik', in *Herder Today. Contributions from the International Herder Conference 1987*, ed. by Kurt Müller-Vollmer (Berlin: De Gruyter, 1990), pp. 85–96; also Michael Maurer, 'Nemesis-Adrastea oder Was ist und wozu dient Geschichte?', in ibid., pp. 46–63.

This criticism applies in particular to those historical laws which Herder propounds in the fifteenth book of the *Ideas*.[124] He takes his lead here from the attempts of the mathematician Johann Heinrich Lambert to apply mechanical concepts such as equilibrium, steady states and pendular oscillation to non-mechanical phenomena—for example, social systems—and himself claims to detect a regular cycle in world history whereby reason and order are repeatedly restored in spite of all threats and will in the long term increasingly prevail over unreason and disorder. He writes, for example: 'All destructive forces in nature must in the course of time [...] give way to the forces of preservation'[125] and 'abuses will punish themselves, and disorder will with time become order through the tireless efforts of an ever-growing rationality'.[126] In the historical 'laws' themselves, such propositions as these are simply reformulated by the addition of metaphors from mechanics, as when Herder declares 'that when a being or system of beings is displaced from this steady state of its truth, goodness, and beauty, it will return to this state through inner force, either in oscillations or in an asymptote'.[127] But no mechanical metaphors or analogies can lend such assertions credibility, because the pairs of concepts they contain (order/disorder, destruction/preservation, abuses/rationality) have no reference to any objectively definable conditions; they are rather the result of subjective value judgements.

It must admittedly not be overlooked that metaphors and analogies from the realm of science were particularly popular in Herder's day.[128] Kant employed such analogies, as already noticed. in order to designate supposedly progressive tendencies in history, for which he expected statistical evidence to emerge in the future. But in the absence of such evidence, he took care not to formulate historical 'laws', and simply expressed the hope that some future student of history might discover a law of this kind. But Herder had no such inhibitions. He formulates several so-called 'natural laws' of history; and although he uses the same

---

124 SW XIV, 213–52.
125 Ibid., p. 213.
126 Ibid., p. 249.
127 Ibid., p. 226.
128 Cf. Ulrich Dierse, 'Der Newton der Geschichte', *Archiv für Begriffsgeschichte*, 30 (1986–87), 158–82; also Ahlrich Meyer, 'Mechanische und organische Metaphorik politischer Philosophie', *Archiv für Begriffsgeschichte*, 13 (1969), 128–99.

analogy as Kant for the discovery of such laws (namely the attempts of astronomers to track the scarcely perceptible course of the sun through the Milky Way), he does not apply this analogy to objectively identifiable political conditions such as Kant was particularly interested in, but to 'the scarcely visible progress of the good in history'[129]—that is, of a moral tendency which can hardly be identified by objective means. The scientific terminology which Herder makes use of in the *Ideas* accordingly offers no prospect of a new method of scientific explanation of historical processes. It serves rather as a rhetorical means of support for the historical and metaphysical optimism of his later years. This is confirmed by the fact that, towards the end of the fifteenth book of the *Ideas*, he abandons the language of mechanics in favour of traditional teleological concepts such as 'providence', 'fate', 'wise goodness', etc.[130] Thus, like his teacher Kant, he outlines a teleology of history which claims to be based on a 'natural' providence; but he does not supply those methodological reservations and qualifications which distinguish the critical philosophy from pre-critical metaphysics.

Although the foregoing account of Herder's attempts to explain the development of history as a natural process may seem all too one-sided and negative, it must not be forgotten that these attempts form only a small part of his work as a philosopher of history, and that the earlier and more original of his two works on that subject, namely *Another Philosophy of History* has not been considered here. So long as he confined himself to other means of understanding history than those of science, he wrote with genuine originality, as when he conjures up past ages with vivid imagination and empathetic understanding in *Another Philosophy* or describes alien forms of culture and their geographical determinants as phenomena of natural history in the ethnological chapters of the *Ideas*. And in *Another Philosophy*, he does not yet seem to feel the need to set up quasi-scientific natural laws of history: his metaphors, which are in part drawn from the realm of natural history and science, are still unmistakably metaphors, and his analogies are plainly nothing other than analogies. Thus he compares the natural development of individual nations and their succession in the world-historical process to the stages of human life or the growth of a tree and its branches.[131]

---

129 SW XIV, 235.
130 SW XIV, 244.
131 SW V, 499, 512, 528f., 566, 575, etc.

On the other hand, he describes the interruption or obstruction of this natural development by violent or regressive means with the help of metaphors from mechanics: thus, the absolutist Prussian state, for example, is likened to a machine, just as modern culture as a whole has allegedly lost its former spontaneity and likewise become mechanical. But when he attempts in the third part of the *Ideas* to identify linear causal processes in world history by analogy with mechanics and combines them with a theory of moral progress, he places excessive demands on his basically very loose comparisons. His 'physics of history' remains, as before, a completely utopian aim.

Human History: Goethe

No single writer had so much influence on Goethe's historical thought as Herder.[132] But simply because Goethe absorbed this influence above all in his early years (namely around the time of Herder's *Another Philosophy*), he remained relatively unaffected by Herder's later efforts in the third part of the *Ideas* to discover quasi-mechanical laws of world history. Goethe's conception of history remains indebted, until his final years, to the historical scepticism of Herder's early treatise, which had attacked Enlightenment optimism and recommended historical relativism and an empathetic understanding of earlier ages of history.

Goethe nevertheless does share the older Herder's view in the *Ideas* that nature is a unitary swhole, of which both the lives of individuals and human history in general form integral parts. He is consequently no less ready than Herder to discover analogies between different levels of organisation (for example, in the novel *The Elective Affinities* between human behaviour patterns and the reactions of chemical compounds). Like Herder, he makes no sharp distinctions between natural necessity and human freedom, and declares that 'there is yet everywhere only *one* nature, and the traces of dismal, passionate necessity also run inexorably through the realm of serene, rational freedom'.[133] For him, as for Herder, the healthy development of both the individual and society at large is analogous to the growth of living organisms, and he likes to describe such processes with the help of

---

132 Cf. Nisbet, 'Goethes und Herders Geschichtsdenken', passim.
133 Goethe, HA VI, 621.

biological metaphors.[134] Conversely, mechanical metaphors have for him—as for the young Herder—a predominantly negative range of meaning: in their application to nature and history, he therefore usually associates them with violent and destructive occurrences.[135]

Since world history contains all too many events of this kind, it is fully understandable that Goethe in general passes very negative judgements on it. He sees in it no regular development and consequently makes no attempt to propound historical laws in analogy to the laws of physics. Quasi-mechanical laws of progress like those in Herder's *Ideas* are quite unthinkable for him; like nature itself, world history is in his opinion far too complex to be reduced to a few simple formulas of this kind. The kind of historiography which most appeals to him sets itself more modest aims, as for example in cultural history, which depicts the quasi-organic development of a single, clearly defined era in culture or art such as that of ancient Greece, Persia, or the Florentine Renaissance.[136]

Even in cultural history, such eras are, of course, rather the exception than the rule; they are all too often interrupted or extinguished by unforeseen and violent incursions from outside. The older Goethe consequently gives great weight to the role of chance and unforeseen events in history, whereby the noblest endeavours are frustrated by human folly or arbitrary intervention. But this sceptical attitude towards history—especially political history—is already apparent in his early works, above all in the dramas *Götz von Berlichingen* and *Egmont*, and it was later intensified by the experience of the French Revolution. The important role which what he calls 'the incommensurability of history' plays in his final years is, of course, in direct contradiction to the historical optimism of the late Enlightenment as defended by Kant and the later Herder. If history really is influenced by regular laws, it is in Goethe's view difficult, or even impossible, to distinguish these from the contingent and the arbitrary: 'Law and chance interact, and the individual spectator often ends up by confusing the two, as is particularly evident in biased historians'.[137]

---

134 Cf. *Goethes Werke*, Weimar edition (henceforth WA), 133 vols (Weimar: Böhlau, 1889–1919), I. Abteilung, XL/I, 217 and VII, 51; cf. Nisbet, 'Goethes und Herders Geschichtsdenken', p. 120.

135 Cf. WA I. Abt., XXVIII, 68–70; LA I. Abt., IV, 221; also Nisbet, *Goethe and the Scientific Tradition*, pp. 54–58

136 Cf. Nisbet, 'Goethes und Herders Geschichtsdenken', pp. 115f.

137 WA II. Abt., III, 134 (1810).

Although Goethe, no less than Herder, is theoretically convinced that nature and history are equally important parts of the world as a harmonious whole, it is nevertheless comprehensible why he often presents nature as the realm of the law and history as the realm of the arbitrary. He was, of course, always aware (especially in his final years) that chaos, or 'the aimless power of unbridled elements' may break in at any time upon the peaceful life of nature.[138] But such convulsions remain rather the exception than the rule, whereas chance seems to him in principle to play a considerably greater role in history than in nature, since human actions are more variable and unpredictable than most natural processes. (Unlike Kant, for example, Goethe does not appear to have considered the possibility that at least statistically predictable regularities might be present in collective human behaviour.) But Goethe is also aware of the fact that there is a certain methodological difference between natural science and the study of history, a difference which the young Herder had recognised in *Another Philosophy of History*, but apparently lost sight of in the later *Ideas*.[139] For the role of the observer of history is in an important respect different from that of the observer of nature. Each individual has their own necessarily incomplete perspective on events, which coincides only partially with that of other individuals; and the process of history itself cannot be distinguished nearly so easily as that of nature from the subjective viewpoint of the observer, because history can only be constituted by the reports of contemporary observers, each of whom saw the events from their own point of view and in terms of their own teleology. There is consequently no privileged, absolute perspective, and all general judgements on history are necessarily dubious. For this reason, Goethe confines himself in his *History of Colour Theory* to a sparse commentary on the extensive extracts he includes from the source materials, through which he lets the work of past colour theorists speak directly to the reader. For the same reason, he tends to favour those forms of historical writing which focus on personal experience, such as biography, autobiography, memoirs, travelogues,

---

138 HA III, 309 (*Faust*, Part II, line 10,219).

139 Cf. Hans Dietrich Irmscher, 'Die geschichtsphilosophische Kontroverse zwischen Kant und Herder', in *Hamann–Kant–Herder. Acta des vierten Internationalen Hamann-Kolloquiums 1985*, ed. by Bernhard Gajek (Frankfurt a. M.: Lang, 1987) pp. 111–92 (p. 153).

etc., and in which history is viewed from an unambiguously personal perspective.

The one kind of regularity which Goethe recognises in the process of history is the simple alternation of opposite tendencies such as constructive and destructive eras or (particularly in cultural history) the cycle of growth, efflorescence, and decline.[140] Any reference to a teleology of providence or moral progress, such as Herder and Kant in their different ways claimed to detect, is for him out of the question. It is therefore no wonder that he was not impressed when the young historian Heinrich Luden told him in 1806 that he had given up mathematics for history. Goethe commented: 'what the historian [...] regards as truth is always only truth for him, only subjective truth [...]. But mathematical truth is the same for everyone'.[141] In short, a historical science in the proper sense is for Goethe an impossibility. His historical scepticism finally becomes so extreme in his last years that he can describe history as 'a web of nonsense' or 'a mass of follies and wickedness'.[142]

If we disregard such ill-tempered outbursts, history ultimately consists for Goethe of the events themselves, although these are inevitably communicated through the necessarily biased reports of individual observers. The best we can obtain is a more or less factual description of the events, which we interpret from our own perspective. And the most we can hope for is to project ourselves to some extent, by empathy and imagination, into past epochs of culture. All theoretical initiatives are one-sided and inadequate, and every attempt to discover a linear development and to explain past events by causal or teleological models must result in a simplification, or indeed distortion, of the indeterminable multiplicity of the events in question.

Finally, we may conclude that Goethe's views on science and the study of history are internally consistent and mutually compatible, although he can accept only with major reservations that the methods of each are transferable to the other. Nature does indeed have a history,

---

140 Cf. Arnold Bergstraesser, 'Die Epochen der Geistesgeschichte in Goethes Denken', in Bergstraesser, *Staat und Dichtung* (Freiburg: Rombach, 1967), pp. 87–97; see also WA I. Abt., VII, 157; WA I. Abt., XXVII, 98f.; WA II. Abt., III, 133; etc.

141 Conversation with Heinrich Luden, 19 August 1806, in *Goethes Gespräche*, ed. by Wolfgang Herwig, 5 vols (Munich: Deutscher Taschenbuch Verlag, 1998), II, 121.

142 Conversation with Friedrich von Müller, 17 Decenber 1824, in *Goethes Gespräche*, III/1, 742.

but the empirical knowledge necessary for its reconstruction were in his day so limited that suspense of judgement often seemed to him the only alternative to arbitrary speculation. In any case, causal explanation is not, in his opinion, the proper task of science. The scientist is for him primarily still a natural historian in the older sense of that term, and not a historian of nature, because he ought rather to be occupied with description and classification than with explanation and prediction.

If Goethe then has strong reservations about applying historical and linear ways of thinking to nature, he is no less sceptical regarding the possibility of applying scientific methods to human history—firstly, because he sees linear modes of explanation as no less inadequate in a historical context than in natural history, and secondly, because the observer of history cannot possibly attain the degree of objectivity required by the observer of nature. In other words, there cannot be a science of history, but at most a natural history, on the model of Herder's historicism, of certain clearly defined aspects of the past (and particularly cultural history).

Conclusion

The foregoing comparisons between Goethe's, Kant's, and Herder's thought set out to present, among other things, Goethe's ideas on nature and history in their historical context. It has been shown that Goethe's views are by no means typical of his times. His scientific beliefs are idiosyncratic and opposed to that Newtonian tradition which underpinned Kant's theory and practice of science; and although his view of nature is based on the same Neo-Platonic premises as that of Herder, Herder's own views on science are fundamentally different from those of Goethe, both in respect of his readiness to speculate beyond the limits of experience and in his essential agreement with the aims of Newtonian science. Goethe's historical thought is likewise remote from that of Kant's (albeit regulative) teleological optimism and his efforts to apply scientific models and methods to history. And although he was strongly influenced by the young Herder's historical relativism and scepticism towards the Enlightenment's theories of progress, he parts company with the older Herder's attempts—which, despite the latter's rejection of the critical philosophy, are closely related to those of Kant—to detect quasi-scientific laws of progress or moral retribution in history.

From today's perspective, the views of all three thinkers are, of course, essentially obsolete. Kant's philosophy of science remains, as before, an intellectual achievement of the highest order. But the theory of relativity has superseded the whole of Newtonian physics, on which both Kant's *Critique of Pure Reason* and *Metaphysical Elements of Science* were based, and Kant's assumption of a firm *a priori* structure of space and time as the foundation of all empirical knowledge has likewise been refuted; and since the theory of relativity and quantum mechanics have applied two quite different principles to different aspects of nature, a consistent unitary theory of nature as a whole is no longer available. It follows from this that no single theory of science can now claim absolute validity; its validity can only be partial and provisional. The Neo-Platonic metaphysics which underpins Herder's and Goethe's image of nature was already obsolete by the end of the eighteenth century, and is of only historical interest today, while the individual scientific theories of the three thinkers here discussed were soon superseded by the progress of geology, the theory of evolution, and other branches of science.

It is therefore not at first sight obvious why Goethe's view of nature still holds a much stronger attraction today than that of Kant or Herder. The main reason for this is that Kant's and Herder's views of nature are far more heavily indebted to the now obsolete science of the eighteenth century than Goethe's, whereas Goethe's view is fundamentally different both from the dominant scientific tradition of his age and from modern science in general. Although his individual theories are indeed for the most part obsolete, his image of nature as an organic whole of which human beings are an essential part and his rejection of all linear models of explanation still strike a sympathetic note with many readers for whom modern science has acquired too many negative associations. It is therefore not surprising that the ecological movement of recent decades has awakened a new interest in Goethe's science. The instrumentalisation of nature by modern technology, which itself owes its origin to that linear and mechanistic way of thinking to which Goethe was strongly opposed, has had disastrous consequences for the environment; and these have understandably created a demand for an alternative view of nature that treats it not just as a means, but as an end in itself. For those in search of an image of nature of this kind, Goethe's writings on science therefore have obvious advantages. But this fact does not provide a justification for condemning modern science itself as misguided and presenting Goethe's view of nature as alone correct. Such judgements are applicable at most to certain ethical attitudes that are often—but by no means necessarily—associated with this or that attitude towards nature. The two views of nature are in fact not so much mutually exclusive alternatives as complementary perspectives from which nature can be viewed with different purposes in mind.[143] For it is entirely possible to consider nature as a whole as an end in itself, and at the same time to regard particular parts of it as means of realising our current aims by developing and applying the requisite technology which modern science has made possible.

In the philosophy of history too, the thought of Kant and Herder seems to some extent more antiquated from today's point of view than that of Goethe (although Kant's political philosophy is still rightly taken seriously). For the moral optimism and teleological belief in providence of Kant and the later Herder cannot readily be reconciled with the catastrophes of the twentieth century, while the negative political effects of the allegedly 'scientific' theories of history of Marx and others, along with the manifest failure of predictions of the future based on such theories, have aroused widespread distrust of the supposedly necessary historical laws and scientific claims of the corresponding philosophies of history. Against this background, Goethe's sceptical thoughts on history and his holistic view of nature still retain their attraction.

---

143 Cf. Karl Robert Mandelkow, 'Natur und Geschichte bei Goethe im Spiegel seiner Rezeption im 19. und 20. Jahrhundert', in *Geschichtlichkeit und Aktualität. Studien zur deutschen Literatur seit der Romantik. Festschrift für Hans-Joachim Mähl*, ed. by Klaus-Detlef Müller, Gerhard Pasternak, Wulf Segebrecht und Ludwig Stockinger (Tübingen: Niemeyer, 1988), pp. 69–96 (p. 95).

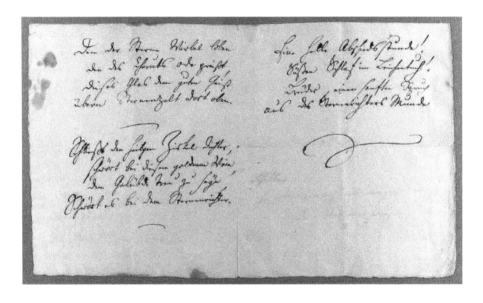

Autograph of Schiller's 'Ode to Joy' (1785). Photograph by Historiograf (2011), Wikimedia, Public Domain, https://upload.wikimedia.org/wikipedia/commons/2/2d/Schiller_an_die_freude_manuskript_2.jpg

10. Schiller's 'Ode to Joy'

A Reappraisal[1]

Freude, schöner Götterfunken[2]
Tochter aus Elysium,
Wir betreten feuertrunken
Himmlische, dein Heiligtum.
Deine Zauber binden wieder,
Was der Mode Schwert geteilt;
Bettler werden Fürstenbrüder,
Wo dein sanfter Flügel weilt.

Chor
Seid umschlungen, Millionen!
Diesen Kuß der ganzen Welt!
Brüder—überm Sternenzelt
Muß ein lieber Vater wohnen.

Wem der große Wurf gelungen,
Eines Freundes Freund zu sein;
Wer ein holdes Weib errungen,
Mische seinen Jubel ein!
Ja—wer auch nur *eine* Seele
Sein nennt auf dem Erdenrund!
Und wer's nie gekonnt, der stehle
Weinend sich aus diesem Bund!

1   An earlier version of this chapter was originally published as 'Friedrich Schiller. "An
     die Freude". A Reappraisal', in Peter Hutchinson (ed.), *Landmarks in German Poetry*
     (Oxford, Berne, Berlin, etc.: Peter Lang, 2000), pp. 73–96.
2   The text is that of the original version published in 1786, as reproduced (with
     spelling and punctuation largely modernised), in Friedrich Schiller, *Sämtliche Werke*
     (henceforth SW), ed. by Gerhard Fricke and Herbert G. Göpfert, 5 vols, 7th edn
     (Munich: Hanser, 1984), I, 133–36.

https://doi.org/10.11647/OBP.0180.10

Chor
Was den großen Ring bewohnet,
Huldige der Sympathie!
Zu den Sternen leitet sie,
Wo der *Unbekannte* thronet.

Freude trinken alle Wesen
An den Brüsten der Natur,
Alle Guten, alle Bösen
Folgen ihrer Rosenspur.
Küsse gab sie *uns* und *Reben*,
Einen Freund, geprüft im Tod.
Wollust ward dem Wurm gegeben,
Und der Cherub steht vor Gott.

Chor
Ihr stürzt nieder, Millionen?
Ahndest du den Schöpfer, Welt?
Such ihn überm Sternenzelt,
Über Sternen muß er wohnen.

Freude heißt die starke Feder
In der ewigen Natur.
Freude, Freude treibt die Räder
In der großen Weltenuhr.
Blumen lockt sie aus den Keimen,
Sonnen aus dem Firmament,
Sphären rollt sie in den Raümen,
Die des Sehers Rohr nicht kennt.

Chor
Froh, wie seine Sonnen fliegen,
Durch des Himmels prächtgen Plan,
Laufet, Brüder, eure Bahn,
Freudig wie ein Held zum Siegen.

Aus der Wahrheit Feuerspiegel
Lächelt *sie* den Forscher an.
Zu der Tugend steilem Hügel
Leitet *sie* des Dulders Bahn.
Auf des Glaubens Sonnenberge
Sieht man *ihre* Fahnen wehn,

Durch den Riß gesprengter Särge
Sie im Chor der Engel stehn.

> Chor
> Duldet mutig, Millionen!
> Duldet für die beßre Welt!
> Droben überm Sternenzelt
> Wird ein großer Gott belohnen.

Göttern kann man nicht vergelten,
Schön ists, ihnen gleich zu sein.
Gram und Armut soll sich melden,
Mit den Frohen sich erfreun.
Groll und Rache sei vergessen,
Unserm Todfeind sei verziehn,
Keine Träne soll ihn pressen,
Keine Reue nage ihn.

> Chor
> Unser Schuldbuch sei vernichtet!
> Ausgesöhnt die ganze Welt!
> Brüder—überm Sternenzelt
> Richtet Gott, wie wir gerichtet.

Freude sprudelt in Pokalen,
In der Traube goldnem Blut
Trinken Sanftmut Kannibalen,
Die Verzweiflung Heldenmut –
Brüder, fliegt von euren Sitzen,
Wenn der volle Römer kreist,
Laßt den Schaum zum Himmel sprützen:
Dieses Glas dem guten Geist.

> Chor
> Den der Sterne Wirbel loben,
> Den des Seraphs Hymne preist,
> Dieses Glas dem guten Geist
> Überm Sternenzelt dort oben!

Festen Mut in schwerem Leiden,
Hülfe, wo die Unschuld weint,
Ewigkeit geschwornen Eiden,

Wahrheit gegen Freund und Feind,
Männerstolz vor Königsthronen –
Brüder, gält es Gut und Blut, –
Dem Verdienste seine Kronen,
Untergang der Lügenbrut!

> Chor
> Schließt den heilgen Zirkel dichter,
> Schwört bei diesem goldnen Wein:
> Dem Gelübde treu zu sein,
> Schwört es bei dem Sternenrichter!

Rettung vor Tyrannenketten,
Großmut auch dem Bösewicht,
Hoffnung auf den Sterbebetten,
Gnade auf dem Hochgericht!
Auch die Toten sollen leben!
Brüder trinkt und stimmet ein,
Allen Sündern soll vergeben,
Und die Hölle nicht mehr sein.

> Chor
> Eine heitre Abschiedsstunde!
> Süßen Schlaf im Leichentuch!
> Brüder—einen sanften Spruch
> Aus des Totenrichters Munde!

English translation:

Joy, thou lovely spark immortal,
Daughter from Elysium,
Drunk with fire we dare to enter
Heavenly one, thy holy shrine.
Your magic spells have reunited,
What the sword of custom cleft;
Beggars become princes' brothers,
Where your gentle wings alight.

> Chorus
> We embrace you, all ye millions!
> Let all the world receive this kiss!
> Brothers—above the starry heavens
> There must dwell a loving father.

Whoever met the weighty challenge,
Of giving friendship to a friend;
Whoever won a lovely woman,
Let him mix his joy with ours!
And even him who on this earth
Has just one soul to call his own!
But let who never passed this test
Steal weeping from this league of ours!

    Chorus
    May all who dwell in this great ring
    Pay homage now to sympathy!
    To the stars it leads the way,
    To the unknown being's throne.

Joy is drunk by every creature
Drunk by all at nature's breasts,
All the good, and all the evil
Follow down her rosy path.
She gave us both vines and kisses,
And a friend, loyal unto death.
Even the worm is rapture given,
The cherub stands in face of God.

    Chorus
    You fall before him all ye millions!
    Do you the world's creator sense?
    Seek him beyond the starry vault,
    Above the stars he has his dwelling.

Joy is yet the mighty mainspring
In eternal nature's realm.
For by joy the wheels are driven
In the universal clock.
From the buds she draws the flowers,
Suns out of the firmament,
Spheres she rolls within the spaces
That no seer's lens can scan.

    Chorus
    Happy, as his suns are flying,
    On the heavens' splendid plane,

Run, ye brothers, on your courses,
Joyful, like a conquering hero.

Out of truth's refulgent mirror
The researcher sees her smile.
To the steep hillside of virtue
The endurer's path she guides.
Up on faith's high sunlit mountain
One can see her banners fly,
Through the crack of bursting coffins
See her in the angels' choir.

       Chorus
       Suffer bravely, all ye millions!
       Suffer for a better world!
       Up above the starry vault
       You'll find a great God's recompense.

Gods can never be requited;
To be like them is beautiful.
Let grief and poverty come hither,
And with the happy ones rejoice.
Let rage and vengeance be forgotten,
Forgiven be our mortal foe,
Not one teardrop shall oppress him,

       Chorus
       Let our book of debts be cancelled!
       Let all the world be reconciled!
       Brothers—above the starry vault
       God will judge as we have judged.

Joy will sparkle in the goblets,
In the golden blood of grapes
Cannibals may drink sweet temper
And desperation courage take—
Brothers, leap from where you're sitting,
When the brimming glass goes round,
Let the foam spray up to heaven:
To the good spirit drink this toast.

Chorus
Whom the constellations honour,
Whom the seraph's hymn applauds,
Drink this glass to the good spirit
Beyond the starry vault above!

Courage firm in sore affliction,
Succour where the innocent weep,
Eternity to words of honour,
Truth to friend and foe alike,
Manly pride in royal presence –
Brothers, if goods and blood it cost, –
Crowns to those who best deserve them,
Downfall to the lying brood!

Chorus
Close the sacred circle tighter,
Swear upon this golden wine:
To be faithful to the vow,
Swear it by the judge above!

Rescue from the chains of tyrants,
Kindness towards the villain too,
Hope for those who lie on deathbeds,
Pardon those condemned to death!
The dead shall also join the living!
Brothers, drink and join the song,
Every sin shall be forgiven,
Hell itself shall cease to be.

Chorus
A serene hour of departure!
Peaceful sleep beneath the shroud!
Brothers—and a gentle verdict
On the dead the judge may utter!

When Schiller's poem 'An die Freude' ('Ode to Joy') first appeared in 1786, it was an immediate popular success. It soon became, as Schiller later acknowledged, 'to some extent a folksong'.[3] It was set to music over

---

3   Schiller to Körner, 21 October 1800, in *Schillers Werke, Nationalausgabe* (henceforth NA), ed. by Julius Petersen and Gerhard Fricke (Weimar: Böhlau,1943-), XXX, 206f.).

a hundred times,[4] and its fame received an extra boost when Beethoven incorporated it—or more precisely, less than half of it—in the fourth movement of his Ninth Symphony. Along with 'The Song of the Bell', it remained Schiller's best known poem throughout the nineteenth century; and well into the twentieth century, its popular appeal—by now inseparable from that of Beethoven's symphony—remained undiminished. In the second half of the century, however, a reaction set in. The poem came to be regarded, especially in Germany, as at best of historical interest[5] and at worst as an embarrassment: significantly, a popular edition of Schiller's poetry, still in print,[6] which includes over 150 items, omits it altogether. 'An die Freude' now survives, in Beethoven's abbreviated version—and in the English-speaking world mainly in archaic or incompetent translations[7]—as the text of the choral section of the Ninth Symphony, whose music still manages to bring some of the poem's emotional charge back to life. But the words, images, and concepts which first transmitted that charge to the composer are no longer an equal partner in the symphony's overall effect—they are simply part of its archaeology. The fact that Beethoven's famous melody is now often performed on its own, without Schiller's text,[8] is a sure sign that this text is now widely considered superfluous.

My aim in this essay is to examine the poem's origins, ancestry, and reception, with a view to discovering why it enjoyed such immense popularity when it first appeared, what Beethoven found so attractive about it, and what kept it alive until relatively recent times. And finally, I shall ask what, if anything, it still has to offer us today.

---

4   See the editors' commentary in Friedrich Schiller, *Werke und Briefe*, Frankfurt edition (henceforth FA), ed. by Otto Dann and other hands, 12 vols (Frankfurt a. M.: Deutscher Klassiker Verlag, 1988–2004), I, 1038; *Schiller-Handbuch*, ed. by Helmut Koopmann (Stuttgart: Kröner, 1998), p. 311; Julius Blaschke, 'Schillers Gedichte in der Musik', *Neue Zeitschrift in der Musik* (1905), 397–401.

5   See *Schiller-Handbuch*, p. 889.

6   Friedrich Schiller, *Gedichte*, ed. by Norbert Oellers (Stuttgart: Reclam, 2009).

7   The best known version is still the nineteenth-century rendering by Lady Natalia Macfarren, reproduced in C. P. Magill, 'Schiller's "An die Freude"', in *Essays in German Language, Culture and Society*, ed. by Siegbert S. Prawer, R. Hinton Thomas and Leonard Forster (London: Institute for Germanic Studies, 1969) pp. 36–45 (pp. 37f.). Typically marred by errors and infelicities is that in Nicholas Cook, *Beethoven: Symphony No. 9* (Cambridge: Cambridge University Press, 1993), pp. 109.

8   See Andreas Eichhorn, *Beethovens Neunte Symphonie. Die Geschichte ihrer Aufführung und Rezeption* (Kassel: Bärenreiter, 1993), pp. 296ff.

The 'Ode to Joy' was composed in the late summer or autumn of 1785, when Schiller, living a hand-to-mouth existence as a fugitive from his native Württemberg, at last found security and happiness in a circle of friends around Christian Gottfried Körner.[9] Along with others of Schiller's works, it was published in February 1786 as the opening item of the second issue of his periodical *Thalia*, with a musical setting by Körner, himself an amateur musician.[10] But although the poem's theme and mood plainly reflect Schiller's personal experience, it is in no sense an autobiographical statement in the manner of Goethe, or even of Klopstock.[11] On the contrary, its poetic currency is largely conventional. In fact, five or more poems by various authors entitled 'Die Freude' or 'An die Freude' had appeared over the previous half century, most of them personifying joy as a goddess or divine being and equating it with that feeling of elation or happiness which accompanies a life of modest virtue and cheerful conviviality among a small circle of friends.[12] Schiller's poem is full of echoes of these earlier works, from the opening line of Hagedorn's poem ('Freude, Göttin edler Herzen')[13] to that of Uz's equivalent work ('Freude, Königinn der Weisen').[14] Schiller's metrical scheme is in fact identical with that of Uz, apart from his addition of a chorus after each verse. Several of the earlier poems belong to the Anacreontic phase of mid-eighteenth-century German poetry, which, in a light-hearted spirit, celebrated the trinity of wine, love, and friendship; the third verse of Schiller's poem, with its references to roses and kisses, grapes and friendship, faithfully reproduces this older idiom. But the 'Ode to Joy' is equally indebted to another traditional class of lyric, namely the Masonic song, as performed by Freemasons at festive gatherings in celebration of their brotherhood and its beliefs; for example, Schiller's references to the creator above the stars echo such lines as 'Up above the starry host/Our Master rules on high' in the Masonic songbooks

---

9   See FA I, 1036; also *Schiller-Handbuch*, p. 13.

10   See *Schiller-Handbuch*, p. 750; also Schiller to Georg Joachim Göschen, 29 November 1785 and 23 February 1786 in NA XXIV, 28f. and 35f.

11   Cf. Hans Mayer, 'Schillers Gedichte und die Tradition deutscher Lyrik', in *Jahrbuch der Deutschen Schiller-Gesellschaft*, 4 (1960), 72–89 (p. 87).

12   See FA I, 1037 and Franz Schulz, 'Die Göttin Freude. Zur Geistes- und Stilgeschichte des 18. Jahrhunderts', *Jahrbuch des Freien Deutschen Hochstifts* (1926), 3–38 (pp. 5–27).

13   Text in Schulz, 'Die Göttin Freude', pp. 5f.

14   Text in ibid., pp. 19f.

of the day.[15] His astronomical references likewise recall the poetry of Brockes and Haller early in the century, with its praise of the Newtonian universe and its creator. In short, precedents can be found in the lyric of the German Enlightenment for most of the motifs and images in the 'Ode to Joy'. The poem's originality consequently lies not so much in its detail but, as I shall try to show, in two other, more general qualities—firstly, in the rhetorical power with which the familiar material is put across, and secondly, in the remarkable concentration of eighteenth-century themes and allusions which Schiller achieves in so short a work.

But before I examine these qualities, I shall give a brief outline of the poem's structure and development, relating it to the modes and genres of poetry current in Schiller's time. In its original form as reproduced here, the poem consists of nine verses, each followed by a chorus; Schiller himself shortened it, in the second version published in 1805, by deleting the final verse and chorus, at the same time making minor alterations to the first verse.[16] The first verse addresses joy directly as a divine being and unifying force promoting human brotherhood, and then the chorus at once expands the frame of reference to the universe at large and its benevolent creator. The second verse celebrates human friendship, with a concluding reprimand for unsociable individuals who have failed to establish a bond of friendship with others. The second chorus, like all the subsequent choruses, again enlarges the perspective to the astronomical universe and its architect, who is given different names from one chorus to the next, from 'God' and 'the unknown being' to 'the good spirit' and 'the judge of the dead'. The third verse refers to joy in the third person, as the animating force in all created beings from the worm to the cherub, and as the inspiration imparted by love, wine, and friendship. (The references here to grapes and drinking prepare the way for the drinking ritual of the last three verses.) Verse four again invokes joy as a cosmic power, this time as the driving force of the physical and biological universe. The fifth verse adopts an older didactic idiom, that of allegorised abstraction, and returns to the world of human experience: joy is now coupled with personified values such

---

15   See Hans Vaihinger, 'Zwei Quellenfunde zu Schillers philosophischer Entwicklung', *Kant-Studien*, 10 (1905), 373–89 (p. 388); also Gotthold Deile, *Freimaurerlieder als Quellen zu Schillers Lied 'An die Freude'* (Leipzig: Verlag Adolf Weigel, 1907), pp. 88–112.

16   See p. 234 below for the revised version.

as truth, virtue and faith, while the last two lines, with their reference to bursting coffins, contain a somewhat incongruous reminiscence of sepulchral poetry and the Gothic novel. The sixth verse includes a further series of abstract concepts, this time calling on those oppressed by deprivation or destructive passions to rise above their affliction in a spirit of joyful forgiveness; these hopeful and conciliatory sentiments, addressed to mankind at large, are echoed in the choruses to verses five and six. Verses seven to nine form a relatively self-contained unit: this is the climax of the poem, in which all the positive sentiments of the preceding verses become the object of joyful celebration in a fraternal company bound together by an oath of loyalty. This company rises to its feet to drink a series of toasts, first to the creator—now described as 'the good spirit'—and then to a series of human virtues and worthy causes such as courage in adversity, succour for the innocent, freedom from tyranny, etc. The last two verses consist entirely of such toasts, culminating in a series of eschatological references to death and the Last Judgement; the formula 'The dead shall also join the living' ingeniously combines the traditional 'vivat!' formula of the salutation or toast with the idea of resurrection from the dead. This final section of the poem contains further incongruities: secular jollification combines with religious solemnity, Christian with pagan allusions, a series of moral, political, and religious values are invoked, and—with a touch of *Sturm und Drang* extravagance and an allusion to the voyages of discovery—we are even invited in verse seven to imagine the spectacle of wine-bibbing cannibals.

The poem was clearly intended from the start for choral performance, for its choruses are specifically labelled as such, and there are several internal references to song and music. Its moral content, its praise of the creator and his works, and its eschatological conclusion lend it affinities to the Christian hymn: it indeed refers explicitly to the seraph's hymn and to the choir of angels. But its Anacreontic associations, its toasts, and the fraternal company addressed in the concluding verses link it no less strongly with the drinking songs of the student fraternities ('Brothers, drink and join the song') and—as already mentioned—with the Masonic song, in which secular conviviality and deistic religiosity traditionally come together. But for all its religious references, the sentiments and values in Schiller's poem are basically secular: it is in fact a kind of secular hymn.

Apart from its external structure, with its regular metre, rhyme, verses, and choruses, the poem also has an internal structure in the way in which its ideas, images, and sentiments are organised. This internal organisation is largely responsible for its rhetorical power, which is one of its two most memorable features. As in many of his later poems, Schiller's imagination follows an architectonic, spatial model:[17] the unifying power of joy embraces not only present friends, but expands horizontally outwards to embrace the whole of humanity in an immense ring or circle, as in the lines 'We embrace you, all ye millions!' and 'all who dwell in this great ring'. At the same time, joy extends upwards through a vertical hierarchy from the lowest forms of life to the supreme being beyond the stars. This vertical axis of height and depth, which is invoked in every chorus, and the interaction of extremes which it entails, is, of course, the stuff of Schiller's dramatic as well as his lyrical imagination: the aesthetic modality here is that of sublimity, and both of the two varieties of sublimity later distinguished by Kant are present: on the one hand, we have what Kant calls the 'mathematical' sublimity of number and size, both in the 'Millionen' of all humanity and in the vastness of the stellar universe which transcends the limits of the imagination and fills us with awe; and on the other, we have Kant's 'dynamic' sublimity of overwhelming power as the millions fall prostrate before the might of the creator (third chorus).[18] Similarly, the poem includes those two sublime objects to which Kant famously refers at the end of his second *Critique* of 1788, namely 'the starry heaven above me and the moral law within me';[19] for Schiller repeatedly invokes the starry heavens in his choruses, and the moral law is a constant presence in the second half of the poem. This association between joy and sublimity remained a real one for Schiller for the rest of his life; it appears once more in the concluding line of *The Maid of Orleans*, in which the heroine triumphs over human weakness to declare 'Short is the pain, and eternal is the joy.'

---

17   Cf. his use of an imaginary landscape of varying heights and depths in his poem 'Der Spaziergang' ('The Walk') in SW I, 228–34 and his comments on the poetic function of landscape in his review of Matthisson's poems in SW V, 997f. See also Martin Dyck, *Die Gedichte Schillers* (Berne: Francke, 1967), pp. 60 and 73.

18   See Immanuel Kant, *Kritik der Urteilskraft* §§ 25–29, in Kant, *Gesammelte Schriften*, Akademie-Ausgabe (henceforth AA), (Berlin: Königlich-Preußische Akademie der Wissenschaften, 1900–), V, pp. 248–78; cf. also Eichhorn, *Beethovens Neunte Symphonie*, p. 226.

19   Kant, AA V, 161.; cf. Eichhorn, *Beethovens Neunte Symphonie*, p. 233.

This contrast of extremes inherent in the experience of sublimity is matched by other kinds of opposition and conflict both within this poem and between it and other early poems by Schiller. In the same issue of his *Thalia* which opened with the 'Ode to Joy', he included two poems of diametrically opposite character, namely 'Freethinking of Passion' and 'Resignation', whose mood is respectively one of nihilistic defiance and black despair. The agonistic tensions which run throughout Schiller's work[20] are also present in the 'Ode to Joy' itself, although in this case, they are invoked only to be decisively overcome. The all-conquering power of joy transcends or vanquishes Grief, Poverty, Rage, Vengeance, Repentance, Debts, Desperation, Affliction, Death, and even Hell itself— if only in the poetic imagination and in moments of high euphoria. It is nevertheless the extreme contrasts in which this poem abounds[21]—and their triumphant resolution in joyful solidarity—which lend the 'Ode to Joy' an exuberance and rhetorical power rarely equalled in any of the lyrical traditions which influenced it.

So much for the poem's rhetorical power. Before I look at its other most original feature, namely its unusual concentration of eighteenth-century themes and allusions, I should like to call to mind its immediate historical context. It was written in the second half of 1785, around the mid-point of the final decade of the *ancien régime*. This was on the whole a propitious time in the history of European culture. There had been no major wars in continental Europe for the last twenty years; Mozart and Haydn, Reynolds and Gainsborough were at the height of their powers; Beaumarchais' *Marriage of Figaro* had just caused a sensation at the Comédie Française; and Part II of Herder's *Ideas on the Philosophy of History*, with its celebration of all the world's peoples, had just been published. There was an atmosphere of expectancy in Europe: the Enlightenment felt that it had come of age, and it was time for its promises to be delivered. Only a year before, Kant had delivered an optimistic answer to the question 'What is Enlightenment?', predicting a further enlargement of those human liberties which enlightened rulers like Frederick the Great had inaugurated. There were, it is true, some

---

20 See Günter Schulz, 'Furcht, Freude, Enthusiasmus. Zwei unbekannte philosophische Entwürfe Schillers', *Jahrbuch der Deutschen Schillergesellschaft*, 1 (1957), 103 and 113–19.

21 Cf. Hans H. Schulte, *'Werke der Begeisterung'. Friedrich Schiller—Idee und Eigenart seines Schaffens* (Bonn: Bouvier, 1980), p. 271.

clouds on the horizon: the affair of the necklace was about to cause serious disquiet in France; and in Germany, the Bavarian government had already begun to suppress the secret society of Illuminati, which represented the radical wing of the *Aufklärung*. But enlightened rulers still sat on the thrones of Prussia, Austria, and Russia, and no one could yet foresee the chaos that would engulf the continent a few years later. Schiller, who shared the prevailing mood of optimism, was already at work on *Don Carlos*, with its stirring appeal for political freedom. This same mood of hope and self-confidence pervades the 'Ode to Joy', which embodies a set of metaphysical and ethical principles derived from the popular philosophy of the time—principles which Schiller expounds more fully in his *Philosophical Letters*, a work which he published only a few months after the poem.

The metaphysics of both works is essentially that of Leibniz, as expounded in his *Théodicée* and other related writings.[22] The continuous chain of being extends, as Schiller puts it, from the worm to the cherub. Evil and suffering do exist, but they are only a subordinate part of the best of possible worlds, and with time and human effort, they can be further reduced, if not wholly eliminated. Although Leibniz himself did not presume to do so, some proponents of his optimism in the later eighteenth century, such as the Berlin theologian Johann August Eberhard, had proceeded to reject the doctrine of eternal punishment, and hence the eternity of hell itself.[23] Schiller appears to endorse Eberhard's position in the last verse of his poem with the lines 'Every sin shall be forgiven,/Hell itself shall cease to be.' It was this same metaphysical optimism which made it impossible for Goethe's Faust, like Lessing's Faust before him,[24] to end his career in eternal damnation.

When we try, however, to discover why Schiller came to regard joy not simply as a human emotion but as a metaphysical principle of cosmic significance, no easy answer presents itself. In his *Philosophical Letters*, it is love (*Liebe*) rather than joy (*Freude*) which links all beings together—a

---

22   Cf. SW V, 357 and editors' commentary in ibid., pp. 1094 and 1098.

23   In his *Neue Apologie des Sokrates oder Untersuchung der Lehre von der Seligkeit der Heiden*, 2 vols (Berlin: Nicolai, 1772–78); cf. Lessing's riposte to this work in his essay 'Leibniz von den ewigen Strafen', in Lessing, *Sämtliche Schriften* (henceforth LM), ed. by Karl Lachmann and Franz Muncker, 23 vols (Stuttgart: Göschen, 1886–1924), XI, 461–87.

24   Cf. Lessing, LM III, 384–90.

sentiment which is not uncommon in pre-critical German philosophy.[25] It goes back to the Neo-Platonic doctrine of cosmic sympathy, which received a new lease of life in the eighteenth century when the success of Newton's theory of gravity as a unitary explanation of the physical universe encouraged philosophers to look for a parallel principle in the moral world. We know that Schiller encountered such ideas in Adam Ferguson's *Institutes of Moral Philosophy*, which he read in Christian Garve's translation.[26] But even in the *Philosophical Letters*, he endows not just love but also joy with a metaphysical significance, declaring that insight into the harmony and perfection of the natural universe fills us with joy by making us aware of our affinity with the creative spirit which produced it.[27] As such, 'Freude' appears as an emotionally heightened, ecstatic form of love, which is itself described as a joyful emotion in others of Schiller's early works.[28]

The older literature on Schiller often maintains, however, that the concept of 'Freude' as encountered in the many poems on joy from Hagedorn to Schiller is derived from, and a virtual synonym for, Shaftesbury's concept of 'enthusiasm' as defined in his *Letter Concerning Enthusiasm* of 1708.[29] It is true that Shaftesbury's work was well received in Germany from an early date,[30] and that the term 'Enthusiasmus' is often used in the *Sturm und Drang* period in that positive sense of creative enthusiasm associated with Shaftesbury.[31] But it is hard to believe that the term 'Freude' had the same semantic content as 'Enthusiasmus' for Schiller and the other poets who sang its praises, not least because the word 'Enthusiasmus' continues to be used as a separate term alongside

---

25   For further details, see Wolfgang Riedel, *Die Anthropologie des jungen Schiller* (Würzburg: Königshausen & Neumann, 1985), pp. 182–98.

26   See David Pugh, *Dialectic of Love. Platonism in Schiller's Aesthetics* (Montreal, QC: Queen's-McGill University Press, 1996), pp. 173–76.

27   SW V, 344f.

28   See, for example, the poem 'Die Freundschaft' (1782), in SW I, 91ff., with its reference to the 'ewgen Jubelbund der Liebe' and its 'freudemutig' enthusiasm.

29   See, for example, Schulz, 'Die Göttin Freude', pp. 7 and 31f.; also Ernst Cassirer, 'Schiller und Shaftesbury', *Publications of the English Goethe Society*, 11 (1935), 35–59 (p. 52).

30   See, for example, Leibniz's favourable reception of Shaftesbury in Leibniz, *Philosophische Schriften*, ed. by C. I. Gerhardt, 7 vols (Berlin: Weidmann:, 1875–90), III, 424f.

31   Cf. Schulte, *'Werke der Begeisterung'*, passim and ibid., 'Zur Geschichte des Enthusiasmus', *Publications of the English Goethe Society*, 39 (1969), 85–122.

'Freude'[32] and hardly ever appears in poetry itself. Schiller's debt to the popular philosophy of his age is still underexplored,[33] and I do not propose to explore it further here. But it does strike me as significant that, as one critic has pointed out,[34] there is no evidence that Schiller encountered any of Shaftesbury's works before his move to Weimar in 1787. Besides, the term 'Freude' had already acquired philosophical and even metaphysical significance before anyone had heard of Shaftesbury in Germany—not least in the writings of Leibniz, who uses it in one of the few works he wrote in German to denote that sentiment which arises out of insight into the divine wisdom of creation, and which itself promotes increased perfection, in this world and the next, among those who experience it.[35] I am not suggesting here that Schiller knew this work by Leibniz, which in fact remained unpublished until after Schiller's death.[36] I am merely arguing that, by the beginning of the eighteenth century, the term 'Freude' already carried sufficient philosophical weight to account for its subsequent prominence in reflective poetry from Hagedorn onwards.

The apex of Schiller's metaphysical universe is, of course, the divine being above the stars. It is not difficult to identify this being with the God of Christianity, for the poem is full of Biblical references, from the cherub who stands before God to the choir of angels, the seraph, and above all the 'judge above' or the judge at the end of the poem who passes judgement on the dead or resurrected. On the other hand, the poem begins with an address to joy as a goddess or 'spark immortal' and a daughter of Elysium, the pagan equivalent of heaven. This mingling of Christian and pagan mythology is not uncommon in post-Renaissance poetry, but by Schiller's time, it is often a sign that *all* the references in question are merely symbolic expressions of basically secular beliefs and values. For in the first place, the god of the 'Ode to Joy' is the god

---

32   See, for example, SW V, 344 and 350.
33   Cf. Wolfgang Riedel's comments in *Schiller-Handbuch*, pp. 155f.
34   Ibid., p. 164.
35   Leibniz, 'Von der Glückseligkeit', in *Philosophische Schriften*, ed. by Hans-Heinz Holz and other hands, 4 vols in 6 (Frankfurt a. M.: Insel: 1965–92), I, 391–401 (p. 396).'it follows from this that, the more one understands the beauty and order of God's works, the more one enjoys delight and joy, and of such a kind that one becomes oneself more enlightened and perfect and, by means of the present joy, secures the joy of the future too.'
36   See the editor's comments in Leibniz, *Philosophische Schriften*, I, 389f.

of the astronomers, of natural religion, the supreme being of the deists and Freemasons. Secondly, the references to resurrection and judgement are there merely to furnish a traditional underpinning for that belief in human immortality and the rectification of injustice in the afterlife to which most of the *Aufklärer*, including Kant, still clung—if only as a sheet anchor for morality, as a 'hope for those who lie on deathbeds', as Schiller puts it, and a bulwark against despair: 'Up above the starry vault/You'll find a great God's recompense.'[37] And the third, and most important article of natural religion is also present: the freedom of the human will to choose between good and evil. In short, this poem is a small part of that great endeavour in late eighteenth- and early nineteenth-century Germany to translate the human and moral substance of Christianity into a new and secular idiom which was to become that of German idealism, simultaneously conserving that substance, raising it up, and superseding it in all three senses which Hegel packs into the German verb *aufheben*.

But the most important part of Schiller's natural religion, in common with that of Kant, is its ethical content. The drinking ritual at the end of the poem is not, as some critics have argued,[38] an incongruous intrusion. It is a secular ceremony, akin to a Masonic gathering, in celebration above all of ethical values, which are an essential part of the young Schiller's philosophy of universal love, and the toasts in the last two verses are all in honour of moral virtues. This coupling of joy with moral virtue is, of course, nothing new; it is to be found in all the German poems on joy from Hagedorn onwards, but in Schiller's case, it is derived from the moral philosophy which he absorbed at the Carlsschule from his teacher Abel and from Ferguson's treatise on ethics. The moral philosophy in question goes back to Hutcheson and Shaftesbury, both of whom saw virtue as the product of natural human benevolence;[39] and the pursuit of virtue leads in turn to moral perfection and personal happiness. These ideas, once again derived from the Neo-Platonic tradition, likewise underlie Adam Ferguson's doctrine of 'sympathy', to which Schiller explicitly alludes in the second chorus. In all of these eudaemonistic doctrines, virtue and happiness—which in Schiller's poem is elevated to

---

37   Cf. Pugh, *Dialectic of Love*, pp. 178f.
38   See, for example, Magill, 'Schiller's "An die Freude"', p. 42.
39   Cf. Riedel, *Die Anthropologie des jungen Schiller*, pp. 125 and 131.

its fullest expression in the emotion of joy—are regarded as inseparable:[40] in the happy man (or woman), the purpose of existence, indeed of the whole universe, is fully realised,[41] and in moments of joy, those who experience it feel at one with the whole of creation. As Schiller puts it in his *Philosophical Letters* (with numerous verbal parallels to his poem): 'There are moments in life when we are inclined to press to our bosom every flower and every distant star, every worm and every higher spirit whose existence we sense—an embrace of all of nature as our beloved.'[42]

Predominant among the moral virtues which the poem celebrates is that of friendship. In the mid-eighteenth century, effusive demonstrations of friendship between males, either in a small group or between individuals, is a central feature of the literature of sensibility. The young Schiller's letters and lyric poetry—as in his poem 'Die Freundschaft' of 1782[43]—perpetuate this tradition. In the latter part of the century, however, such friendship is more often expressed in larger groups or formally constituted societies such as the literary 'Hainbund' founded in 1773 in Göttingen.[44] The Freemasons in particular became associated with the ideal of friendship, as in Lessing's Masonic dialogues *Ernst and Falk*,[45] and it was no doubt partly for this reason that Schiller's poem was warmly welcomed in Masonic circles.[46] The liberal and charitable aims of the Freemasons, as well as the deistic framework within which these aims were pursued, accord very well with Schiller's poem, and especially with the drinking ritual of the last three verses.

---

40 Cf., Schiller's Carlsschule address 'Virtue Considered in its Consequences' in SW V, 280–87 (p. 282).

41 Goethe expresses this same belief in his essay 'Winckelmann' of 1805, in *Goethes Werke*, Hamburg Edition, ed. by Erich Trunz (Hamburg: Wegner, 1948—64), XII, 96–129 (p. 98).

42 SW V, 350.

43 SW I, 91ff.

44 Cf. Schulte, 'Zur Geschichte des Enthusiasmus', p. 104; see also the article 'Freundschaft' in the *Lexikon der Aufklärung*, ed. by Werner Schneiders (Munich: C. H. Beck, 1995), pp. 139–41.

45 On the significance of friendship in this work, see Peter Michelsen, 'Die "wahren Taten" der Freimaurer. Lessings *Ernst und Falk*', in Michelsen, *Der unruhige Bürger. Studien zu Lessing und zur Literatur des 18. Jahrhunderts* (Würzburg: Konigshausen & Neumann, 1990), pp. 137–59 (pp. 157ff.).

46 Cf. Zerboni di Sposetti to Schiller, 14 December 1792, in Schiller, NA XXXIV/, 208. Despite numerous approaches by Freemasons, Schiller resolutely refused to join the order himself; see Deile, *Freimaurerlieder*, pp. 20–30 and Hans-Jürgen Schings, *Die Brüder des Marquis Posa. Schiller und der Geheimbund der Illuminati* (Tübingen: Niemeyer, 1996), pp. 108f.

In a kind of secular equivalent of the Eucharist, the circle of friends pledges its faith in humanity and its potential for constructive moral action. And significantly, the wine they drink is drunk not for anything it represents, but for its physical effects: the young Schiller's morality has no hint of Kantian rigorism about it, for human benevolence springs spontaneously from the psycho-physical harmony of well-adjusted human nature—and alcohol and convivial company can only enhance this process. The ideal of personal friendship is accordingly enlarged, in this poem, to encompass the entire human race[47] in the cosmopolitan spirit of the Enlightenment and of German literary *Humanität*.

It is this wider ethical relevance which gave this poem its popular appeal from the 1780s to recent times. For it celebrates not just individual moral values such as courage, charity, and honesty, but also the political values of liberty, equality, and fraternity—although Schiller does not group these together as a trinity as happened soon afterwards in France. Liberty, as a liberal rather than a revolutionary ideal,[48] is invoked in the lines 'Manly pride in royal presence' (verse eight) and especially 'Rescue from the chains of tyrants' (verse nine). In the nineteenth century, Schiller was regularly hailed as a champion of freedom, whether of the nation (as in *Wilhelm Tell*) or of the self-determining individual (as in the tragedies and later philosophical writings). This even gave rise, in the case of the 'Ode to Joy', to the myth that his original title for the poem was 'An die Freiheit' ('Ode to Freedom'), later changed by the censor to 'An die Freude'.[49] In the euphoria of 1989 in Berlin, Leonard Bernstein actually conducted a performance of Beethoven's Ninth Symphony in which the word 'Freiheit' replaced 'Freude' throughout the choral section.[50] This inspired one misguided Germanist[51] to revive the myth of the censor's intervention, an absurd claim which ignores not only the long tradition of earlier poems on the theme of 'Freude' but also the fact that Schiller himself explicitly gives the poem its present title in the covering letter

---

47 Cf. T. J. Reed in the *Schiller-Handbuch*, p. 13.
48 Cf. Rudolf Dau, 'Friedrich Schillers Hymne "An die Freude". Zu einigen Problemen ihrer Interpretation und aktuellen Rezeption', *Weimarer Beiträge*, 24 (1978), Heft 10, 38–60 (pp. 43 and 50).
49 See Gottfried Martin, 'Freude Freiheit Götterfunken. Über Schillers Schwierigkeiten beim Schreiben von Freiheit', *Cahiers d'Études Germaniques*, 18 (1990), 9–18 (9f.); cf. Eichhorn, *Beethovens Neunte Symphonie*, pp. 320f.
50 *Schiller-Handbuch*, p. 181; also Martin, 'Freude Freiheit Götterfunken', p. 9.
51 Martin, ibid..

with which he sent it to his publisher in 1785.[52] Nevertheless, political liberty does appear in the list of ethical ideals celebrated in the poem, especially in the final verse, which Schiller deleted after events in France had invested it with unintended revolutionary overtones.[53]

Social and political equality are likewise commended in the poem. In the second half of the first verse, Schiller praises the power of joy to efface those distinctions which the divisive force of class conventions ('the sword of custom')[54] imposes: 'Beggars become princes' brothers,/ Where your gentle wings alight'. Here again, he took fright after the French Revolution, and the second version of the poem removes both the hint of violence in 'the sword of custom' and the suggestion of social and political upheaval implicit in the reference to beggars by recasting the lines in question as follows:

> Your magic spells have reunited,
> What strict custom split apart;
> Every man becomes a brother,
> Where your gentle wings alight.

But it is the last, and most neglected,[55] of the three aspirations of the revolutionary era—namely fraternity—which is by far the most prominent in Schiller's poem in both its versions. The word 'brother' occurs no fewer than eight times, both in the sense of personal friendship as pledged in the German ceremony of 'drinking brotherhood' and in that of universal brotherhood as the supreme ideal of the Enlightenment. In the first of these senses, Schiller's references to brotherhood reflect that ideal of personal friendship which runs through the literature of sensibility in Germany; such friendship defines itself in those years as a middle-class virtue, as the opposite of aristocratic insincerity and courtly intrigue,[56] an opposition which is hinted at in verse eight of the poem

---

52 Schiller to Göschen, 29 November 1785, in Schiller, NA XXIV, 29.
53 Cf. Schiller's circumstantial condemnation of the French Revolution in his conversation of 1793–94 with Friedrich Wilhelm von Hoven, in Schiller, NA XLII, 179.
54 On the political significance of the term 'Mode' (custom), see Hans Mayer, 'Neunte Symphonie and Song of Joy', in Mayer, *Ein Denkmal fur Johannes Brahms. Versuche über Musik und Literatur* (Frankfurt a. M.: Suhrkamp, 1983), pp. 28–39 (pp. 28ff.).
55 See the article 'Fraternity' in *The Blackwell Companion to the Enlightenment*, ed. by John W. Yolton and other hands (Oxford: Blackwell, 1991), pp. 173f.
56 See the article 'Freundschaft' in the *Lexikon der Aufklärung*, ed. Schneiders, p. 140; also the article 'Friendship' in the *Encyclopedia of the Enlightenment*, ed. by Alan

('Manly pride in royal presence/ [...] Downfall to the lying brood!'). In its second, universal sense, the ideal of fraternity as human brotherhood pervades the entire poem, and the principal function of God as 'a loving father' is to provide a head for the fraternal family of mankind (and, in a cosmic sense, of all created beings).[57] Although this family exists as yet only as an ideal, it may one day be realised in practice ('Suffer bravely, all ye millions!/Suffer for a better world!'). In short, the poem embodies the basic political as well as moral ideals of the Enlightenment; but they are formulated in such general terms that no specific political programme can be abstracted from them.

The critical reception of the poem has not been helped by the fact that Schiller himself, in 1800, condemned it in no uncertain terms. As he wrote to Körner:[58]

> [The Ode to] *Joy* [...] is also thoroughly faulty, according to my present taste, and even if it does recommend itself by a certain emotional fire, it is nevertheless a bad poem and signifies a stage of education which I certainly had to leave behind me in order to accomplish anything worthwhile. But because it appealed to the defective taste of its time, it received the honour of becoming something of a folksong. Your liking for this poem may be based on the period of its origin; but this also lends it the only value it has, and it has it only for *us*, and not for the world or for the art of poetry.

In other words, its only value is personal and particular, as a reminder of a moment of happiness shared by Schiller, Körner, and their circle. Schiller had several reasons for dismissing the poem in this way. I have already mentioned his unease over certain lines which, after 1789, might be construed in a revolutionary sense. It is also possible that the references to hell, resurrection, etc. in the final verse which he deleted in the second edition sounded too exclusively Christian for his liking in later years. And the eudaemonistic ethics of cosmic sympathy alluded to throughout the poem must have struck him as naive and old-fashioned after his studies of Kant's moral philosophy in the early 1790s.[59] But

---

Charles Kors, 4 vols (Oxford: Oxford University Press, 2003), II, 91–96.

57   Cf. Schiller's remarks on the family of mankind in his address 'Virtue Considered in its Consequences' (1780), in SW V 283; also Riedel, *Die Anthropologie des jungen Schiller*, p. 177.

58   See note 3 above; cf. also Körner's reply defending the poem, in Schiller, NA XXXVIII/1, 393.

59   Cf. the editor's comments in Schiller, FA I, 1039.

above all, he rejected the poem for aesthetic reasons. Its popular tone and direct appeal to the emotions reminded him of the popular ballads and Masonic songs which he now openly despised;[60] and in describing the work as a *Volkslied*, he was implicitly putting it in the same class as the poems of Gottfried August Bürger, with their down-to-earth echoes of the folksong, which he condemned in his scathing review of the latter's works in 1791[61]—a review whose harshness owes as much to his disapproval of his own early poetry as to his distaste for that of Bürger. His classical aesthetics of the 1790s demanded reflective distance, refinement, and emotional restraint in poetry, and the 'Ode to Joy' now appeared far too immediate, homespun, and effusive for his liking.

The faults which Schiller found in it—its popular idiom, lack of refinement, and autobiographical origins—are not necessarily faults by today's standards. But even today, it is difficult not to find deficiencies in the poem. It lacks that combination of simplicity and originality which we admire in Goethe's lyric, and it has none of the complexity and multiplicity of meaning we associate with Hölderlin or Rilke. Its idealistic optimism and rhetorical enthusiasm are alien to our age, and for historical reasons, they are viewed with particular suspicion in Germany. As already mentioned, it also draws heavily on earlier poems, both in theme and in expression: many of its pronouncements are commonplaces, or even clichés.[62] It is full of incongruous images and allusions, and has been described by one critic as a confused 'jumble of pietist emotion, *Sturm und Drang* ranting and *Aufklärung* lore'.[63] Yet it does have a dynamic coherence, as I have tried to show: but its organising principle is not so much logical as cumulative and climactic, as its joyful exuberance expands outwards and upwards to embrace an ever wider range of experience, and as its tempo accelerates with a concluding series of one-line acclamations. This cumulative character, this richness of reference, inevitably generates incongruities, but it is at the same time one of the poem's greatest strengths—even by Schiller's

---

60   See, for example, Schiller's letters to Goethe, 24 May 1803, to Körner, 10 June 1803, and to Wilhelm von Humboldt, 18 August 1803, in NA XXXII, 42, 45, and 63.

61   SW V, 970–85.

62   Cf. Dyck, *Die Gedichte Schillers*, p. 10; also ibid., 'Klischee und Originalität in Schillers Gedichtsprache', in *Tradition und Ursprünglichkeit. Akten des III. Internationalen Germanisten-Kongresses 1965 in Amsterdam*, ed. by Werner Kohlschmidt and Herman Meyer (Berne and Munich: Francke, 1966), pp. 178f.

63   Magill, 'Schiller's "An die Freude"', p. 42.

own classical standards. For in that same review in which he condemns Bürger's poems, he defines the task of poetry as follows: 'It ought to collect together the manners, character, and entire wisdom of its age in its mirror, and create, with its idealising art, a model, refined and ennobled, for its century from the century itself.'[64]

The 'Ode to Joy' fulfils the spirit of this requirement more completely than any other German lyric poem of the half-century from 1740 to 1790 that I know. It is a microcosm and summation of the culture and aspirations of the German Enlightenment, from sensibility and Anacreontic frivolity to the *Sturm und Drang* and Gothic revival, from Leibnizian metaphysics to Hutchesonian moral sense, from *Aufklärung* didacticism and Newtonian astronomy to Klopstockian fervour and pietistic devotion, from the literature of travel to the cosmopolitan secret societies and the declarations of the rights of man. Its incongruities are those of the age and culture which produced it. But when Schiller defined the task of poetry in 1791, he was aware that the age which he now called on poetry to represent was no longer the age he had known in 1785: the political revolution in France and the intellectual revolution of the critical philosophy had generated new problems and new attitudes which called for a new poetic currency, even if popular poetry continued to employ the old one.

I therefore conclude that the historical importance of Schiller's 'Ode to Joy' is greater than its critics, from Schiller himself onwards, have generally acknowledged. As for its relevance today, such life as it still possesses it owes almost entirely to Beethoven's setting of 1824. Beethoven knew and loved the poem from his years in Bonn onwards, and he planned to set it to music as early as 1793.[65] Several attempts remained fragments or no longer survive, and when he finally composed his choral symphony, the text he had before him was Schiller's second version, which ends rather lamely in the middle of the drinking ritual at the end of the eighth chorus. The poem was, of course, still too long for Beethoven's purposes, and he retained only those parts—namely the first three verses and the choruses to verses one, three, and four—which he considered most important. He also changed their order by grouping

---

64 SW V, 971.
65 See the *Schiller-Handbuch*, p. 179; Magill, 'Schiller's "An die Freude"', p. 39; and Eichhorn, *Beethovens Neunte Symphonie*, p. 225.

the verses together as a separate body, followed by the choruses as a second group including two repeats of the first verse.[66] The effect of this change was to accentuate Schiller's polarity between the earthly hierarchy, united in joy, and the mighty creator of the universe before whom the millions prostrate themselves—in short, to accentuate that contrast of height and depth, power and powerlessness, which is inherent in the aesthetic experience of sublimity. Beethoven, who can rarely resist the heroic mode, also brings in the chorus of verse four with its lines 'Run, ye brothers, on your courses/ Joyful, as a conquering hero' as a link between his two main sections, accompanying it with a triumphant march (marked *alla marcia*) as humanity proceeds towards its goal of joyful brotherhood.[67] The concluding repeat of the first verse and its chorus rounds off Beethoven's text as a more tightly unified entity than Schiller's longer, enumerative poem, and the penultimate line of the first verse in its revised form, 'Every man becomes a brother', re-emphasises the ideal of human brotherhood. It is this central ideal of the Enlightenment, and its sublime representation in Schiller's poem, that inspired the last movement of Beethoven's symphony.

To do justice to Beethoven's setting would require more space and greater competence than I can lay claim to. I shall simply conclude with a few comments on the reception of Schiller's text in Beethoven's setting and its residual significance today. In the years immediately before and after the revolution of 1848, the choral symphony was acclaimed by various liberal and radical voices, from Bruno Bauer to the young Richard Wagner.[68] Surprisingly, it already possessed that strong association with the cause of liberty which it has never entirely lost,[69] despite the fact that Schiller's overt allusions to liberty occur only in those verses of the poem which Beethoven left out. The symphony was adopted by socialist groups in the early decades of the twentieth century as an anthem of proletarian solidarity, and was regularly performed by workers' choirs in the 1920s.[70] In more recent times, its theme of fraternity has usually—and with more justification—been interpreted in terms of international rather than proletarian co-operation ('Let *all the world*

---

66   For a detailed account, see Eichhorn, pp. 230–35.
67   Ibid., p. 271.
68   Ibid., pp. 307–12.
69   Cf. Martin's flawed attempt to renew this connection (note 48 above).
70   Eichhorn, *Beethovens Neunte Symphonie*, pp, 296 and 320–26.

receive this kiss'); and Beethoven's melody, with—and increasingly often without—Schiller's text, has been adopted at various times as an anthem by the Council of Europe, by NATO, by the Olympic team of the two Germanies in the 1950s and 60s, and as the preferred choice of a sizeable minority of Germans in 1990 for a new national anthem.[71] Some of these associations are distinctly odd: universal brotherhood is not the most obvious aspiration of a military alliance, and the 'Ode to Joy' is not perhaps the most suitable anthem for the European Union, at least at the present moment—hence, no doubt, the current preference for instrumental renderings of Beethoven's melody. But at a more fundamental level, this preference is probably motivated by a distrust of words and concepts which have become hackneyed by overuse and tainted by misuse. More disquietingly, indifference towards them can easily be bred once the ideals they represent—freedom from oppression, equality before the law, and international co-operation—have become realities, at least for the fortunate majority in the western world, or when they are enforced by the deadening discipline of political correctness, which devalues common sense and inhibits spontaneity. These ideals soon recover their life and emotional content, of course, when they are seriously challenged, or when they are rescued from grave danger, as happened at the fall of the Berlin Wall in 1989 and the liberation of Kosovo in 1999. But fortunately, there is another alternative: we can at any time re-experience something of their original power by enjoying the major works of art which they inspired, such as Beethoven's Ninth Symphony—and also perhaps, with a little more effort of the historical imagination, the poem which inspired Beethoven to write it.

---

71   See *Schiller-Handbuch*, p. 181 and Eichhorn, *Beethovens Neunte Symphonie*, pp. 296f.

'Laocoon and his sons', also known as 'the Laocoon Group'. Marble, copy after an Hellenistic original from ca. 200 BC. Found in the Baths of Trajan in 1506. Museo Pio Clementino, Octagon, Laocoon Hall, Vatican Museums. Photograph by Marie-Lan Nguyen (2009), Wikimedia, Public Domain, https://upload.wikimedia.org/wikipedia/commons/1/17/Laocoon_Pio-Clementino_Inv1059-1064-1067.jpg

11. Laocoon in Germany:
The Reception of the Group since Winckelmann[1]

The Laocoon group in the Vatican, reputedly the work of the three Rhodian sculptors Hagesandros, Athanodorus, and Polydorus, is one of the most famous sculptures to have come down to us from antiquity. It depicts the Trojan priest Laocoon and his sons being bitten and strangled to death by two enormous serpents. There are various versions of the legend, but the most familiar is that of Virgil, who, in the *Aeneid*, Book II, describes Laocoon's fearful death as a punishment imposed on him by Minerva, the protectress of the Greeks, for his temerity in warning his fellow Trojans against bringing the Wooden Horse into Troy. Since its discovery in a vault on the Esquiline Hill in Rome on 14 January 1506, the Laocoon group has been the subject of controversy, probably more so than any other ancient sculpture.[2] But it was in Germany, between the middle of the eighteenth and the first decades of the nineteenth century, that the controversy reached its height. After Winckelmann, in

---

1 An earlier version of this chapter was originally published as 'Laocoon in Germany. The Reception of the Group since Winckelmann', in *Oxford German Studies*, 10 (1979), 22–63.

2 On the Laocoon debate in general, see Margarete Bieber, *Laocoon. The Influence of the Group since its Rediscovery*, rev. edn (Detroit, MI: Wayne State University Press, 1967); Hellmut Sichtermann, *Laokoon*, Werkmonographien zur bildenden Kunst, 101 (Stuttgart: Reclam, 1964); Horst Althaus, *Laokoon. Stoff und Form* (Berne: Francke, 1968); William Guild Howard, *Laokoon. Lessing, Herder, Goethe. Selections* (New York, NY: Henry Holt & Co., 1910); and Carl Justi, *Winckelmann und seine Zeitgenossen*, 3rd edn, 3 vols (Leipzig: F. C. W. Vogel, 1923), I, 474–98. I have not attempted to discuss all the German writers who took part in the debate after 1800; other contributions, mainly by art historians of the nineteenth century, are listed in Hugo Blümner's edition of *Lessings Laokoon*, 2nd edn (Berlin: Weidmann, 1880), pp. 722–74.

   https://doi.org/10.11647/OBP.0180.11

1755, proclaimed it an exemplary instance of that Greek beauty which he urged his contemporaries to emulate, it played a central part in the rise of the neo-classical movement; and for over fifty years, many of the foremost intellects in Germany contributed to the debate over its significance and its relationship to their own aesthetic and philosophical principles. Perhaps the most remarkable feature of the controversy is the diversity of opinion which the statue generated. Indeed, it is not too much to say that, during this period, it became a touchstone of taste. But in one respect, nearly all the participants were united: they regarded this sculpture as of paradigmatic value in art and aesthetic theory, and they spoke of it with reverence.

The object of this essay is not to provide a history of the neo-classical movement in Germany, a subject that has been amply treated in the past.[3] Its aim is rather, by examining salient points in the reception of a particular work of art, to furnish a more concentrated, if more limited, perspective on some of the changes in attitude towards art and life which took place during the age of Goethe and its aftermath. I should add that I have chosen the Laocoon group rather than any other work not merely because so much was written about it at that time. It has for long struck me as strange that so drastic a spectacle as the group affords should have fascinated so rational an age as the eighteenth century, and that it was able to captivate such devotees of classical beauty and serenity as Winckelmann and the older Goethe. None of the explanations hitherto advanced for this phenomenon has impressed me as satisfactory, and it may be that, if we can discover why so many leading minds responded to the work's challenge, we stand to learn something significant about their attitudes and the times they lived in, and perhaps also about the statue itself. Such problems as to when precisely the statue originated, and which version of the Laocoon myth it represents—problems about which art historians and archaeologists have continued to argue[4]—I

---

3   See, for example, Walther Rehm, *Griechentum und Goethezeit* (Leipzig: Dieterichsche Verlagsbuchhandlung, 1936); the same author's *Götterstille und Göttertrauer* (Berne: Francke, 1951); E. M. Butler, *The Tyranny of Greece over Germany* (Cambridge: Cambridge University Press, 1935); and H. C. Hatfield, *Winckelmann and his German Critics* (New York, NY: King's Crow Press, 1943).

4   On various stages of the debate see Gisela M. A. Richter, *The Sculpture and Sculptors of the Greeks*, 4th edn (New Haven, CT and London: Yale University Press, 1970), pp. 237ff.; Bieber, *Laocoon*, pp. 37–41; A. F. Stewart, 'To Entertain an Emperor. Sperlonga, Laokoon and Tiberius at the Dinner Table', *Journal of Roman Studies*, 76 (1977) 76–94.

shall mention only in so far as they impinge upon the interpretations of the group by the writers in question.

The Laocoon debate in Germany begins with Winckelmann's essay 'Thoughts on the Imitation of the Greek Works in Painting and Sculpture' of 1755. It was this short essay, more than Winckelmann's later *History of the Art of Antiquity*, which caught the imagination of his contemporaries, and expressed most strikingly his vision of the ancient Greeks as a happy and ideal race whose sculptures embodied consummate beauty, a beauty to which artists of every period should look as an unsurpassed model. The first such masterpiece which Winckelmann mentions, and the main example of the qualities he admires, is the Laocoon group. The group remains today what it was in antiquity, he says, 'a perfect rule of art'.[5] And in his celebrated lines on the excellence of the ancient statues, it is again the Laocoon which serves as his example:[6]

> Finally, the universal and predominant characteristic of the Greek masterpieces is a noble simplicity and quiet greatness, both in posture and expression. Just as the depths of the sea remain forever calm, however much the surface may rage, so does the expression of the Greek figures, however strong their passions, reveal a great and dignified soul. Such a soul is depicted in the face of Laocoon, and not only in his face, despite his most violent torments. The pain which is evident in his every muscle and sinew, and which, disregarding his face and other parts of his body, we can almost feel ourselves simply by looking at his painfully contracted abdomen—this pain, I maintain, nevertheless causes no violent distortion to his face or to his general posture. He raises no terrible clamour, as in Virgil's poetic account of his fate. His mouth is not wide enough open to allow this, and he emits instead an anxious and oppressed sigh [...]. The physical pain and spiritual greatness are diffused with equal intensity throughout his entire frame, and held, as it were, in balance. Laocoon suffers, but he suffers like the Philoctetes of Sophocles: his misery touches us to the heart, but we envy the fortitude with which this great man endures it.

'A noble simplicity and quiet greatness'—these are the qualities which Winckelmann glorifies in the statues of the Greeks and which became

---

5   Johann Joachim Winckelmann, *Sämtliche Werke* (subsequent references to this edition are identified by the abbreviation WW), ed. by Joseph Eiselein, 12 vols (Donaueschingen: Verlag Deutscher Klassiker, 1825–29), I, 9.

6   WW I, 30f.

the ideals of the neo-classical movement in Germany. He holds them up in opposition to the Baroque art of the preceding century with its movement, passion, and extravagance—the art of Bernini, whom he explicitly attacks in the essay.[7] For the state in which 'noble simplicity and quiet greatness' are seen to their best advantage is not that of motion, but of rest.

On the face of it, the Laocoon group is scarcely the most obvious instance Winckelmann could have chosen to demonstrate his thesis. Numerous other Greek sculptures were known, even then, which display the simplicity and tranquillity he admires in a far higher degree than the complex and contorted Laocoon—the Belvedere Apollo, for example, to which he refers briefly, or the so-called Antinous, both of which Hogarth had praised two years before as models of classical perfection.[8] As one critic remarks, 'why he should have chosen this particular group as an example of the very qualities it lacks, is no easy question to answer'.[9]

It is simply not enough to say, as some scholars have done, that the Laocoon group seemed moderate to Winckelmann in comparison with the excesses of Bernini, Puget, Falconet, and other sculptors of the Baroque and Rococo eras.[10] This may well be true, but it does not alter the fact that more moderate examples still were available, to which the terms Winckelmann uses would have been much more appropriate. And as for E. M. Butler's explanation that, 'dazzled by a flash of a great revelation', Winckelmann 'was in fact in a trance; and like many another clairvoyant, he was uttering truths which did not apply to the object before him, but were associated with it in his mind', this does not answer the problem at all, but simply evades it. By such reasoning, Winckelmann might just as well have chosen one of the ecstatic figures of Bernini as his example.

The true explanation is that Winckelmann had *no choice* but to show that his thesis applied to the Laocoon; and the reason for this lies in the work's earlier reception. For it was realised, from the moment of its discovery in 1506, that this was the very work which Pliny, in his

---

7   WW I, 20.

8   William Hogarth, *The Analysis of Beauty* (London: J. Reeves, 1753), pp. 66, 86, 128, etc.

9   Butler, *The Tyranny*, p. 47.

10 See, for example, Justi, *Winckelmann und seine Zeitgenossen*, I, 484 and 496; see also Bieber, *Laocoon*, p. 33.

Natural History, had described as *opus omnibus et picturae et statuariae artis praeponendum* ('the greatest of all works in painting and sculpture');[11] and for the Renaissance, Pliny's judgement was axiomatically valid. When his praise was echoed by Michelangelo, who was present immediately after the discovery, the work's reputation was further enhanced. Not only Michelangelo, however, but Titian, Rubens, and other great artists revered and copied the group,[12] and the verdicts passed upon it down to the time of Winckelmann are one long succession of superlatives. Since it influenced the art of the late Renaissance and Baroque periods directly, its affinity with Baroque sculpture is a very real one—indeed, the period of Greek art from which it dates is often described as 'Hellenistic Baroque'. The artists of the seventeenth century saw in it an example of extreme naturalism and unrestrained emotion,[13] and it is not at all surprising that Bernini himself, no less than his detractor Winckelmann, regarded it as the greatest masterpiece of antiquity.[14]

Given the immense reputation of the Laocoon, Winckelmann had at least to accommodate the work to his thesis, if not to use it as his principal example. To ignore it would have been to lay himself open to immediate refutation. He opted for the bolder alternative, that of undermining his opponents' case from within, and based his argument squarely upon the Laocoon. In order to succeed, however, he had to demonstrate that, for all its Baroque affinities, its greatness lay not in those aspects which Bernini and his successors admired, but in the precise opposite of these. And if he could persuade his readers that this extreme case was indeed characterised by 'noble simplicity and quiet greatness', his thesis would automatically be accepted for almost any other Greek work he cared to name. Just how successful his gamble was is shown by the subsequent history of neo-classicism in Germany.

Winckelmann could not deny the obvious, however. He readily admits that every muscle and sinew of Laocoon is racked by violent torment, and that his body is by no means at rest. But this physical upheaval is counterbalanced (*abgewogen*) by certain qualities of mind which counteract the pain and reduce its expression to the minimum

---

11   Pliny, *Natural History*, XXXVI, 37.
12   Bieber, *Laocoon*, pp. 18f.
13   Bieber, *Laocoon*, p. 12.
14   See Max Pohlenz, 'Laokoon', in *Die Antike*, 9 (1953), 54.

consistent with the priest's predicament. This is the sense of his famous metaphor of the sea, so often repeated by later writers: what really matters is not the visible surface of the water, which may rage and boil as it will, but the unseen depths, which are forever calm. Not the superficial appearance of the group, but its spiritual significance, is what counts, and by implication, the Baroque artists who venerated the group were themselves of a superficial turn of mind. In short, the qualities which Winckelmann detects are moral rather than aesthetic, and the only tangible evidence he adduces for them is the fact that Laocoon does not cry out, and therefore appears to restrain his emotions. His argument transcends those of his adversaries because it accommodates their case, along with his own, in a series of antitheses: motion and rest, passion and composure, pain and nobility, body and soul, are the co-determinants of the sculpture. And in each case, the second is not only the more important of the two—its connotations are spiritual rather than physical, which makes it a relatively intangible quality.

The triumph of Winckelmann's idealistic aesthetics was made possible, however, not just by his skill in dialectics, but also by the temper of his age, the age of the Enlightenment. By showing that the Laocoon group embodied an idea, a stoical ethos, he succeeded in rationalising a respected but disquieting work. This strongly recommended both his own cult of Hellenism, and the statue itself, to his countrymen. It has rightly been observed that his conception of the Greeks and their moral excellence is of literary, rather than artistic origin, and that he derived it rather from Plato and Sophocles than from the much later products of Hellenistic art.[15] His fondness for allegorical art reflects the same didactic bias.

In his later *History of the Art of Antiquity*, Winckelmann discusses ancient art much more fully and empirically, and the work is rightly regarded as a milestone in art history.[16] But although his analysis of the

---

15 See Hatfield, *Winckelmann and his German Critics*, p. 9. Winckelmann suggests as much himself when he comments in his 'Thoughts on the Imitation': 'The *noble simplicity* and *quiet greatness* of the *Greek statues* is also the true hallmark of the Greek writings of the best periods, the writings of the Socratic school' (WW I, 34).

16 So convinced was Winckelmann, however, that the values he discerned in the Laocoon group were identical with those of the Socratic age that he allowed this belief, rather than archaeological or epigraphical evidence, to determine its date. He placed it as far back in time as possible, in the age of Alexander the Great (WW VI, 16).

Laocoon group is more detailed, he again dwells on Laocoon's facial expression. As in the earlier essay, the physical is significant only in so far as it reflects the spiritual conflict:[17]

> The paternal heart reveals itself in the mournful eyes, and pity seems to swim on them in a dim vapour. His face is plaintive, but not clamorous, and his eyes turn upwards in search of higher help. His mouth is full of sadness, and his depressed lower lip is heavy with it; but in his raised upper lip, it is mixed with pain, which rises with a surge of vexation, as if at an undeserved and unworthy injury, into his nose, making it swell up and revealing itself in the dilated and upturned nostrils. In his lower brow the conflict between pain and resistance, as if united in a *single* point, is fashioned with great wisdom [...].

He does proceed to emphasise the statue's 'beauty' soon afterwards,[18] but comes no nearer than in the previous essay to defining what constitutes it.[19] This passage, in fact, is an exercise in physiognomy rather than objective description, and it was no doubt on such models as this that the physiognomist Lavater, in the 1770s, based his own fanciful interpretations of Greek and Roman countenances.[20]

The success of Winckelmann's arguments began a fateful trend in German criticism of the Laocoon, and indeed of ancient art in general. His visionary approach encouraged his successors to speculate, to read their own ideas into the work, and his concern with its ethical significance and exemplary status as a product of Greek humanity aroused enthusiasms which bore little relation to historical fact. As the archaeologist Heyne ruefully commented in 1779 on Winckelmann's description:[21]

> It is not designed to provide a clear concept and representation of the group: and one must already know this figure precisely and have

---

17   WW VI, 22.
18   WW VI, 23.
19   Cf. Blümner, *Lessings Laokoon*, p. 496: 'For Winckelmann, beauty is a somewhat indefinable substance, of which it is easier to say what it is not than what it is.'
20   See Johann Caspar Lavater, *Physiognomische Fragmente*, 4 vols (Leipzig and Winterthur: Weidmanns Erben und Reich, 1775–78), II, 254–59, 'Helden der Vorzeit'; III, 48–57, 'Ueber griechische Gesichter'; and IV, 169–75, annotated extracts from Winckelmann.
21   Christoph Gottlob Heyne, 'Examination of Some Reports and Assertions on the Belvedere Laocoon', in Heyne, *Sammlung antiquarischer Aufsätze*, 2 vols (Leipzig: Weidmanns Erben und Reich, 1778–79), II, 1–52 (p. 18).

reflected on it before this description can produce its proper effect; otherwise, one risks falling into that state to which so many of our young compatriots succumbed a few years ago, by working themselves up, like the knight of La Mancha, into a transport of enthusiasm lacking in nothing except—a real, or at least a definite object.

To Winckelmann's immediate successor in the Laocoon debate, however, Heyne's strictures do not apply. For Lessing's *Laocoon, or On the Limits of Painting and Poetry* of 1766 is renowned for its precise reasoning, and what Lessing has to say on the beauty of Greek sculpture betrays nothing of Winckelmann's Platonic enthusiasms.

Nevertheless, Lessing does adopt several of Winckelmann's most important premises. Like his predecessor, he regards the Greeks as representatives of an ideal humanity, even if his opinion of them differs in some respects from Winckelmann's; and he agrees with him that the Greek masterpieces provide a standard against which the art of all subsequent ages should be measured. For both writers, the highest beauty is that of the human form, and its supreme expression is found in the sculpture of the Greeks.

Lessing's primary purpose in *Laocoon*, of course, is not to discuss the statue of that name, but to define the respective provinces of poetry and visual art. But in this enterprise, the Laocoon group serves as his main example in the visual arts, to which he contrasts Homer, and to a lesser extent Virgil, as his criteria in poetry. In placing the statue on a level with the greatest epics of antiquity, he implicitly acknowledges Winckelmann's opinion of its merit. Indeed, the first works of art which the latter had named, in conjunction, in his essay of 1755, were the Laocoon group and the epics of Homer, and in his central passage on the group (already quoted above), the statue was compared with Virgil's rendering of the Laocoon episode in the *Aeneid*. Lessing, then, respected Winckelmann as the foremost German authority on ancient art, and in choosing the title *Laocoon* for his treatise, he is both complimenting Winckelmann and endorsing his admiration of the statue.

Immediately after his preface, Lessing opens his treatise with Winckelmann's words on the Laocoon group as an example of 'noble simplicity and quiet greatness'.[22] Winckelmann, it will be remembered,

---

22   Gotthold Ephraim Lessing, *Sämtliche Schriften* (subsequent references to this edition are identified by the abbreviation of the editors' initials LM), ed. by Karl Lachmann and Franz Muncker, 23 vols (Stuttgart, Leipzig and Berlin: Göschen, 1886–1924), IX, 6.

paid much attention to Laocoon's face and had relatively little to say about the group as a whole. This followed from his interpretation of Laocoon as a paragon of fortitude, for which his face, more than his stricken body and struggling sons, furnished the main evidence. Lessing, however, is more specific still: the one feature which he stresses throughout the first thirty pages of his work is Laocoon's mouth, and the fact that it is not wide open as if to emit a cry, despite his obvious anguish, but half closed, as if he were merely sighing. Here again, he concurs with Winckelmann—except that he rejects Winckelmann's explanation of the half-closed mouth as a sign of noble simplicity and quiet greatness.

Lessing suggests another reason, or rather two reasons, for Laocoon's apparent restraint; and both of them are aesthetic, rather than ethical, in character. Having cited examples from Homer and Sophocles of Greek heroes who did not hesitate to cry out in pain, he concludes that Laocoon's heroic qualities cannot account for his suppressing his cries: and the first reason he advances is the law of beauty, by which, he argues, all Greek sculpture was governed. He explains this further in the following passage, which contains some of his central observations on the statue:[23]

> The master worked towards the highest beauty, under the given circumstances of bodily pain. This, in all its disfiguring violence, could not be combined with the former. He therefore had to diminish it; he had to reduce crying to sighing; not because crying betrays an ignoble soul, but because it distorts the face in a repellent way. For just imagine Laocoon's mouth forced open, and judge the effect. Let him cry out, and see the result. We had an image which aroused pity, because it combined beauty and pain; now, it has become an ugly and abhorrent image from which one would rather avert one's gaze, because the spectacle of pain arouses displeasure without allowing the beauty of the suffering subject to transform our displeasure into the sweet feeling of pity.
>
> The wide open mouth [...] is a blemish in painting and a hollow in sculpture, which produces the most adverse possible effect.

It could well be argued, however, that Lessing's disagreement with Winckelmann is more apparent than real. For in his *History of the Art of Antiquity* of 1764, Winckelmann had himself declared that the visual artist, unlike the poet, is constrained by the imperative of beauty: 'In

---

23   LM IX, 17.

the representation of the *hero*, the artist is allowed less freedom than the poet [...]. Since the former [...] must choose the most beautiful of beautiful forms, he is confined to a certain degree of expression of the passions which must not have an adverse formal effect.'[24] And the examples he gives of such restraint actually include the Laocoon group. Lessing was undoubtedly aware of this, for he writes in one of the drafts of his *Laocoon*: 'Besides, Winckelmann has supplied more detail on Laocoon's state of rest, and he shares my opinion that beauty was the reason for it'.[25] Despite this, he kept up the fiction that he had first encountered Winckelmann's *History* only after his own treatise was virtually completed,[26] and stuck to his original intention of refuting the argument in Winckelmann's earlier essay of 1755 on Laocoon as a 'great soul'. Various reasons have been given by critics for Lessing's pretended ignorance of the *History*.[27] Perhaps he merely wished to emphasise that he had discovered the law of beauty independently of Winckelmann. Or perhaps there was something about Winckelmann's original moral interpretation which he wished at all costs to oppose.

Whatever the reasons for his subterfuge, the beauty which Lessing discerns in the Laocoon group is much more clearly defined than Winckelmann's, although it is still of a very general nature. As he remarks in one of his drafts, Winckelmann's beauty is a quality which he appears to have abstracted from the works he admired; Lessing, on the other hand, concludes by an *a priori* deduction that it is a necessary property of the visual arts, since they alone can render it: 'For since the visual arts are alone capable of rendering the beauty of form; since they require the help of no other art in order to do so; and since other arts must dispense with it completely; it is surely indisputable that this beauty can be nothing other than their specific task.'[28] Given that his treatise is built upon the antithesis between visual art and poetry, it is very much

---

24 WW IV, 204f.

25 LM XIV, 380.

26 LM IX, 156.

27 See, for example, Elida Maria Szarota, *Lessings Laokoon. Eine Kampfschrift für eine realistische Kunst und Poesie* (Weimar: Arion Verlag, 1959), p. 11. Szarota's reasons are that the Laocoon group is more central to Winckelmann's earlier work, that Lessing wished to keep off technical matters he knew little of, that he wished to avoid a full-scale polemic against the respected Winckelmann, and that he may in any case have preferred Winckelmann's earlier to his later work.

28 LM XIV, 411.

in Lessing's interest to account for Laocoon's facial expression by the nature of the art in question; for Winckelmann's moral argument, which could apply just as well to poetry, blurs the distinction which Lessing wishes to make. Furthermore, the explanation by the law of beauty has the virtue of economy. For although Winckelmann's moral explanation is not necessarily incompatible with the argument from beauty, it is logically superfluous: *principia praeter necessitatem non sunt muliplicanda.* Finally, Winckelmann's concept of beauty is empirically vague as well as logically imprecise, whereas Lessing, who declares that violent passions distort the body and 'the beautiful lines which outline it in a state of rest',[29] has observable, linear properties in mind. And when he says later in his treatise that Virgil's description of the serpents wound repeatedly round Laocoon's neck would destroy 'the pyramidal pointed shape of the group which is so agreeable to the eye',[30] it is obvious that his conception of beauty is close to that of Hogarth, for whom it is associated with serpentine lines and pyramidal figures. Hogarth, whose *Analysis of Beauty* Lessing had reviewed favourably in 1754,[31] had in fact singled out the pyramidal shape of the Laocoon group for special praise.[32]

The second reason which Lessing suggests for Laocoon's failure to cry out is again derived from the nature of the art in question. But although he does not say so, it is very much a secondary reason, for it is valid only for sculptures or paintings which, like the Laocoon group, represent an action in time in such a way as to create an illusion of reality.

Works which represent an action can represent only a single moment within it. This being so, the artist must select the most fruitful or 'pregnant' moment possible—that is, the moment which affords the greatest scope for the imagination, the moment 'from which the preceding and subsequent actions become most intelligible'.[33] And since it is to be given an unnatural permanence in the work of art, it must correspond to a state which is more than fleeting or instantaneous. For these reasons, the moment represented in Laocoon's conflict with the serpents is not the climax of his agony, the final cry before his collapse, but a moment just before it, to which the imagination can readily add

---

29   LM IX, 14.
30   LM IX, 41.
31   LM V, 405–07.
32   Hogarth, *Analysis of Beauty*, p. 21.
33   LM IX, 19f. and 95.

the climax, and in which Laocoon's expression is more compatible with the permanence of statuary than a momentary shriek of pain would be.

Like Winckelmann, Lessing sees the group as governed by two opposing, but balancing principles. Since it depicts an action, it has motion as well as rest, 'expression' as well as beauty. And the expression—in this case, of pain—is tempered both in the interests of beauty, which is the overriding principle in all visual art, and because it must be appropriate to the most suggestive moment in the action depicted.

Lessing's secondary argument concerning the 'pregnant moment', unlike his reflections on beauty, reveals a peculiarity of the group which neither he nor Winckelmann chose to acknowledge—namely that it is a thoroughly untypical sculpture. For it portrays a highly dramatic event which, as Lessing knew,[34] had been the subject of a lost tragedy by Sophocles. This, far more than its abstract, linear beauty, is why it appealed so much to the dramatist Lessing. For him, it is a tragedy *in nuce*, which lends itself admirably to a literary approach. Accordingly, he even proceeds to apply his own neo-Aristotelian theory of tragedy to it. His concept of the 'pregnant moment', which suggests as much as possible of the preceding and succeeding action, and which in the case of Laocoon corresponds to the peripeteia of a tragedy, itself underlines the group's dramatic qualities. And as the first quotation from his *Laocoon* above makes clear, the emotion which the statue arouses is that of pity. Here, perhaps, is the main reason why he decided to attack Winckelmann's original interpretation of Laocoon's restraint as a sign of stoic self-control,[35] and to feign ignorance of his revised interpretation. Like Corneille's theory of tragedy, Winckelmann's picture of Laocoon as a stoic hero and 'great soul' demands admiration, not pity. And admiration is an unproductive emotion which cannot further the cause of human brotherhood:[36]

> Everything stoical is untheatrical; and our pity is always proportionate to the suffering expressed by the object of our interest. If we see him

---

34   See LM IX, 7f.

35   Cf. E. H. Gombrich, 'Lessing. Lecture on a Master Mind', *Proceedings of the British Academy*, 43 (1957), 133–56, who sees Lessing's opposition to Winckelmann as a veiled attack on the Cornelian theory of tragedy with its ideal of nobility as an object of admiration (pp. 143f.).

36   LM IX, 10.

bearing his misery with a great soul, this great soul will indeed arouse our admiration, but admiration is a cold emotion whose inactive amazement excludes every other warmer passion as well as every other clear impression.

That Winckelmann had chosen the Laocoon group as his main example in 1755 was a godsend to Lessing, whose dramatic theory enabled him to rationalise the group even more fully than the law of beauty did. Winckelmann's admiration lacked that 'clear impression' which Lessing was looking for, in visual art as well as in poetry. And the fact that the dramatic qualities which Lessing praised in this particular statue are purely contingent, and absent in countless other sculptures and paintings which must rely on beauty alone for their appeal, is one of the reasons why the visual arts come off so poorly in his treatise in comparison with poetry, which can represent actions much more fully and effectively.[37]

The only other aspect of the group which Lessing discusses in detail is the date of its origin, a question which he treats at considerable length. It is not so much the date itself which interests him, for he is no archaeologist. What interests him is whether the statue is earlier or later than Virgil's *Aeneid*, and whether Virgil's narration of this episode is influenced by the group or vice versa. Although he concedes that the two works may have been created independently, or derived from an earlier common source, he does everything he can to show that the statue is based on Virgil. His principal evidence, which is purely hypothetical, is that Virgil, had he followed the sculptors, would have had no need to diverge from them in the way he does, with Laocoon uttering terrible cries, the serpents wrapped round his body instead of his limbs, etc.; whereas the sculptors, had they followed Virgil, would have been compelled by the nature of their art to make precisely the kind of alterations they appear in fact to have made.[38] But why does Lessing argue at such length in support of a theory to which, as he is aware, there are equally possible alternatives?

He admits, near the beginning of his work, that the first thing which provoked him to disagree with Winckelmann was the latter's

---

37 Gombrich, 'Lessing', p. 140, even declares: 'The more one reads the *Laocoon*, the stronger becomes the impression that it is not so much a book about as against the visual arts.'

38 LM IX, 34–50 and 156–62

condemnation of Virgil for allowing his Laocoon to cry out, instead of controlling his anguish like the Laocoon of the statue.[39] The controversy began, then, as a defence of Virgil against Winckelmann, and of literature against visual art. It could well be that Lessing's determination to establish the primacy of poetry in range of expression led him to argue in turn for its priority in time, and that the more limited he perceived the statue to be in its rendering of a temporal action, the more it came to look like a pale reflection of the poetic version which interested him more profoundly.

Lessing's comments on the Laocoon group, despite his excessively literary approach and circumscribed view of the visual arts, had far-reaching effects. For he is one of those writers who are often just as impressive when they are wrong as when they are right. His arguments on the date of the statue, for example, have the excitement of a detective story, and it is from them that the debate on this question, a debate which continues today, takes it proper beginning. Similarly, his theory of the 'pregnant moment', which applied the criterion of verisimilitude to the sculpture with unprecedented rigour, started another controversy over precisely which moment in Laocoon's death throes the work represents, and inaugurated a fashion for increasingly realistic interpretations of the group. (These, a few decades later, were taken to extremes which Lessing would never have dreamed of.) But the main effect of his comments on the statue, apart from enhancing its already immense prestige, was to reinforce Winckelmann's cult of Greek beauty, while narrowing its already narrow scope still further. The Baroque view of the group was now completely refuted, and the other extreme of a restrained, and in the last resort empty beauty had been reached. No one before or since Lessing has rationalised this strange monument so ruthlessly or completely. With his law of beauty, 'pregnant moment', and tragic pity, Lessing pressed the statue, with its carefully balanced form and expression, into a logical system which fitted it as neatly as the pyramidal box into which Hogarth had said it could be packed. For Lessing, it held no further mystery. Gripped fast by the coils of the serpents and the straitjacket of Lessing's system, Laocoon was bound as firmly as Prometheus. But just as surely, he was to show that he still had life in him, and the struggle he was soon to put up was the greatest

---

39   LM IX, 7.

in his career. The first, tentative stirrings are to be found in the writings of Herder.

Herder mentions the Laocoon group on several occasions. His first extended reference to it is the poem 'Laocoon's Head!', written at some time before he left Riga in 1769.[40] The following extracts should convey its temper:

> O thou, in a great sigh
> soaring heavenwards! drawest from deepest heart's abyss
> the souls of thine on this sigh
> heavenwards up with thee!
>
> The serpent-bound earthly body,
> how venom-swollen it succumbs! [...]
>
> O thou, of the high gods of heaven
> a dumb image of compassion! amid all heavens
> abandoned!—of all poor humanity
> the highest majesty
>
> Of suffering! [...]
>
> And all angels fetched thee in,
> And with open mouth, loud in voice, the angels thee, thy children
> embraced! The serpents' knot
> of fate was shattered [...]
>
> [...] Be, o head, my messenger
> Of the deity!—Image of suffering!—like majesty of pain
> on their soul of other soul
> heavenwards draws and rests!

The spirit of this poem is remote from Lessing's cool deliberations. The style is exclamatory and incoherent—the young Herder cultivates the manner of Klopstock—and the emphasis is on the group's pathos, to which Herder gives a religious slant which is totally absent from Lessing's and Winckelmann's descriptions. Laocoon here appears as an innocent sufferer on the point of death—a victim of cruel fate, or cruel gods, as in the classical myths; yet his passion, like that of Christ, is

---

40 Johann Gottfried Herder, *Sämtliche Werke* (henceforth SW), ed. by Bernhard Suphan, 33 vols (Berlin: Weidmann, 1877–1913), XXIX, 303f. See also the editor's introduction to this volume on the date of the poem.

somehow representative of suffering mankind. His soul, as he expires, is received by angelic embraces. In short, Herder's poem is an incongruous mixture of classical and Christian elements, and its hero is a composite of Prometheus[41] and Christ.

What Herder has done is to isolate and amplify the pathetic side of Winckelmann's description of the statue. His references to Laocoon's 'sigh', which he emphasises nearly every time he mentions the group in his works,[42] and to the effects of the poison, point to Winckelmann's essay of 1755.[43] In his critique of Lessing's *Laocoon* in the first of his *Critical Silvae* of 1769, he in fact cites Winckelmann's description (although he has surprisingly little to say on the statue itself); but significantly, he omits Winckelmann's initial sentences on Greek self-control, and quotes only the passage on Laocoon's suffering.[44] For it is neither the hero's supposed stoicism and restraint, nor the beauty, balance, and symmetry of the group which captivates the young Herder, but its emotional expressiveness. In his poem, Laocoon has become the pretext for a sentimental effusion at a time when literary *Empfindsamkeit* (sensibility) was at its height.

But Herder has discerned something else which Winckelmann was careful not to mention—namely the Christian associations which the group had acquired during the late Renaissance and Baroque eras, when artists had found in it a religious pathos akin to their own.[45] Whether Herder knew it or not, theologians of the Counter-Reformation had commended Laocoon to painters as a model for the passion of Christ and the sufferings of saints and martyrs,[46] and numerous examples of Christian art had been influenced by it: for instance, the figures of Christ and St Sebastian in Titian's altarpiece of the Resurrection in the Church of SS Nazaro e Celso at Brescia reflect the artist's studies of the group,[47]

---

41   See Hatfield, *Winckelmann and his German Critics*, p. 91.

42   See, for example, SW VIII, 20; XVII, 351; XXVIII, 281; etc.

43   Winckelmann, WW I, 32, quotes Bernini's theory that the effects of the venom can be detected in Laocoon's thigh.

44   SW, III, 74.

45   See Bieber, p. 12.

46   See L. D. Ettlinger, 'Exemplum Doloris. Reflections on the Laocoon Group', in *De Artibus Opuscula XL. Essays in Honor of Erwin Panofsky*, ed. by Millard Meiss, 2 vols (New York, NY: New York University Press, 1961), I, 121–26 (p. 136).

47   See Bieber, p. 17; also Harold E. Wethey, *The Paintings of Titian. Complete Edition. I: The Religious Paintings* (London: Phaidon, 1969), p. 127.

as does the Christ in Rubens' 'Elevation of the Cross' in Antwerp Cathedral.[48]

In later discussions of the group, Herder again presents Laocoon in a pathetic light, as an anguished father and innocent martyr.[49] But in his *Letters on Humanity* (*Humanitäts-Briefe*) of 1795, in keeping with his increasingly secular leanings in his later years, Laocoon is cited as an example of 'pure forms of humanity'.[50] On this occasion, Laocoon is explicitly likened to the Christian martyrs, but it is a further sign of Herder's growing secularism that he now regards the statue as *superior* to its Christian counterparts: 'It is scarcely possible to imagine a martyr as purer, more affecting, and at the same time more significantly beautiful in the sphere of art. The serpents disfigure nothing, and in their coils the dumb sigh of the sufferer creates an effect which Sts Sebastian, Laurence, and Bartholomew cannot produce'. In the commentary to his poem 'Pygmalion' of 1801, Herder again stresses the expressive qualities of the group—its movement and its pathos. By this time, however, the Promethean aspect has ousted the Christian associations completely. Laocoon, though close to death, is no longer so passive as before: he rightly resists the punishment of the gods—not in the cause of religion, of course, but of secular morality. He is a 'martyr of patriotism and truth'.[51] For Herder bases his interpretation on Virgil, but unlike Lessing, he considers that Virgil's priest is in no sense a tragic hero. Laocoon's sole offence is that he defended his country, and he dies as the innocent victim of a vengeful deity. By implication, the undeserved fate of this virtuous man is an indictment of the gods. In these last, moralistic observations on the group, Herder is in fact taking issue with Goethe, who interprets the work in purely aesthetic terms and dismisses the legend, with all the awkward questions it raises, as irrelevant (see p. 273 below).

To sum up: with Herder, the reception of the Laocoon group in Germany enters a new phase. In his sentimental poem, the enthusiasm which Winckelmann had aroused becomes divorced from the statue as

---

48   See Wolfgang Stechow, *Rubens and the Classical Tradition* (Cambridge, MA: Harvard University Press, 1968), pp. 22ff.
49   Cf. SW VIII, 20 (1778).
50   SW XVII, 351.
51   SW XXVIII, 280f.; like so many of his contemporaries, Herder now emphasises Laocoon's activity, expressed in his 'posture of *struggling activity*' (Herder's italics).

a work of art, and its emotional potential is cultivated for its own sake. The Christian pathos of the Baroque era is revived, and reinforced by the *Empfindsamkeit* of the 1760s. But along with this emotionalism, another characteristic begins to make itself felt. Herder's Laocoon is the innocent, at first passive, victim of higher powers. But in the commentary of 1801 he is less submissive, and 'seems [...] to dispute with the gods'.[52] He now dies fighting for values he holds dear, and those values are human rather than divine. This new, defiant quality of Laocoon comes truly into its own, however, with Wilhelm Heinse's novel *Ardinghello* of 1787.

A device sometimes employed by those who have offered new interpretations of the sculpture has been to look to other versions of the myth. Winckelmann, Lessing, and Herder, although they were acquainted with other versions, followed that of Virgil, in which Laocoon dies as a valiant patriot who has unwittingly crossed the plans of Minerva. But Heinse, through the mouth of the artist-hero of his novel, turns first to that of the fabulist Hyginus, whose Laocoon is a priest of Apollo, punished for marrying and siring children against the wishes of the god.[53] He at once rejects this version, however, in favour of the more colourful explanation of the grammarian Servius in his commentary to Virgil: 'Servius, however, gives the better explanation and says that it happened *because he* [...] *made love to his wife through incontinence in the temple of Apollo* (p. 239; Heinse's italics).

From this beginning, Heinse constructs a picture of Laocoon as an audacious opportunist who exploited his priestly office to increase his power, and to indulge his carnal pleasures:

> His facial appearance with his fine curly beard is entirely Greek, and felt by a deeply perceptive man on the basis of everyday contact; it expresses an astute individual who respects little other authority than his own advantage and pleasure, and has duly chosen the best position in civil society for this purpose; full of energy and strength of body and soul.

In the statue, we see him punished for his final outrage, perpetrated within sight of the altar; and lest we forget the nature of his offence,

---

52   SW XXVIII, 280.

53   Wilhelm Heinse, *Ardinghello und die glückseligen Inseln*, ed. by Max L. Baeumer (Stuttgart: Reclam, 1975), p. 237. All subsequent references to the novel are to this edition.

Heinse, towards the end of his description, draws attention to the appropriate part of his anatomy (pp. 239f.):

> The whole of Laocoon shows a man who is punished and whom the arm of divine justice has at last reached; he sinks into the night of death under the terrible judgement, and round his lips the recognition of his sins is still visible [...].
>
> Even the genitalia of the father are stretched upwards by the overall tension, with scrotum and member contracted [...].

Heinse's Laocoon dies, then, as a Dionysian criminal and public enemy. But he is neither an object of pity, nor of condemnation. On the contrary, his death is a glorious one, which is described with unconcealed admiration: 'There suffers here a mighty rebel against society and the gods, and one shudders with joyous sorrow at the terrible downfall of this splendid criminal' (p. 240).

It is hard to avoid the impression, however, that Heinse's Laocoon is rebelling not against the majesty of Apollo, but against the moral idealism of Winckelmann.[54] Admittedly, both the statue, as a work of art, and Laocoon, as a man, are just as much objects of admiration for Heinse as they were for Winckelmann. But they are admired for precisely the opposite reasons. The morality of Heinse's priest—if morality it can be called—is one of unscrupulous and sensual egotism. In his coarse vitality and flouting of religion, he is as far removed from Winckelmann's noble stoic as he is from Herder's seraphic martyr, and his apotheosis foreshadows Nietzsche's cult of the powerful and ruthless individual. Similarly, the aesthetic qualities which Heinse celebrates are the reverse of those praised by Winckelmann. The description of the statue, as of many other works of art analysed by the hero of Heinse's novel, serves to illustrate the long dialogues on aesthetics which take up much of the work. And although it is set in Renaissance Italy, the problems it deals with and the terminology employed are those of Lessing, Winckelmann, and the eighteenth century. Movement, expression, sensuality, and individual character, not immobile serenity and idealised abstraction, are what Heinse values in the art of antiquity: 'every form is individual,

---

54   CF. Max L. Baeumer, 'Heinse und Nietzsche. Anfang und Vollendung der dionysischen Ästhetik', in Baeumer, *Heinse-Studien* (Stuttgart: Metzler, 1966), pp. 116f.

and none is abstract; a purely ideal human figure, whether of a man or a woman or a child or an old man, is inconceivable' (p. 12). Such are the qualities he discovers in the statue and holds up in conscious opposition to Winckelmann (pp. 239f.):

> His entire body trembles and shakes and burns, swelling up under the agonising deadly venom which spreads like a river [...].
>
> The serpents carry out the orders from on high, solemn and naturally huge of their kind, like earthquakes devastating the lands.
>
> The flesh is wonderfully alive and beautiful; all the muscles rise from within, like waves in a storm at sea. He has done with crying and is in the process of recovering his breath. The son on his right is gone, the one on his left is meanwhile held fast, and the dragons will soon make short work of him.

With its picture of unmitigated violence, its vigorous, colloquial language, its reversal of Winckelmann's metaphor of the sea, and its mischievous suggestion that, although Laocoon is not crying out, he is merely drawing breath to renew his screams, this account is a counterblast to Winckelmann, and a parody of his image of classical restraint. As if to underline this, the last sentence on the main figure, 'The left side may well belong to the highest achievement art has attained', ironically affirms Winckelmann's 'this part of the body can be described as a miracle of art'.[55]

What is not apparent from the novel is that Heinse probably gave more thought to the group than any of his contemporaries. The commonplace books of his Italian journey, which were not published until the twentieth century, are full of conflicting interpretations of the group, in which he anticipates some of the main arguments of the nineteenth-century critics. For whereas most of Heinse's contemporaries are content to admire Laocoon's heroism in face of his punishment, regardless of what its cause may have been, or to feel secure in the knowledge that Sophocles had written a tragedy in which Laocoon's fate would no doubt have been adequately explained, Heinse recognised that the statue posed essentially the same problem as the Lisbon earthquake, the problem of theodicy (his use of the metaphor of an earthquake underlines this connection): 'If Laocoon is a criminal, why is he so beautiful in his physique, and so wise and intelligent in his features?

---

55   WW VI, 23.

And if he is virtuous, are the gods not then unjust?'[56] Plagued by such doubts, Heinse concludes in turn that the group is an empty exercise in technical virtuosity,[57] and, in another of his inimitable passages, that it is utterly contrived and devoid of beauty:[58]

> I do not know whether the Laocoon group is really as beautiful as is claimed; the more I look at it, the more artificial it seems to me, and like a dancing-master's pose, as if the serpents were trained for one of them to descend through the arms and the other to ascend between the legs, so as to bind, as it were, the father and the two little sons into a marble fan; and to give it a handle, Papa must sit on the altar.

Set as it is amidst notes on Lessing's *Laocoon*, this irreverent outburst is clearly directed as much at German neo-classicism as against the group itself, and Heinse decided not to publish it. He finally included in his novel the one interpretation which not only expressed the Dionysian philosophy of his hero Ardinghello, and at the same time struck out at Winckelmann, but seemed to do most justice to the problem of evil and providence. For as he writes in his notebooks:[59]

> No evils give pleasure which do not belong to the best of a larger whole, even in imitation [...]. Laocoon can most kindly be interpreted as nothing more than the divine execution of an infamous voluptuary, along with the brats he sired in licentiousness in the temple of Apollo [...]. The Greeks never depicted an evil which did not contribute to the good of a whole; perhaps with the exception of their Oedipus.

Heinse's rebellious Laocoon marks a further step away from neo-classical idealism towards a more naturalistic interpretation of the group. The graphic description of his physical torments foreshadows an increasing interest in the pathology of Laocoon's death. And for all its exaggeration, this exuberant portrait cannot be dismissed as poetic fantasy. Laocoon's aggressively virile nakedness, and its incongruity with his priestly function before the altar, has often proved an embarrassment, and one of the fullest archaeological accounts of the group in the twentieth century

---

56 Wilhelm Heinse, *Sämtliche Werke*, ed. by Carl Schüddekopf, 10 vols (Leipzig: Insel Verlag, 1903–25), VIII (1), 516. All subsequent references are to this volume, in which the main discussions of Laocoon occur on pp. 282ff., 295–301, 311–14, 433f., 516f., 536 and 562f.

57 VIII (1), 516f.

58 VIII (1), 536.

59 VIII (1), 433f.

suggests that the erotic version of the myth may well have influenced the statue.[60] Moreover, several commentators mention other ancient representations of the legend in which Laocoon is accompanied by a winged Cupid.[61] Be that as it may, Heinse's discussion tells us as much about the author and his age as it does about the statue. His Laocoon is a *Kraftgenie*, like the hero of *Ardinghello*, a work which Goethe bracketed together with Schiller's *The Robbers*.[62] He represents a protest against the social and religious constraints of the times, and the rage of Apollo found a sympathetic echo in the reactions of many scandalised readers.[63]

The Laocoon of Friedrich Schiller, however, is of a different stamp from Heinse's irresponsible priest. For the Schiller who celebrates Laocoon's heroism is no longer the dramatist of protest and author of *The Robbers*; he is the mature theorist of tragedy for whom greatness consists not in heroic deeds as such, but in the moral freedom which manifests itself in them. Apart from a short tribute to the statue in his *Letter of a Danish Traveller* of 1785, in which he praises it as a 'model of the highest truth and beauty',[64] Schiller does not discuss the work at length until 1793, in his essay *On the Pathetic*. That he should select this work of sculpture, along with Virgil's narrative of the legend, as his chief illustration in an essay on tragedy indicates just how immense the reputation of the group had become in Germany by the final years of the century.

Schiller's Laocoon is conceived in the tradition of Winckelmann and Lessing rather than that of Herder or Heinse. Like Winckelmann's hero, he is caught up in a conflict of mind and body, and it is his strength of will which transforms his physical defeat into a moral triumph; to reinforce this point, Schiller quotes the description from Winckelmann's *History of the Art of Antiquity* in full.[65] At the same time, his account resembles

---

60   R. Foerster, 'Laokoon', *Jahrbuch des Kaiserlichen Deutschen Archäologischen Instituts*, 21 (1906), 1–32 (p. 23).

61   See, for example, WW VI, 23; Heyne, 'Examination', II, 45; Blümner (ed.), *Lessings Laokoon*, p. 706; and Foerster, pp. 28f.

62   *Goethes Werke*, Hamburger Ausgabe (henceforth HA), ed. by Erich Trunz, 14 vols (Hamburg: Christian Wegner Verlag, 1948–69), X, 538.

63   See, for example, the comments on Heinse's *Ardinghello* by Stolberg, F. L. W. Meyer, Herder, Jacobi and others in Baeumer's edition of that novel, pp. 563–65, 573, etc.

64   Friedrich Schiller, *Sämtliche Werke*, ed. by Gerhard Fricke and Herbert G. Göpfert, 7th edn, 5 vols (Munich: Hanser, 1984), V, 881. All subsequent references to Schiller are to this edition.

65   Schiller V, 251.

that of Lessing, in that his Laocoon evokes a reaction comparable to that which we experience on witnessing a tragedy. Laocoon controls the effects of his suffering by a supreme effort of will, and according to Schiller, it is through overcoming his natural inclinations in this way that the hero rises to tragic stature: 'to retain one's freedom in a storm which agitates the whole of sensuous nature requires a capacity for resistance that is infinitely exalted [*erhaben*] above all the power of nature'.[66]

The word '*erhaben*' (sublime) is fundamental to Schiller's interpretation. The first ingredient of tragic art is suffering, and the greater the suffering, the greater the moral victory of the hero who resists it. In so doing, he attains sublimity.[67] What Schiller admires in Winckelmann's description is not the beauty found in the statue, but precisely this conflict of spiritual and physical principles: 'How truly and finely the conflict between intelligence and the suffering of sensuous nature is developed in this description, and how aptly the phenomena are specified in which animality and humanity, natural coercion and rational freedom are revealed!'[68] Schiller's Laocoon is altogether a more exalted character than his predecessors: for he has passed through the school of Kant's moral philosophy. By substituting Kant's terminology for Winckelmann's, Schiller assimilates him to his own theory of tragedy, which is based on Kantian premises; and he goes on to show, with reference to Virgil, how Laocoon evokes our pity by choosing to suffer in a virtuous cause—that is, by attempting to rescue his children.[69] The sculptor, unfortunately, cannot render this active sublimity (*das Erhabene der Handlung*), as it is not in his power to indicate whether an action is freely chosen or not—in other words, the categorical imperative cannot be expressed in marble. He can only depict a more passive kind of sublimity, whereby the hero retains his moral freedom while submitting to his inevitable fate.[70] Laocoon, then, is a close relative of Schiller's Maria Stuart. Like her, he displays '*das Erhabene der Fassung*'.

Though an eminently virtuous character, Schiller's Laocoon has at least one thing in common with Heinse's defiant rebel: the accent lies more on his *freedom* than on his morality. As a true Schillerian hero, it

---

66 Ibid., V, 412.
67 Ibid., V, 515 and 517.
68 Ibid., V, 521.
69 Ibid., V, 526.
70 Ibid., V, 527.

is more important that he should be morally free than that he should be freely moral. But unlike Heinse, Schiller does not go into the rights and wrongs of Laocoon's punishment. That he regards it as unmerited, however, is clear from his poem 'Das Ideal und das Leben' ('The Ideal and Life') of 1795:[71]

> When the sufferings of man assail you
> When Laocoon against the serpents
> Defends himself with nameless agony,
> Let man be outraged! May his protest
> Strike against the heavenly vault above
> And tear the fabric of your feeling heart!

Like Herder a few years later. Schiller here suggest that Laocoon's fate cannot be reconciled with divine providence. But he does not pursue the question further, and nothing more is heard of the Kantian Laocoon.

The best known contribution to the Laocoon debate in eighteenth-century Germany, after those of Winckelmann and Lessing, is that of Goethe.[72] It is not surprising that he was fascinated by the statue and followed with interest the controversy which Lessing's *Laocoon* aroused over the limits of poetry and the visual arts.[73] For as a young man, he had still not decided whether to devote his main energy to poetry or to painting.

He first saw a plaster cast of the entire group in the collection of statuary at Mannheim in October 1769. In his letter to Langer of 30 November 1769, he describes the visit, and tells how the Laocoon in particular aroused his enthusiasm: 'Among lots of pretty things I

---

71 Ibid., I, 204.

72 Since a good chronological survey of Goethe's many utterances on the group is provided by Gottfried von Lücken, 'Goethe und der Laokoon', in *Natalicium. Johannes Geffcken zum 70. Geburtstag* (Heidelberg: [n.p.], 1931), pp. 85–99, I shall confine myself here to the principal ones. See also Ernst Grumach, *Goethe und die Antike*, 2 vols (Berlin: De Gruyter, 1949), II, 547ff. As for Heinrich Keller's *Goethe und das Laokoon-Problem* (Frauenfeld and Leipzig: Huber & Co., 1935), it deals not with Goethe's views on the statue, but with his attitude to the problem discussed in Lessing's *Laocoon*, namely the distinction between poetry and visual art.

73 On Goethe's enthusiastic reaction to Lessing's *Laocoon*, and his interest in the ensuing debate, see HA IX, 316 (*Dichtung und Wahrheit*) and *Goethes Briefe*, Hamburg edition (henceforth HA Briefe), ed. by Karl Robert Mandelkow, 6 vols, 4th edn (Munich: C. H. Beck, 1988), I, 98, to Langer, 30 November 1769. See also Georg Rosenthal, 'Das Laokoonproblem in Goethes *Dichtung und Wahrheit*', *Neue Jahrbücher für das klassische Altertum*, 23 (1920), 171–77 (p. 172).

encountered [...] nothing was able to attract my entire being so much as the Laocoon group [...]. I was entranced by it, so that I forgot all the other statues'.[74] He has set down some reflections on the group, he informs Langer, which should throw new light on the controversy, and has communicated these discoveries to his teacher Oeser, with whom he studied art at Leipzig. He hopes to put the finishing touches to his essay (*'ce petit ouvrage'*) in the following year. Unfortunately, this work is now lost.

Although Goethe may have visited Mannheim again in 1771, his remarks concerning that visit in his *Dichtung und Wahrheit* (*Poetry and Truth*), composed many years later, probably apply to the earlier occasion, which he had by that time forgotten.[75] These remarks, at any rate, contain some clues as to what the discoveries he mentioned to Langer may have been:[76]

> I resolved for myself the famous question as to why he [Laocoon] does not cry out by telling myself that he was unable to do so. All the actions and movements of the three figures were in my view derived from the initial conception of the group. The entire posture of the main body, as violent as artistically accomplished, was composed of two elements, namely the striving to resist the snakes and the recoil from the momentary bite. To reduce this pain, the abdomen had to be drawn inwards, making it impossible to cry out. Hence I also decided that the younger son had not been bitten [...].

He adds, however, that Oeser was not greatly impressed by his findings; and it is indeed understandable that this friend and teacher of Winckelmann should have looked askance at the young Goethe's account, since it eschews Winckelmann's moral interpretation completely in favour of a purely physical, anatomical explanation. For Goethe, the group is governed by a tension of opposites, just as it was for Winckelmann and Lessing. But the opposites he has in mind are not those of pain and a moral or aesthetic restraint upon its expression, but pain and physical resistance to its source. Undeterred by Oeser's neo-classical teachings, the young Goethe simply follows the evidence of his

---

74   HA Briefe, I, 97f.; this letter is in French, translated here into English.
75   See the editor's comments in HA XII, 584f. and Humphry Trevelyan, *Goethe and the Greeks* (Cambridge: Cambridge University Press, 1941), pp. 38f. on the dates of the two visits.
76   HA IX, 502.

senses. If he did indeed formulate these conclusions in 1769, he was the first to explain Laocoon's contracted abdomen and consequent silence not as the result of a conscious effort, but as an involuntary reflex. This interpretation was to be widely accepted in the following century.

Goethe had now come to believe, as a gloss on Lessing's *Laocoon* in his *Ephemerides* of 1770 confirms, that truth, rather than beauty, is the governing principle in ancient art: 'The ancients [...] shunned not so much the ugly as the false, and understood how to transform even the most terrible distortions in beautiful faces into beauty'.[77] He adds even more plainly a few lines further on 'that the excellence of the ancients should be sought in something other than the formation of beauty'. The position he has now reached is the one he develops a few years later in the essays *On German Architecture* and *After Falconet and on Falconet*, where he rejects the cult of beauty ('the soft doctrine of recent beautification') altogether and glorifies realistic and 'natural' forms of art instead.[78] To the ideal, the abstract, and the typical, the young Goethe opposes an art informed by individual character and expression, such as Gothic architecture and Dutch painting—an art which he describes as 'characteristic'. 'This characteristic art', he declares, 'is then the only true one'.[79]

Given these sentiments, it is ironic that Goethe's chief work on the Laocoon group, the essay *On Laocoon* of 1797, should have been written to refute a theorist who summed up the essence of the group as 'characteristic'. The theorist in question was Aloys Hirt, the authority on ancient art who acted as Goethe's guide to the antiquities of Rome during his Italian journey.

Goethe was not the first, as has been maintained, to apply the term 'characteristic' to the visual arts.[80] Hogarth, for example, speaks of the 'characteristic beauty' of Glycon's statue of Hercules, by which he means that its beauty is not that of a general ideal, but of an individual character,

---

77 *Der junge Goethe*, ed. by Hanna Fischer-Lamberg, 6 vols (Berlin: De Gruyter, 1963–74), I, 431.

78 HA XII, 7–15 and 23–28.

79 HA XII, 13.

80 See E. C. Mason, 'Schönheit, Ausdruck und Charakter im ästhetischen Denken des 18. Jahrhunderts', in *Geschichte–Deutung–Kritik. Literaturwissenschaftliche Beiträge dargebracht zum 65. Geburtstag Werner Kohlschmidts*, ed. by Maria Bindschedler and Paul Zinsli (Berne: Francke, 1969), pp. 91–108 (p. 97).

appropriate to the exceptional physique of Hercules.[81] Christian Garve, in 1769, similarly declares: 'Thus, when it was a question of making certain persons and beings recognisable, the artist often had to make exceptions to his supreme law and give the characteristic precedence over the beautiful.'[82] And Herder also applies the term to sculpture in that same year.[83] The significance of the word varies somewhat from one writer to the next, sometimes denoting a purely individual quality, and sometimes that of a particular type; but in all cases, it is distinct from, and often the antithesis of, the concept of beauty as a universal ideal. Fluctuations of this kind also occur in Goethe's use of the term[84]—but 'the characteristic' for him is always distinct from beauty in an ideal sense, and indeed is often synonymous with Winckelmann's and Lessing's term *'Ausdruck'* (expression).[85]

For Aloys Hirt, truth and expression are the basis of all great art, particularly that of antiquity. Its excellence lies in its ability to express individual characters and emotions rather than abstract ideals:[86]

> In all the works of the ancients without exception, both at rest, and in movement and expression, individuality of significance—the characteristic—is evident. All other laws were subordinate to this in every representation, in every figure [...]. Truth, as the first requirement of the characteristic, must therefore be predominant in every work of art. It remains, and is, the basic law of beauty and of goodness.

From these remarks, it is obvious that Hirt's naturalistic aesthetic is akin to that of the young Goethe.[87] What distinguishes it is not its conception, but the one-sided way in which Hirt applies it. For despite his premise

---

81   Hogarth, *Analysis of Beauty*, p. 15.

82   Review of Lessing's *Laokoon*, reprinted in Blümner (ed.), *Lessings Laokoon*, p. 691.

83   Herder, SW III, 90, *Erstes Kritisches Wäldchen*. Herder uses it in a rather different sense, however, to represent that which characterises a god as the god of war, love, or the like, rather than as an ordinary individual, so that the sculptor may have to represent such figures as 'more characteristic than individual'. Once again, however, a particular rather than a general quality is envisaged.

84   On Goethe's use of the term, see Otto Harnack, 'Goethes Kunstanschauung in ihrer Bedeutung für die Gegenwart', *Goethe-Jahrbuch*, 15 (1894), 187–205 (pp. 198f.) and Ferdinand Denk, 'Ein Streit um Gehalt und Gestalt des Kunstwerks in der deutschen Klassik', *Germanisch-Romanische Monatshefte*, 18 (1930), 427–42 (p. 435).

85   See Mason, 'Schönheit, Ausdruck und Charakter', p. 98.

86   'Über Laokoon', in *Die Horen*, XII, 10. Stück (1797), 1–26 (pp. 12 and 23f.). On Hirt's definition of 'Karakteristik' see also his earlier essay 'Versuch über das Kunstschöne', in *Die Horen*, XI, 7. Stück (1797), 1–37 (esp. pp. 34–36).

87   See Lücken, 'Goethe und der Laokoon', p. 92.

of the 'characteristic', Hirt is no *Stürmer und Dränger*, but a literal-minded rationalist who pursues his theory to whatever extremes it may lead. Humourless and lacking in elegance—'He is a pedant, but knows a lot', was Goethe's succinct judgement[88]—he is inflexibly opposed to Winckelmann and Lessing, and determined to banish the last vestige of ideal beauty from the ancient statues. The 'characteristic' is to take its place. His main example, needless to say, is the Laocoon, which is the subject of one of his two essays published by Schiller in 1797 in his journal *Die Horen*: 'But what—if Laocoon's expression were neither that of sighing nor of crying? if the artist gave no thought either to reflection on quiet greatness or to a beauty which moderated expression, but fixed his choice rather on the moment of the highest degree of expression?'[89] By arguing against Winckelmann that pain, and pain alone, determines the expression and attitude of the main figure, and against Lessing that the moment represented is the climax of Laocoon's agony, immediately before his collapse, Hirt draws a horrifying picture which outdoes even Heinse's in violence,[90] and from which all heroic elements, even those of the rebel, are lacking. What we have here is not so much an aesthetic analysis as a pathologist's report, in which, for good measure, not one but multiple causes of death are enumerated:[91]

> Laocoon does not cry out, because he is no longer able to cry [...]. The paroxysm, the highest tension, the raging convulsions are visible in all his limbs [...]. The blood, which rushes in complete turmoil into the outermost parts and makes all the vessels swell up, disrupts the circulation and prevents inhalation: the lungs, through the compression and impeded circulation of the blood, are progressively distended; the corrosive venom from the serpent's bite helps to accelerate the violent

---

88 Ludwig Geiger, 'Briefe von Goethe und Hirt', *Goethe-Jahrbuch*, 15 (1894), 68–81 and 96–108 (p. 97). Compare Schiller's comment to Goethe on one of Hirt's essays he had accepted for *Die Horen*: 'We must indeed set something up to counteract the dreadful ponderousness of Hirt's essay': 25 October 1796, in *Briefwechsel zwischen Schiller und Goethe*, ed. by Franz Muncker, 4 vols (Stuttgart: Cotta, 1892), II, 21.

89 Hirt, 'Über Laokoon', p. 7.

90 Although I have no positive evidence, I strongly suspect that Hirt's account is influenced by Heinse's. For example, Hirt's comment on 'the greatest possible contraction of his abdomen, which causes even his genitals to project' ('Über Laokoon', p. 8), is all too reminiscent of his predecessor. Hirt may have read *Ardinghello*, or he may have met Heinse in Rome, where Hirt was in residence from September 1782 and which Heinse left in July 1783.

91 'Über Laokoon', p. 8.

fermentation; a stifling pressure stupefies the brain, and an apoplexy seems to effect a sudden death [...].

After continuing for several paragraphs in this vein, Hirt concludes, with disarming modesty, 'I believe I have shown that the masters represented the most strenuous degree of expression'.[92]

Writing such as this, of course, lent itself to satire. In his novella 'The Collector and his Circle' of 1799, Goethe puts Hirt's arguments into the mouth of the boorish and dogmatic guest, who is dubbed 'the characteristician',[93] and against whom the mild and civilised collector vainly defends the beauty of ancient art. And although the guest is eventually worsted in argument by another visitor, 'the philosopher' (whose views are modelled on those of Schiller),[94] his thesis is refuted less by logic than by ridicule. His following remarks are a pastiche of Hirt's description: 'Step before the Laocoon, and see nature in complete upheaval and despair, the final stifling pain, convulsive tension, raging spasms, the effects of a corrosive venom, violent fermentation, impeded circulation, stifling pressure and paralytic death.'[95] To this, the philosopher caustically replies that, if Laocoon really were as the guest describes him, he would deserve to be smashed to pieces on the spot.

The unfortunate Hirt was further satirised on two occasions by August Wilhelm Schlegel,[96] who labelled his method 'the surgical approach', and took the only step which remained to be taken beyond his diagnosis of apoplexy: is it not possible that Laocoon is already dead?[97] After repeating Winckelmann's and Lessing's contention that Laocoon's condition is tempered by nobility of expression and beauty of execution, Schlegel concludes: 'Of course he cannot cry out, otherwise he would raise his voice against so disfiguring a description and failure to recognise his heroic greatness'.[98] And although Hirt attempted to

---

92   Ibid.

93   HA XII, 78.

94   Compare, for example, the views of 'the philosopher' on the treatment of horrific subjects in poetry (HA XII, 80f.) with those of Schiller in his letter to Goethe of 7 July 1797 (*Briefwechsel zwischen Schiller und Goethe*, II, 122f.).

95   HA XII, 76.

96   *Athenaeum*, ed. by A. W. and F. Schlegel, 1798–1800 (reprinted Stuttgart, 1960), I, 2. Stück, 261ff. (Athenaeumsfragment No. 310) and II, 2. Stück, 226f. ('Über Zeichnungen zu Gedichten und John Flaxmans Umrisse').

97   Ibid., I, 2, p. 261.

98   Ibid., I, 2, p. 263.

refute these accusations,[99] Schlegel offered only mockery in reply: 'Since I then indicated that I did not consider Laocoon's condition as yet quite so desperate, he [Hirt] made such an immoderate fuss in reply that he almost changed places with his hero.'[100]

Hirt's views were completely at odds with those of Goethe, who had long since outgrown his youthful love of 'the characteristic', and whose classical ideals, since his Italian journey, had filled him with a new respect for Winckelmann. Why then, one may ask, did he and Schiller go out of their way to publish Hirt's essay in the journal *Die Horen*, of which Schiller was the editor?

Schiller welcomed the essay, for he believed the time was ripe for the 'characteristic'—that is, expressive and realistic—elements of Greek art to be brought to the fore:[101]

> for in general, Winckelmann's and Lessing's conception is still prevalent, and our most recent aestheticians, on both poetry and sculpture, are at great pains to free the beauty of the Greeks from all characteristic elements and to make these a hallmark of modernity. It seems to me that the more recent analysts, in their efforts to isolate the concept of the beautiful and to set it up in a certain purity, have almost emptied it of content and turned it into an empty sound [...].

He is thinking above all of Friedrich Schlegel, whose eulogies of Goethe and high-handed criticisms of Schiller had irritated them both, and who, in his pre-Romantic years, was outdoing even the Weimar Classicists in his cult of Greek beauty. In his *On the Study of Greek Poetry* of 1797, Schlegel described the state of modern poetry, whose hallmark is 'the characteristic', as anarchic and decadent. The only way to salvation was to follow the beginnings Goethe had made, and to cultivate 'the highest beauty', devoid of individual expression, as found in Greek poetry and art.[102] To this extreme classicism, Hirt's essay offered the perfect antidote: the two extremes would cancel each other out. Besides, Schiller must have found Hirt's arguments a good deal more sympathetic than

---

99 In *Berlinisches Archiv der Zeit und ihres Geschmacks* (1798), 11. Stück, 439.

100 *Athenaeum*, II, 2. Stück, 227.

101 Schiller to Goethe, 7 July 1797, in *Briefwechsel zwischen Schiller und Goethe*, II, 122.

102 *Über das Studium der griechischen Poesie*, in Friedrich Schlegel, *Kritische Schriften*, ed. by Wolfdietrich Rasch (Munich: Hanser, 1964), pp. 126, 148, and 154. On this whole episode see also Mason, 'Schönheit, Ausdruck und Charakter', pp. 100–04 and John William Scholl, 'Friedrich Schlegel and Goethe, 1790–1802', *PMLA*, 21 (1906), 40–192 (pp. 106–18).

those of Schlegel, for as we have seen, he had himself stressed not the beauty of the group, but its sublimity and the extreme suffering which Laocoon has to endure. Goethe readily agreed that Hirt's essay should be published,[103] not least because he saw the benefits which he stood to reap: as Schiller pointed out, the way would be open for Goethe and his ally Heinrich Meyer[104] to carry the day with their more balanced views, before a public already disposed in their favour.[105]

Provoked by Hirt's ideas, Goethe had by now almost completed his own essay *On Laocoon*, reviving his plans of almost thirty years before. He published it in the first number of his periodical *Propyläen* in the following year. Since Goethe avoided naming him, Hirt could only reply in the most general and indirect terms. Completely outmanoeuvred, he had only time to defend himself in a feeble postscript to his own essay in *Die Horen*,[106] before August Wilhelm Schlegel's ridicule and the satire of Goethe's 'The Collector and his Circle' descended on him in turn. His more detailed reply, in which he conceded many of Goethe's points but stuck firmly to his own theory of 'Karakteristik', remained unpublished.[107]

Like most of the previous theorists, Goethe was interested in the Laocoon group for its exemplary qualities, and as a means of illustrating his own aesthetic principles. The way in which he and Schiller treated Hirt was far from admirable, but for the classicist Goethe, his theories posed a greater threat than Friedrich Schlegel's insipid cult of beauty, for they implied that the group had no exemplary status whatsoever, and reduced it to an interesting, but purely individual case—a study of extreme physical pain. Such heresies could not be left unchecked. And the method Goethe chose was the same as that which Winckelmann had successfully employed before him: he would transcend his opponent's views by incorporating them into his own, broader thesis, for Hirt had failed to realise 'that only Lessing's, Winckelmann's and his, and indeed

---

103 To Schiller, 8 July 1797, *Briefwechsel zwischen Schiller und Goethe*, II, 124.

104 Heinrich Meyer's 'Einige Bemerkungen über die Gruppe Laokoons und seiner Söhne', in *Propyläen*, I, 1. Stück (1799), 175f. was written, however, in 1796 and does not take issue with Hirt. In his much later *Geschichte der bildenden Künste bei den Griechen*, 4 vols (Dresden: Waltersche Buchhandlung, 1824–36), Meyer dismisses Hirt, without naming him, as a past writer whose exaggerated notion of 'das Charakteristische' has now disappeared without trace (I, 206), but does not mention him in his discussion of the Laocoon (III, 65–79).

105 See Schiller to Goethe, 7 July 1797, in *Briefwechsel zwischen Schiller und Goethe*, II, 123.

106 'Nachtrag über Laokoon', in *Die Horen*, XII, 12. Stück (1797), 19–28.

107 Hirt's remarks were first published in Denk, *Das Kunstschöne*, pp. 110–16.

several further pronouncements, together exhaust this work of art'.[108] Heinrich Meyer understood Goethe's tactic precisely when he wrote of his essay: 'It stands so well in the middle between the two extremes which have in turn been asserted, namely *beauty* without sympathy and passion as the supreme purpose and goal of art, and *truth* which was meant to be represented'.[109] Goethe's essay is open to fundamental objections, but as one might expect, it is masterfully written, and contains many original observations on the group. As so often, he has learnt from the limitations of his predecessors, and at the same time availed himself of their positive achievements. One of the main insights he brings to his study, and with which he introduces the work, is an awareness of how limited the rational understanding is in face of a complex work of art, whose significance is not finite, but inexhaustible.[110] Accordingly, he does not apply a rigid conceptual framework to it, as Lessing had done. The concepts he does employ are not narrow or restrictive, but of a general kind, and he uses several of them, not just one or two as others had done—knowledge of anatomy, individual character, degree of movement, idealisation, and appeal to the senses (*Anmut*) are among the qualities he looks for, as well as the traditional *Schönheit*.[111] And aware of the excesses to which Winckelmann's physiognomical approach had led, he refuses to speculate on Laocoon's spiritual state, and warns against reading our own reactions into the work itself. In these, and in other respects, he has benefited from the work of the Göttingen archaeologist Heyne, whose essay of 1779 on the group is distinguished by its common sense, its careful scrutiny of the evidence, and its refusal to speculate.[112]

---

108 To Schiller, 5 July 1797, in *Briefwechsel zwischen Schiller und Goethe*, II, 121. Precisely the same point is made by Carl Ludwig Fernow, another neo-classicist, in his remarks on the Laocoon in his essay 'Über das Kunstschöne', in Fernow, *Römische Studien*, 3 vols (Zurich: H. Gessner, 1806–08), I, 291–450. Winckelmann, Lessing, and Hirt discern 'Idealität', Schönheit', and 'Karakter' respectively in the statue: in fact, all three are present (p. 430). This essay was no doubt intended to support Goethe.

109 To Goethe, 26 July 1797, in *Goethes Briefwechsel mit Heinrich Meyer*, ed. by Max Hecker, *Schriften der Goethe-Gesellschaft*, 34 (1919), 15.

110 HA XII, 56.

111 Ibid.

112 For example, Heyne argues that the struggle is at its height, not at its end, and that the ways in which the group can be interpreted are infinite. He also applies the formula of unity in variety to it: 'Just think of the different postures of the three

Goethe is also the first to consider the statue almost exclusively in aesthetic terms as a work of sculpture. For even Lessing, although his analysis is primarily aesthetic, supplemented it with long historical reflections and an elaborate philological apparatus, and his poetic interests influenced his interpretation considerably. As on his first visit to Mannheim, Goethe is guided above all by his senses. And unlike most of his predecessors, he treats the group throughout as an organic whole, instead of concentrating his attention on the main figure. The properties he is most concerned with are formal ones—symmetry, balance, gradation, co-ordination, and unity in variety—and it is in this emphasis on form that the classical values he has espoused since his journey to Italy, as well as the limitations of his aesthetics, become most apparent.

Goethe's interpretation resembles those of Winckelmann and Lessing in that he sees the statue as governed by a tension of opposites, the main ones being beauty on the one hand, and passion and expression on the other. But since the latter qualities had been given so much prominence by Hirt, Goethe takes more account of them than the other neo-classicists had done, and, doubtless as a concession to Hirt, even refers to them as 'das Charakteristische'. The counterbalancing 'Schönheit' is not, however, a distinct quality of attractiveness existing side-by-side with the group's expressive qualities—Goethe reserves the separate term 'Anmut' (grace) for that which is visually agreeable. It consists rather in the restraint or moderation with which the—inherently violent— expression of the group is executed. But he realises that the group is far too complex to be comprehended by a simple antithesis such as that of beauty and expression. This is merely the dominant polarity within which a whole series of subordinate contrasts can be discerned, and these in turn call forth contrasting emotional reactions in the beholder:[113]

> I therefore venture to repeat once again that the group of Laocoon, along with all its other acknowledged merits, is also a model of symmetry and diversity, of rest and movement, of contrasts and gradations, which

---

individuals, their different emotions, their different ages, their different expressions, their contrast and yet union through their entrapment by the snakes. What variety, and yet how many points of unity!' (Heyne, *Sammlung antiquarischer Aufsätze*, II, 20 and 27f. Otto Harnack, 'Zu Goethes Laokoonaufsatz', *Vierteljahrsschrift für Litteraturgeschichte*, 6 (1893) 156–58, also notices Heyne's influence on Goethe.

113 HA XII, 58.

present themselves to the viewer in part sensuously, in part spiritually, and together with the high pathos of the spectacle excite an agreeable sensation and moderate the storm of suffering and passion through grace and beauty.

There is a similar conflict of opposites in the actions of all three figures. Each of them performs not one, but two separate actions. The elder son attempts to extricate himself from the coils, while reacting in horror to his father's plight; the younger son fights for air with one hand, and fends off the serpent with the other; and Laocoon himself struggles actively with his arms, while his body reacts convulsively as he is bitten in the loins. 'There thus arises a combined effect of striving and yielding, of action and passivity, of effort and surrender, which would perhaps be impossible under any other circumstances'.[114] This theory that everything is determined by the bite, which is administered at the very centre of the group, is of course the one that Goethe had framed on his visit to Mannheim almost thirty years earlier.

In analysing the temporal dimension of the group, Goethe is able to reformulate Lessing's idea of the 'pregnant moment'. Like Lessing, he believed that the moment represented is not the climax of Laocoon's agony, as Hirt had maintained, but the moment preceding it. Yet unlike Lessing, he argues that this moment is both fleeting and climactic—the statue resembles 'a fixed stroke of lightning',[115] and what we see is 'the climax of the moment represented'.[116] But the climax Goethe has in mind is not the climax which Hirt spoke of: it is the climax of the action, not of the agony; and like Lessing's 'pregnant moment', it is a transitional phase between two separate actions—the struggle against the serpents, and the reaction to the bite.

In Laocoon himself, therefore, two successive actions are represented simultaneously. And as Goethe points out, the three figures have succumbed in varying degrees to the serpents' attack, from the peripheral involvement of the elder son to the fatal wound of the father. The group thus conveys an extended temporal sequence, and Goethe, like Lessing and Schiller, is aware of its dramatic qualities. The elder son, the father, and the younger son evoke fear, terror, and pity respectively,[117] and the

---

114 HA XII, 61.
115 HA XII, 60.
116 HA XII, 63.
117 HA XII, 65.

elder son is not only a participant in the action, but also a spectator.[118] The group as a whole can be likened to a tragedy: it is in fact 'a tragic idyll'.

It is at this point that the limitations of Goethe's classicism become most obvious. Despite his concessions to Hirt, he cannot bring himself to admit that the group has anything remotely horrific about it—he therefore denies that the younger son has been bitten at all,[119] although it has always been accepted that he has, and he denies that any effect of the venom can be seen in the father's body.[120] Similarly, his convictions demand that the statue, like all great works of art, should represent a universally intelligible condition—in short, that it should be ideal rather than 'characteristic'. It accordingly depicts not a specific event which can be understood only by those who know the myth of Laocoon, but a scene of universal human relevance:[121]

> of his priesthood, of his Trojan-national and all poetic and mythological accretions, the artists have divested him [...] It is a father with two sons, in danger of succumbing to two dangerous animals. Thus there are also no divinely sent serpents, but purely natural ones [...] A father was asleep with his two sons, they were enwrapped by two serpents and now struggle, as they awake, to tear themselves out of the living net.

Here, for once, Goethe is demonstrably wrong. Apart from the fact that the block on which Laocoon sits is plainly an altar, it was known before Goethe's essay was written that he originally wore a laurel wreath, as a groove around his head testifies;[122] this at once identifies him as a priest of Apollo. And as for the serpents, they are zoological monstrosities, being too thin for constrictors, and too long to be venomous.[123] As Herder drily observed, 'an ordinary snake event does not explain this representation';[124] to understand its significance, we have to know the legend—and even then, we have to decide which version of it to follow.

---

118 HA XII, 64.

119 HA XII, 60.

120 HA XII, 61.

121 HA XII, 59.

122 See Ennius Quirinus Visconti, *Œuvres: Musée Pie-Clémentin*, 7 vols (Milan: J. P. Giegler, 1818–22), II, 277. The volume in question first appeared in 1792.

123 See A. W. Lawrence, *Greek and Roman Sculpture* (London: Jonathan Cape, 1972), p. 250.

124 Herder, SW XXVIII, 281.

Despite all Goethe's efforts, an unexplained residue remains. This late attempt, at the end of the eighteenth century, to restore Laocoon to the neo-classical niche which Winckelmann had created for him did not succeed. It was to no avail that C. L. Fernow, in his *Roman Studies* of 1806, tried to defend the neo-classical interpretation against the doubts which Hirt had disseminated,[125] because the tide of opinion on the statue had already begun to turn. One of the first signs of this change came, in fact, from within the neo-classical camp itself: as early as 1787, F. W. B. Ramdohr, after reiterating the verdict of Winckelmann and his followers that the statue displays unity in variety and expression tempered by beauty, confessed, after many apologies and hesitations, 'that this group, despite all its undoubted advantages, has not awakened in me the pleasant impression which I have experienced at the beauty of other statues'.[126] Try as he might, Ramdohr could not discover in the Laocoon that beauty and restraint which he recognised in the Antinous and the Belvedere Apollo. And though the Schlegels joined Goethe in opposing the views of Hirt, they were allies whose services he could well have done without. For Friedrich Schlegel, who had defined the essence of modern art as 'the characteristic' and condemned it as inferior to 'the highest beauty' of Greek art, soon reversed his position entirely and held up 'the characteristic', for which he now preferred the near-synonym of 'the Romantic', as the ideal to which modern art should aspire. In other words, Schlegel's aesthetic values were by this time close to those of Hirt, who must therefore be regarded as a forerunner of Romanticism;[127] the main difference was that Hirt saw these values as fulfilled in ancient art, and Schlegel in modern art. In short, the Romantic era had begun, and it faced the task of explaining those aspects of the group which Goethe's elegant analysis had failed to account for.

In the nineteenth century, more interpretations of the group than ever before appeared, but few of them were as independent or original as those of the previous century. They began as reactions to, or developments of, earlier points of view, and thenceforth, a few themes were enlarged upon with a remarkable degree of continuity. Instead of analysing individual

---

125 Fernow, II, 415–50.

126 F. W. B. Ramdohr, *Ueber Mahlerei und Bildhauerkunst in Rom*, 3 vols (Leipzig: Weidmann, 1787), I, 56–68 (p. 64).

127 See Denk, *Das Kunstschöne...*, p. 108.

contributions separately, in chronological sequence, it will therefore be more convenient to follow each of the main tendencies within the nineteenth century debate to the point where they converge; that is, the point where the Laocoon debate ceased to be an issue of importance in Germany.

One of the few facts of the Laocoon myth on which everyone agreed was that his death was divinely ordained. Yet apart from Herder and Heinse, none of the writers hitherto discussed had seriously considered the religious implications of the statue. Goethe had, indeed, flatly denied that it had any. They seem not to have been unduly troubled that the divine wrath may have struck down an innocent victim.[128] But in the nineteenth century, two questions of a religious nature were discussed again and again: is Laocoon's punishment justified? and does his death, as represented in the statue, have any religious or spiritual significance?

For the classical scholar F. G. Welcker, whose study of the group first appeared in 1827, Laocoon is above all a man of religion: his expression has 'something priestly and pious' about it.[129] To justify Laocoon's punishment, Welcker argues that the statue is based on the lost tragedy of Sophocles, in which Laocoon doubtless died for an erotic misdemeanour such as that reported by Hyginus and Servius. But Welcker does not try, as Heinse had done, to endow the death itself with any positive significance—it is not the apotheosis of a Dionysian hero, but merely 'affecting, exciting pity, and hopeless'.[130] Like Herder, he makes much of 'the pathetic quality of the scene',[131] and does his best to arouse compassion in us for the dying priest. Indeed his efforts to extenuate Laocoon's transgression, which he describes as 'a youthful precipitation',[132] are so successful that we are left with the impression that the punishment, after all, scarcely fits the crime. Welcker is therefore aware of the problem which had troubled Heinse, but he does not solve it satisfactorily. The same applies to the art historian Heinrich

---

128 Compare Visconti, II, 268, for whom Laocoon is satisfied with the knowledge that he is innocent: 'He does not repent [...] for his zeal [in attacking the Wooden Horse], and he prefers the evidence of his conscience to the anger of the gods and the opinion of men.'

129 F. G. Welcker, *Alte Denkmäler*, 5 vols (Göttingen: Dieterich, 1849–64), I, 322–51 (p. 326). An earlier version of his remarks appeared in 1827.

130 Ibid., I, 325.

131 Ibid., I, 326

132 Ibid., I, 346.

Brunn, who interprets the group in a similar way in his *Geschichte der griechischen Künstler*, and cites Welcker in support.[133]

Needless to say, later writers were not convinced by such explanations. Adolf Stahr, in 1855, discerns 'a lack of reconciliation [...], something oppressive, frightening, agonising' in the group, and calls Laocoon's death a 'hopeless martyrdom'.[134] And three years later, Johannes Overbeck, while acknowledging that the serpents are unmistakably divine emissaries, denies that any moral idea whatsoever can be gleaned from the statue; for even if some versions of the myth attempt to justify Laocoon's death on ethical grounds, none of this can be perceived from the group itself.[135] In short, Welcker, Brunn and other religious apologists do not carry conviction, because the statue depicts only the terrible punishment, but gives us no means of telling whether it is merited or not. Furthermore, the best known version of the myth, that of Virgil, portrays Laocoon as entirely innocent. This, perhaps, is why Novalis had declared: 'it is an *immoral* work of art.'[136]

But there is a further reason why many nineteenth-century writers saw Laocoon's death in a negative light. As Walther Rehm has shown, after Fritz Stolberg visited Italy in 1791–92 and judged the ancient statues unfavourably from a Christian point of view,[137] the opinion steadily gained ground that even the most serene sculptures of gods and goddesses were spiritually empty. It is unfortunate that Novalis's comments on the group, jotted down after a reading of Goethe's essay, remained fragmentary. From what he does say, however, it appears that, at a time when Friedrich Schlegel was still paying homage to Greek beauty and defending Winckelmann's views, Novalis had already found the group spiritually deficient; not only does he describe it as immoral, he also feels that Laocoon is not passive enough in his suffering: 'Is not a more comprehensive, in short more exalted moment in the Laocoon

---

133 2 vols (Stuttgart: Ebner & Seubert, 1857–59), I, 494.

134 Adolf Stahr, *Torso, Kunst, Künstler und Kunstwerke des griechischen und römischen Alterthums*, 2nd edn, 2 vols (Brunswick: Vieweg, 1878), II, 83–95 (p. 93). The first edition appeared in 1855.

135 Johannes Overbeck, *Geschichte der griechischen Plastik*, 4th edn, 2 vols, (Leipzig: J. C. Hinrichssche Buchhandlung, 1893–94), II, 296–336 (pp. 318–22); the work first appeared in 1857–58.

136 Novalis, *Schriften*, ed. by Paul Kluckhohn and Richard Samuel, 2nd edn, 4 vols (Stuttgart: Kohlhammer, 1960–75), III, 412.

137 Rehm, *Götterstille*, p. 141.

drama conceivable—perhaps that in which the highest pain turns into rapture—resistance into surrender—the highest life into stone'.[138]

Friedrich Thiersch, whose history of Greek art was published in 1825, goes even further. He sees Laocoon's death not as a moral victory, but as a spiritual failure, and says that the statue reveals 'a mind succumbing in the grimmest struggle, already close, indeed surrendering, to the terror of despair'.[139] But once again, it was one of the greatest intellects of the age who expressed the new attitude most memorably. Hegel, in his *Lectures on Aesthetics* (1818–28), contends that Christian art is superior to that of antiquity because it offers a hope of liberation and redemption through love, even in suffering and death:[140]

> In the ideals of the ancients, on the other hand, we [...] may well see only the expression of pain in nobler natures such as Niobe and Laocoon; they do not dissolve in laments and despair, but preserve their great and high minded nature in this state; but this self-preservation remains empty, for the suffering and pain are as it were the final state, and in place of reconciliation and satisfaction there is a cold resignation, in which the individual, without breaking down, gives up what it had held on to [...]. Only Romantic religious love attains the expression of bliss and freedom.

It is ironic that the philosopher Hegel, rather than the Schlegels or Novalis, pronounced the most characteristically Romantic verdict on the group. He also declares that, in the works of the Italian masters, Christ's spiritual, as distinct from physical suffering, shows itself in a facial expression of gravity—not, as in the figure of Laocoon, in a contraction of the muscles which could be interpreted as a cry.[141]

For Winckelmann, Lessing, and Schiller, Laocoon's death was a triumph of the spirit over matter. For Hegel, almost the reverse is true. Just as Laocoon had been pressed a few decades earlier into the service of Kantian idealism, so now is he made to typify a phase in Hegel's world-historical process. For as Hegel remarks elsewhere in

---

138 Novalis, *Schriften*, III, 412f.

139 Friedrich Thiersch, *Ueber die Epochen der bildenden Kunst unter den Griechen*, 2nd edn (Munich: Literarisch-Artistische Anstalt, 1829); the first edition appeared in 1825.

140 G. W. F. Hegel, *Vorlesungen über die Ästhetik*, ed. by H. G. Hotho, 2nd edn, 3 vols (Berlin: Duncker und Humblot, 1842–43), III, 35f. For other negative judgements on Greek art during the Romantic era see Rehm, *Götterstille*, pp. 151–67. Most of these writers criticise the Ancients' view of death as inadequate in comparison with that of Christianity.

141 Ibid., II, 43.

his lectures,[142] the statue is the product of 'a late period', so that the death of Laocoon represents the downfall of an era before a new age of the World Spirit dawns.

As a corollary to this belief that the group is devoid of spiritual significance, the critics shifted their attention more and more to Laocoon's physical state. Hirt's opinions were reiterated and confirmed: the group is nothing more than a study in extreme physical pain, in which the involuntary reflexes of the main figure show little or no trace of heroic restraint.[143] Hebbel, in his poem 'Before the Laocoon', is clearly of this opinion. He blames Michelangelo for having praised the group excessively, and sees the fact that Laocoon rebelled against Apollo as symbolic: not beauty, but truth is the criterion which the artists followed, and the group is criticised by implication as a piece of unvarnished naturalism:[144]

> Michelangelo as a wonder of art bid you welcome
> Since you served to counterbalance the beauteous Apollo
> Who bore Raphael aloft and denied Michelangelo's merit;
> Some repeated his praise, but they protested too much.
> What truth can accomplish you show all too clearly, o Group
> Even more clearly you show that it cannot achieve everything!

At around the same time, the argument as to whether or not Laocoon is crying out was renewed, and it seemed to some writers that physical agony such as Laocoon's must be matched by the loudest possible clamour. This was denied, however, in 1862, when P. J. W. Henke, on the strength of a medical diagnosis of the stricken priest, concluded that the moment represented is that between inhalation and exhalation.[145] The criteria of nineteenth-century realism were applied to the group so uncompromisingly that it began to seem as if it were made not of marble, but of flesh and blood, despite the fact that Schopenhauer had already supplied the necessary *reductio ad absurdum*:[146]

---

142 Ibid., II, 439.

143 See Thiersch, *Ueber die Epochen*, p. 375; Brunn, *Geschichte*, I, 488; Overbeck, *Geschichte*, II, 312; etc.

144 Friedrich Hebbel, *Sämtliche Werke*, ed. by Richard Maria Werner, 12 vols (Berlin: Behr, 1901–03), VI, 334. On the influence of the group on Michelangelo, see Arnold von Salis, *Antike und Renaissance* (Erlenbach-Zurich: Rentsch, 1947), pp. 143ff.

145 P. J. W. Henke, *Die Gruppe des Laokoon* (Leipzig and Heidelberg: Winter, 1862), pp. 20–25.

146 Arthur Schopenhauer, *Die Welt als Wille und Vorstellung* (1818), in Schopenhauer, *Sämtliche Werke*, ed. by Wolfgang von Löhneysen, 5 vols (Stuttgart: Cotta, 1960–65),

> One could not produce a crying Laocoon in marble, but only an open-mouthed Laocoon fruitlessly attempting to cry out, with his voice stuck in his throat [...]; this would result in the invariably ridiculous spectacle of an effort with no result, exactly parallel to that which a practical joker produced when he plugged with wax the horn of a sleeping night-watchman whom he then awoke with cries of 'fire!', only to enjoy the latter's fruitless efforts to sound the alarm.

The realistic evaluations continued, and brought down new censures on the group in 1876, when the anatomist Friedrich Merkel, after minute measurements of the group, discovered that many of its proportions are wrong: by their stature, the two sons should be around seven to eight and four to six years old, yet their proportions resemble those of a man and a youth respectively; besides, the necks of all three figures are too long. Merkel may, however, have hit upon the true reason why Laocoon failed to escape from the serpents: he had a severe limp, for his right leg is at least seven centimetres shorter than his left.[147]

By the end of the century, the excesses of realism were over. But it was now widely accepted that the sculptors set out to express physical anguish by every means at their disposal, and that they selected the moment of maximum muscular tension in Laocoon's body in order to display their virtuosity.[148] This conviction that the physical aspects of the group are all-important could only further diminish the work's already diminished reputation.

Another factor which helped to bring Laocoon down from his eminence was the increase in knowledge of Greek art. When the Parthenon sculptures were brought to England and purchased for the nation in 1816,[149] art historians began to realise that the restraint and serenity which Winckelmann had admired are more evident in the works of the Periclean age than in the much later and more exaggerated sculptures of the Hellenistic era. It could no longer be doubted that most of the works from the Roman collections, including the Laocoon,

---

I, 320f. Cf. Gombrich, 'Lessing. Lecture on a Master Mind', p. 140: 'To ask [...] what noise the poor priest emits is as useless as to ask after the colour of his hair.'

147 Friedrich Merkel, 'Bemerkungen eines Anatomen über die Gruppe des Laokoon', *Zeitschrift für bildende Kunst* II (1876), 353–62 (pp. 355 and 358).

148 See Foerster, 'Laokoon', p. 32 and Wilhelm Klein, *Geschichte der griechischen Kunst*, 3 vols (Leipzig: Veit & Co., 1904–07), III, 315.

149 See William St Clair, *Lord Elgin and the Marbles* (London: Oxford University Press, 1967), pp. 250–62.

were of a much later date than the masterpieces of Phidias and his contemporaries; and although some writers tried for a time to place the familiar works on the same level as the newly discovered older sculptures,[150] their efforts were fruitless. It was not that the Aegina marbles or the Parthenon frieze received the same kind of adulation with which Winckelmann had greeted the later sculptures: Theseus and Poseidon did not replace Laocoon, they merely reduced and diluted his appeal.

As the nineteenth century progressed, more and more was written on the Laocoon, as on other ancient sculptures, but fewer and fewer of the writers were anything other than art historians and archaeologists. The fragmentation of knowledge into specialised disciplines is, of course, one of the main reasons why Laocoon was left at the mercy of the specialists. Few now dared to indulge in the dilettantism of the previous century, when everyone of classical education—and that meant practically every scholar—felt entitled to pronounce on works of art which, more often than not, they knew only from engravings. Hegel ridicules the armchair scholars ('Stubengelehrte') of that era who had taken part in the debate without ever having set eyes on the sculptures they held forth upon. Besides, the growth of science and positivism left little room for physiognomical speculation in classical archaeology, and the literary associations which had made the statue so attractive to philological critics such as Lessing served only to alienate those who valued art for art's sake.[151] All these advances entailed losses as well as gains, for the literary quality of what was written on the statue was never again to reach its former standards, or the symbolic potentialities of the statue to be explored so profoundly.

Spiritually empty, of doubtful morality, anatomically inaccurate, contrived, calculated, and inferior to earlier Greek art, the Laocoon group was now reviled on every side. The standard verdict around the turn of the century was that it was 'an outstanding work of Greek

---

150 Thiersch, *Ueber die Epochen*, p. 384, following Visconti, admits that the Laocoon and other Hellenistic works are much later than those of the Periclean era, but maintains that they are of no less merit.

151 Overbeck, *Geschichte der griechischen Plastik*, II, 320ff., for example, sees it as one of the group's major faults that it is not fully intelligible as a work of art in its own right.

decadence',[152] mannered and sensational, lacking depth of feeling,[153] and even sinister and brutal, displaying 'a wily cruelty of taste'.[154] The neo-classicists of Victorian times condemned it as alien to true Greek values, and the painter Karl Stauffer-Bern blamed Laocoon, rather than Michelangelo, for all the extravagances of Baroque art since the group's discovery: 'It seems to me as if no work of art has caused so much damage in the world as the Laocoon group; I can virtually see Baroque art asleep in it [...]. From this point onwards, people began to sculpt potato sacks and pass them off as heroes [...].'[155] As the reverence with which the group had once been held evaporated, it became an object not just of abuse, but of caricature.[156] One of the earliest of these (Titian's famous parody, with apes instead of human figures, was aimed not at the group itself, but at Bandinelli's imitation)[157] is a characteristic poem of Heine, in which his mistress takes the place of the serpents:[158]

> You ought with love to embrace me,
> Beloved, beautiful girl!
> Embrace me with arms and with feet then,
> And with your flexible shape.
>
> Vigorously she has enlaced me,
> Entwined me and wrapped me around,
> The sweetest of all the serpents,
> The happiest Laocoon.

Such dignity as the group still possessed in Germany it owed mainly to Lessing's *Laocoon*, which was a standard work for senior pupils at

---

152   Karl Stauffer-Bern to Lydia Escher, 29 August 1889, in Otto Brahm, *Karl Stauffer-Bern. Sein Leben, seine Briefe, seine Gedichte*, 12th edn (Berlin: Meyer & Jessen, 1912), p. 293.

153   Heinrich Bulle, *Der schöne Mensch im Altertum*, 2nd edn (Munich and Leipzig: G. Hirth, 1912), p. 503.

154   August Schmarsow, *Erläuterungen und Kommentar zu Lessings Laokoon* (Leipzig: Quelle & Meyer, 1907), p. 38. Compare the negative judgements of English-speaking writers such as Lucy M. Mitchell, *A History of Ancient Sculpture* (London: Kegan Paul, Trench & Co., 1883), p. 605, who speaks of 'the revolting scene' the group affords, and Fred O. Nolte, *Lessing's Laokoon* (Lancaster, PA: Lancaster Press, 1940), p. 34, who says that the merit of the snakes is 'about equal to dislocated plumbing'.

155   Brahm, *Karl Stauffer-Bern*, pp. 293f.

156   See Klein, *Geschichte*, III, 315.

157   See Heyne, *Sammlung antiquarischer Aufsätze*, II, 41.

158   Heinrich Heine, *Historisch-kritische Gesamtausgabe der Werke*, ed. by Manfred Windfuhr, 16 vols (Hamburg: Hoffmann & Campe, 1973–97), I/1, 461.

the classically oriented *Gymnasien* in the later nineteenth century and helped to keep the earlier neo-classical values alive.[159]

By the early twentieth century, however, occasional voices were already protesting that the group was not decadent at all,[160] and that it might well now be underrated.[161] But by this time, one can no longer speak of the reception of the work in Germany in isolation, for the German writers were now reacting not so much to the earlier Laocoon cult in their own country as to current opinions in European archaeology at large. Negative judgements continue to be heard down to recent times,[162] but the critics are now on the whole more charitable. As one authority says—and the first three words are significant—'we must admit that it is a magnificent creation'.[163]

The group is now rarely mentioned outside the world of classical studies. Nevertheless, there is evidence that its symbolic potential is not yet exhausted, and that even the creative writer may still find a use for it. Peter Weiss, in his address of 1965 'Laocoon, or On the Limits of Language', discovers a new antithesis within the group: the father and the younger son have lost all ability to communicate, but the elder son, who will perhaps escape to tell of what he has seen, may symbolise our hopeless yet hopeful attempts to transcend the limitations of language:[164]

> In this sculpture, the dichotomy is expressed between that which is dumb and static, and that which turns towards the outside world and attracts its attention through movement. Laocoon and his younger son no longer presuppose any onlooker. They now merely constitute a monument to their own destruction. They will never again utter a sound. But the older son still belongs to an animated world, and he breaks out of the statuesque realm to give a report to those who will perhaps come to his aid.

---

159 A work written for this school public is Julius Ziehen, *Kunstgeschichtliches Anschaungsmaterial zu Lessings Laokoon*, 2nd edn (Bielefeld and Leipzig: Velhagen & Klasing, 1905), first published in 1899. Ziehen lists other works on *Laokoon* useful to schoolteachers.

160 See Klein, *Geschichte*, III, 315.

161 See Foerster, 'Laokoon', p. 1.

162 See, for example, Walter Herwig Schuchardt, *Die Epochen der griechischen Plastik* (Baden-Baden: Bruno Grimm Verlag, 1959), p. 126, who sees the work as 'in its contrived and elaborated quality lacking in full and genuine life'.

163 Richter, *The Sculpture and Sculptors of the Greeks*, p. 236.

164 Peter Weiss, *Rapporte* (Frankfurt a. M.: Suhrkamp, 1968), pp. 170–87 (pp. 180f.); note also Zoltan Imre's ballet 'Laocoon', written for the Ballet Rambert and first performed on 14 February 1978.

Such was the reception of the Laocoon group in Germany since Winckelmann. We have seen how, during the nineteenth century, it fell completely from its former eminence. What still has to be considered is why, apart from the fact that it was championed by Winckelmann, it had been held in such esteem during the previous century. The Renaissance and Counter-Reformation, of course, had little difficulty in assimilating it to their own scheme of values, both because of its provenance and its subject matter. It was a genuine relic of antiquity, authenticated by Pliny himself. And its subject was congenial to those already accustomed to the martyrdoms and crucifixions of Christian art, of which it could be seen as a typological forerunner. To the eighteenth century, however, it presented more of a challenge. The authority of antiquity was as binding as ever, and in some ways even more so than before. But the subject of the group, as traditionally understood, made it less tractable to a rationalistic and increasingly secular age. One of the problems the eighteenth century faced was that of making sense of an extreme case of suffering, with strong religious overtones, but without invoking religion to explain it. Only the young Herder resorted to Christian analogies, but he later abandoned them. It is more symptomatic of the times that Winckelmann, in his essay of 1755, warned artists against depicting saints, and recommended the classical—that is, heathen—myths instead.[165] Laocoon appealed to the eighteenth century as a representative figure of human suffering—but unlike its Christian equivalents, the suffering of Laocoon could no longer be given any transcendental significance.

With the exception of Hirt, all of the eighteenth-century writers discussed here, even those who, like Lessing and Goethe, stuck mainly to aesthetic questions, regarded Laocoon as a hero and exemplary figure. They saw in him a victory of the human spirit, whether over bodily weakness, an unjust fate, or the restraints of moral convention. According to the *Aeneid*, he defied the gods by hurling his spear at the Wooden Horse, which he refused to accept on trust, and he questioned the arguments of those who were prepared to do so. For Laocoon was a sceptic, and this assuredly helped to endear him to the century of the Enlightenment. But it was in his death that he seemed to display his greatest strength: for the main difference between Laocoon and the Christian martyrs—and, I would submit, the secret of his appeal to the

---

165 WW, I, 50.

eighteenth century—is that he does not accept his suffering, any more than he did the Wooden Horse, with resignation. His face, in which the Greek artists have combined all the traditional signs of pain, admittedly has much in common with the Christian art of the Baroque. But he is no St Sebastian, immobile and submissive, for his body is still full of resistance. Lessing took great trouble to show that the moment depicted is that *before* Laocoon succumbs to his torment, as did Goethe when Hirt dared to suggest that Laocoon has already succumbed. Heyne, too, stressed that he is struggling with all his might.[166] And we must not forget that, in Montorsoli's restoration by which the group was known until the original right arm, bent back behind Laocoon's head, was discovered in 1906, Laocoon held the serpent high above him, in what might be interpreted as a last, self-assertive gesture of defiance.[167] For most writers of the eighteenth century, then, the group was a glorification of the human spirit and its essential freedom, even in the direst of predicaments, and it was in this freedom that they found a sense in Laocoon's terrible fate.

The other main reason why the group was so greatly revered was that, from Winckelmann onwards, it was associated with those values which the neo-classicists claimed to have found in ancient Greece. Despite the terror of the scene, balance and restraint were preserved. Reason—whether moral or artistic—presided over the catastrophe, and conferred a unity and harmony on the whole. But it was possible to discover other, opposing principles in the work, just as the Baroque era had done, and, in Hegelian fashion, the antithesis was soon to claim its rights. For Heinse already, it represented not harmony and restraint, but violent and uncontrolled expression.

Once it had been identified with neo-classicism, however, it had to be defended, and the conflict of Goethe, Schiller, and their allies with Hirt was a campaign against a threat to their classicistic principles. But on several counts, the position they held was untenable. Apart from the reasons already given, the fact that people ceased to require the sanction of antiquity to justify their aspirations rendered Laocoon superfluous in aesthetic theory. It is appropriate that nearly all of the

---

166 Heyne, *Sammlung antiquarischer Aufsätze*, II, 20.
167 See Wolfgang Helbig, *Führer durch die öffentlichen Sammlungen klassischer Altertümer in Rom*, 4th edn, 4 vols (Tübingen: E. Wasmuth, 1963–72), I, 164.

eighteenth-century commentators emphasise how precarious the group's situation is. The balance cannot for long be maintained, and destruction must shortly supervene. The group may therefore stand as a symbol of neo-classicism itself,[168] as an interlude, a 'pregnant moment', between Baroque extravagance and Romantic self-abandon.

One of the most remarkable things about the Laocoon debate is the number of different interpretations it has generated. And another is the extreme way in which they diverge, and the vehemence with which they have been defended. The debate, in fact, has been conducted in superlatives, with very few signs of compromise. The group has been pronounced both the greatest and the most pernicious work of art of all time. Part of the reason for this is that the spectacle it affords is itself an extreme and dire eventuality, which is bound to evoke a forceful reaction. The bizarre and horrible death of a father and one or both of his sons, of whose agony their violent reactions can leave us in no doubt, produces a powerful initial shock. As Winckelmann said, we can almost feel the pain of the bite ourselves, accentuated as it is by Laocoon's complete nudity and the sensitivity of the area affected. To this shock, we can either respond with revulsion, or master it by finding some aesthetic or moral justification for the work.

If we analyse the spectacle further, we see that, as Goethe realised, it was full of paradoxes and antitheses. Here is life at its most intense at the moment of death. Here, with grim irony, a priest is immolated upon his own altar. The three figures themselves are full of contrasts: youth contrasts with age, the younger son is dying, the elder is almost free: the right hands are expressive and gesturing, the left hands are active in defence. There are movements throughout, voluntary and involuntary, human and animal, and yet all the participants are bound together and rooted to the spot. In the organisation of the group, we find variety and unity, dissonance and harmony, expression and formal control. And in this fearful conflict of man against nature, of mind against matter, there are signs both of resistance and capitulation, of defiance and resignation. To this, we ourselves react with admiration and revulsion, pity and horror, hope and fear, so that a series of conflicts is set up within us in turn.

---

168 Cf. Butler, *The Tyranny of Greece over Germany*, p. 81.

In order to resolve these, we must decide which of our emotions have priority, or—and this amounts to the same thing—which poles of which antitheses within the group are more important than their opposites. This task is made no easier by the fact that the group has undergone numerous alterations and restorations since it was discovered, and that we do not even know for what purpose it was originally created. In short, we have to interpret the work's significance, and since the event it depicts is intelligible only in terms of the myth it is based on, we have to decide which version of the myth to follow. And it is here that our troubles really begin, because the different versions are diametrically opposed or internally contradictory. In some, Laocoon is an innocent hero, punished only for defending his fatherland; in others, he is first and foremost a reprobate who desecrated the temple of the god he served; and in others again, he is both a patriot and a criminal. We turn once more to the group to measure the conflicting versions against it, and we are confronted with the same ambiguities as before. Is Laocoon a rebel or a martyr, a hero or a criminal? Is his punishment just or unjust? does he bear it with fortitude or despair, with indignation or remorse? does he indeed display any conscious emotion at all, or is he even in a position to do so? Some have contended that he is not, and yet others have read almost every kind of expression, short of hilarity, into his face.

In the last resort, our interpretation will be guided by yet another set of variables, those of our own predispositions and background. Indeed, when we evaluate the interpretations of past critics, it is usually possible to relate them to the background and outlook of the writers concerned. But we must be wary of reducing what they say to straightforward social determinants—for example, Winckelmann's interpretation to his discontent with Germany, his penurious circumstances, and his need for a heroic ideal; Lessing's to his revolt against the French influence, typified by rigid Cornelian heroism; and so on. For although these were no doubt contributory factors, the case of Heinse provides a salutary warning against such simplifications: as we have seen, Heinse came up with several variant interpretations of the group within a short space of time, some of which later reappeared in the works of others of completely different backgrounds and attitudes. The reception of the Laocoon group in Germany has been a complex process, in which the ambiguous evidence of the group itself, the various versions of the myth, and the personalities of the critics, along with their individual circumstances, the ideological influences to which they were subject, and the general state of learning at the time at which they wrote, have interacted with one another—and with a further factor of even greater significance than the rest: the reception of the group by their predecessors. In almost every case, the critics were replying to earlier critics, and the most important factor within the debate has been the debate itself.[169]

Given the nature of the group, it is not surprising that the debate consisted of a movement between extremes, the chief of which were the idealistic and naturalistic modes of interpretation. Both could point to evidence in support of their case, but it was the failure of the former to give a morally convincing account of the work which helped to tip the balance in favour of the latter. Many writers from the nineteenth century onwards have felt that the myth, as here depicted, is ethically incommensurable, and that technical virtuosity was therefore the artists' principal consideration. But the conclusion does not necessarily follow from the premise: perhaps it was the power, rather than the justice, of the gods which the sculptors wished to commemorate. Be that as it may, critics of the group are still wary of interpreting its content, and they usually have more to say on its style and its place in the history of art. This is certainly not because the earlier enigmas have been disposed of. It is because writers are more conscious than before of the complexity of the issues, the number of variables involved, and the failure of their predecessors to produce an interpretation which might comprehend them all without leaving an intractable residue. One twentieth-century writer refuses to reopen the questions of which moment is depicted, what feelings are expressed, and which version of the legend is followed, and decides instead that *all* past interpretations are justified.[170] For those who constructed them, they of course were. But in that case, any other interpretation, however arbitrary, must be equally justified, and we are left with a complete relativism which must

---

169 Compare Karl Robert Mandelkow, 'Probleme der Wirkungsgeschichte', in Mandelkow, *Orpheus und Maschine. Acht literaturgeschichtliche Arbeiten* (Heidelberg: Stiehm, 1976), pp. 103–17 (p. 113): 'The reception history of a work or author is always from the start the reception history of the reception history [...] One's own horizon of expectation is modified by one's reaction to other horizons of expectation.'

170 Sichtermann, *Laokoon*, p. 23.

inhibit all further initiatives. In short, critics now hesitate to interpret the group not because the problems have been solved, but because they have despaired of conclusively solving them.[171]

The Laocoon group is in this respect a paradigmatic case—not of the limits of poetry and visual art, but of the limits of interpretation. For if no comprehensive interpretation can be found, there are two equally good, but incompatible reasons why this must be so: either the work itself may have no coherent conception which can be reduced to a unitary explanation; or we, through lack of evidence or perspicacity, have failed to discover one. And even if we do succeed to our own satisfaction, the former possibility can never be completely eliminated.

When all is said and done, we may well ask why so much intellectual effort has been expended on what now seems to many so undeserving an object. The villain of the piece, if there is a villain, is surely Pliny, who convinced at least three centuries that this was the greatest sculpture of all time. And the hero, if there is a hero, is perhaps the sceptical archaeologist Heyne, whose words of warning, like those of the Trojan priest Laocoon, went unheeded by his countrymen: 'It is very much to be doubted that the Greek artists ever had in mind the thousandth part of all the fine aesthetic reasonings on quiet grandeur with which they are credited.'[172]

---

171 The fullest and most impressive account to date of the current *impasse* in Laocoon studies is Richard Brilliant's book *My Laocoon* (Berkeley, CA: University of California Press, 2000).

172 Heyne, *Sammlung antiquarischer Aufsätze*, II, 22 (1779).

List of Illustrations

Chapter 1

Chapter 2

Chapter 3

Chapter 4

Chapter 5

Chapter 6

Chapter 7

Chapter 8

Darstellung der Urpflanze. Woodcut by Pierre Jean François Turpin   162
based on a concept by Johann Wolfgang von Goethe (1837), scanned
from Anita Albus, *Die Kunst der Künste. Erinnerungen an die Malerei*
(Frankfurt am Main: Eichborn Verlag 1997). Photograph by JuTa
(2010), Wikimedia, Public Domain, https://commons.wikimedia.
org/wiki/File:Urpflanze.png

Chapter 9

Portrait of Immanuel Kant by Johann Gottlieb Becker (1768), oil on   178
canvas, Schiller-Nationalmuseum, Marbach am Neckar, Germany.
Photograph by UpdateNerd (2018), Wikimedia, Public Domain,
https://upload.wikimedia.org/wikipedia/commons/f/f2/Kant_
gemaelde_3.jpg

Chapter 10

Autograph of Schiller's 'Ode to Joy' (1785). Photograph by   214
Historiograf (2011), Wikimedia, Public Domain, https://upload.
wikimedia.org/wikipedia/commons/2/2d/Schiller_an_die_freude_
manuskript_2.jpg

Chapter 11

'Laocoon and his sons', also known as 'the Laocoon Group'. Marble,   240
copy after an Hellenistic original from ca. 200 BC. Found in the
Baths of Trajan in 1506. Museo Pio-Clementino, Octagon, Laocoon
Hall, Vatican Museums. Photograph by Marie-Lan Nguyen (2009),
Wikimedia, Public Domain, https://upload.wikimedia.org/
wikipedia/commons/1/17/Laocoon_Pio-Clementino_Inv1059-1064-
1067.jpg

Bibliography

Adickes, Erich, *Kant als Naturforscher*, 2 vols (Berlin: De Gruyter, 1924–25).

Adler, Jeremy, *'Eine fast magische Anziehungskraft'. Goethes 'Wahlverwandtschaften' und die Chemie seiner Zeit* (Munich: C. H. Beck, 1987).

Aesch, Alexander Gode-von, *Natural Science in German Romanticism* (New York: Columbia University Press, 1941).

Albertsen, Leif Ludwig, *Das Lehrgedicht. Eine Geschichte der antikisierenden Sachepik in der neueren deutschen Literatur* (Aarhus: Akademisk Boghandel, 1967).

Allgemeine Deutsche Biographie, 56 vols (Leipzig: Duncker & Humblot, 1875–1912).

Allison, Henry E., *Lessing and the Enlightenment* (Ann Arbor, MI: University of Michigan Press, 1966).

Althaus, Horst, *Laokoon. Stoff und Form* (Berne: Francke, 1968).

Amory, Thomas, *The Life and Opinions of John Buncle Esquire*, ed. by Ernest A. Baker (London: Routledge, 1904).

——, [published anonymously], *The Life of John Buncle, Esq.; Containing Various Observations and Reflections, Made in several Parts of the World; and Many Extraordinary relations*, 2 vols (London: J. Noon, 1756–66).

Anderson, James, *The Constitutions of the Ancient and Honourable Fraternity of Free and Accepted Masons*, rev. edn, ed. by John Entick (London: J. Scott, 1767).

Antognazza, Maria Rosa, *Leibniz. An Intellectual Biography* (Cambridge: Cambridge University Press, 2009).

Assmann, Jan, *Religio duplex. Ägyptische Mysterien und europäische Aufklärung* (Berlin: Verlag der Weltreligionen, 2010).

Athenaeum. Eine Zeitschrift von August Wilhelm und Friedrich Schlegel, ed. by Ernst Behler (Stuttgart: Cotta, 1960, originally Berlin: Vieweg, 1798; Unger, 1799–1800).

Augustine, St, *The Trinity*, translated by Stephen McKenna, *The Fathers of the Church*, 45 (Washington, D.C.: Catholic University of America Press, 1970).

Baeumer, Max L., *Heinse-Studien* (Stuttgart: Metzler, 1966).

Bahr, Ehrhard, et al. (eds.), *Humanität und Dialog. Lessing und Mendelssohn in neuer Sicht* (Detroit, MI and Munich: Wayne State University Press and edition text+kritik, 1982).

——, 'The Pursuit of Happiness in the Political Writings of Lessing and Kant', *Studies on Voltaire and the Eighteenth Century*, 151 (1976), 167–74.

Bapp, Karl, 'Goethe und Lukrez', *Jahrbuch der Goethe-Gesellschaft*, 12 (1926), 46–67.

Barnard, Frederick M., *Self-Direction and Political Legitimacy. Rousseau and Herder* (Oxford: Clarendon Press, 1988).

Barner, Wilfried, 'Geheime Lenkung. Zur Turmgesellschaft in Goethes Wilhelm Meister', in *Goethe's Narrative Fiction*, ed. by William J. Lillyman (Berlin and New York: De Gruyter, 1983), pp. 85–109.

——, and other hands, *Lessing: Epoche–Werk–Wirkung*, 5th edn (Munich: C. H. Beck, 1987).

Baumgarten, Siegmund Jacob, *Theologische Lehrsätze von den Grundwahrheiten der christlichen Lehre* (Halle: Gebauer, 1747).

Beierwaltes, Werner, *Platonismus und Idealismus* (Frankfurt a. M.: Klostermann, 1972).

Bergstraesser, Arnold, 'Die Epochen der Geistesgeschichte in Goethes Denken', in Bergstraesser, *Staat und Dichtung* (Freiburg: Rombach, 1967), pp. 87–97.

Berthold, Gustav, Friedrich von Oppeln-Bronikowski, and Adolph Menzel, *Die Werke Friedrichs des Großen in deutscher Übersetzung*, 10 vols (Berlin: R. Hobbing, 1913–14).

Bieber, Margarete, *Laocoon. The Influence of the Group since its Rediscovery*, rev. edn (Detroit, MI: Wayne State University Press, 1967).

Blackwell Companion to the Enlightenment, The, ed. by John W. Yolton and other hands (Oxford: Blackwell, 1991).

Blaschke, Julius, 'Schillers Gedichte in der Musik', *Neue Zeitschrift in der Musik* (1905), 397–401.

Blümner, Hugo, *Lessings Laokoon*, 2nd edn (Berlin: Weidmann, 1880).

Böhme, Gernot, *Alternativen der Wissenschaft* (Frankfurt a. M.: Suhrkamp, 1980).

——, 'Ist Goethes Farbenlehre Wissenschaft?', *Studia Leibnitiana*, 9/1 (1977), 27–54.

Bohnen, Klaus, ed., *Lessings 'Nathan der Weise'* (Wege der Forschung, 587) (Darmstadt: Wissenschaftliche Buchgesellschaft, 1984).

——, *Geist und Buchstabe. Zum Prinzip des kritischen Verfahrens in Lessings literaturästhetischen und theologischen Schriften* (Cologne: Böhlau, 1974).

Brahm, Otto, *Karl Stauffer-Bern. Sein Leben, seine Briefe, seine Gedichte*, 12th edn (Berlin: Meyer & Jessen, 1912).

Brecht, Bertolt, *Gesammelte Werke*, 20 vols (Frankfurt a. M.: Suhrkamp, 1967).

Brilliant, Richard, *My Laocoön* (Berkeley, CA: University of California Press, 2000).

Broder, Henryk M., *Kritik der reinen Toleranz*, 2nd edn (Munich: Pantheon, 2009).

Brunn, Enrico, *Geschichte der griechischen* Künstler, 2 vols (Stuttgart: Ebner & Seubert, 1857–59).

Bulle, Heinrich, *Der schöne Mensch im Altertum*, 2nd edn (Munich and Leipzig: G. Hirth, 1912).

Butler, E. M., *The Tyranny of Greece over Germany* (Cambridge: Cambridge University Press, 1935).

Cassirer, Ernst, 'Schiller und Shaftesbury', *Publications of the English Goethe Society*, 11 (1935), 35–59.

Catt, Henri de, *Frederick the Great. The Memoirs of his Reader*, translated by F. S. Flint, 2 vols (London: Constable & Co., 1916).

Chladenius (Chladni), Johann Martin, *Einleitung zur richtigen Auslegung vernünftiger Reden und Schriften* (Leipzig: Lankisch, 1742).

Contiades, Ion, *G. E. Lessing: 'Ernst und Falk'. Mit den Fortsetzungen J. G. Herders und F. Schlegels* (Frankfurt a. M.: Insel Verlag, 1968).

Cook, Nicholas, *Beethoven: Symphony No. 9* (Cambridge: Cambridge University Press, 1993).

Coreth, Emerich, *Trinitätsdenken in neuzeitlicher Philosophie*, Salzburger Universitätsreden, 77 (Salzburg: A. Pustet, 1986).

Cranz, August Friedrich, 'Fragment eines Schreibens über den Ton in den Streitschriften einiger teutschen Gelehrten und Schöngeister' [no author, place of publication or publisher named], (1779).

Creuz, C. C. von, *Oden und andere Gedichte*, 2 vols (Frankfurt a. M.: Varrentrapp, 1769).

Cusa, Nicholas of, *Nicholas of Cusa on Learned Ignorance* [*De docta ignorantia*, 1440], ed. by Jasper Hopkins (Minneapolis: Arthur J. Banning Press, 1981).

——, *Nicholas of Cusa on Interreligious Harmony* [*De pace fidei*, 1453], edited and translated by James E. Biechler and H. Lawrence Bond (Lewiston, Queenston and Lampeter: Edwin Mellen, 1990).

Dacier, M., 'Examen de l'Histoire de la Matrone d'Ëphèse', *Mémoires de littérature, tirés des Registres de l'Académie Royale des Inscriptions*, 41 (1780), 523–45.

Dalzell, Alexander, 'Lucretius', in *The Cambridge History of Classical Literature*, Vol. II, Part 2, 'The Late Republic', ed. by E. J. Kenney (Cambridge: Cambridge University Press, 1982), pp. 33–55.

Darwin, Erasmus, *The Botanic Garden*, 2 vols (London: Jones & Co., 1789–91).

Dau, Rudolf, 'Friedrich Schillers Hymne "An die Freude". Zu einigen Problemen ihrer Interpretation und aktuellen Rezeption', *Weimarer Beiträge*, 24 (1978), 38–60.

Daunicht, Richard, *Lessing im Gespräch* (Munich: Fink, 1971).

Deile, Gotthold, *Freimaurerlieder als Quellen zu Schillers Lied 'An die Freude'* (Leipzig: Verlag Adolf Weigel, 1907).

Denk, Ferdinand, 'Ein Streit um Gehalt und Gestalt des Kunstwerks in der deutschen Klassik', *Germanisch-Romanische Monatshefte*, 18 (1930), 427–42.

——, *Das Kunstschöne und Charakteristische von Winckelmann bis Friedrich Schlegel* (Munich: A. Huber, 1925).

Deppermann, Klaus, 'Die Kirchenpolitik des Großen Kurfürsten', *Pietismus und Neuzeit*, 6 (1981), 99–114.

d'Hondt, Jacques, *Hegel Secret. Recherches sur les sources cachées de la pensée de Hegel* (Paris: Presses universitaires de France, 1968).

Dickey, Laurence, *Hegel. Religion, Economics, and the Politics of Spirit 1770–1807* (Cambridge: Cambridge University Press, 1987).

Die Religion in Geschichte und Gegenwart, ed. by Hans Dieter Betz, Don S. Browning, Bernd Janowski, and Eberhard Jüngel, 3rd edn, 7 vols (Tübingen: Mohr, 1957–65).

Dierse, Ulrich, 'Der Newton der Geschichte', *Archiv für Begriffsgeschichte*, 30 (1986–87), 158–82.

Dülmen, Richard van, 'Die Aufklärungsgesellschaften in Deutschland als Forschungsproblem', *Francia*, 5 (1977), 251–75.

——, *Der Geheimbund der Illuminaten* (Stuttgart-Bad Cannstatt: Frommann, 1975).

Durzak, Manfred, 'Gesellschaftsreflexion und Gesellschaftsdarstellung bei Lessing', *Zeitschrift für deutsche Philologie*, 93 (1974), 546–60.

Dusch, Johann Jakob, *Briefe zur Bildung des Geschmacks*, 6 vols, rev. edn (Leipzig: Meyer, 1773).

Dyck, Martin, *Die Gedichte Schillers* (Berne: Francke, 1967).

Eberhard, Johann August, *Neue Apologie des Sokrates oder Untersuchung der Lehre von der Seligkeit der Heiden*, 2 vols (Berlin: Nicolai, 1772–78).

Eibl, Karl, '"kommen würde" gegen "nimmermehr gekommen wäre". Aufklärung des "Widerspruchs" von § 4 und § 77 in Lessings Erziehung des Menschengeschlechts', *Germanisch-Romanische Monatsschrift*, 65 (1984), 461–64.

Eichhorn, Andreas, *Beethovens Neunte Symphonie. Die Geschichte ihrer Aufführung und Rezeption* (Kassel: Bärenreiter, 1993).

Einsiedel, August von, *Ideen* ed. by Wilhelm Dobbek (Berlin: Akademie-Verlag, 1957).

Encyclopedia of the Enlightenment, ed. by Alan Charles Kors, 4 vols (Oxford: Oxford University Press, 2003).

Engelhardt, Dietrich von, *Historisches Bewusstsein in der Naturwissenschaft* (Freiburg: Karl Alber, 1979).

Ettlinger, L. D., 'Exemplum Doloris. Reflections on the Laocoon Group', in *De Artibus Opuscula XL. Essays in Honor of Erwin Panofsky*, ed. by Millard Meiss, 2 vols (New York: New York University Press, 1961).

Fabian, Bernhard, 'Lucrez in England im siebzehnten und achtzehnten Jahrhundert', in *Aufklärung und Humanismus*, ed. by Richard Toellner (Heidelberg: Schneider, 1980).

——, 'Pope and Lucretius: Observations On An Essay On Man', *The Modern Language Review*, 74 (1979), 524–37, https://doi.org/10.2307/3726701

——, 'Das Lehrgedicht als Problem der Poetik', in *Die nicht mehr schönen Künste*, ed. by H. R. Jauss (Munich: Fink, 1968), pp. 67–89.

Faust, Ulrich, *Mythologien und Religionen des Ostens bei Johann Gottfried Herder* (Münster: Aschendorff, 1977).

Fernow, Carl Ludwig, *Römische Studien*, 3 vols (Zurich: H. Gessner, 1806–08).

Fink, Gonthier-Louis, 'Lessings Ernst und Falk. Das moralische Glaubensbekenntnis eines kosmopolitischen Individualisten', *Recherches Germaniques*, 10 (1980), pp. 18–64.

Fink, Karl J., *Goethe's History of Science* (Cambridge: Cambridge University Press, 1991).

Fleischmann, Wolfgang Bernard, 'Zum Anti-Lucretius des Kardinals de Polignac', *Romanische Forschungen*, 77 (1965), 42–63.

——, *Lucretius and English Literature 1680–1740* (Paris: Nizet, 1964).

——, 'The Debt of the Enlightenment to Lucretius', *Studies on Voltaire and the Eighteenth Century*, 25 (1963), 631–43.

Foerster, R., 'Laokoon', *Jahrbuch des Kaiserlichen Deutschen Archäologischen Instituts*, 21 (1906), 1–32.

Forst, Rainer, *Toleranz im Konflikt. Geschichte, Gehalt und Gegenwart eines umstrittenen Begriffs* (Frankfurt a. M.: Suhrkamp, 2003).

Frenzel, Elisabeth, *Stoffe der Weltliteratur* (Stuttgart: Kröner, 1962).

Frick, R. H., *Die Erleuchteten. Gnostisch-theosophische und alchemistisch-rosenkreuzerische Geheimgesellschaften bis zum Ende des 18. Jahrhunderts* (Graz: Akademische Druck- und Verlagsanstalt, 1973).

Friedman, Michael, 'Causal Laws and the Foundations of Natural Science', in *The Cambridge Companion to Kant*, ed. by Paul Guyer (Cambridge: Cambridge University Press, 1992), pp. 161–99.

——, *Kant and the Exact Sciences* (Cambridge, MA: Harvard University Press, 1992).

Fusil, C.-A., 'Lucrèce et les littérateurs poètes et artistes du XVIIIe siècle', *Revue d'Histoire littéraire de la France*, 37 (1930), 161–176.

——, 'Lucrèce et les philosophes du XVIIIe siècle', *Revue d'Histoire littéraire de la France*, 35 (1928), 194–210.

Gadamer, Hans-Georg, *Wahrheit und Methode. Grundzüge einer philosophischen Hermeneutik*, 4th edn (Tübingen: Mohr, 1975).

Gale, Thomas, ed., *Opuscula mythologica physica et ethica, graece et latine* (Amsterdam: Henricus Wetsteinius, 1688).

Gay, Peter, *The Enlightenment: An Interpretation, I, The Rise of Modern Paganism* (New York: Knopf Doubleday, 1967).

Geiger, Ludwig, 'Acht Briefe F. A. Wolfs, sieben Briefe A. Hirts, vier Briefe Goethes an Hirt', *Goethe-Jahrbuch*, 15 (1894), 54–110.

Gerstenberg, Heinrich Wilhelm von, *Ugolino*, ed. by Christoph Siegrist (Stuttgart: Reclam, 1966).

Geschichtliche Grundbegriffe, ed. by Otto Brunner, Werner Conze, and Reinhart Koselleck, 8 vols (Stuttgart: Klett, 1972–97).

Gloy, Karen, *Die Kantische Theorie der Naturwissenschaft* (Berlin: De Gruyter, 1976).

Goethe, Johann Wolfgang, *Goethes Gespräche*, ed. by Wolfgang Herwig, 5 vols (Munich: Deutscher Taschenbuch Verlag, 1998).

——, *Goethe-Handbuch*, ed. by Bernd Witte, and other hands, 5 vols (Stuttgart: Metzler, 1996–99).

——, *Goethes Briefe und Briefe an Goethe* [HA Briefe], ed. by Karl Robert Mandelkow, 6 vols, 4th edn (Munich: C. H. Beck, 1988).

——, *Goethes Gespräche*, ed. by Wolfgang Herwig, 4 vols (Zurich and Stuttgart: Artemis Verlag, 1965–72).

——, *Der junge Goethe*, ed. by Hanna Fischer-Lamberg, 6 vols (Berlin: De Gruyter, 1963–74).

——, *Werke, Hamburg edition* [HA], ed. by Erich Trunz, 14 vols (Hamburg: Wegner, 1948–64).

——, *Die Schriften zur Naturwissenschaft* [LA], ed. by the Deutsche Akademie der Naturforscher, 17 vols (Weimar: Böhlau, 1947–70).

——, *Goethes Gespräche mit Eckermann*, ed. by Franz Deibel (Leipzig: Insel-Verlag, 1921).

——, *Goethes Briefwechsel mit Heinrich Meyer*, ed. by Max Hecker, Schriften der Goethe-Gelleschaft, 34 (Weimar: Goethe-Gesellschaft, 1917–1922).

——, *Briefwechsel zwischen Schiller und Goethe*, ed. by Franz Muncker, 4 vols (Stuttgart: Cotta, 1892).

——, *Werke, Weimar edition* [WA], 133 vols (Weimar: Böhlau, 1889–1919).

——, *Briefwechsel zwischen Goethe und Knebel (1774–1832)*, ed. by Gottschalk Eduard Guhrauer, 2 vols (Leipzig: Brockhaus, 1851).

Gögelein, Christoph, *Zu Goethes Begriff von Wissenschaft auf dem Wege der Methodik seiner Farbstudien* (Munich: Hanser, 1972).

Goldenbaum, Ursula, 'Einleitung', in *Appell an das Publikum. Die öffentliche Debatte in der deutschen Aufklärung 1687–1796*, ed. by Ursula Goldenbaum (Berlin: Akademie Verlag, 2004), pp. 1–118.

Golinski, J. V., 'Science in the Enlightenment', *History of Science*, 24 (1986), 411–24.

Goltz, Alexander von der, 'Lessings Fragment Das Christentum der Vernunft. Eine Arbeit seiner Jugend', *Theologische Studien und Kritiken*, 30 (1857), 56–84.

Gombrich, E. H., 'Lessing. Lecture on a Master Mind', *Proceedings of the British Academy*, 43 (1957), 133–56.

Gräf, H. G., *Goethe über seine Dichtungen* (Frankfurt a. M.: Rütten & Loening, 1901–14).

Grisebach, Eduard, *Die Wanderung der Novelle von der treulosen Witwe durch die Weltliteratur*, 2., vermehrte Ausgabe (Berlin: Lehmann, 1889).

Grumach, Ernst, *Goethe und die Antike. Eine Sammlung*, 2 vols (Berlin: De Gruyter, 1949).

Grumach, Renate, and Grumach, Ernst, *Goethe, Begegnungen und Gespräche* (Berlin: De Gruyter, 1965).

Grundmann, Herbert, *Studien über Joachim von Floris* (Leipzig: Teubner, 1927).

Guggisberg, Hans R., *Religiöse Toleranz. Dokumente zur Geschichte einer Forderung* (Stuttgart–Bad Cannstatt: frommann-holzboog, 1984).

Guignes, Joseph de, ed., *Le Chou-King, un des livres sacrés des Chinois* (Paris: N.M. Tilliard, 1770).

Gunton, Colin E., *The One, the Three and the Many* (Cambridge: Cambridge University Press, 1993).

Guthke, Karl S., 'Lessings Rezensionen. Besuch in einem Kartenhaus', *Jahrbuch des Freien Deutschen Hochstifts* (1993), 1–59.

——, 'Lessing und das Judentum', *Wolfenbütteler Studien zur Aufklärung*, 4 (1977), 229–71.

——, 'Lessings "Sechstes Freimaurergespräch"', *Zeitschrift für deutsche Philologie*, 86 (1966), 576–97.

Hadzsits, George Depue, *Lucretius and his Influence* (New York: Cooper Square Publishers, 1963).

Hales, Steven D., and Rex Welshon, *Nietzsche's Perspectivism* (Urbana and Chicago, IL: University of Illinois Press, 2000).

Haller, Albrecht von, *Gedichte*, ed. by Ludwig Hirzel, 2 vols (Frauenfeld and Leipzig: Huber, 1917).

Hammermayer, Ludwig, *Der Wilhelmsbader Freimaurerkonvent von 1782* (Heidelberg: Schneider, 1980).

Harnack, Otto, 'Goethes Kunstanschauung in ihrer Bedeutung für die Gegenwart', *Goethe-Jahrbuch*, 15 (1894), 187–205.

——, 'Zu Goethes Laokoonaufsatz', *Vierteljahrsschrift für Litteraturgeschichte*, 6 (1893) 156–58.

Harris, H. S., *Hegel's Development. Toward the Sunlight 1770–1801* (Oxford: Clarendon Press, 1972).

Hatfield, H. C., *Winckelmann and his German Critics* (New York: King's Crow Press, 1943).

Haupt, Johann Thomas, *Gründe der Vernunft zur Erläuterung und zum Beweise des Geheimnisses der Heiligen Dreieinigkeit* (Rostock and Wismar: J. A. Berger and J. Boedner, 1752).

Hay Colligan, J., *The Arian Movement in England* (Manchester: Manchester University Press, 1913).

Haym, Rudolf, *Herder*, 2nd edn (Berlin: Aufbau Verlag, 1954), 2 vols.

——, *Die romantische Schule*, 4th edn (Berlin: Weidmann, 1920).

Hebbel, Friedrich, *Sämtliche Werke*, ed. by Richard Maria Werner, 12 vols (Berlin: Behr, 1901–03).

Hedley, Douglas, 'Coleridge's Intellectual Intuition, the Vision of God, and the Walled Garden of "Kubla Khan"', *Journal of the History of Ideas*, 54 (1998), 115–34.

Hegel, Georg Willhelm Friedrich, *Lectures on the Philosophy of World History. Introduction: Reason in History*, translated by H. B. Nisbet (Cambridge: Cambridge University Press, 1975).

——, *Theorie-Werkausgabe*, ed. by Eva Moldenhauer and Karl Markus Michel, 20 vols (Frankfurt a. M.: Suhrkamp, 1970).

——, *Briefe von und an Hegel*, ed. by Johannes Hoffmeister, 5 vols (Hamburg: Meiner, 1952–54).

——, *Vorlesungen über die Ästhetik*, ed. by H. G. Hotho, 2nd edn, 3 vols (Berlin: Duncker und Humblot, 1842–43).

——, *Werke*, ed. by Phillip Marheineke and other hands, 18 vols (Berlin: Duncker und Humblot, 1832–45).

Heine, Heinrich, *Historisch-kritische Gesamtausgabe der Werke*, ed. by Manfred Windfuhr, 16 vols (Hamburg: Hoffmann & Campe, 1973–97).

Heinse, Wilhelm, *Ardinghello und die glückseligen Inseln*, ed. by Max L. Baeumer (Stuttgart: Reclam, 1975).

——, *Sämtliche Werke*, ed. by Carl Schüddekopf, 10 vols (Leipzig: Insel Verlag, 1903–25).

Heinz, Marion, 'Existenz und Individualität. Untersuchungen zu Herders Gott', in *Kategorien der Existenz. Festschrift für Wolfgang Janke*, ed. by Klaus Held and Jochem Hennigfeld (Würzburg: Königshausen & Neumann, 1993), pp. 160–78.

Heise, Wolfgang, 'Lessings Ernst und Falk', *Weimarer Beiträge*, 11 (1979), 5–20.

Helbig, Wolfgang, *Führer durch die öffentlichen Sammlungen klassischer Altertümer in Rom*, 4th edn, 4 vols (Tübingen: E. Wasmuth, 1963–72).

Henke, P. J. W., *Die Gruppe des Laokoon* (Leipzig and Heidelberg: Winter, 1862).

Herder, Johann Gottfried, *Briefe. Gesamtausgabe 1763–1803*, ed. by Karl-Heinz Hahn, Wilhelm Dobbek and Günter Arnold, 10 vols (Weimar: Böhlau, 1977–2001).

——, *Ausgewählte Werke in Einzelausgaben. Schriften zur Literatur*, 2 vols (Berlin and Weimar, Aufbau Verlag, 1985–90).

——, *Sämtliche Werke* [SW], ed. by Bernhard Suphan, 33 vols (Berlin: Weidmann, 1877–1913).

——, *Von und an Herder: ungedruckte Briefe aus Herders Nachlaß*, ed. by Ferdinand Gottfried von Herder and Heinrich Düntzer, 3 vols (Leipzig: Dyk'sche Buchhandlung, 1861–62).

——, *Bibliotheca Herderiana* (Weimar: privately printed, 1804).

Hettner, Hermann, *Geschichte der deutschen Literatur im achtzehnten Jahrhundert*, ed. by Georg Witkowski, 4 vols (Leipzig: Paul List Verlag, 1928).

Heyne, Christoph Gottlob, *Sammlung antiquarischer Aufsätze*, 2 vols (Leipzig: Weidmanns Erben und Reich, 1778–79).

Hillen, Gert, *Lessing-Chronik. Daten zu Leben und Werk* (Munich: Hanser, 1979).

Hirt, Aloys, 'Über die Characteristik als Hauptgrundsatz der bildenden Künste bei den Alten', *Berlinisches Archiv der Zeit und ihres Geschmacks*, 2 (1798), 437–51.

——, 'Nachtrag über Laokoon', *Die Horen*, XII, 12. Stück (1797), 19–28.

——, 'Über Laokoon', *Die Horen*, XII, 10. Stück (1797), 1–26.

——, 'Versuch über das Kunstschöne', *Die Horen*, XI, 7. Stück (1797), 1–37.

Historisches Wörterbuch der Philosophie, ed. by Joachim Ritter, 13 vols (Darmstadt: Wissenschaftliche Buchgesellschaft, 1971–2007).

Hocke, Gustav René, *Lukrez in Frankreich von der Renaissance bis zur Revolution* (Cologne: Kerschgens, 1935).

Hodgson, Leonard, *The Doctrine of the Trinity* (London: Nisbet, 1943).

Hoensbroech, Marion Gräfin, *Die List der Kritik. Lessings kritische Schriften und Dramen* (Munich: Fink, 1976).

Hogarth, William, *The Analysis of Beauty* (London: J. Reeves, 1753).

Höpfner, Felix, *Wissenschaft wider die Zeit. Goethes Farbenlehre aus rezeptionsgeschichtlicher Sicht* (Heidelberg: Winter, 1990).

Howard, William Guild, *Laokoon. Lessing, Herder, Goethe. Selections* (New York: Henry Holt & Co., 1910).

Humboldt, Alexander von, *Kosmos. Entwurf einer physischen Weltbeschreibung*, 5 vols (Stuttgart and Tübingen: Cotta, 1845–62).

Hüskens-Hasselbeck, Karin, *Stil und Kritik. Dialogische Argumentation in Lessings philosophischen Schriften* (Munich: Fink, 1978).

Ingensiep, Hans Werner, 'Die biologischen Analogien und die erkenntnistheoretischen Alternativen in Kants Kritik der reinen Vernunft B, §27', *Kant-Studien*, 85 (1994), 381–93.

Irmscher, Hans Dietrich, 'Die geschichtsphilosophische Kontroverse zwischen Kant und Herder', in *Hamann–Kant–Herder. Acta des vierten Internationalen Hamann-Kolloquiums 1985*, ed. by Bernhard Gajek (Frankfurt a. M.: Lang, 1987) pp. 111–92.

——, 'Grundlagen der Geschichtsphilosophie Herders', in *Bückeburger Gespräche über Johann Gottfried Herder*, ed. by Brigitte Poschmann (Rinteln: Bösendahl, 1984), pp. 12–19.

——, 'Beobachtungen zur Funktion der Analogie im Denken Herders', *Deutsche Vierteljahrsschrift für Literaturwissenschaft und Geistesgeschichte*, 55 (1981), 64–97.

Irmscher, Hans Dietrich, and Emil Adler, *Der handschriftliche Nachlass Johann Gottfried Herders. Katalog* (Wiesbaden: Harrasowitz, 1979).

Jablonski, Paul Ernst, *Pantheon Aegyptiorum*, 3 vols (Frankfurt an der Oder: Christian Kleyb, 1750–52).

Jacob, Margaret C., *The Radical Enlightenment. Pantheists, Freemasons and Republicans* (London: Allen & Unwin, 1981).

Jacobi, Friedrich Heinrich, *Werke*, 6 vols (Leipzig: G. Fleischer, 1812–25).

Jones, G. L., 'Lessing and Amory', *German Life and Letters*, 20 (1966–67), 298–306.

Jussieu, Antoine Laurent de, *Genera plantarum* (Zurich: Ziegler, 1791; first published Paris, 1789).

Justi, Carl, *Winckelmann und seine Zeitgenossen*, 3rd edn, 3 vols (Leipzig: F. C. W. Vogel, 1923).

Kamen, Henry, *The Rise of Toleration* (London: Weidenfeld & Nicolson, 1967).

Kant, Immanuel, *Political Writings*, ed. by Hans Reiss, 2nd edn (Cambridge: Cambridge University Press, 1991).

——, *Werkausgabe* [WW], ed. by Wilhelm Weischedel, 12 vols (Frankfurt a. M.: Suhrkamp, 1968).

——, *Gesammelte Schriften* [AA], ed. by Königlich-Preußische Akademie der Wissenschaften, 29 vols (Berlin: Reimer, 1902–).

——, *Allgemeine Naturgeschichte und Theorie des Himmels* (Königsberg: Petersen, 1755).

Keller, Heinrich, *Goethe und das Laokoon-Problem* (Frauenfeld and Leipzig: Huber & Co., 1935).

Keudell, Elise, *Goethe als Benutzer der Weimarer Bibliothek* (Weimar: Böhlau, 1931).

Klein, Wilhelm, *Geschichte der griechischen Kunst*, 3 vols (Leipzig: Veit & Co., 1904–07).

Knebel, Karl Ludwig von, *K. L. von Knebels literarischer Nachlaß und Briefwechsel*, ed. by K. A. Varnhagen von Ense and Theodor Mundt (Leipzig: Gebrüder Reichenbach, 1840).

Knigge, Adolf von, *Sämtliche Werke*, ed. by Paul Raabe, 24 vols (Nendeln, Liechtenstein: KTO Press, 1978–93).

Kondylis, Panajotis, *Die Aufklärung im Rahmen des neuzeitlichen Rationalismus* (Stuttgart: Klett-Cotta, 1981).

Koselleck, Reinhart, *Futures Past. On the Semantics of Historical Time*, translated by Keith Tribe (Cambridge, MA and London: MIT Press, 1985).

Košenina, Alexander, 'Zur deutschen Übersetzung zweier Romane Thomas Amorys und der sich anschliessenden Fehde zwischen Wieland und Nicolai', *Daphnis*, 18 (1989), 179–98.

La Fontaine, Jean de, *Contes et Nouvelles en vers*, ed. by Georges Couton (Paris: Garnier, 1961).

La Mettrie, Julien Offray de, *Œuvres philosophiques*, 2 vols (Hildesheim: Georg Olms Verlag, 1970).

La Motte, Houdar de, *Oeuvres*, 10 vols (Paris: Prault, 1753–54).

La Réunion du Christianisme, ou la manière de rejoindre tous les chrétiens sous une seule confession de foy, [published anonymously], (Saumur: René Pean, 1670).

Lamport, F. J., *Lessing and the Drama* (Oxford: Oxford University Press, 1981).

Lavater, Johann Caspar, *Physiognomische Fragmente*, 4 vols (Leipzig and Winterthur: Weidmanns Erben und Reich, 1775–78).

Lawrence, A. W., *Greek and Roman Sculpture* (London: Jonathan Cape, 1972).

Leibniz, Gottfried Wilhelm, *Writings on China*, ed. by Daniel J. Cook and Henry Rosemont Jr. (Chicago and La Salle, IL: Open Court 1994).

——, *Philosophische Schriften*, ed. by Hans Heinz Holz, 4 vols in 6 (Frankfurt a. M.: Suhrkamp, 1965–92).

——, *Philosophische Schriften*, ed. by C. I. Gerhardt, 7 vols (Berlin: Weidmann, 1875–90).

——, *Opera omnia, nunc primum collecta*, ed. by Louis Dutens, 6 vols (Geneva: De Tournes, 1768).

——, *Oeuvres philosophiques latines et françoises de feu M. de Leibnitz*, ed. by Rudolf Erich Raspe (Amsterdam and Leipzig: Schreuder, 1765).

——, *Recueil de diverses Pièces sur la Philosophie*, ed. by Christian Kortholt (Hamburg: publisher unknown, 1734).

Lepenies, Wolf, *Das Ende der Naturgeschichte* (Munich: Hanser, 1976).

Lessing, Gotthold Ephraim, *Werke und Briefe*, ed. by Wilfried Barner and other hands, 12 vols (Frankfurt a. M.: Deutscher Klassiker Verlag, 1985–2003).

——, *Meine liebste Madam. Lessings Briefwechsel mit Eva König 1770–1776*, ed. by Günter Schulz and Ursula Schulz (Munich: C. H. Beck, 1979).

——, *D. Faust; Die Matrone von Ephesus*, ed. by Karl S. Guthke (Stuttgart: Reclam, 1968).

——, *Sämtliche Schriften* [LM], ed. by Karl Lachmann and Franz Muncker, 23 vols (Stuttgart, Leipzig and Berlin: Göschen, 1886–1924).

Lexikon der Aufklärung, ed. by Werner Schneiders (Munich: C. H. Beck, 1995).

Locke, John, *'A Letter concerning Toleration' in Focus*, ed. by John Horton and Susan Mendus (London and New York: Routledge, 1991); text of Letter, pp. 12–56.

Lovejoy, Arthur O., *The Great Chain of Being* (Cambridge, MA: Harvard University Press, 1933).

Lucretius (Titus Lucretius Carus), *De Rerum Natura*, ed. by W. H. D. Rouse and Martin Ferguson Smith (Cambridge, MA and London: Harvard University Press and William Heinemann, 1975).

——, *Titus Lukretius Carus Von der Natur der Dinge*, trans. by Franz Xaver Mayr, 2 vols (Leipzig and Vienna: Johann Georg Mössle, 1784).

——, *The Epicurean Philosopher: His Six Books, De Natura Rerum*, with Notes by Thomas Creech (Oxford: Anthony Stephens, 1682).

Lücken, Gottfried von, 'Goethe und der Laokoon', in *Natalicium. Johannes Geffcken zum 70. Geburtstag* (Heidelberg: [n.p.], 1931), pp. 85–99.

Ludz, Peter Christian, ed., *Geheime Gesellschaften* (Heidelberg: Schneider, 1979).

Lüpke, Johannes von, *Wege der Weisheit. Studien zu Lessings Theologiekritik* (Göttingen: Vandenhoeck & Rupprecht, 1989).

Marquard, Odo, *Abschied vom Prinzipiellen. Philosophische Studien* (Stuttgart: Reclam, 1981).

Magill, C. P., 'Schiller's "An die Freude"', in *Essays in German Language, Culture and Society*, ed. by Siegbert S. Prawer, R. Hinton Thomas and Leonard Forster (London: Institute for Germanic Studies, 1969) pp. 36–45.

Magnus, Rudolf, *Goethe as a Scientist* (New York: Henry Schuman, 1949).

Mandelkow, Karl Robert, *Goethe in Deutschland. Rezeptionsgeschichte eines Klassikers*, 2 vols (Munich: C. H. Beck, 1980–89).

——, 'Natur und Geschichte bei Goethe im Spiegel seiner Rezeption im 19. und 20. Jahrhundert', in *Geschichtlichkeit und Aktualität. Studien zur deutschen Literatur seit der Romantik. Festschrift für Hans-Joachim Mähl*, ed. by Klaus-Detlef Müller, Gerhard Pasternak, Wulf Segebrecht und Ludwig Stockinger (Tübingen: Niemeyer, 1988), pp. 69–96.

——, *Orpheus und Maschine. Acht literaturgeschichtliche Arbeiten* (Heidelberg: Stiehm, 1976).

Manuel, Frank E., *The Eighteenth Century Confronts the Gods* (Cambridge, MA: Harvard University Press, 1959).

Margalit, Avishai, 'Der Ring. Über religiösen Pluralismus', in *Toleranz. Philosophische Grundlagen und gesellschaftliche Praxis einer umstrittenen Tugend*, ed. by Rainer Forst (Frankfurt a. M. and New York: Campus Verlag, 2000) pp. 162–76.

Marolles, Michel de, *Le Poète Lucrèce, latin et français* (Paris: T. Quinet, 1650).

Martin, Gottfried, 'Freude Freiheit Götterfunken. Über Schillers Schwierigkeiten beim Schreiben von Freiheit', *Cahiers d'Études Germaniques*, 18 (1990), 9–18.

Marx, Karl, *Karl Marx, Frühe Schriften*, ed. by Hans-Joachim Lieber and Peter Fürth (Stuttgart: Cotta, 1962).

Mason, E. C., 'Schönheit, Ausdruck und Charakter im ästhetischen Denken des 18. Jahrhunderts', in *Geschichte–Deutung–Kritik. Literaturwissenschaftliche Beiträge dargebracht zum 65. Geburtstag Werner Kohlschmidts*, ed. by Maria Bindschedler and Paul Zinsli (Berne: Francke, 1969), pp. 91–108.

Mayer, Hans, *Ein Denkmal fur Johannes Brahms. Versuche über Musik und Literatur* (Frankfurt a. M.: Suhrkamp, 1983).

——, 'Schillers Gedichte und die Tradition deutscher Lyrik', *Jahrbuch der Deutschen Schiller-Gesellschaft*, 4 (1960), 72–89.

McManners, John, *Death and the Enlightenment* (Oxford: Oxford University Press, 1981).

Meinecke, Friedrich, *Die Entstehung des Historismus*, 2 vols (Munich and Berlin: R. Oldenbourg, 1936).

Mendelssohn, Moses, *Gesammelte Schriften. Jubiläumsausgabe*, ed. by Michael Brocke and other hands, c. 38 vols (Stuttgart/Bad Cannstatt: frommann-holzboog, 1971–).

Merkel, Friedrich, 'Bemerkungen eines Anatomen über die Gruppe des Laokoon', *Zeitschrift für bildende Kunst II* (1876), 353–62.

Metzger, Michael M., *Lessing and the Language of Comedy* (The Hague: Mouton, 1966).

Meyer, Ahlrich, 'Mechanische und organische Metaphorik politischer Philosophie', *Archiv für Begriffsgeschichte*, 13 (1969), 128–99.

Meyer, Heinrich, *Geschichte der bildenden Künste bei den Griechen*, 4 vols (Dresden: Waltersche Buchhandlung, 1824–36).

——, 'Einige Bemerkungen über die Gruppe Laokoons und seiner Söhne', *Propyläen*, I, 1. Stück (1799), 175–76.

Meyer, Herman and Werner Kohlschmidt, *Tradition und Ursprünglichkeit. Akten des III. Internationalen Germanisten-Kongresses 1965 in Amsterdam* (Berne and Munich: Francke, 1966).

Michelsen, Peter, 'Die "wahren Taten" der Freimaurer. Lessings Ernst und Falk', in Michelsen, *Der unruhige Bürger. Studien zu Lessing und zur Literatur des 18. Jahrhunderts* (Würzburg: Konigshausen & Neumann, 1990), pp. 137–59.

——, 'Ist alles gut? Pope, Mendelssohn und Lessing. Zur Schrift Pope ein Metaphysiker!', in *Mendelssohn-Studien*, ed. by Cécile Lowenthal-Hensel and Rudolf Elvers (Berlin: Duncker & Humblot, 1979), pp. 81–109.

Mitchell, Lucy M., *A History of Ancient Sculpture* (London: Kegan Paul, Trench & Co., 1883).

Moltmann, Jürgen, *History and the Triune God. Contributions to Trinitarian Theology* (London: SCM Press, 1991).

Montesquieu, Charles-Louis de Secondat, *De l'Esprit des lois* (Geneva: Barillot & Fil, 1748).

——, *Lettres persanes* (Cologne: Pierre Marteau, 1721).

Müller, Paul, *Untersuchungen zum Problem der Freimaurerei bei Lessing, Herder und Fichte* (Diss. Berne: Haupt, 1965).

Müller-Vollmer, Kurt, ed., *Herder Today. Contributions from the International Herder Conference 1987* (Berlin: De Gruyter, 1990).

Needham, Joseph, *Science and Civilisation in China*, vol. II (Cambridge: Cambridge University Press, 1956).

Neubauer, John, '"Die Abstraktion, vor der wir uns fürchten". Goethes Auffassung der Mathematik und das Goethebild in der Geschichte der Wissenschaft', in *Versuche zu Goethe. Festschrift für Erich Heller*, ed. by Volker Dürr and Géza von Molnár (Heidelberg: L. Stiehm, 1976), pp. 305–20.

New Catholic Encyclopedia, The, Catholic University of America (New York: McGraw-Hill, 1967).

Nicolai, Friedrich, *Ein paar Worte betreffend Johann Bunkel und Christoph Martin Wieland*, (Berlin and Stettin: no publisher named, 1779).

——, *Leben Bemerkungen und Meinungen Johann Bunkels nebst den Leben verschiedener merkwürdiger Frauenzimmer. Aus dem engländischen übersetzt*, 4 vols (Berlin: Nicolai, 1778).

——, [advertisement and call for subscriptions], *Allgemeine Deutsche Bibliothek*, 31 (1777), unpaginated notices at end of this volume.

——, *Monthly Review*, 35 (1766), 34.

——, 'Nachricht', *Allgemeine Deutsche Bibliothek*, 37 (1779), Erstes Stück, 295–316.

Nietzsche, Friedrich, *Werke in drei Bänden*, ed. by Karl Schlechta (Munich: Hanser, 1965–67).

Nisbet, Hugh Barr, *Gotthold Ephraim Lessing. His Life, Works, and Thought* (Oxford: Oxford University Press, 2013).

——, 'On the Rise of Toleration in Europe. Lessing and the German Contribution', *Modern Language Review*, 105 (2010) xxviii–xliv (Presidential Address of the Modern Humanities Research Association, delivered on 21 May 2010).

——, ed., *Gotthold Ephraim Lessing, Philosophical and Theological Writings* (Cambridge: Cambridge University Press, 2005).

——, 'Die ethische Grundlage von Goethes Naturwissenschaft', in Thomas Jung and Birgit Mühlhaus (eds.), *Über die Grenzen Weimars hinaus—Goethes Werk in europäischem Licht* (Oxford, Berne, Berlin, etc.: Peter Lang, 2000), pp. 171–83.

——, 'Friedrich Schiller. "An die Freude". A Reappraisal', in Peter Hutchinson, ed., *Landmarks in German Poetry* (Oxford, Berne, Berlin, etc.: Peter Lang, 2000), pp. 73–96.

——, 'Herder. The Nation in History', in *National History and Identity*, ed. by Michael Branch (Helsinki: Finnish Literature Society, 1999), pp. 78–96.

——, 'Naturgeschichte und Humangeschichte bei Goethe, Herder und Kant', in Peter Matussek (ed.), *Goethe und die Verzeitlichung der Natur. Goethe-Sonderband in der Reihe Kulturgeschichte der Natur* (Munich: C. H. Beck, 1998), pp. 15–43.

——, 'The Rationalisation of the Holy Trinity from Lessing to Hegel', *Lessing Yearbook*, 31 (1999), 115–35.

——, 'Lessing's Ethics', *Lessing Yearbook*, 25 (1993), 1–40.

——, 'Goethes und Herders Geschichtsdenken', *Goethe-Jahrbuch*, 110 (1993), 115–33.

——, 'The German Reception of an Irish Eccentric. The Controversy over Thomas Amory's "Life of John Buncle, Esq.", 1778–79', in P. Skrine, R. E. Wallbank-Turner and J. West (eds.), *Connections. Essays in Honour of Eda Sagarra on the Occasion of her 60th Birthday* (Stuttgart: Heinz Verlag, 1993), pp. 179–89.

——, 'Die naturphilosophische Bedeutung von Herders "Ältester Urkunde des Menschengeschlechts"', in Brigitte Poschmann (ed.), *Bückeburger Gespräche über Johann Gottfried Herder 1988* (Rinteln: Bösendahl, 1989), pp. 210–26.

——, 'Lessing and Misogyny. "Die Matrone von Ephesus"', in *Texte, Motive und Gestalten. Festschrift für Hans Reiss*, ed. John L. Hibberd and H. B. Nisbet (Tübingen: Niemeyer, 1989), pp. 13–31.

——, 'Karl Ludwig von Knebel's Hexameter Translation of Lucretius', *German Life and Letters*, 41/4 (1988), 413–25.

——, 'Herder und Lukrez', in *Johann Gottfried Herder 1744–1803*, ed. by Gerhard Sauder (Hamburg: Meiner, 1987), 77–87.

——, 'Lucretius in Eighteenth-Century Germany. With a Commentary on Goethe's "Metamorphose der Tiere"', *Modern Language Review*, 81 (1986), 97–115.

——, 'Zur Funktion des Geheimnisses in Lessings "Ernst und Falk"', in Peter Freimark, Franklin Kopitzsch and Helga Slessarev (eds.), *Lessing und die Toleranz* (Detroit, MI and Munich; Wayne State University Press and edition text + kritik, 1986), pp. 291–309.

——, 'Laocoon in Germany. The Reception of the Group since Winckelmann', *Oxford German Studies*, 10 (1979), 22–63.

——, *Goethe and the Scientific Tradition* (London: Institute of Germanic Studies, University of London, 1972).

——, *Herder and the Philosophy and History of Science* (Cambridge: MHRA, 1970).

——, 'Herder and Francis Bacon', *Modern Language Review*, 62 (1967), 267–83.

——, 'Herder, Goethe and the Natural "Type"', *Publications of the English Goethe Society*, 37 (1967), 83–119.

Nisbet, Hugh Barr and John L. Hibberd (eds.), *Texte, Motive und Gestalten der Goethezeit. Festschrift für Hans Reiss* (Tübingen: Niemeyer, 1989).

Nolte, Fred O., *Lessing's Laokoon* (Lancaster, PA: Lancaster Press, 1940).

Novalis, *Novalis Schriften: die Werke Friedrich von Hardenbergs*, ed. by Paul Kluckhohn and Richard Samuel, 2nd edn, 4 vols (Stuttgart: Kohlhammer, 1960–75).

Oehlke, Waldemar, *Lessing und seine Zeit*, 2 vols (Munich: C. H. Beck, 1919).

Osswald, Bernhard, *Anton Günther. Theologisches Denken im Kontext einer Philosophie der Subjektivität* (Paderborn and Munich: Schoningh, 1990).

Otto, Regine, '"Lukrez bleibt immer in seiner Art der Einzige": Karl Ludwig von Knebel an Goethe. Ungedruckte Briefe aus den Jahren 1821 und 1822', in *Impulse. Aufsätze, Quellen, Berichte zur deutschen Klassik und Romantik, Folge 5*, ed. by Walter Dietze and Peter Goldammer (Berlin and Weimar: Aufbau-Verlag, 1982), pp. 229–63.

Otto, Wolf Dietrich, 'Toleranzkultur und Pädagogik oder: Wie reden deutsche Pädagogen über Toleranz?', in *Kulturthema Toleranz. Zur Grundlegung einer interdisziplinären und interkulturellen Toleranzforschung*, ed. by Alois Wierlacher (Munich: Iudicium, 1996), pp. 565–631.

Overath, Angelika, Navid Kermani, and Robert Schindel, *Toleranz. Drei Lesarten zu Lessings Märchen vom Ring* (Göttingen: Wallstein, 2003).

Overbeck, Gertrud, 'Goethes Lehre von der Metamorphose der Pflanzen und ihre Widerspiegelung in seiner Dichtung', *Publications of the English Goethe Society*, 31 (1961), 38–59.

Overbeck, Johannes, *Geschichte der griechischen Plastik*, 4th edn, 2 vols, (Leipzig: J. C. Hinrichssche Buchhandlung, 1893–94).

Pelters, Wilm, *Lessings Standort. Sinndeutung der Geschichte als Kern seines Denkens* (Heidelberg: L. Stiehm, 1972).

Perkins, Franklin, *Leibniz and China. A Commerce of Light* (Cambridge: Cambridge University Press, 2004).

Petronius, Gaius, *Satyricon*, and Seneca, L. Annaeus, *Apocolocyntosis*, translated by Michael Heseltine and W. H. D. Rouse, revised by E. H. Warmington. Loeb Classical Library 15. (London: Heinemann, 1956).

Petsch, Robert, 'Die Matrone von Ephesus. Ein dramatisches Bruchstück von Lessing', *Dichtung und Volkstum*, 41 (1941), 87–95.

Plath, Margarete, 'Der Goethe-Schellingsche Plan eines philosophischen Naturgedichts: Eine Studie zu Goethes "Gott und Welt"', *Preußische Jahrbücher*, 106 (1901), 44–74.

Pohlenz, Max, 'Laokoon', *Die Antike*, 9 (1953), 54.

Pons, Georges, *G. E. Lessing et le christianisme* (Paris: Didier, 1964).

Poschmann, Brigitte, ed., *Bückeburger Gespräche über Johann Gottfried Herder 1988* (Rinteln: Bösendahl, 1989).

Prawer, S. S., *Karl Marx and World Literature* (Oxford: Oxford University Press, 1976).

Price, Lawrence Marsden, *The Reception of English Literature in Germany* (Berkeley, CA: University of California Press, 1932).

Pugh, David, *Dialectic of Love. Platonism in Schiller's Aesthetics* (Montreal, QC: Queen's-McGill University Press, 1996).

Pütz, Peter, *Die Leistung der Form. Lessings Dramen* (Frankfurt a. M.: Suhrkamp, 1986).

Ramdohr, F. W. B., *Ueber Mahlerei und Bildhauerkunst in Rom*, 3 vols (Leipzig: Weidmann, 1787).

Ranke, Leopold von, *Über die Epochen der neueren Geschichte*, ed. by Theodor Schieder and Helmut Berding (Munich: Historische Kommission der Bayerischen Akademie der Wissenschaften, 1971).

Rattansi, P. M., and J. E. McGuire, 'Newton and the "Pipes of Pan"', *Notes and Records of the Royal Society*, 21–22 (1966–67), 108–43.

Rawlinson, A. E. J., ed., *Essays on the Trinity and the Incarnation* (London: Longmans, 1928).

Realencyclopädie für protestantische Theologie und Kirche, ed. by J. J. Herzog, 3rd edn, 24 vols (Leipzig: Hinrichs, 1896–1913).

Reed, T. J., *The Classical Centre: Goethe and Weimar 1775–1832* (London: Croom Helm, 1980).

Rehm, Walther, *Götterstille und Göttertrauer* (Berne: Francke, 1951).

——, *Griechentum und Goethezeit* (Leipzig: Dieterichsche Verlagsbuchhandlung, 1936).

Reinalter, Helmut, ed., *Freimaurer und Geheimbünde im 18. Jahrhundert in Mitteleuropa* (Frankfurt a. M.: Suhrkamp, 1986).

Reiss, Hans, *Formgestaltung und Politik. Goethe-Studien* (Würzburg: Königshausen & Neumann, 1993).

Ribe, Neil M., 'Goethe's Critique of Newton. A Reconsideration', *Studies in the History and Philosophy of Science*, 16 (1985), 315–55.

Richter, Gisela M. A., *The Sculpture and Sculptors of the Greeks*, 4th edn (New Haven, CT and London: Yale University Press, 1970).

Riedel, Wolfgang, *Die Anthropologie des jungen Schiller* (Würzburg: Königshausen & Neumann, 1985).

Ries, Paul, 'Die Insel Pines: Philosophie, Pornographie oder Propaganda?', in *Literatur und Volk im 17. Jahrhundert*, ed. by Wolfgang Brückner and other hands (Wiesbaden: Harrassowitz, 1985), pp. 753–76.

Roberts, J. M., *The Mythology of the Secret Societies* (London: Secker and Warburg, 1972).

Rosenthal, Georg, 'Das Laokoonproblem in Goethes *Dichtung und Wahrheit*', *Neue Jahrbücher für das klassische Altertum*, 23 (1920), 171–77.

Ross, Ian Campbell, 'Thomas Amory, John Buncle, and the Origins of Irish Fiction', *Éire—Ireland*, 18/3 (1983), 71–85.

Rouché, Max, *Herder précurseur de Darwin? Histoire d'un mythe* (Paris: Imprimerie Nouvelle Thouars, 1940).

——, *La Philosophie de l'histoire de Herder* (Paris: Société d'édition: Les Belles Lettres, 1940).

Ruffini, Francesco, *Religious Liberty*, translated by J. Parker Heyes, with a preface by J. B. Bury (London and New York: Williams & Newgate, 1912).

Runte, Roseann, 'The Matron of Ephesus in Eighteenth-Century France. The Lady and the Legend', *Studies in Eighteenth-Century Culture*, 6 (1977), 361–75.

Ruppert, Hans, *Goethes Bibliothek, Katalog* (Weimar: Arion Verlag, 1958).

Ruskin, John, *The Works of John Ruskin*, ed. by E. T. Cook and Alexander Wedderburn (London and New York: George Allen and Longmans Green & Co., 1903–12).

Sagarra, Eda, 'Die "grüne Insel" in der deutschen Reiseliteratur. Deutsche Irlandreisende von Karl Gottlob Küttner bis Heinrich Böll', in *Europäisches Reisen im Zeitalter der Aufklärung*, ed. by Hans-Wolf Jäger (Heidelberg: Carl Winter, 1992), pp. 182–95.

Saine, Thomas P., 'Was ist Aufklärung?', in *Aufklärung, Absolutismus und Bürgertum in Deutschland*, ed. by Franklin Kopitzsch (Munich: Nymphenburger Verlagshandlung, 1976).

Sakai, Kiyoshi, 'Leibnizens Chinologie und das Prinzip der Analogie', in *Das Neueste über China. G. W. Leibnizens "Nova Sinica" von 1697*, ed. by Wenchao Li and Hans Poser (Stuttgart: Steiner, 2000), pp. 275–93.

Salewski, Michael, 'Europa, der tolerante Kontinent?', in *Religiöser Pluralismus und Toleranz in Europa*, ed. by Christian Augustin, Johannes Wienand and Christiane Winkler (Wiesbaden: Verlag für Sozialwissenschaften, 2006), pp. 12–27.

Salis, Arnold von, *Antike und Renaissance* (Erlenbach-Zurich: Rentsch, 1947).

Sauder, Gerhard, *Der reisende Epikuräer: Studien zu Moritz August von Thümmels* 'Reise in die Mittäglichen Provinzen von Frankreich' (Heidelberg: C. Winter, 1968).

——, *Empfindsamkeit, Vol. I, Voraussetzungen und Elemente* (Stuttgart: Metzler, 1974).

Schatzberg, Walter, *Scientific Themes in the Popular Literature of the German Enlightenment*, 1720–1760 (Berne: Herbert Lang, 1973).

Schelling, F. W. J., *Werke*, ed. by Manfred Schröter, 6 vols (Munich: Beck Verlag, 1927).

——, *Werke*, ed. by Manfred Schröter, 6 vols (Munich: Beck Verlag, 1927), 4. Ergänzungsband (1959).

——, *Sämtliche Werke*, ed. by K. F. A. Schelling, 14 vols (Stuttgart: Cotta, 1856–61).

Schiller, Friedrich, *Gedichte*, ed. by Norbert Oellers (Stuttgart: Reclam, 2009).

——, *Schiller-Handbuch*, ed. by Helmut Koopmann (Stuttgart: Kröner, 1998).

——, *Werke und Briefe, Frankfurt edition* [FA], ed. by Otto Dann and other hands, 12 vols (Frankfurt a. M.: Deutscher Klassiker Verlag, 1988–2004).

——, *Sämtliche Werke*, ed. by Gerhard Fricke and Herbert G. Göpfert, 5 vols, 7th edn (Munich: Hanser, 1984).

——, *Anthologie auf das Jahr 1782*, ed. by Katharina Mommsen (Stuttgart: J. B. Metzler, 1973).

——, *Briefwechsel zwischen Schiller und Körner*, ed. Klaus L. Berghahn (Munich: Winkler, 1973).

——, *Werke, Nationalausgabe* [NA], ed. by Julius Petersen and Gerhard Fricke , 42 vols (Weimar: Böhlau, 1943–).

Schilson, Arno, *Geschichte im Horizont der Vorsehung. G. E. Lessings Beitrag zu einer Theologie der Geschichte* (Mainz: Matthias Grünewald Verlag, 1974).

Schimank, Hans, 'Der Aspekt der Naturgesetzlichkeit im Wandel der Zeiten', in *Das Problem der Gesetzlichkeit*, ed. by the Joachim-Jungius-Gesellschaft der Wissenschaften, Vol. II (Hamburg: Richard Meiner, 1949), pp. 139–86.

Schings, Hans-Jürgen, *Die Brüder des Marquis Posa. Schiller und der Geheimbund der Illuminati* (Tübingen: Niemeyer, 1996).

Schlegel, Friedrich, *Kritische Schriften*, ed. by Wolfdietrich Rasch (Munich: Hanser, 1964).

Schlitt, Dale M., *Hegel's Trinitarian Claim. A Critical Reflection* (Leiden: Brill, 1984).

Schmarsow, August, *Erläuterungen und Kommentar zu Lessings* Laokoon (Leipzig: Quelle & Meyer, 1907).

Schmidt, Erich, *Lessing. Geschichte seines Lebens und seiner Schriften*, 4th edn, 2 vols (Berlin: Weidmannsche Buchhandlung, 1923).

Schmidt, Gerhart, 'Der Begriff der Toleranz im Hinblick auf Lessing', *Wolfenbütteler Studien zur Aufklärung*, 2 (1975), 121–36.

Schmidt, Johan Werner, 'Diderot and Lucretius: The De rerum natura and Lucretius's Legacy in Diderot's Scientific, Aesthetic, and Ethical Thought', *Studies on Voltaire and the Eighteenth Century*, 208 (1982), 183–294.

Schmidt, Wolfgang, 'Lucrez und der Wandel seines Bildes', *Antike und Abendland*, 2 (1946), 193–219.

Schneider, Heinrich, *Lessing. Zwölf biographische Studien* (Berne: Francke, 1950).

Scholem, Gershom, 'The Curious History of the Six-Pointed Star', *Commentary. A Jewish Review*, 8 (1949), 243–51.

Scholl, John William, 'Friedrich Schlegel and Goethe, 1790–1802', *PMLA*, 21 (1906), 40–192.

Schöne, Albrecht, *Goethes Farbentheologie* (Munich: C. H. Beck, 1987).

Schopenhauer, Arthur, *Sämtliche Werke*, ed. by Wolfgang von Löhneysen, 5 vols (Stuttgart: Cotta, 1960–65).

Schrimpf, Hans Joachim, 'Über die geschichliche Bedeutung von Goethes Newton-Polemik und Romantik-Kritik', in *Gratulatio. Festschrift für Christian Wegner*, ed. by M. Honeit and M. Wegner (Hamburg: C. Wegner, 1963), pp. 63–82.

Schröder, Jürgen, *Gotthold Ephraim Lessing. Sprache und Drama* (Munich: Fink, 1972).

Schuchardt, Walter Herwig, *Die Epochen der griechischen Plastik* (Baden-Baden: Bruno Grimm Verlag, 1959).

Schulte, Hans H., *'Werke der Begeisterung'. Friedrich Schiller—Idee und Eigenart seines Schaffens* (Bonn: Bouvier, 1980).

——, 'Zur Geschichte des Enthusiasmus', *Publications of the English Goethe Society*, 39 (1969), 85–122.

Schulz, Franz, 'Die Göttin Freude. Zur Geistes- und Stilgeschichte des 18. Jahrhunderts', *Jahrbuch des Freien Deutschen Hochstifts* (1926), 3–38.

Schulz, Günter, 'Furcht, Freude, Enthusiasmus. Zwei unbekannte philosophische Entwürfe Schillers', *Jahrbuch der Deutschen Schillergesellschaft*, 1 (1957), 103–41.

Schumpeter, Joseph A., *History of Economic Analysis*, ed. by Elizabeth Boody Schumpeter (London: Allen & Unwin, 1954).

Schwarz, Reinhard, 'Lessings Spinozismus', *Zeitschrift für Theologie und Kirche*, 65 (1968), 271–90.

Schwinger, Richard, *Friedrich Nicolais Roman 'Sebaldus Nothanker'* (Weimar: Felber, 1987).

Sebald, W. G., 'Die Zweideutigkeit der Toleranz. Anmerkungen zum Interesse der Aufklärung an der Emanzipation der Juden', *Der Deutschunterricht*, 36, Heft 4 (1984), 27–47.

Seeba, Hinrich C., '"Der wahre Standort einer jeden Person". Lessings Beitrag zum historischen Perspektivismus', in *Nation und Gelehrtenrepublik. Lessing im europäischen Zusammenhang*, ed. by Wilfried Barner and Albert M. Reh (Detroit, MI and Munich: Wayne State University Press and edition text + kritik, 1984), pp. 193–214.

Semler, Johann Salomo, ed., *Evangelische Glaubenslehre*, 3 vols, (Halle: Gebauer, 1759–60).

Sepper, Dennis, *Goethe contra Newton. Polemics and the Project for a New Science of Color* (Cambridge: Cambridge University Press, 1988).

Sichtermann, Hellmut, *Laokoon*, Werkmonographien zur bildenden Kunst, 101 (Stuttgart: Reclam, 1964).

Siegrist, Christoph, *Das Lehrgedicht der Aufklärung* (Stuttgart: Metzler, 1974).

Sloterdijk, Peter, *Gottes Eifer. Vom Kampf der drei Monotheismen* (Frankfurt a. M. and Leipzig: Insel, 2007).

Snow, C. P., *The Two Cultures and the Scientific Revolution, The Rede Lecture, 1959* (Cambridge: Cambridge University Press, 1959); new edition, with an introduction by Stefan Collini (Cambridge: Cambridge University Press, 1993).

Spaemann, Robert, 'Genetisches zum Naturbegriff des 18. Jahrhunderts', *Archiv für Begriffsgeschichte*, 11 (1967), 59–74.

Spencer, T. J. B., 'Lucretius and the Scientific Poem in English', in *Lucretius*, ed. by D. R. Dudley (London: Routledge, 1965).

Splett, Jörg, *Die Trinitätslehre G. W. F. Hegels* (Freiburg and Munich: Alber, 1965).

St Clair, William, *Lord Elgin and the Marbles* (London: Oxford University Press, 1967).

Stahr, Adolf, *Torso, Kunst, Künstler und Kunstwerke des griechischen und römischen Alterthums*, 2nd edn, 2 vols (Brunswick: Vieweg, 1878).

Stammen, Silvia, 'Geschichte der Zerstörung—Zerstörung der Geschichte. Nathans Tod im Textvergleich mit Nathan der Weise', in *Theater gegen das Vergessen. Bühnenarbeit und Drama bei George Tabori*, ed. by Hans-Peter Bayerdorfer and Jörg Schönert (Tübingen: Niemeyer, 1997), pp. 283–318.

Stechow, Wolfgang, *Rubens and the Classical Tradition* (Cambridge, MA: Harvard University Press, 1968).

Steffens, Henrik, *Was ich erlebte*, 10 vols (Breslau: Max, 1840–44).

Stein, Andreas, [published anonymously], *Geschichte einiger Esel oder Fortsetzung des Lebens und der Meynungen des Weltberühmten John Bunkels*, 3 vols (Hamburg and Leipzig: no publisher named, 1782–83).

Stewart, A. F., 'To Entertain an Emperor. Sperlonga, Laokoon and Tiberius at the Dinner Table', *Journal of Roman Studies*, 76 (1977) 76–94.

Stockum, T. C. van, 'Lessings Dramenentwurf Die Matrone von Ephesus', *Neophilologus*, 46 (1962), 125–34.

Strich, Fritz, *Die Mythologie in der deutschen Literatur von Klopstock bis Wagner*, 2 vols (Halle: Niemeyer, 1910).

Szarota, Elida Maria, *Lessings Laokoon. Eine Kampfschrift für eine realistische Kunst und Poesie* (Weimar: Arion Verlag, 1959).

Taylor, Charles, 'Gadamer on the Human Sciences', in *The Cambridge Companion to Gadamer*, ed. by Robert J. Dostal (Cambridge: Cambridge University Press, 2002), pp. 126–42.

——, 'The Politics of Recognition', in *Multiculturalism. A Critical Reader*, ed. by David Theo Goldberg (Cambridge, MA and Oxford: Blackwell, 1994), pp. 75–106.

Thiersch, Friedrich, *Ueber die Epochen der bildenden Kunst unter den Griechen*, 2nd edn (Munich: Literarisch-Artistische Anstalt, 1829).

Tillich, Paul, *Gesammelte Werke*, ed. by Renate Albrecht, 14 vols (Stuttgart: Evangelisches Verlagswerk, 1959–75).

Trevelyan, Humphry, *Goethe and the Greeks* (Cambridge: Cambridge University Press, 1941).

Trois imposteurs, *Le Traité des trois imposteurs: manuscrit clandestin du début du XVIIIe siècle*, ed. by Pierre Rétat (Saint-Étienne: Universités de la Région Rhône-Alpes, 1973).

Ure, Peter, 'The Widow of Ephesus. Some Reflections on an International Comic Theme', *Durham University Journal*, 49 (1956–57), 1–9.

Vaihinger, Hans, 'Zwei Quellenfunde zu Schillers philosophischer Entwicklung', *Kant-Studien*, 10 (1905), 373–89.

Vierhaus, Rudolf, 'Aufklärung und Freimaurerei in Deutschland', in *Das Vergangene und die Geschichte. Festschrift für Reinhard Wittram zum 70. Geburtstag*, ed. by Rudolf von Thadden, Gert von Pistohlkors und Hellmut Weiss (Göttingen: Vandenhoeck & Ruprecht, 1973), pp. 23–41.

Visconti, Ennius Quirinus, *Œuvres: Musée Pie-Clémentin*, 7 vols (Milan: J. P. Giegler, 1818–22).

Voltaire, François-Marie Arouet, *Treatise on Tolerance*, translated by Brian Masters, ed. by Simon Harvey (Cambridge: Cambridge University Press, 2000).

——, *Letters on England*, translated by Leonard Tancock (London: Penguin Books, 1980).

Walker, D. P., *The Ancient Theology. Studies in Christian Platonism from the Fifteenth to the Eighteenth Century* (London: Duckworth, 1972).

Weisse, Christian Felix, *Lustspiele*, 3 vols (Leipzig: Dykische Buchhandlung, 1783).

——, *Weissens Lustspiele*, 3 vols (Karlsruhe: Schmieder, 1778).

Weiss, Peter, *Rapporte* (Frankfurt a. M.: Suhrkamp, 1968).

Welcker, Friedrich Gottlieb, *Alte Denkmäler*, 5 vols (Göttingen: Dieterich, 1849–64).

Wells, George A., 'What is Wrong with Emilia Galotti?', *German Life and Letters*, 37 (1983–84), 163–73.

——, 'Goethe's Geological Studies', *Publications of the English Goethe Society*, 35 (1965), 92–137.

Wenzel, Manfred, '"Die Abstraktion, vor der wir uns fürchten". Goethe und die Physik', *Freiburger Universitätsblätter*, 35, Heft 133 (1996), 55–79.

Wethey, Harold E., *The Paintings of Titian. Complete Edition. I: The Religious Paintings* (London: Phaidon, 1969).

Whaley, Joachim, 'A Tolerant Society? Toleration in the Holy Roman Empire, 1648–1806', in *Toleration in Enlightenment Europe*, ed. by Ole Peter Grell and Roy Porter (Cambridge: Cambridge University Press, 2000), pp. 175–95.

Wieland, Christoph Martin, *Geschichte des Agathon* (first version), ed. by Fritz Martini (Stuttgart: Reclam, 1979).

——, 'Sechs Fragen zur Aufklärung', in *Was ist Aufklärung? Thesen und Definitionen*, ed. by Ehrhard Bahr (Stuttgart: Reclam, 1974), pp. 23–28.

——, *Werke*, ed. by Fritz Martini and Hans Werner Seiffert, 5 vols (Munich: Hanser, 1964–65).

——, *Gesammelte Schriften*, ed. by the Königlich-Preußische Akademie der Wissenschaften, 23 vols in progress (Berlin: Weidmann, 1909–).

——, 'Abgenöthigter Nachtrag zur Johann-Bunkliade', *Der Teutsche Merkur* (1779), Erstes Vierteljahr, 154–72.

——, 'Die Bunkliade', *Der Teutsche Merkur* (1778), Drittes Vierteljahr, 77–90 and 165–72; Viertes Vierteljahr, 55–75, 158–73, and 248–60.

Wierlacher, Alois, ed., *Kulturthema Toleranz: Zur Grundlegung einer interdisziplinären und interkulturellen Toleranzforschung* (Munich: iudicium, 1996).

Winckelmann, Johann Joachim, *Sämtliche Werke*, ed. by Joseph Eiselein, 12 vols (Donaueschingen: Verlag Deutscher Klassiker, 1825–29).

Wokler, Robert, 'Multiculturalism and Ethnic Cleansing in the Enlightenment', in *Toleration in Enlightenment Europe*, ed. by Ole Peter Grell and Roy Porter (Cambridge: Cambridge University Press, 2000), pp. 69–85.

Wollgast, Siegfried, 'Zu den philosophischen Quellen von Gottfried Arnold und zu Aspekten seines philosophischen Systems', in *Gottfried Arnold (1666–1714). Mit einer Bibliographie der Arnold-Literatur ab 1714*, ed. by Dietrich Blaufuss and Friedrich Niewöhner (Wiesbaden: Harrossowitz, 1995), pp. 301–35.

Wordsworth, William, *Poetical Works*, ed. by Thomas Hutchinson, revised by Ernest de Selincourt (London: Oxford University Press, 1950).

Wüst, Wolfgang, 'An der Toleranzgrenze. Der frühmoderne "Ernstfall" für Aufklärung, Toleranz und Pluralismus', in *Religiöser Pluralismus und Toleranz in Europa*, ed. by Christian Augustin, Johannes Wienand and Christiane Winkler (Wiesbaden: Verlag für Sozialwissenschaften, 2006), pp. 53–68.

Zeuch, Ulrike, ed., *Lessings Grenzen* (Wiesbaden; Harrassowitz, 2005).

Ziehen, Julius, *Kunstgeschichtliches Anschaungsmaterial zu Lessings Laokoon*, 2nd edn (Bielefeld and Leipzig: Velhagen & Klasing, 1905).

Zimmermann, Robert, 'Der Cardinal Nicolas Cusanus als Vorläufer Leibnizens', *Sitzungsberichte der Kaiserlichen Akademie der Wissenschaften*, 8 (Vienna, 1852), 306–28.

Zimmermann, Rolf Christian, *Das Weltbild des jungen Goethe. Studien zur hermetischen Tradition des deutschen 18. Jahrhunderts*, 2 vols (Munich: Fink, 1969–79).

Zumbach, Clark, *The Transcendental Science. Kant's Conception of Biological Methodology* (The Hague: Martinus Nijhoff, 1984).

Index

About the Team

Alessandra Tosi was the managing editor for this book.

Melissa Purkiss performed the copy-editing and proofreading.

Anna Gatti designed the cover. The cover was produced in InDesign using the Fontin font.

Luca Baffa typeset the book in InDesign and produced the paperback and hardback editions. The text font is Tex Gyre Pagella; the heading font is Californian FB. Luca produced the EPUB, MOBI, PDF, HTML, and XML editions — the conversion is performed with open source software freely available on our GitHub page (https://github.com/OpenBookPublishers).

This book need not end here...

Share

All our books — including the one you have just read — are free to access online so that students, researchers and members of the public who can't afford a printed edition will have access to the same ideas. This title will be accessed online by hundreds of readers each month across the globe: why not share the link so that someone you know is one of them?

This book and additional content is available at:

https://doi.org/10.11647/OBP.0180

Customise

Personalise your copy of this book or design new books using OBP and third-party material. Take chapters or whole books from our published list and make a special edition, a new anthology or an illuminating coursepack. Each customised edition will be produced as a paperback and a downloadable PDF.

Find out more at:

https://www.openbookpublishers.com/section/59/1

Like Open Book Publishers

Follow @OpenBookPublish

Read more at the Open Book Publishers BLOG

You may also be interested in:

**The Life of August Wilhelm Schlegel,
Cosmopolitan of Art and Poetry**

Roger Paulin

https://doi.org/10.11647/OBP.0069

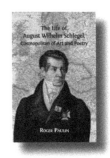

Exploring the Interior
Essays on Literary and Cultural History

Karl S. Guthke

https://doi.org/10.11647/OBP.0126

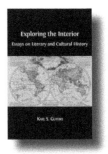

Hyperion, or the Hermit in Greece

Howard Gaskill

https://doi.org/10.11647/OBP.0160

Lightning Source UK Ltd.
Milton Keynes UK
UKHW020454040621
384876UK00001B/49